THE BILL OF THE CENTURY

THE
BILL OF THE
CENTURY
· · ·

THE EPIC BATTLE FOR
THE CIVIL RIGHTS ACT

CLAY RISEN

BLOOMSBURY PRESS

NEW YORK · LONDON · NEW DELHI · SYDNEY

Published by Bloomsbury Press, New York

Bloomsbury is a trademark of Bloomsbury Publishing Plc

All papers used by Bloomsbury Press are natural, recyclable products made
from wood grown in well-managed forests. The manufacturing processes
conform to the environmental regulations of the country of origin.

Bloomsbury books may be purchased for business or promotional use.
For information on bulk purchases please contact Macmillan Corporate
and Premium Sales Department at specialmarkets@macmillan.com.

LIBRARY OF CONGRESS CATALOGING-IN-PUBLICATION
DATA HAS BEEN APPLIED FOR.

ISBN: 978-1-60819-824-5

First U.S. Edition 2014

1 3 5 7 9 10 8 6 4 2

Typeset by Hewer Text UK Ltd., Edinburgh
Printed and bound in the U.S.A. by Thomson-Shore, Inc. Dexter, Michigan

To Elliot and Talia

CONTENTS

INTRODUCTION

AT 8:00 A.M. ON JULY 3, 1964, a thirteen-year-old boy in Kansas City, Missouri, named Eugene Young went into the barbershop at the historic Muehlebach Hotel to get a haircut. He hopped into the chair of Lloyd Soper, one of the barbers, and gave him two dollars. A few minutes later, Young left, another satisfied customer. Young's satisfaction went beyond the mere follicular: he was black, and the day before he had been refused service at the same shop.

In the intervening hours and a thousand miles away, President Lyndon B. Johnson had signed into law the Civil Rights Act of 1964, which among other things forbade places of public accommodation—including restaurants, hotels, theaters, and barbershops—from discriminating on the basis of race. Who knows how many countless black men had been denied service at the Muehlebach since it opened in 1915. And now, suddenly, the doors were opened, as if they had never been closed. "I didn't mind cutting that little boy's hair," Soper said.[1]

Young's story was repeated across the country that day, and in the weeks that followed. An entire social system built on oppressing and excluding blacks had been outlawed with the stroke of a pen, and blacks were amazed to find how easy it fell apart. A black civil rights leader in Atlanta walked into the restaurant at the Henry Grady, an exclusive downtown hotel formerly the segregated terrain of the city's white elite, and was served like he had been coming there for years. In Birmingham an aging black chauffeur went for dinner at the Dinkle-Tutweiler Hotel, where he had driven white customers for more than three decades but never himself been allowed to eat.[2]

There were pockets of resistance: a few hours after Johnson signed the bill, an Atlanta motel filed a suit against the Department of Justice, claiming the new law was unconstitutional. In Greenwood, Mississippi, officials drained a formerly whites-only public pool rather than open it to black children. In Tuscaloosa, Alabama, a mob of whites chased the actor Jack Palance from a movie theater because they thought he had been sitting with a black man. And an Atlanta restaurant owner named Lester Maddox vaulted himself into the national spotlight by not only refusing to serve blacks, but chasing them away, in front of photographers, with a gun. Yet overall the fall of Jim Crow was rapid and peaceful. As a Department of Justice report concluded at the end of the month, "The general picture is one of large-scale compliance."[3]

The Civil Rights Act of 1964 was the most important piece of legislation passed by Congress in the twentieth century. It reached deep into the social fabric of the nation to refashion structures of racial order and domination that had held for almost a century—and it worked. Along with banning segregation in public accommodations, it banned discrimination in the workplace—and not only on the basis of race, but sex, religion, and national origin as well. It permitted the attorney general to sue school districts that failed to integrate, finally giving teeth to the Supreme Court's 1954 *Brown v. Topeka Board of Education* ruling. And it barred federal funds from going to state or local programs that practiced discrimination—effectively withholding billions of dollars from the Jim Crow South, until the South got rid of Jim Crow. The act put the political, economic, and moral power of the federal government firmly behind black America, in a single step demolishing white supremacy's stranglehold on public policy.

While racism and discrimination are still facts of American life, the profound effects of the Civil Rights Act are evident in every facet of contemporary society, from the expansion of the black middle class to the election of black officials to the highest offices in the land. Less well known is the full story behind the act's passage.

The basic outlines of the bill's biography are of course familiar. President John F. Kennedy introduced it in June 1963 in response to growing racial tension across the South, in particular the violent crackdown against black protesters in Birmingham. As the bill moved through the House that year, it was spurred along by events like the March on Washington in August, the bombing of the 16th Street Baptist Church in Birmingham in September, and the assassination of President Kennedy in November. Once the House passed the bill the next February, Southern Democrats in the Senate tried to kill it by refusing to allow a vote on it, also known as filibustering. Despite sinking dozens of bills before, this time the Southerners failed, and the bill became law.

We think we know this story, because we know so well the two men most often associated with it: the Reverend Dr. Martin Luther King Jr. and Kennedy's successor, Lyndon B. Johnson. Every biography of King and Johnson tells how one or the other, or sometimes both, made the bill a reality—King with his moral force on the streets of Birmingham and before the Lincoln Memorial, Johnson with his political lever-pulling behind the scenes on Capitol Hill.

Their combined efforts overcame the Southerners' historic filibuster and demonstrated what great men can achieve when the stars align, as they did in Washington that year.

This story, however, is in need of significant updating. King and Johnson were great men, and they played critical roles in the bill's passage. But neither deserves all the credit, or even the bulk of it. On the contrary, the bill came to pass thanks to a long list of starring and supporting players: men like Senate Minority Leader Everett Dirksen, Deputy Attorney General Nicholas Katzenbach, and Republican representatives William McCulloch and John Lindsay. Outside Congress and the White House, dozens of civil rights, labor, and religious groups brought enormous pressure on the government to create and then strengthen the bill, and later provided the manpower and coordination to pull the bill through the record-breaking filibuster it faced in the Senate—led by men like labor leader Walter Reuther, the National Association for the Advancement of Colored People (NAACP)'s Clarence Mitchell and Roy Wilkins, and the National Council of Churches president, J. Irwin Miller. The Civil Rights Act is often explained like a one-man play, when in fact it had a cast of thousands.

The idea that either King or Johnson was the dominant figure behind the Civil Rights Act distorts not only the history of the act but the process of American legislative policymaking in general. The purpose of this book is to correct that distortion.

Again, King and Johnson played important roles. Without King's Birmingham protest campaign in the spring of 1963, in which the city's police were goaded into siccing dogs on schoolchildren, Attorney General Robert Kennedy and his Justice Department advisers could not have persuaded President John F. Kennedy to submit the original civil rights bill to Congress. And King's magnificent "I Have a Dream" speech during the March on Washington helped persuade white America that the time had come for federal action on civil rights. But King did not plan the march, and the speech itself had little direct impact on Congress. And King played no role whatsoever in the writing of or lobbying for the bill. Instead, that work was done by men like Mitchell, the head lobbyist for the NAACP, and Whitney Young, the head of the Urban League, both of whom had deep contacts in Congress and quietly but forcefully worked for the bill's passage.

Likewise, Johnson's repeated public demands that Congress pass the entire bill were vital. Had he even once called on the bill's backers to compromise, the fragile edifice of support for the legislation might well have crumbled. But Johnson's role has been greatly exaggerated, while the momentum generated by his predecessor, and the tireless work done by

Justice Department officials and members of Congress on both sides of the aisle, has been ignored. Johnson was not, in this instance, the "master of the Senate": he persuaded exactly one senator, Carl Hayden of Arizona, to switch his vote on the filibuster, and in that case Hayden simply moved from a "nay" to being conspicuously absent during the first roll call. Meanwhile, Johnson tried and failed to win over several members of the Southern Democratic bloc, including Al Gore Sr. of Tennessee and J. William Fulbright of Arkansas. And the Senate leadership behind the bill, under Mike Mansfield of Montana, stubbornly rejected Johnson's demand to play hardball against the filibusterers by forcing the Senate into round-the-clock sessions. Rather than directing the bill from on high, Johnson, like everyone else, was trying to make sense of a fluid situation, and was often reacting to and channeling—and being channeled himself by—the many different figures and forces arrayed for and against the bill.

Rather than focusing on King and/or Johnson as the prime movers behind the bill, this book emphasizes the pluralism of the process, the complex and contradictory cast of characters who pushed and pulled the bill toward (or away from) the president's desk. There was the Republican representative William McCulloch, the deeply conservative small-town Ohio lawyer whose quiet passion for civil rights helped save the bill from being derailed in the House Judiciary Committee. There was Everett Dirksen, whose support for the bill brought over enough Republicans to defeat the filibuster. And there was Representative Howard Smith, the archsegregationist from Virginia who amended the bill so that it banned sex discrimination—a move that he hoped would turn off congressional male chauvinists but that actually opened the door to equality for millions of American women. It was the varied efforts of these and other men, not the genius of a single historical actor, that made the Civil Rights Act.

An exclusive focus on King and Johnson also marginalizes the important efforts of thousands of labor, civil rights, and religious activists to win passage. One of the central but often forgotten stories behind the bill is how it catalyzed a nationwide movement behind black equality, drawing in retired white parishioners in Iowa, auto workers in Detroit, black college students in South Carolina, and Jewish seminarians in New York City. In many cases, particularly among whites outside the South, lobbying for the bill—either through letter writing, or local demonstrations, or trips to Washington—was their first involvement with civil rights, and with social activism (as the rest of the 1960s and later decades can attest, for many it would not be their last). Yet the bill could not have passed without their sheer numbers and relentless effort. As Georgia senator Richard Russell, the leader of the filibuster, wrote to a friend after the bill passed, "We had been able to hold the line until all the churches joined the civil rights lobby in 1964."[4]

Finally, because neither King nor Johnson played much of a role in writing or negotiating the bill, telling the story of the Civil Rights Act through them obscures the significant ways in which the bill changed over the year between its submission by Kennedy and its signature by Johnson. In a March 1964 article in the *Nation*, Martin Luther King Jr. called the civil rights bill "the child of a storm, the product of the most turbulent motion the nation has ever known in peacetime." Kennedy did not want a ban on employment discrimination in the bill at all, and his initial version did not include Title VII. But civil rights lobbyists persuaded House Judiciary Committee chairman Emanuel Celler to add it. After that, though, the means of enforcing the ban were whittled back by the administration and congressional Republicans. Separately, the idea of adding significant federal spending on jobs and worker training to help poor blacks was heavily debated during the early months of the bill, but it was left on the drafting room floor. Why? Only a history that focuses on the bill itself, and not merely on one of the people involved in it, can give the whole picture in all its complexity.[5]

AT THE OUTSET of 1963, few expected anything more than token federal action on civil rights, and even then no one expected it to pass. Civil rights supporters had seen too many promising advances—the 1954 *Brown* decision to end school segregation, the 1957 and 1960 civil rights acts—fail to deliver. President Kennedy had paid scant attention to civil rights as a domestic policy issue, and he was expected to do the bare minimum necessary to secure the black vote before the 1964 election. Just over a year later, President Johnson sat down in the East Room of the White House and signed the most sweeping single piece of legislation passed by Congress since the end of the Civil War.

The bill did have its shortcomings—it left alone things like de facto school and housing segregation, and it paid short shrift to voting discrimination; in fact, less than nine months after Johnson signed the Civil Rights Act, he and the Senate Democrats introduced a separate bill to address voting discrimination more fully, culminating in the Voting Rights Act of 1965. Nor did it address the problems facing blacks aside from discrimination, like the lack of well-paying jobs in urban areas or the low levels of educational attainment in African American communities, problems that may have been rooted in racism but would not be solved simply by its eradication.

Nevertheless, the Civil Rights Act is a monument to the capacity of American democracy to tackle knotty, long-standing social and political problems through peaceful, reasonable means. Particularly at a time when, in the early twenty-first century, Americans despair over partisan gridlock and uncompromising political positions, the passage of the act offers an example of what the country's legislative machinery was once capable of, and what it may well be able to achieve again. The act did not solve American racism, something the country is still dealing with—and may never fully overcome. But it moved America forward to an extent that no one, at its outset, could have expected. How that happened is the subject of this book.

CHAPTER I

BAD BEGINNINGS
TO A BIG YEAR

THE GUESTS BEGAN TO LINE up outside the Southwest Gate of the White House in the early evening of February 12, 1963. The temperature, barely above zero all day, was dropping fast. The queue, eleven hundred invitees long, moved slowly; women shivered in their cocktail dresses, men popped their suit collars. They had come from all corners of the country—Atlanta, Chicago, Texas—but few grumbled at the inconvenience. They were about to be received by President and Mrs. Kennedy themselves before proceeding to a lavish reception in the East Wing.[1]

The event, an hour-long reception to mark Lincoln's birthday during the centennial year of the Emancipation Proclamation, had brought together a nearly comprehensive roster of the nation's black leadership: college presidents, ministers, and civil rights leaders rubbed elbows with government officials and black entertainers. Howard University president James Nabrit was there; so was Sammy Davis Jr. The poet Langston Hughes filed in, as did NAACP president Roy Wilkins.[2]

Well-stocked bars and an extensive buffet—shrimp creole, curried chicken, roast turkey, tongue—kept the guests occupied while they waited to have their photographs taken with the president. Others danced to the sounds of the Marine Corps band. "It would be impossible for any reporter to name all the 'big shots' who were there," wrote an unnamed "special correspondent" for the *New Journal and Guide*, a black newspaper from Norfolk, Virginia, "simply because he could not possibly have seen them all in the mass of humanity that flowed in and out of a dozen corridors and ballrooms."[3]

To many observers, the function was a blatant, brilliant attempt by Kennedy's Democrats to co-opt the legacy of Abraham Lincoln, the nation's first Republican president and the man whose memory still brought millions of black voters to the GOP. Lincoln's birthday had long been a high point in the party's political calendar, a day when Republican legislators headed home to their states and districts to trumpet their successes and lambast their opponents. This year was no different: at a reception in Binghamton, New York, Senator Jacob Javits attacked the Kennedy administration as "stand pat" and "lacking in impulse and the momentum to innovate." But while reports of similar criticism filtered back into the nation's leading newspapers, they were drowned out by coverage of the White House event. "Pity the poor Republicans!" chided *Jet* magazine. "Once they had a day for themselves— Lincoln's birthday. Now the Dems have snatched this away."[4]

But the real political theater—darker, cynical, less interested in the morality of civil rights than its political advantages and risks—played out behind the scenes. Kennedy, aware of how racial discrimination in America was hurting the country's global image, had stormed into office promising to make real progress on civil rights, only to drop the issue before even taking office. But by late 1962, Kennedy's inner circle had begun to take seriously the liberals' warning that inaction on civil rights could hurt the president in the 1964 election. The black vote had arguably put him over the top in 1960, and he would need it again in his run for reelection, especially if he were pitted against a liberal Republican like New York governor Nelson Rockefeller. To win over blacks, his advisers said, the president had to do something high profile and substantive to show that he took civil rights seriously.

Not everyone in the White House agreed. Kennedy had a broad agenda— tax cuts, space exploration, urban renewal, education—all of which, they calculated, could be derailed by a divisive campaign for civil rights legislation. So far, Kennedy, while sympathetic on civil rights, seemed to concur. He had offered a milquetoast voting rights bill in mid-1962 that had withered under a Southern filibuster, and he had signed a weak executive order banning discrimination in new homes built with federal subsidies—at the time a small fraction of the nation's housing stock. Kennedy made clear that those measures were as far as he would go for the moment.

The complaints against Kennedy were legion: not only had he failed to send major civil rights legislation to Congress, as he had promised to do in his campaign speeches, but by appointing a series of federal judges with demonstrated racist proclivities (as a sop to Southern Democrats), he had in fact made the situation worse for blacks in the South. W. Harold Cox, whom Kennedy appointed in June 1961 to the Southern District of Mississippi, was a particular embarrassment, given to using gross racial epithets on the bench. (In 1964 Cox would dismiss charges against all but two of the men indicted for the murder of three civil rights workers in Neshoba County, Mississippi.)

Some black journalists even spoke of a political revolt against the Democratic Party. "President Kennedy will impose a great strain on his Negro supporters and on Democratic left wingers in general if he bypasses civil rights action in the coming session of Congress," wrote the *Chicago Defender*, a black newspaper.[5]

Kennedy wasn't alone in looking beyond civil rights; the country in general seemed to have let the issue slip from its consciousness. In an article that spring for the *Nation*, Martin Luther King Jr. wrote that 1962 was "the year that civil rights was displaced as the dominant issue in domestic politics." Despite the violent clashes in October 1962 over integration at Ole Miss, "there was a perceptible diminishing in the concern of the nation to achieve a just solution to the problem." Part of the blame "must be laid to the adminis- tration's cautious tactics," King wrote. "Even in the shadow of Cuba, such issues as trade legislation and tax reform took the play away from civil rights in editorial columns, public debate and headlines." But it was also the unin- tended consequence of Kennedy's sunny New Frontier promise: who wanted to dwell on an intractable problem when the nation seemed to be moving forward, fast, in almost every other pursuit? The nation was moving forward, but it was leaving black Americans behind.[6]

Civil rights leaders continued to push for further action. The president's admin- istration overlapped with the centennial of Lincoln's, and among other things King had been lobbying Kennedy to issue a "Second Emancipation Proclamation," to come one hundred years after the first. He had even sent the president a suggested text, much revised after internal debates among King's advisers, in May 1962. Though this final version was short and unremarkable, even then it was too strong for the cautious Kennedy. The president did not respond.[7]

Still, as the new year began, Kennedy agreed that something needed to be done. He fastened on to an idea put forth by two members of his inner circle, his in-house intellectual Arthur M. Schlesinger Jr. and Louis E. Martin, the deputy chairman of the Democratic National Committee: rather than a pithy statement that would upset the president's allies among both the Southern conservatives and the racial liberals, why not a social event, pegged to Lincoln's birthday? There had never been anything like it, Martin said, a fact sure to push the black press into positive coverage. At the same time, it would not leave a trace—managed correctly, the white press would ignore it, and a few days later it would be forgotten by all but the attendees. Tellingly, only one momentary crisis marred the evening in the president's eyes: at one point Kennedy saw Sammy Davis Jr. with his Swedish wife May Britt, who was white. "Who invited them?" he fumed at his aides. The couple was a hot item in the press, both for their celebrity status and, much more so, their differing skin tones. If a photographer caught the president with them on film, the resulting coverage could stick him on the front page—and in the middle of the "race issue" the president had sought so assiduously to avoid. Kennedy ducked and weaved around the crowd, and managed to avoid the pair completely—at least when the cameras were around.[8]

Kennedy may have won points with some members of the black elite with the Lincoln Day cocktail hour, but those with a sharp political eye knew the event was a distraction, a PR stunt. Even *Jet* magazine, which otherwise fawned over the White House's attention on Lincoln Day, issued a warning to Kennedy at the end of its coverage of the reception: "The VIPs appreciate the hospitality but for the rest of the year they'll be quietly paying for the air tickets, the clothes, and the hotel reservations. The brother who didn't get to see the inside of the White House wants some civil rights relief."[9]

Missing from the crowd that night were three civil rights leaders who would do more than most to shape the remaining months of Kennedy's term: A. Philip Randolph, the head of the Brotherhood of Sleeping Car Porters and the patriarch of the civil rights movement; Clarence Mitchell, the chief lobbyist for the NAACP; and Martin Luther King Jr. himself. All three had declined the invitation in polite protest of the administration's weak record on civil rights. While many of the guests inside the White House were flattered by Kennedy's hour of attention, these three took it as a challenge: if the president offered shrimp creole in lieu of efforts to address racial injustice, they would find new ways to make the political system turn in their direction. By that point King was already well into his plans for a mass demonstration in Birmingham, Alabama. Randolph was beginning to formulate his own demonstration plans, this time for a rally in Washington that summer. And Mitchell was brainstorming ideas for forcing the White House to act on civil rights legislation. By the year's end, these three, acting separately, would combine to push the White House and Congress toward civil rights legislation more sweeping than anyone at the president's reception that cold February evening could have predicted.[10]

SEASONED CIVIL RIGHTS leaders were used to disappointment. Though the 1950s and early '60s were later remembered for a string of incremental civil rights victories, the era was a series of frustrations for those who lived through it. It is striking to consider that on the eve of the Civil Rights Act, civil rights as a cause was in every way stymied, compromised, and ignored by the government and large swaths of the American public.

The postwar years had started out optimistically. Though Franklin D.

Roosevelt had hardly been a close friend of the civil rights movement, his administration had taken a few small but important steps to help blacks, most notably a series of executive orders during World War II that created and strengthened the Fair Employment Practices Commission. That body, which was intended to root out employment discrimination in companies with government contracts, enjoyed mixed success. But after almost a decade of New Deal legislation that largely excluded blacks at the behest of Southern legislators, the FEPC showed that Roosevelt was not completely ignorant or unmoved by the plight of African Americans, and it offered hope that more action might soon follow.

His successor, Harry S. Truman, at first built on and seemed to exceed his predecessor's commitment to helping blacks. In June 1947 he stood in front of a civil rights rally at the Lincoln Memorial, 10,000 strong, to declare "new concepts of civil rights . . . not the protection of the people against the government, but the protection of the people by the government." That October his Civil Rights Committee issued a landmark report, "To Secure These Rights," which laid out the case for government action against discrimination and outlined a federal infrastructure to do it, including the creation of a Civil Rights Division in the Department of Justice, a permanent Civil Rights Commission, and a joint standing committee on civil rights in Congress. And in July 1948, Truman issued both Executive Order 9980, which established a fair employment practices office within the Civil Service Commission to monitor discrimination within the federal government, and Executive Order 9981, which banned discrimination in the armed forces.[11]

Truman and the federal government were not the only ones pressing civil rights in the postwar era. States and cities were active as well, particularly in the industrial North. In March 1945, New York State passed the Ives-Quinn Act, which vested a fair employment commission with cease-and-desist powers, modeled on the National Labor Relations Board. That body in turn became the basis for similar state-level agencies across the country. In 1949 states enacted more civil rights laws than ever before; by the turn of the decade, eight of them had their own employment discrimination laws.[12]

But the burst of activism in the 1940s was short-lived. Truman's words, however heartfelt, were just words, and after his paper-thin victory in the 1948 election, and a failed campaign to reform the Senate's filibuster rules, there was almost no chance of seeing those words turned into deed. Truman and his allies in Congress submitted a sheaf of civil rights bills anyway—including measures against the poll tax and lynching—only to see them defeated, one by one. In May 1950 Southern senators even filibustered an FEPC proposal that made compliance strictly voluntary. Nor were the state and municipal laws a

clear sign of success: many were voluntary, staffed by unpaid or part-time officials, given meager legal recourse, and starved of funding—in other words,
window dressing for cities with growing populations of black voters.

And for every step forward, it often seemed like there was at least one step
back. On Christmas Day 1951 the Florida NAACP coordinator, Harry T.
Moore, and his wife were assassinated, two of scores of black activists killed in
the wave of violence and intimidation that crashed over the South in the late
1940s and early '50s.[13]

It did not help that most of official Washington preferred to ignore civil
rights during the 1950s. President Dwight D. Eisenhower, though hardly a
defender of Jim Crow, believed that aside from protecting voting rights and
enforcing court orders, the federal government had no obligations in the
field. And the Democrats, after adopting an aggressive civil rights plank in
their 1948 platform—and seeing a sizable chunk of the South bolt for the
Dixiecrat ticket—beat a broad retreat at the next election, adopting a much
weaker plank and nominating Alabama senator John Sparkman, a segregationist New Dealer, to run as vice president alongside Adlai Stevenson, the
governor of Illinois.[14]

Stevenson was joined by such public moralists as the theologian Reinhold
Niebuhr, who called on liberals to slow their civil rights activities because the
South had made "steady progress in racial justice" and it would "be a calamity
if this progress were arrested by heedless action." Southern moderates had
succeeded in convincing liberals like Niebuhr that the region's advances were
real but fragile, that the South was particularly sensitive to pressure or criticism from the outside, and too much noise from liberal Democrats could kill
off those buds like an early April frost. Such realism and practical moderation
were the new watchwords, said Eleanor Roosevelt: "It means going ahead one
step at a time in accordance with the realities, and the priority of importance."
Niebuhr and Roosevelt were not being callous; they did in fact believe strongly
in civil rights. But like most Americans in the 1950s, they also believed that
the postwar spirit of centrist consensus, right-thinking liberalism, and steady,
pro-growth economic policies would soon alleviate, if not eliminate, America's
racial shortcomings.[15]

And in any case, the liberals argued, there was little point in pushing for
civil rights legislation when there was no chance of it passing. The experiences
under Truman were seared into the liberal brain. The Southerners had batted
away bill after bill with brutal, effortless efficiency. The caucus had held a full
nelson on the American legislative process for decades, but never was it more
effective than in the 1950s. Under the leadership of Georgia senator Richard
B. Russell, the Southerners—who by 1963 were technically bipartisan, having

added Texas Republican John Tower to their caucus in the 1962 midterms—were the true masters of the Senate. They controlled the majority of the Senate committees, including Judiciary, Armed Services, and Finance, giving them almost total control of the flow of legislation through the upper chamber.

Southern politicians and voters alike understood the overarching value of seniority in Congress, and they made sure their elected officials had a lock on it. Turnover in their ranks was rare, brought on only by death or the occasional retirement."[16]

Though many Southern senators would develop individual interests—Russell and his Louisiana colleague Allen Ellender were both foreign policy wonks—their primary commitment remained the preservation of the intricate web of laws and customs that kept whites and blacks separate and unequal. Over the years they had beaten back bills to make lynching a federal crime, to end the poll tax, and to loosen literacy test requirements; in all, 120 bills had died either in the Judiciary Committee, overseen by Mississippi senator James Eastland, or under the withering fire of a full-on filibuster since the end of World War II.[17]

Even the two civil rights acts passed under the Eisenhower administration—one in 1957, one in 1960—proved to be more demonstrations of Southern power than successes by their opponents. The debate over the 1957 act centered around its third section, or title, which gave the attorney general the power to file suit against the denial of constitutional rights. The bill was introduced in 1956 and easily cleared the liberal-leaning House of Representatives. But when it reached the Senate, on the last day before Congress adjourned for the year, it was diverted to the Judiciary Committee at the behest of Lyndon Johnson, then the majority leader, who wanted to make the liberals cool their heels until he could devise a strategy for getting some form of the bill through. The bill was revived in 1957—and almost immediately set upon by Russell, who charged that Title III was "a potential instrument of tyranny and persecution" that could be used "to jail, imprison and mistreat American citizens." And Russell had a point: Title III was technically an amendment to an existing part of the federal code that allowed the president "or such person as he may empower for that purpose," including the attorney general, to use the military to enforce civil rights. In other words, Title III would give the attorney general not just legal power over the South, but military power as well.[18]

But even without Russell's damning insight, the bill was guaranteed a haircut; Johnson, wanting a token civil rights bill under his belt for a future presidential run, had worked out a deal with Russell to whittle the bill to a nub, then allow it to pass. In short order, Title III was axed, and another provision, which allowed the Justice Department to sue over a denial of the right to vote, was weakened by the addition of a requirement that cases be tried in front of a jury—which, in the South, meant white defendants would inevitably be judged by all-white juries.[19]

President Eisenhower signed the bill on September 9, 1957, but the civil rights community had long since disowned it. "It has been the advocates of segregation and of white domination who have won the major triumph," said Senator Douglas. Many blamed Johnson for trimming the bill so closely, a suitable trophy for his own career but of little use to its intended beneficiaries. "I was so mad at Johnson I was speechless, for gutting the bill so much," said the civil rights lawyer and activist Joe Rauh.[20]

But others were less pessimistic. Though the bill did not amount to much in substance, symbolically it was a breakthrough. Even before the bill passed, the *New York Times* predicted that its passage would "result in a more or less permanent coalition of Republican and Democratic liberals to act as a slight counterbalance to the conservative coalition . . . Both the political as well as the social demand for better race laws has reached a point where they can no longer be ignored." Many supported the bill not because of what it did, but what it made possible. "All of a sudden you started hearing it all over the place: 'We've got to break the virginity,'" recalled Representative Richard Bolling, a liberal Democrat from Missouri. "You heard guys saying things about 'once they do it the first time, it won't be so hard to get them to do it the next time.'"[21]

But that "next time" did not arrive for a long time. Almost immediately, journalists and activists were predicting a wave of new civil rights legislation in 1958. When nothing happened that year, the *New Journal and Guide* ran a headline predicting NEW LAWS EXPECTED WHEN CONGRESS CONVENES IN '59. That article appeared on December 27; just over two weeks later, Eisenhower said he would not support civil rights legislation during the coming year, save for an effort to strengthen voting rights.[22]

That bill, when it did arrive, amounted to little more than a weak echo of the 1957 act. Though it took sixteen months to work its way through Congress, in its final form the Civil Rights Act of 1960 merely allowed courts to appoint voting referees—glorified observers, really—and required the preservation of voting records. "It is almost certain that this bill, again designed ostensibly to give southern negroes the ballot, will enfranchise only a handful of the thousands who are voteless today," wrote the *Washington Post.*[23]

On the floor of the Senate, the bill's supporters wallowed in self-pitying theatrics. After Arkansas senator John McClellan boasted that "we have repelled, for the time being at least, vicious assaults on the rights and liberties of our people," Senator Joseph S. Clark Jr. lamented: "The roles of Grant and Lee at Appomattox have been reversed." Turning to Richard Russell, he said,

"Dick, here is my sword. I hope you'll give it back to me so I can bend it into a plowshare." Clark then read "The Battle Hymn of the Republic" as Russell looked up in a silent gloat at the galleries.[24]

CLARK MAY HAVE been milking the scene for melodrama, but he was not wrong. Despite increased racial activism across the South, things during the late 1950s, remembered as the early years of the "high tide" of the civil rights movement, were actually getting worse for blacks.

Take voting rights. Between 1940 and 1946, an estimated four hundred thousand blacks registered to vote in the South, bringing the total to some six hundred thousand. Returning black veterans had pushed against Jim Crow, and in a few places, Jim Crow stepped backward. But the white South soon recovered its stance and tightened the vise of segregation. In Louisiana the number of registered black voters dropped from 10 percent in 1956 to 6.9 percent in 1962. In Mississippi it went from 1.4 percent to 1.1 percent. According to a 1959 study by the Southern Regional Council, the number of registered black voters in eight Southern states dropped by nearly forty-six thousand between 1956 and 1958 alone.[25]

To be fair, the 1957 act did two important things: it gave the Department of Justice the power to sue over voting rights violations, and it elevated the department's Civil Rights Section to division level, with a commensurate increase in funding and staffing. But while that looked like progress on paper, in practice it was a shuffle-step forward, wholly dependent on the men in charge at Justice. In October 1957 Herbert Brownell Jr., Eisenhower's pro-civil-rights attorney general, resigned, replaced by William Rogers. Under Rogers the new Civil Rights Division became a backwater, at a time when working at Justice was already low on the wish list of ambitious young lawyers headed to the federal government. Between 1957 and 1964 the department brought a mere fifty-five suits under the 1957 and 1960 acts. And it could take years for a suit to work through the court system, leaving blacks with little real relief. House Judiciary Committee Chairman Emanuel Celler declared in January 1964 that "the right-to-vote section of the 1957 civil rights law has been a failure."[26]

A similar story could be heard about education. In 1954 the Supreme Court handed down its decision in *Brown v. Topeka Board of Education*, ruling that school segregation was unconstitutional. But a year later, in the so-called *Brown II* decision, it ruled that school desegregation should proceed with "all deliberate speed," be implemented by local school boards, and be overseen by district courts. While some border states and cities did in fact move ahead with desegregation plans, across much of the South, *Brown II* made the 1954 decision a dead letter. In the four years after the initial *Brown* decision, Southern states passed 196 statutes against school integration.[27]

As a result, by 1962, eight years after *Brown*, only 7.8 percent of black students in the South attended integrated schools. Of the 3,058 Southern school districts with both black and white students, only 972 qualified as even minimally desegregated, and 815 of those were in border states. Three Southern states lacked even a single integrated school district. The specifics were even more damning: while half of all blacks in the border state of Kentucky attended integrated schools, only 1 percent of blacks in North Carolina did. In Virginia, out of 217,000 school-age black children, only 533 attended an integrated school on the eve of the Civil Rights Act of 1964.[28]

A different kind of school segregation, in some ways equally as insidious as the de jure system of the South, affected districts in other parts of the country. From Los Angeles to Chicago to the Boston suburbs, blacks were excluded from vast tracts of residential neighborhoods, even as they were subtly but blatantly discriminated against in the workplace. The result was de facto segregation, in which blacks and whites lived, worked, and studied separately—and because whites got the better-paying jobs, their neighborhoods and schools were significantly better off. As the historian Thomas J. Sugrue documented in his book *Sweet Land of Liberty*, as early as the 1920s, Northern blacks were launching sizable protest movements against de facto school segregation in places like Chester, Pennsylvania; Benton Harbor, Michigan; and Shaker Heights, Ohio. In tiny Hillburn, New York, black families boycotted the 1943–44 school year to protest school district lines that intricately divided whites and blacks. On October 22, 1963, as the Judiciary Committee debated the civil rights bill in the House of Representatives, nearly a quarter of a million black students boycotted school in Chicago to protest de facto segregation and unequal resources.[29]

And while the postwar economic situation for blacks was rising in absolute terms through the 1950s and early '60s, they were falling further behind whites in every corner of the country. Again, early gains proved elusive: median black household income rose from below half to about 60 percent of that of white families in the early 1950s—and then began to taper off over the following decade. As late as 1966, the legal scholar Michael Sovern lamented in a report for the Century Foundation: "Perhaps the most poignant evidence of the Negro's subordinate role in our economy is the extent to which Negro newspapers regard as newsworthy the opening of the most ordinary jobs to members of their race."[30]

WITHIN THE MOVEMENT itself, by the early 1960s the mood was one of frustration. "I think 1962 was perhaps the lowest moment for the civil rights movement during the Kennedy years," said NAACP president Wilkins. Enormous energies had been unleashed, milestones seemingly achieved. Yet the energies were spent to little end. The *Brown* decision was a landmark in American judicial history, but what seemed like the goal for so long—the end to legal segregation—turned out to be just the beginning.[31]

Even outside the South, progress was uneven at best. James P. Davis, a black state legislator from Kansas City, Kansas, told of a car trip his family took to North Dakota, which took him across Kansas and into Nebraska. As long as they remained in his state, the Davises could not find service at a single restaurant; as soon as they crossed into Nebraska, where discrimination in public accommodations was illegal, they had no problem. (Davis and a colleague then led a successful campaign to get a similar accommodations law passed in Kansas.)[32]

Such progress was unpredictable; in early 1963, four years after the predominantly rural, conservative state of Kansas opened up its public accommodations, the middle-class, liberal Chicago suburb of Oak Park refused to desegregate its symphony—because, the president of the symphony association said, "Nothing is integrated in Oak Park, you know."[33]

Time and again, behind the headlines of progress one could find complications, reversals, standstills, and only the occasional step forward. In February 1960, four black students in Greensboro, North Carolina, took seats at a Woolworth's lunch counter and asked for service. When the wait, staff ignored them, they remained in their seats until closing time—and in doing so launched a new wave of sit-ins. Black protesters across the country copied and adapted the "-in" model for their own purposes: wade-ins at segregated swimming pools, kneel-ins at segregated churches, play-ins at segregated parks. The Greensboro action also inaugurated a surge of student and youth activism that would resonate through the black movement—and deep into white culture as well. The next year black students and other activists boarded buses for the Freedom Rides through the South, enduring violence and arrests as they passed deeper into the region and, eventually, forcing intervention by a reluctant Kennedy administration. Largely as a result, in September 1961, Attorney General Robert Kennedy issued new rules banning segregation in interstate travel—though even that was a small accomplishment, since it simply added federal muscle to a six-year-old ban by the Interstate Commerce Commission.[34]

Indeed, such signs of progress were valuable largely for their symbolism. The Kennedy rules were intended to signal that the administration supported black demands for freedom of movement around the country, without

offending the administration's Southern Democratic allies. The 1957 and 1960 civil rights acts symbolized congressional intent to protect black voting rights, but as substance they meant little. As the *Cleveland Call and Post*, a black newspaper, wrote in a September 1961 editorial, "At the present rate of progress, without the help of new and stronger federal laws, it could well be another century before all of the barriers erected by Southern states against Negro voting are shattered."[35]

Complicating things further was the fact that there was no single, unified civil rights movement, but many: there were the establishment organizations like the NAACP and the Urban League; the Southern, religiously inflected groups like the Southern Christian Leadership Conference (SCLC); the brasher groups of students and other young people, like the Congress of Racial Equality (CORE) and the Student Nonviolent Coordinating Committee (SNCC); and the urban, radical outfits like the Black Muslims. And those were just at the national level; at the state, local, and neighborhood level, a constellation of civil rights groups focused on specific goals using specific methods—picketing segregated work sites, keeping their children out of segregated schools, and boycotting segregated department stores.

By the early 1960s, these frustrations and competing energies threatened to undermine the fragile unity of the movement. At the national level, at least, a fragile alliance bound together the mainstream organizations. But many of the secular, establishment leaders, like Wilkins of the NAACP and Whitney Young of the Urban League—men most effective in the banquet halls and Capitol Hill offices of Washington, men who had worked for decades to build a national movement—felt challenged by, and a bit envious of, the upstart success of the Southern-focused, religious Martin Luther King Jr. and his even younger comrades-in-arms in SNCC. "We talked of the need to coordinate our work, not duplicate it or divide our forces, but except for some good results on voter education and registration in the South, we were not really pulling together," Wilkins said later. King and SNCC eschewed politics for bearing moral witness; forcing confrontation with segregation in its rawest, ugliest form, they felt, was the only way to effect real change. And yet even then there was tension—the impatient students in SNCC saw King, a few years older, but a generation apart, as too square, too self-conscious, too focused on his own moral righteousness; behind his back they called him "Da Lawd." To his face they paid fealty to his organizing prowess, but the rifts—regional, generational, theological—kept the different strands of the movement from cohering into a national force.[36]

ONE THING, MAYBE the only thing, almost everyone in the movement could agree on was the need for presidential leadership. And so perhaps the biggest frustration of the early 1960s came from the White House. On July 15, 1960, less than forty-eight hours after John F. Kennedy won the Democratic nomination for president and less than a day after he announced Lyndon Johnson as his running mate, the two men sat down in the Rendezvous Room of the Biltmore Hotel in downtown Los Angeles with a klatch of the party's leading black officials, organized by Representative William Dawson of Chicago. The group, already wary of Kennedy's lily-white background and Johnson's spotty civil rights history, rained questions on the duo. Much of the skepticism focused on Johnson. "How can you account for the fact that Senator Johnson is perhaps a symbol against the sit-ins?" asked a convention delegate from Detroit. The Reverend E. Franklin Jackson, of Washington, D.C., asked, in reference to the special session of Congress that Johnson would oversee, as majority leader, when he returned from the convention: "What assurance can you give us that we will get some help from Senator Johnson in the next six weeks? That's when we are going to need it, if the Negro is going to get any help."[37]

Kennedy asked them to follow him in implementing the strong civil rights plank that, just days before, the party had written into its platform. "What we are interested in is the support of all those who support the platform," the candidate said. "What we are interested in is the program. It was written by people associated with me. In the final analysis I bear the responsibility." The next day, Kennedy's words were there for all to read on the front page of the *New York Times*.[38]

They were words Kennedy came to regret. He had just committed himself to carrying out the most extensive civil rights program adopted by either of the two main parties since 1948—a program that, given the power of the Southern Democratic bloc, was virtually impossible to achieve. Among other things, it called for an end to literacy tests and poll taxes; a requirement that school districts submit detailed desegregation plans to begin no later than 1963, offering technical compliance to do so; full Title III powers for the attorney general; a fair employment practices commission; and an end to discrimination in federally assisted housing programs—all under "the strong, active, persuasive, and inventive leadership of the President of the United States."[39]

But rather than backing down, Kennedy doubled down. On October 7, during his second debate with Vice President Richard M. Nixon, Kennedy said that Americans were entitled to know "what will be the leadership of the president in these areas to provide equality of opportunity for employment.

Equality of opportunity in the field of housing, which could be done in all federal-supported housing by a stroke of the president's pen." Less than three weeks later, at the instigation of his advisers Louis Martin and Harris Wofford, he called Martin Luther King Jr.'s wife, Coretta, after her husband had been sentenced to prison in Georgia. The call was just a gesture, and widely interpreted as a campaign move; nonetheless it was welcomed, especially since it stood in contrast to the actions of the Nixon campaign, which had decided to stay removed from the issue. The call was of a part with Kennedy's act-fast charisma, the force of his language, and the energy of his campaign, all of which seemed to promise the world to African Americans.[40]

"When John F. Kennedy became President later that year," recalled NAACP president Roy Wilkins, "everyone expected him to come in and tear up the pea patch for civil rights." He just had to—after all, it was the black vote in places like Chicago, and thus Illinois, that made the difference in key states; without it, Richard Nixon would become president. In September, Kennedy had asked Senator Joseph Clark and Representative Emanuel Celler to develop legislation to implement the Democratic platform on civil rights in 1961.[41]

Disappointment, when it came, was swift and severe. "Within ten days of the election, Clarence Mitchell had taken careful readings around Washington and found that Kennedy had no intention of beginning his new administration with a full-scale legislative program for civil rights," recalled Wilkins. Kennedy may have owed his election to the black vote, but he and his advisers believed he would owe his legislative success to the Southern Democrats in Congress.[42]

Kennedy was not ignorant or callous about civil rights; he simply saw it for what it was: a morally important issue that was almost impossible, politically, to address. One early incident reveals much about his thinking. On February 10, 1961, three weeks after Kennedy, in his inaugural address, implored his "fellow citizens of the world" to "ask not what America will do for you, but what together we can do for the freedom of man," he sat down with a three-man delegation from Americans for Democratic Action to discuss how to pursue the "freedom of man" at home. The ADA was the leading organization on the anticommunist left, led by such liberal luminaries as Adlai Stevenson, Eleanor Roosevelt, Walter Reuther, and Joe Rauh—the last of whom, one of the leading liberal lawyers in Washington, was among the three meeting with Kennedy that day.[43]

First to speak was Robert Nathan, a New Deal economist who had chaired the ADA in the 1950s. He argued that in order to jump-start the national economy—a recession that had begun in April 1960 was just coming to an end that February, though no one in the room yet knew it—the federal government needed to spend an additional $50 billion, even though doing so would boost the deficit by over 60 percent. Kennedy laughed. "Bob, I want you to keep this up," he said. "It's very helpful now for you to be pushing me this way." Though hardly an intellectual himself, Kennedy loved engaging with them, challenging them, drawing from them. Meetings like this were fun for him, and fun for men like Nathan, who enjoyed trading urbane banter with the leader of the free world.

Then it was Rauh's turn. "Well, Mr. President, I hope that the spirit with which you have treated Bob's pressure from the left, on the issue for which he speaks for the ADA, will go equally for the issue on which I speak for the ADA: civil rights."

The smile dropped from the president's face. "Absolutely not," Kennedy said. "It's a totally different thing. Your criticism on civil rights is quite wrong."

Rauh was stunned. "Oh shit," he thought. "Nothing is going to happen. How did we let this happen?" He withdrew, and the conversation moved on.

But later, reflecting on the incident, Rauh realized that something more was going on in the president's head. Kennedy was not naïve, nor was he unaware of how meager his "achievements" really were. "It seems pretty clearly," Rauh told an interviewer later, "that it was a kind of guilty conscience because he felt that he wasn't doing enough in there, that this was a moral issue."

Over the next several months Wilkins and Rauh sent Kennedy numerous proposals for executive orders on employment and housing, but with nothing to show for it. Wofford, Kennedy's civil rights adviser, did the same—though after a while, he was told not to expect any follow-up to his memos. After Kennedy failed to sign an executive order banning housing discrimination, as he had promised to do in the debate with Nixon, with the "stroke of the presidential pen," thousands of people took part in the "Ink for Jack" campaign, inundating the White House mail room with pens.[44]

The administration's single biggest offense against civil rights, in its advocates' eyes, had come a few weeks before the Lincoln's birthday event, when Kennedy refused to back a move by Senate liberals to reform the Senate's infamous filibuster rules. The particular rule in question, number 22, set the requirements for bringing an end to a debate and moving to a vote on legislation—in other words, how many votes it would take to end a filibuster, the Southerners' most powerful and effective tool against civil rights legislation. The rule required two thirds of the senators present in the chamber to vote for an end to the debate, or "cloture," meaning that just handful of senators could prevent the majority from working its will.[45]

Given that the Southern-bloc senators could almost always draw on conservative Republicans for the balance of those votes, the liberals argued that the current rule set too high a bar. And indeed it did: the filibuster was almost never defeated, and had never been broken on a civil-rights-related matter. Liberals had pressed for changing Rule 22 at the start of every session for the past fourteen years, only to see their efforts quashed for lack of broad support in the Senate and executive leadership in the White House.[46]

But now, in early 1963, civil rights forces thought things would be different. Although the liberals continued to lose their annual reform campaigns, the vote counts were getting closer each time. In 1957 Johnson, as majority leader, had tabled a similar motion to reform Rule 22, but it had failed by only seventeen votes—its best showing yet. And in 1958 a wave of young, liberal senators had won office, including Phil Hart of Michigan, Edmund Muskie of Maine, and Eugene McCarthy of Minnesota. By 1963, these men had begun to figure out how the Senate worked, and they were eager to make a renewed push for Rule 22 reform.[47]

Still, for all the changes in the Senate, the decision over whether and how the body's internal rules were applied still rested, to a great degree, with the White House, and in particular with Vice President Lyndon Johnson. Not only did Johnson still pull weight in the chamber that he had dominated as majority leader during the 1950s, but as the president of the Senate he ruled over procedural questions. Civil rights leaders hoped that Johnson's commitment to the 1960 Democratic platform, which called for allowing a simple majority of senators to amend the body's governing rules, meant that this time they could count on him.

The debate over Rule 22 opened on January 14 with a motion by New Mexico Democrat Clinton Anderson, and almost immediately the Democrats ran into trouble. Johnson would once again disappoint the liberals: that afternoon he had his lieutenants out chatting with senators and the press about how the campaign would not only fail, but suck up valuable time and political capital, resources that the White House would rather use for other items on its agenda. The liberals tried repeatedly to get Johnson to issue a statement in their favor, or even any statement at all. Finally, on January 21, Johnson made clear what was already suspected: he would play Pontius Pilate and refuse to rule, which in effect meant siding with the Southerners and their insistence that the current requirement, which was the standing interpretation of the Senate's governing rules, remain. The debate limped on, but on January 31, Anderson's motion was tabled, effectively ending the debate.[48]

Conservatives cheered. The civil rights community mourned. On February 7, Joe Rauh released a statement lambasting Johnson for failing to act on Rule 22 at the moment when, Rauh and others believed, even a little pressure from the executive branch could have made the difference. "Vice President Johnson has demonstrated once again that his first loyalty is to the Southern racists," Rauh wrote. "A majority of the Senate favored a change in the filibuster rule but Vice President Johnson made that impossible."[49]

In a letter to Francis Biddle, a battle-hardened Washington liberal who had mentored him during the Franklin D. Roosevelt administration, Rauh let loose in despair. "I know of no one who has been watching the Senate," Rauh wrote, "who does not feel that Johnson's rulings were inexcusably wrong and cost us our chance at changing the filibuster rule and enacting civil rights legislation." Thanks to the vice president, years of work had been lost. "Some of us who have worked for a decade believing that one day we would have both a majority in the Senate and a favorable vice president and when that day came the rules would be changed," he added. "The heartbreaking thing is that when we finally got a majority of the Senate ready to go, we had lost a favorable vice president." Without a favorable vice president, there could be no Rule 22 change. And with Rule 22 intact, there could be no hope of defeating a Southern filibuster and enacting civil rights legislation. "I personally do not look for any change in this decade," Rauh concluded.[50]

ANY ATTEMPT TO comprehend Kennedy's civil rights position must also be an exploration of the liberal establishment's position. To understand why Kennedy did what he did (or did not do), it is necessary to understand where he was coming from.

By the middle of the twentieth century, the black migration from the rural South to the industrial North was in full tilt, in the process revolutionizing Northern cities and urban politics. But for most Northern whites, the black experience was still an abstraction—particularly for wealthier whites, who were largely insulated from the sharp edge of social change. Even in cities where black populations were already quite large, their day-to-day struggles with poverty, low-wage jobs, and discrimination was filtered and mitigated through a system of political feudalism, in which a few black ward heelers would promise votes to white candidates in exchange for political favors. "Those running for office in the Democratic Party looked to just three or four people who would then deliver the Negro vote," recalled Robert Kennedy, "and you never had to say you were going to do anything on civil rights. You never had to say you were going to do anything on housing. It was mostly just recognition of them."[51]

Moreover, when it came to the South, the Democrats in particular had an enormous incentive to ignore civil rights, lest they run afoul of the powerful Southern Democrats. Every aspiring liberal senator knew first- or secondhand what would happen if he took on the South. In the spring of 1949, the new senator from Minnesota, Hubert H. Humphrey, came into office as a national civil rights celebrity, having made a fiery speech at the 1948 Democratic convention that sealed a place for a strong civil rights plank in the party platform. When he arrived in Washington he had more than seven hundred speaking invitations waiting for him. He dove into the fray immediately; within his first hundred days in office he had called for loosening Rule 22 and submitted legislation to make lynching a federal crime and, separately, to create a federal commission on civil rights.[52]

The Senate leadership, seeing Humphrey as a potential threat, acted preemptively; he was the only new senator not to receive temporary office space, and he was passed over for plum committee assignments, landing on the unimportant Post Office and Government Operations Committees. One day, early in 1949, Humphrey entered the Senate cloakroom to find Russell conversing with a group of other Southerners. Speaking in a way to appear confidential, while still making sure Humphrey heard him, Russell said, "Can you imagine the people of Minnesota sending that damn fool down here to represent them?" As Humphrey—and others who saw or heard of this— quickly realized, "I was not going to make it into the Senate 'Club' on the strength of civil rights." On the contrary, the strict hierarchy of seniority, the collective power of the Southern Democrats, and the culture of compromise that dominated the postwar Senate came together to militate against anyone striking out on an issue as thorny as civil rights—a lesson that someone as savvy as John Kennedy would have absorbed within the first few months of his Senate career, if not before.[53]

The president also understood what it would take to get civil rights legislation through: careful planning, endless negotiations, and the stamina to wait out a Southern filibuster while the rest of his agenda sat on the dock rotting. It was not a question of his commitment, he would tell people, but a matter of political realism. "Nobody needs to convince me any longer," he told Martin Luther King Jr. in early 1961, "that we have to solve the problem, not let it drift into gradualism. But how do you go about it? If we go into a long fight in Congress, it will bottleneck everything else and still get no bill." Nor did anyone he respected try to convince him otherwise: as Kennedy's brother Robert later told the *New York Times* journalist Anthony Lewis, "There wasn't anybody who was calling for civil rights legislation that could really give any leadership in getting it through."[54]

Meanwhile, opposition from the South against his entire agenda proved more robust than the president had expected, even though he came from the Senate and had worked with staunch segregationists like Richard Russell and James Eastland for years. Kennedy simply did not understand how central segregation was to the Southern politician's worldview, a reality upon whose shores his domestic agenda crashed time and again, any time it even came close to challenging Jim Crow: education, health care, rural development, housing. "The Kennedys," said Arthur Fleming, Eisenhower's last secretary of health education and labor and a future chair of the Commission on Civil Rights, "did not anticipate the kind of things that went on in Mississippi. They honestly did not believe the kind of things that people wanted to do to turn back the civil rights initiatives."[55]

That view was rooted in Kennedy's imbibing, long before coming to Congress, the redeemer's myth of the New South: that, left to its own devices, smarter, cooler heads would prevail in the region and, by and by, it would evolve toward racial equality. This was the story he tried to tell in a chapter in his book *Profiles in Courage* about the Mississippi senator and Supreme Court justice L. Q. C. Lamar, who drafted his state's secession ordinance yet later eulogized the abolitionist Massachusetts senator Charles Sumner. (In the same book, Kennedy lambasted the abolitionist Representative Thaddeus Stevens as "the crippled, fanatical personification of the extremes of the Radical Republican movement.")[56]

At the same time, the president and his advisers understood the need for some sort of action on civil rights. In late 1961, Lee White, who took over as Kennedy's point man on civil rights after Wofford's brief tenure, penned a memo for the president arguing for strong action in the coming year. He noted that there was mounting pressure for legislation from the civil rights community, and inaction could hurt the Democrats in the midterm elections. And, he wrote, the Republicans were winning points by criticizing the administration, without offering any proposals of their own. "Javits, Keating, et al. have had great fun twitting the administration," he wrote. "As noted, the pressure surely will increase. It seems obvious the administration must act, the questions being what, how and when." As to the "what," White recommended boldness. "Any package of relatively easy items (e.g. anti-poll tax and literacy legislation) would not satisfy the civil rights groups" while still angering the Southern Democrats. "Thus it should be a strong package or none at all."[57]

But Kennedy remained unconvinced. His congressional liaison, Larry O'Brien, warned that a strong civil rights bill from the president would endanger the rest of his agenda, and still face a strong filibuster. When his brother and Burke Marshall pressed White's case and urged him to issue a voting rights bill, Kennedy told them to go for it—but as a Department of Justice bill, not one from the administration. The bill they sent, introduced in the Senate on January 25, 1962, by Majority Leader Mike Mansfield, was much smaller than what White had urged: it would exempt anyone with a sixth-grade education from having to take a literacy test before registering to vote. Not only did the Southerners filibuster it, but the pro-civil-rights forces in the Senate did almost nothing to defend it. The bill's sponsors brought the filibuster to a vote twice, losing both times, the second by a shockingly low 53–43 vote.[58]

Robert Kennedy was dismayed. "I went up and testified," he later told Anthony Lewis. "Nobody paid the slightest bit of attention to me. We got no place with that. Nobody paid any attention." Though the bill was hardly enough to get civil rights groups motivated, it quickly became clear that nothing short of an all-out war against the Southern Democrats would get a bill through.[59]

The issue, Marshall and others concluded, was that "the Negro and his problems were still pretty invisible to the country as a whole." And without public support, there was little incentive for most senators to risk offending their Southern superiors. Marshall later recalled one particularly revealing conversation with Mansfield. "I asked him what we should tell people that were interested in civil rights legislation," Marshall said, "and he said, 'Tell them the truth.' And I said, 'What is the truth?' And he said, 'That you'll never get a civil rights bill with a Democratic president.'"[60]

To be fair, early on Kennedy did take steps to make the passage of civil rights legislation at least theoretically easier. In 1961 he and Sam Rayburn, the Speaker of the House, drove through an expansion of the House Rules Committee, the panel that decided which legislation made it to the House floor, which had been run for years by the archsegregationist Howard Smith. Enlarging the committee diluted Smith's power, making it easier, at least in theory, to get civil rights bills passed. But for the most part, the president focused his efforts on areas where gradual but concrete achievements could be obtained by the White House on its own: executive orders, Department of Justice litigation, nondiscrimination in government contracts, and the promotion of blacks within the federal bureaucracy.[61]

Kennedy got started on this last step before the sun had even set on his inauguration day. As he watched the parade passing in front of the review stand outside the White House, he noticed that the Coast Guard contingent was completely white. Afterward, he found Richard Goodwin, one of his new special assistants, and ordered him to see why. "Within a few months the Coast Guard Academy was integrated," Goodwin recalled.[62]

Kennedy demanded similar action across the executive branch. Louis Martin, the vice chairman of the Democratic National Committee and the man Kennedy trusted beyond all others on racial issues, kept a list of what he called "superblacks"—three hundred of the most qualified people of color he could find, in a variety of professions—so he could be ready to feed black candidates for any position that came open. And at least at first, the demand for such names was insatiable. "Everyone was scrambling around trying to find himself a Negro in order to keep the President off his neck," recalled Roy Wilkins.[63]

Yet over time the zeal for hiring blacks tapered off. In a March 1963 memo to the president, special adviser Ralph Dungan wrote: "Our effort to recruit outstanding Negroes to fill a representative number of policy level appointive posts in the Administration has had only limited success to date. Moreover, Negro leaders in recent months have publicly registered their disappointment with the slow rate of progress of this Administration."[64]

It is easy to look back at Kennedy's first two and a half years and condemn his performance on civil rights. And there is no doubt he could have done more. But probably not much: until mid-1963, civil rights was not a pressing moral imperative in the eyes of the national leadership. It was one problem among many, and a much more intractable one. Kennedy had a well-stocked plate of priorities, some of his choosing—a big tax cut, a new Housing and Urban Development Department—and some not, like the crises in Berlin and Cuba. All of these required the unified support of the Democratic Party, support that could fall apart if he pushed civil rights too aggressively.

Kennedy had little more success with executive orders. On March 6, 1961, he signed Executive Order 10925, which created the President's Committee on Equal Employment Opportunity and gave it the power to investigate the hiring practices of government contractors and, at its discretion, terminate contracts where discrimination was found. The committee, led by Vice President Johnson, was a big improvement on its previous iteration under the Eisenhower administration, which had lacked any sort of enforcement powers. And it was significantly more active: in its first year it addressed 1,306 cases, more than the number of cases (462) that Eisenhower's committee had dealt with in seven years.[65]

But the Johnson committee shone only by comparison. The committee rarely pursued punitive action; instead, through a program called Plans for Progress, it engaged leading contractors to create internal programs to root out discrimination and promote fair hiring practices. But these were companies with huge budgets, educated workforces, and relatively progressive leadership, and they were glad to get positive PR from the government for pursuing policies they would have undertaken anyway, if they had not already. And the Plans for Progress were completely voluntary, with little oversight by the Johnson committee to make sure the plans were actually put into practice.[66]

As a result, though Johnson had his staff issue regular press releases touting every new company engaged under Plans for Progress, actual progress was halting. A 1963 study by the Department of Labor found that twenty-five thousand of the federal government's thirty-five thousand contractors did not have a single black employee.[67]

Kennedy's other major civil-rights-related executive order was a 1962 edict on housing discrimination, the subject of his audacious presidential debate statement about what a "stroke of the Presidential pen" could achieve, and the cause of much public embarrassment ever since. The idea was to ban discrimination by housing developers and sellers who received federal assistance, either through tax breaks, subsidies, or mortgage guarantees. And it was something Kennedy clearly wanted to do—he had Nicholas deB. Katzenbach, then head of the Office of Legal Counsel in the Justice Department, write up a draft order in the fall of 1961.[68]

But the realities of presidential politics soon intervened. Kennedy had other priorities that fall that would be hurt by spending political capital on housing: among other things, he wanted to create a Department of Housing and Urban Development, a testy subject for Southerners and one they would likely oppose if Kennedy riled them up with an order on housing. After a long beachfront walk at Hyannis Port, Massachusetts, with his brother Robert, Kennedy told Katzenbach to stand down, and the order went on the back burner. It did not matter: Congress rejected the HUD proposal anyway (the department was finally created by President Johnson in 1965).[69]

The experience also revealed for Kennedy the soft underbelly of civil rights support. Even as open-housing advocates pressed him for action, civil rights Democrats in the North were telling him that housing was off-limits. Of course, he did not need politicians to tell him that: over the course of several nights in July 1951, some four thousand white residents of Cicero, Illinois, had attacked an apartment building into which a single black family had moved; eventually Governor Adlai Stevenson had to send in the Illinois National Guard. The Cicero riot was not the first of its kind; nor was it the last—housing integration set off scores of violent episodes across the industrial North throughout the 1950s.[70]

By the early 1960s, the issue was positively radioactive—any politician who advocated open housing risked a drubbing at the polls. That explains why Larry O'Brien, Kennedy's White House congressional liaison, found himself on the receiving end of a scream-filled phone call from Representative Martha Griffiths in September 1962. Griffiths, who represented a suburban Detroit district, was a reliably liberal representative, but she wanted nothing to do with housing: she said she had a team from her office traveling the district asking what was topmost on voters' minds, and the fear that blacks might move into their neighborhood dominated. The president, she demanded, "just couldn't issue that order before the election or we would be dead, politically." O'Brien received similar calls from similarly liberal representatives like James O'Hara, another Detroit-area congressman, and Leonor Sullivan, who represented St. Louis.[71]

Kennedy decided to wait until after the midterm elections to sign the housing order, and even then he had it written in a way to minimize its actual impact. It only applied to primary sales, and it was strictly prospective—sales of existing homes did not count. Although it ostensibly applied to all housing that benefited from federal assistance in any way, it explicitly excluded those backed by federal mortgage insurance, the main way in which the federal government interacted with the housing market. As a result, the order affected only about 25 percent of new housing construction—hardly the sort of bold, pathbreaking action Kennedy had implied would occur with a stroke of his pen. And even then, Kennedy dragged his feet on implementation: it was not until early April 1963 that a committee was formed to put the order into effect.[72]

THE ONE BRIGHT spot in Kennedy's early civil rights forays came in the one place where many in the movement did not place much hope: the Department of Justice and its Civil Rights Division. The office had been created by the 1957 civil rights act—and promptly forgotten. Robert Kennedy had other ideas, though: a well-staffed division, he realized, could bring significant dividends at little political cost to his brother.

Kennedy dismissed out of hand the suggestion that he hire Harris Wofford, the young Notre Dame law professor who had served as the president's civil rights point man during the campaign—but who was also a close associate of several leading civil rights figures, an attachment that might bring charges of bias against the division. Instead, Kennedy chose Burke Marshall, an antitrust lawyer at the firm of Covington and Burling, to run the division. Aside from a teaching a few adjunct classes at Howard University's law school, Marshall had no previous exposure to civil rights, and in temperament and philosophy—cerebral, staid, personally conservative—he was the furthest thing from a "movement" lawyer that Kennedy could find. Which is just what the attorney general wanted.[73]

Marshall rounded out a legal all-star team. Byron White, the deputy attorney general, was a Rhodes scholar, former professional football player, and future Supreme Court justice. Running the Office of Legal Counsel was another Rhodes scholar, Katzenbach, a University of Chicago law professor who had known Marshall as a teenager in suburban New Jersey and later preceded him as editor of the *Yale Law Journal*. Archibald Cox, a professor at Harvard Law School, became solicitor general. Louis Oberdorfer, who ran the tax division, was likewise a Yale law graduate who had clerked for Justice Hugo Black. They were later joined by John Douglas, yet another Rhodes scholar, who took over the Civil Division in mid-1963 and immediately assumed the task of coordinating the government's role in the March on Washington.

These men, noted historian and Kennedy adviser Arthur M. Schlesinger Jr., shared a set of overlapping experiences. Most had fought in World War II; Katzenbach, a navigator on a B-25 Mitchell bomber, was shot down over Italy in 1943 and spent two years in a POW camp. They had gone to the best schools, had clerked for appellate and Supreme Court justices, and had spent time in white-shoe law firms. The result, Schlesinger said, was "a common moral outlook" and a set of qualities—"integrity, judgment, drive, understatement, personal reserve"—that made their reserved natures a counterweight to the passion of the years to come.[74]

Robert Kennedy set the tone of his department's civil rights stand almost immediately. In 1960, school officials in New Orleans had pleaded with the Eisenhower administration to endorse their desegregation plan, as a way of giving them desperately needed political cover in the face of vociferous, at times violent, opposition from white parents. The Republican president was silent, even after the state legislature threatened to restrict financing for the district should it proceed with its plans. But in February 1961, barely three weeks into its term, the Kennedy Justice Department took an existing federal suit and expanded it to demand that the state release hundreds of thousands of dollars for the New Orleans schools, money they needed for their desegregation plan. The legislature relented. And then a dam seemed to break: after hardly budging over nearly seven years after *Brown*, the South began to integrate its schools. Grudgingly, haltingly, and often in heavily urban areas where the risk of white resistance was relatively minor, to be sure—still, at the end of 1960, only 17 Southern school districts were desegregated, but by 1963, 166 were.[75]

The division also went on a hiring spree; though many of the best law school students set to graduate in 1961 had already accepted jobs elsewhere, Marshall and Kennedy were able to persuade several to change their minds, and by 1962 the division's early successes had made it one of the hottest places to work in Washington. Meanwhile, the existing staff kept busy by filing fourteen new civil rights suits in 1961 and launching investigations or negotiations in sixty-one Southern counties. They would hold long strategy sessions in Kennedy's enormous, chaotic office on the fifth floor of the Justice Department, with Brumus, the attorney general's giant black Newfoundland, lying nearby, or out in the courtyard, where Kennedy's wife, Ethel, had set up umbrellas and chairs. John Doar, Marshall's assistant and a Republican holdover from the Eisenhower Justice Department, became a sort of civil rights fireman, showing up in small towns across the Deep South to meet with voting rights litigants and then file suit in the nearest federal courtroom.[76]

But even the success of the Civil Rights Division had its limits. The legal process laid out under the 1957 and 1960 acts was slow and unwieldy. There were not enough lawyers to file more than a token number of legal actions. More important, though, was the attitude among the men gathered around Robert Kennedy. Good, right-thinking men who would have liked to see Jim Crow disappear overnight, they were also prisoners of their own establishment thinking. They had been taught—at home, in college, at law school, in Washington—that as long as the system functions correctly, good will prevail. Like their president, these men did not at first grasp the realities of the black situation, did not understand the totality of the Jim Crow system, its imperviousness to logic, or Southerners' willingness to employ violent means to block even the mildest advance of black rights. As a result, throughout the first years of the Kennedy administration, Marshall and others replied with seeming callousness to the demands of civil rights leaders and their political allies for federal intervention against bombing campaigns, assassinations, and police violence. In June 1962, a group of leaders from the embattled protest movement in Albany, Georgia, traveled all the way to Washington to plead for federal relief. John Doar told them point-blank there was nothing the Department of Justice could do. As one of Robert Kennedy's aides, John Nolan, later told the journalist Victor Navasky, "We weren't trying to solve the civil rights problems of the United States of America. We were just trying to keep people from getting hurt. We wanted to prevent bloodshed. They were lid-keeping operations."[77]

And contrary to the far-right fantasy of power-grabbing bureaucrats run amok, the men in the Civil Rights Division were almost allergic to pushing the boundaries of the federal government's mandate. After repeated demands from congressmen and the NAACP to take action against a wave of antiblack bombings in Birmingham in late 1961, Marshall sent a terse declaration to Clarence Mitchell: "In view of specific provisions contained in the Act, matters of this kind fall within the primary jurisdiction of local law enforcement authorities." On July 2, 1962—two years to the day before the signing of the Civil Rights Act—Burke Marshall gave an address to the annual NAACP convention in Atlanta. "Law exists to serve the needs of men," he said, "and when the needs of men are revolutionary in nature—as has been true of the needs of Negroes in the United States in the past—the courts and the processes of the law are blamed for doing what must be done. Yet the alternative is either chaos or rigid control through dictatorship without regard to the law."[78]

HAD JOHN F. KENNEDY had his way, the civil rights issue would have continued on a low simmer, bubbling up occasionally but otherwise sitting quietly on the back burner. He did not get his wish. The protest movement in Albany, Georgia, was making regular appearances on the nation's front pages: though police chief Laurie Pritchett was too smart to use the cattle prods and mobs that had turned other protest actions into international incidents, he arrested scores of protesters—including King—and refused to negotiate for even the most symbolic weakening of the town's Jim Crow system. Kennedy watched it all with dismay, but did nothing. Finally, on August 1, 1962, he told a weekly press conference: "I find it wholly inexplicable why the city Council of Albany will not sit down with the citizens of Albany, who may be Negroes, and attempt to secure them, in a peaceful way, their rights." After all, his administration was negotiating with its sworn enemy, the Soviet Union. "I can't understand why the government of Albany, the city council of Albany, can't do the same for American citizens."[79]

It was the first time Kennedy had directly endorsed the civil rights demonstrators since he took office. The next day King sent him a telegram from his jail cell in Albany, expressing his gratitude for the "directness of your statement to Albany crisis. I earnestly hope you will continue to use the great moral influence of your office to help this crucial situation. There is no need for another Little Rock here."[80]

King's message was prescient, since the need for "another Little Rock" presented itself just weeks later. On September 10, 1962, Supreme Court Justice Hugo Black upheld a Fifth Circuit Court of Appeals order for the University of Mississippi to admit a black transfer student named James Meredith. The White House quickly reached an agreement with Mississippi governor Ross Barnett to let him register, but when Meredith appeared on campus on September 20, the governor himself was there to block him. Meredith tried again five days later, this time in the company of federal marshals and Justice Department attorneys, and again was blocked. Each time he appeared, the crowd greeting him—mostly students, but with an influx of older, unfamiliar faces—grew larger and angrier.[81]

Challenged, Kennedy acted decisively. On Thursday, September 27, Robert Kennedy declared that "the orders of the federal courts can and will be enforced," and traveled across the Potomac to the Pentagon to explore military options with General Maxwell Taylor, chairman of the Joint Chiefs of Staff. By Sunday the president had federalized and mobilized the state National Guard and sent hundreds of newly deputized marshals into Oxford. That evening, under the direction of Katzenbach and Doar, federal forces escorted Meredith onto campus and into a dormitory, so that he would be ready to register the next morning. All the while, scores, then hundreds of onlookers began to gather on campus. Some carried signs reading "Yankees Go Home." But for the most part, a tense peace held.[82]

As the sun set, though, the insults began to fly, followed by brickbats. Soon a full-scale riot was under way, with squads of burly Ole Miss students taking on unarmed marshals, many of whom were much older and out of shape (and unsure of why they were there to begin with, being mostly white Southerners themselves). By the next morning the toll was staggering: hundreds injured on both sides, two dead, scores of cars upended and burned. But Meredith was registered.[83]

Even as the Kennedys put themselves on the line to defend Meredith's right to attend Ole Miss, they were careful to couch their efforts in legal, not moral, rhetoric. During a phone call with Governor Barnett on September 30, President Kennedy swore off any commitment to Meredith's case beyond the dispassionate application of the law. "I don't know Mr. Meredith, and I didn't put him in there," he said. "But under the Constitution I have to carry out the law. I want your help in doing it." His reasoning was partly strategic—men like Barnett might be more willing to lower their resistance if they saw the administration as a neutral force. But such a position also came naturally to the Kennedys. As Schlesinger noted, they "did not see racial justice as *the* urgent American problem, as *the* contradiction, now at last intolerable, between the theory and the practice of the republic."[84]

And yet, as the year drew to a close, the Justice Department's thinking began to shift, ever so slowly. Imperceptible to the public, the shift showed up in memos and meetings, in end-of-the-year reports and offhand comments. The tumult of 1963 was yet to come, but Ole Miss had capped a year of rising tensions, of small outbursts of violence. And if that were the case, the present approach—piecemeal, conservative, reactive—could not hold. In October, still reeling from his experience at Ole Miss, Katzenbach asked Marshall to submit ideas for civil rights legislation. Marshall minced no words: "The department has had great difficulty in obtaining prompt hearings and decisions in the district courts," he admitted. To that end, his division needed legislation "to expedite civil actions brought by the United States for relief against racial discrimination in voting." But he went further, to endorse what amounted to Title III powers for the attorney general: they needed "a bill to

protect persons from injury, oppression, threats and intimidation in the exercise of rights under the Constitution; to provide punishment, and to authorize
the attorney general to sue for preventative relief." While they were at it, he
said, why not also ask Congress to amend the National Labor Relations Act to
ban discrimination in unions?[85]

Marshall was not the only one in Washington urging action. The day after
the midterm elections, Representative Thomas Curtis, a conservative
Republican from Missouri, called up the GOP congressional aide Fred Sontag
in New York and told him that he and a group of Republicans were going to
make a big push for civil rights legislation in the next congressional term.
Things were already afoot: Robert Kimball, an aide to New York congressman
John Lindsay, was working full-time on drafting a new bill, having been
seconded from Lindsay's office to a new organization called the Republican
Legislative Research Association, a liberal group founded by Charles Taft, the
son of President William Howard Taft, and former Republican presidential
nominee Alf Landon. "There was the feeling on the Republican side that we
were looked upon as naysayers," Kimball recalled. "There was a feeling we
should do something on civil rights."[86]

The bill, which Lindsay introduced on January 30, read like a wish list sent
over from the civil rights leadership: it made the Civil Rights Commission
permanent and gave it the power to investigate election fraud; it established a
federal fair employment commission to oversee government contractors; it
gave the attorney general the power to initiate lawsuits over school segregation; and it exempted anyone with a sixth-grade education from literacy tests.
The bill, Lindsay boasted, was "designed to pass."[87]

Democrats were moving, too. On January 8, four leading liberals—
Humphrey, Paul Douglas of Illinois, Joseph Clark of Pennsylvania, and
Harrison Williams of New Jersey—wrote an impassioned letter to Kennedy
demanding fast action on civil rights. After praising his executive order on
housing, they said, "The time has come for similar forthright action in the
legislative field." Playing to the president's political side, they argued that civil
rights would help, not hurt, the party in 1964. "Many Democratic members of
the Senate class of 1958 believe strongly that their re-election in 1964 will be
materially affected by the Democratic civil rights record compiled by the 88th
Congress." But they could not go it alone. "The eventual success of any such
program undoubtedly depends on your leadership." Louis Martin was even
more blunt. The coming year, he told Kennedy speechwriter Ted Sorensen in
an early 1963 memo, was going to be a hot one: "American Negroes through
sit-ins, kneel-ins, wade-ins, etc. will continue to create situations which involve
the police powers of the local, state and federal government."[88]

Yet for all the activity and chatter about civil rights, 1963 began with an administration believing that a few symbolic acts, like the Lincoln Day reception, were enough to solidify its position vis-à-vis black America. "Our feeling was that the Negro community was pretty much at peace," said Lee White. In a background interview with the journalist Simeon Booker of *Jet* magazine, Kennedy insisted that the problems of African Americans could be addressed largely through the administration's overall agenda of trade promotion and lower taxes. "The president urged groups who hinted of deteriorating race relations to look at the statistics on unemployment, house ownership, education and all the rest to see that the unrest is a general national problem aggravated by conditions," Booker wrote.[89]

And Robert Kennedy was adamant, even in private, that his department was making huge strides on the issue. In a confidential year-end report to the president, he wrote, "1962 was a year of great progress in civil rights." Among his team's many accomplishments, he boasted, were breakthroughs like twenty-nine Southern counties volunteering to make their voting records available. And, he added, "of the approximately 350 assistant United States attorneys appointed in this Administration, 32 are Negroes."[90]

Evidently satisfied with such meager advances, John Kennedy dedicated just two sentences in his State of the Union speech that year to civil rights, and then only to the matter of voting rights: "The most precious and powerful right in the world, the right to vote in a free American election, must not be denied to any citizen on grounds of his race or color. I wish that all qualified Americans permitted to vote were willing to vote, but surely in this centennial year of Emancipation all those who are willing to vote should always be permitted." He spent more time during his speech dwelling on the nation's transportation system.[91]

Still, Kennedy was not deaf to his advisers' entreaties. On February 28, he surprised even his close colleagues with a lengthy statement on civil rights that outdid all previous utterances in its moral seriousness.[92]

Kennedy began by examining, he said, "how far we have come in achieving first-class citizenship for all citizens regardless of color, how far we have yet to go, and what further tasks remain to be carried out." Just weeks after he had refused to discuss Martin Luther King Jr.'s demand for a second Emancipation Proclamation, he addressed King's point directly: "That Proclamation was only a first step—a step which its author unhappily did not live to follow up, a step which some of its critics dismissed as an action which 'frees the slave but ignores the Negro.' Through these long one hundred years, while slavery has vanished, progress for the Negro has been too often blocked and delayed."

He ran through a litany of problems caused by discrimination. It hampers, he said, "our economic growth by preventing the maximum development and utilization of our manpower. It hampers our world leadership by contradict- ing at home the message we preach abroad. It mars the atmosphere of a united and classless society in which this Nation rose to greatness." But these reasons, he said, were largely beside the point. "Therefore," he said, "let it be clear, in our own hearts and minds, that it is not merely because of the Cold War, and not merely because of the economic waste of discrimination, that we are committed to achieving true equality of opportunity. The basic reason is because it is right."

Somewhat hyperbolically, the president claimed that "in the last two years, more progress has been made in securing the civil rights of all Americans than in any comparable period in our history." Still, he conceded, "pride in our progress must not give way to relaxation of our effort. Nor does progress in the Executive Branch enable the Legislative Branch to escape its own obligations."

To that end, the president recommended a series of proposals: expedited voting rights lawsuits, temporary voting referees to monitor elections in coun- ties where there were suits pending and where less than 15 percent of the black population was registered, uniform registration requirements, encourage- ment to pass a constitutional amendment banning poll taxes, an extension of the Civil Rights Commission, and technical assistance for school districts trying to desegregate. He also reintroduced his filibustered bill from 1962 to make the completion of sixth grade sufficient evidence of a voter's literacy to obviate a test at the registrar's desk.

The message was notable for several reasons. Kennedy was the first presi- dent, in fact one of the first national politicians, to say explicitly that ending racial discrimination was a moral issue. That alone, said Wilkins, was enough to give hope that the president would act more forcefully in the coming year. Kennedy had "finally recognized the need for legislative action," he said. "I'm not sure whether we had reached him or whether all those inside agitators down South had gotten his Yankee dander up, but he was beginning to move." Whitney Young, the head of the National Urban League, agreed, calling it "the most comprehensive statement on this complex and sensitive subject ever in our time by a chief executive." Nevertheless, Young added, the statement did fall short. "There is no legislation recommended in the area of racial discrimi- nation in employment to strengthen the program of the President's Committee on Equal Employment Opportunity." A skeptical Martin Luther King Jr. praised the message simply as "constructive."[93]

To judge by the Southern Democrats' reaction, though, Kennedy had just fired the opening salvo of the second Civil War—Richard Russell claimed that the proposed legislation threatened "almost every phase of social and racial relations." But among the civil rights community, Kennedy's proposal fell flat. Even the ADA, no friend of the Republicans, declared that their civil rights proposals "have caught the Administration off guard. In each area of civil rights the Republican proposals have greater comprehension than the administration's recommendations." Indeed, "in contrast with the Republican package, the President sent an eloquent civil rights message to Congress but accompanied it with minimal proposals."[94]

The Republicans gleefully shot holes in the proposal, too. Lindsay called it "thin." Nelson Rockefeller, a likely contender for the GOP presidential nomination in 1964, noted that the president's message included only five of the twenty-eight recommendations made by the Civil Rights Commission in its report earlier that month. The Kennedys, choosing to hear what they wanted, interpreted silence as apathy. "There wasn't any interest" in the bill, Robert Kennedy complained. "There was no public demand for it. There was no demand by the newspapers or radio or television."[95]

A FEW DAYS after Kennedy sent his message, Joe Rauh met with several fellow civil rights leaders in New York. As they commiserated over what they considered unnecessary timidity on the president's part—Rauh later said the message represented "such an inane package of legislation as to make the civil rights movement feel that it wasn't worth going for"—his comrade in arms and the NAACP's head lobbyist, Clarence Mitchell, walked in the door. He was carrying a sheaf of congressional bills under his arm—Republican bills. At least someone's trying to get the ball rolling, Mitchell said, chuckling. With a Democratic president and large Democratic majorities in both houses, the chances of a Republican-authored bill passing, on civil rights no less, were vanishingly small. "If you need to be cheered up with bills like that that can't go anywhere," said Rauh, "you're in pretty bad shape."[96]

It appeared, said King, "a melancholy fact that the administration is aggressively driving only toward the limited goal of token integration." And yet King held out hope that forces of action within the White House—or even within Kennedy himself—would draw out the president soon. "It would be profoundly wrong to take an extreme position either way when viewing the administration."[97]

King wrote those words in an article for the *Nation* in March 1962. By the end of the year he was much less sanguine—the literacy test bill had failed, the housing executive order was a bust, and Kennedy seemed even less interested in civil rights legislation than the year before. Meanwhile, King's Albany campaign had failed spectacularly, with King and his supporters in jail and the Kennedy team praising the nonconfrontational strategy of the Albany police. If Washington was ever to take civil rights seriously, King realized that dark winter, it would take a new, much riskier strategy on the part of the movement.

CHAPTER 2

"A NATIONAL MOVEMENT TO ENFORCE NATIONAL LAWS"

THE MOMENTUM ON CIVIL RIGHTS changed at 1:00 P.M. on May 2, 1963, when the doors of the 16th Street Baptist Church in Birmingham, Alabama, burst open and dozens of schoolchildren poured forth into the warm spring sunlight, singing "We Shall Overcome." Wyatt Tee Walker, the executive director of the Southern Christian Leadership Conference and the strategic visionary behind the protests, sent the children out in waves; a dozen here, a score there, coursing in different directions through and around Kelly Ingram Park, a block-size plaza southeast of the church. Hundreds of onlookers, having heard rumors of the march, were gathered around the park, as was a sizable chunk of the Birmingham police department.[1]

The children were marching without a parade permit, and officers immediately corralled them into waiting police vans. But the children kept coming. When an officer saw Fred Shuttlesworth, a local preacher and one of the Birmingham movement's leaders, standing on the side, he shouted, "Hey Fred, how many more have you got?"

"At least a thousand!" Shuttlesworth replied.

"God almighty."

Shuttlesworth was hardly exaggerating. By the time the day's marches were over, three hours after they had begun, the police had run out of wagons and were resorting to school buses. Six hundred children were taken to jail.

The next day the marches resumed, and the police returned, this time with the fire department, fire hoses, and dogs. The marchers were hit with a light spray from the hoses at first, but when a determined core of them refused to retreat, the police captain in charge ratcheted up the streams to full blast, a hundred pounds of pressure. Many ran but several children did not budge. When the retreating children saw their fellow marchers' example and turned around, K-9 units came at them with dogs.[2]

That afternoon Martin Luther King Jr. sent a telegram to the president. "Will you permit this recrudescence of violence in Birmingham to threaten our lives and deny our rights?" he asked. Kennedy did not respond, at least not that day. But he was watching, like the rest of the world. Photographers had snapped hundreds of pictures of German shepherds, their teeth sinking into young boys and girls. It made him "sick," Kennedy told an aide. And Kennedy was not alone. "A snarling police dog set upon a human being is recorded in the permanent photoelectric file of every human being's brain," said CBS News correspondent Eric Sevareid.[3]

The planning for the Birmingham campaign had begun at a meeting of the SCLC leadership in early January near Savannah, Georgia. King was licking his wounds from the failed Albany protests, but eager to apply the lessons learned. The consensus was to try again, but this time to do so in a way, and a place, that guaranteed a violent response by the police—and promised immediate national exposure. "What I did in Birmingham I learned in Albany," Walker later said.[4]

And yet at first, the Birmingham movement sputtered, precisely because those lessons were not applied. The protests, consisting mostly of lunch counter sit-ins, were to begin in early March. But when the mayoral election, pitting the virulently segregationist commissioner of public safety Eugene "Bull" Connor against the relatively moderate lieutenant governor Albert Boutwell, went into a runoff, the movement's leaders decided to postpone.[5]

Meanwhile, events elsewhere threatened to upstage the Birmingham campaign before it began. In Greenwood, Mississippi, police attacked voting rights protesters with dogs, even as dozens of news photographers snapped pictures that would appear the next day on newspaper front pages nationwide, including the *New York Times*—under a photograph of the congressional Republican leaders who had just introduced a sheaf of strong civil rights proposals.[6]

Greenwood failed to generate the federal response that King was hoping would come from such a vicious display of raw state racism. At an April 2 press conference, Robert Kennedy, while admitting that "the laws are not adequate" to deal with the Greenwood crisis," said, "I don't think legislation per se is going to eliminate this problem for the United States." And President Kennedy, when asked about the protests at an April 3 press conference, responded noncommittally: "There has been a denial of rights, which seems to me evident, but which the court must decide."[7]

That same day, just 65 of the 250 or so people on Walker's "arrest list"—those willing to go to jail as a result of their protest activity—showed up in the church basement of A. D. King, Martin Luther King Jr.'s brother. The problem was timing: Boutwell had won the runoff, but Connor had refused to accept the vote, forcing the election into the courts. Although Shuttlesworth called the moderate Boutwell nothing more than a "dignified Connor," the city's black elders urged restraint until the court ruling. Nor were they eager to see Shuttlesworth and King succeed. Shuttlesworth was already well known around town as the "Wild Man of Birmingham," a verbally and tactically aggressive, at times reckless activist, while they saw King as an outsider who flew in from his home in Atlanta when he was not touring the country speaking and raising funds. The pressure came from outside as well: Burke Marshall called King and urged him to delay the protests, reporting that Robert Kennedy had deemed them "ill-timed."[8]

After King and his deputy, Ralph Abernathy, were arrested on April 12 for violating an injunction against parading handed down the day before, eight local moderate religious leaders wrote a lengthy letter to the *Birmingham News* calling the protests extreme, "unwise" and "untimely." A few days later King began scribbling a response on scraps of paper that he smuggled out to his lawyer, and which would come to be celebrated as the "Letter from Birmingham Jail."[9]

The letter was barely noticed at first, and probably would not have had much effect on the White House anyway. The Kennedys had extra reason to avoid confrontations in the South that spring. During his State of the Union address, the president had proposed a $13.5 billion tax cut as a panacea for the country's problems: lingering unemployment, trade promotion, the deficit, and even racial tensions. But to win the bill, he had to bring over Southern Democrats, who often aligned with Midwest conservative Republicans against spending and tax cut measures, both of which they said would create unsustainable deficits. And Kennedy was already facing a civil rights dustup in Washington: on April 16 the Civil Rights Commission had submitted its study of segregation in Mississippi, recommending that the president should cut off federal funds to the state. Kennedy did his best to distance himself from the proposal, but the report was catnip for Southern politicians—Mississippi senator James Eastland called it "a monstrous libel."[10]

Things grew even more complicated on the night of April 23, when a white postal worker from Baltimore named William Moore, who had been on a peace march to deliver a letter to Mississippi governor Ross Barnett, was found dead on the side of a highway in northeastern Alabama, shot twice at close range. The next day, the president brought up the shooting at a press conference, unprompted. "We had outrageous crime, from all accounts, in the State of Alabama, in the shooting of the postman who was attempting in a very traditional way to dramatize the plight of some of our citizens, being assassinated on the road," he said. "We do not have direct jurisdiction, but we are working with every legislative, legal tool at our command to insure protection for the rights of our citizens, and we shall continue to do so." The killing drew the national reporters away from Birmingham, and it was unclear how many would return.[11]

When King got out of jail, his movement looked to be in tatters. Only a few hundred people had been arrested, far fewer than at the same point during the Albany protests, and much of the country had turned its attention elsewhere. On April 19, Shuttlesworth had flown to Washington to meet with Burke Marshall and request federal intervention, but Marshall, while sympathetic, said not to expect anything. "I told him that there was no basis upon which the federal government could take any action at present," Marshall wrote in a follow-up memo to Robert Kennedy.[12]

The only way to get the federal government to act, King realized, was to take a dramatic step that would bring into sharp relief the everyday violence perpetrated against Birmingham's blacks. Though skeptical at first, King eventually sided with James Bevel, an organizer from Mississippi in town to help with nonviolence training, who believed the choice was clear: send in the children.

Two days after the "children's crusade" began, Robert Kennedy ordered Marshall to go to Birmingham to meet with King. Marshall had already called King twice to get him to call off the latest stage in the protests, and the attorney general had publicly criticized them: "An injured, maimed, or dead child is a price that none of us can afford." But other politicians were more forceful in their denunciations of the Birmingham police. Democratic senator Wayne Morse of Oregon said events like those in Birmingham presented "an infinitely greater threat to American freedom than Cuba"—tough words in a country still recovering from the shock of the missile crisis of October 1962.[13]

Over the next few weeks, Marshall—along with the Justice Deapartment's Joe Dolan and Louis Oberdorfer, a Birmingham native with close ties to the city's business leaders—shuttled between Washington and Alabama, and in Birmingham from King and the moderate black leadership to Mayor Boutwell and various quarters of the white elites, many of whom were willing to make concessions to King. Marshall at first repeated his insistence that King call a truce until the court ruled on the Boutwell-Connor election. King said no, catching Marshall by surprise. Though Marshall insisted in calls back to

Washington that King was "confused," he began to realize that only a broad settlement, involving the desegregation of Birmingham's public accommodations, would end the crisis—and that to avoid replaying the same story in countless cities across the South, blanket federal legislation was needed.[14]

It was precisely the reaction that King and his men were looking for. "Today I was in a room with one of the top men in the Justice Department, who paced the floor, couldn't sit down, changed from chair to chair," bragged Ralph Abernathy during a mass meeting on the night of May 6. "Day before yesterday we filled up the jail. Today, we filled up the jail yard. And tomorrow, when they look up and see that number coming, I don't know what they're gonna do!" The next night, after a long day that saw adult protesters hit back at the police with rocks and bricks, King said in a sermon, "The hour has come for the Federal government to take a forthright stand on segregation in the United States . . . I am not criticizing the president, but we are going to have to help him."[15]

Marshall's fear of multiple Birminghams was not hypothetical. During the week following the beginning of the children's marches, the White House watched nervously as dozens of demonstrations took place around the country. Many of them were held in sympathy with Birmingham—on May 9, fifteen hundred people marched in New York's Times Square—but not all. On May 6, black students from the overwhelmingly black Lincoln High School in Englewood, New Jersey, caught national attention with a sit-in at the majority-white Cleveland High School across town to protest "the total failure of state and local officials to act in any useful way in the past two years to solve Englewood's segregation crisis." Over Memorial Day weekend, tear gas was used in six different cities, and on June 11, some 650 demonstrators shut down construction at an annex to a hospital in Harlem in protest against union discrimination.[16]

In Washington as well, Kennedy was coming under intense pressure to act. On May 4 he met with a delegation from the ADA, who asked him to publicly and personally intervene in Alabama. But Kennedy dodged. "There's no federal law that we could pass that could do anything about that. What law could you pass?" he asked. The delegation, which included the historian and Kennedy adviser Arthur M. Schlesinger Jr., left disappointed. "I must confess that I have found his reaction to Birmingham disappointing," Schlesinger wrote in his journal later that day. "Even if he has no power to act, he has unlimited power to express the moral sense of the people; and, in not doing so, he is acting much as Eisenhower used to act when we denounced him so."[17]

Kennedy's reticence during the Birmingham crisis is understandable, since only much later did the full sweep of the events come into focus. But others could sense full well what was under way. Schlesinger noted in his journal on

June 2: "The civil rights movement has suddenly turned, following Birmingham, into a Negro revolution. It has been a long time since I have felt things to be so vividly in motion in our country. Old institutions and ideas, which have held firm for so long, seem to be giving way all at once." Even the columnist Walter Lippmann, the bellwether of the moderate liberal establishment, called for drastic change: "A revolutionary condition exists," he wrote on May 28. "The cause of desegregation must cease to be a Negro movement, blessed by white politicians from the Northern states. It must become a national movement to enforce national laws, led and directed by the national government."[18]

Things continued to worsen in Birmingham. On May 7, several hundred demonstrators surged into the downtown; the police pushed back with hoses. The jails overflowed with prisoners, so many that serving breakfast was a four-hour affair. Pressure for action mounted in Washington: Republican senator Jacob Javits challenged Kennedy to intervene in Birmingham and "in every community where civil rights are seriously jeopardized."[19]

Finally, on Thursday, May 9, Marshall was able to get the two sides to agree to a truce, followed by a schedule for desegregating the city's lunch counters and dressing rooms. Kennedy was relieved, and took the initiative to go before the cameras to cast the deal as evidence supporting his tack on civil rights. "I am gratified to note the progress in the efforts by white and Negro citizens to end an ugly situation in Birmingham, Alabama," he said. "I have made it clear since assuming the Presidency that I would use all available means to protect human rights, and uphold the law of the land. Through mediation and persuasion and, where that effort has failed, through lawsuits and court actions, we have attempted to meet our responsibilities in this most difficult field where Federal court orders have been circumvented, ignored, or violated."[20]

Two nights later, however, bombs ripped through the home of A. D. King and the Gaston Motel, where many of the movement leaders from out of town liked to stay. No one was killed, but the city fell into chaos as the Birmingham police and state troopers tore into gathered black onlookers.[21]

The next morning, Sunday, May 12, President Kennedy flew back from a weekend at Camp David to meet with Attorney General Nicholas Katzenbach, Press Secretary Ed Guthman, and Burke Marshall—who had been picked up early that morning by helicopter from his farm in Virginia, where he had gone to relax after the stress of the Birmingham negotiations—as well as Secretary of Defense Robert McNamara, Secretary of the Army Cyrus Vance, and Chairman of the Joint Chiefs of Staff Earle Wheeler. Robert Kennedy's dog paced the room as the president tick-tocked in his rocking chair.[22]

President Kennedy, it became clear, had had enough of letting Birmingham solve its own problems. He wanted to send in federal troops, he told the group;

the question was, how? Should they go into Birmingham directly, and precipitate a major crisis in federalism? "You don't have the same situation" as you had in Montgomery, said Robert Kennedy, referring to the white mob that attacked black Freedom Riders in that city in 1962. Making clear that the concern here was law and order, not civil rights, the attorney general added that "the group that's gotten out of hand is not the white people, it's the negroes, by and large."

Moreover, acting in a way that seemed to upstage local and state law enforcement might give Governor George Wallace an excuse to pull back his forces, leaving the Army as a de facto police department. At the same time, Kennedy said, action to check Wallace was imperative. "The governor has virtually taken over the city," he said. Without federal action, "you're going to have his people around sticking bayonets in people." That in turn could precipitate violent protests around the country, led by "black Muslims," a group that took an antagonistic stance on race relations and whose leaders, most notably the preacher Malcolm X, incorporated separatist and often violent rhetoric into their speeches. As Kennedy concluded, "If they feel on the other hand that the government is their friend, and is intervening for them, is going to work for them, this would head some of that off."

The answer, then, was to put troops near but not in Birmingham. In a show of how King had come to occupy a central part of the president's mind, before giving McNamara and Wheeler the order to deploy, Kennedy wanted to know what the civil rights leader would do. "How freely do you talk to King?" he asked Marshall.

"I talk to him freely," Marshall replied. Kennedy then asked him to call King and, without giving away the plans, find out what his expectations were for the next few days. Marshall returned a few minutes later, saying that King simply wanted the White House to get behind the agreement, and to help him stave off further violence. "He didn't say anything about troops, did he?" Kennedy asked.

"No, he didn't," Marshall replied.[23]

That was all Kennedy needed to hear. Just before 9:00 P.M. he went on TV to announce that he was sending troops to Army facilities near Birmingham, dispatching Marshall back to the city, and taking preliminary steps to federalize the Alabama National Guard. "This government will do whatever must be done to preserve order, to protect the lives of its citizens, and to uphold the law of the land," Kennedy said.[24]

THANKS IN PART to Kennedy's strong stand, Birmingham settled down, and the agreement held. By May 15, most of the troops had been withdrawn, and Marshall had returned to Washington.

But with him came new concerns—and ideas. With protests popping up around the country, including a Birmingham-like campaign in Jackson, Mississippi, Marshall and others feared the federal government was going to inevitably play a much larger role in the country's racial tumult than the administration wanted. No longer did Kennedy have the choice of getting involved or staying out; the only question now was, what sort of involvement did he want? For Marshall, the current nonstrategy of putting out spot fires was untenable—Birmingham had almost collapsed into general chaos, despite the indefatigable work of peaceful men like King and Boutwell (and Marshall himself). What if the next crisis involved a less capable black leader, or a less moderate white mayor? What if the campaign were led by the burgeoning bogeyman of the white establishment, the Black Muslims?

By late April the rest of the Justice Department leadership below Kennedy—Katzenbach, press secretary Ed Guthman, Office of Legal Counsel (OLC) head Norbert Schlei, John Doar, Oberdorfer—had concluded that comprehensive federal civil rights legislation was now imperative. "I think without having a meeting or discussion about it, everyone concluded that the president had to act," Marshall said later. More than anyone else, they had been on the front lines of the nation's racial crises in Oxford, Greenwood, and Birmingham. These men—save for Oberdorfer, non-Southerners; save for Guthman, Ivy League–educated—who had been trained to believe that reason would win out over prejudiced passion had seen, in the student mob at Oxford and the police riots in Birmingham, the depths to which the South was willing to go to defend Jim Crow, and they were no longer willing to accept the constricting limits of current federal law as an excuse not to act.[25]

The Justice Department men were not the only people in the executive branch warming to the idea of a big push for civil rights legislation. As early as mid-April, Lee White, who had long favored a more aggressive stance by Kennedy, used the Birmingham protests as an opening to urge action. White had unsuccessfully pressed for Kennedy to issue a strong statement on the Emancipation Proclamation centennial, and had been disappointed when the president soft-shoed the legislation that emerged from his February 28 speech. Now he saw his chance. In an April 17 memo to Larry O'Brien, he wrote: "I suggest you call a meeting at the White House within the next ten days or so to set up formally a working committee"—including key congressmen and representatives from the Departments of Justice and Health, Education, and Welfare—"to ensure coordinated efforts by all to secure civil rights legislation." Knowing that O'Brien would not support him unless he thought the bill had a good chance of passing, White detailed a "basic checklist," including "the mechanics of setting up a campaign headquarters, if one is to be created, and how it is to be staffed, financed and keyed into its basic operations." O'Brien, meanwhile, was counseling Kennedy against legislation, since it would mean running "smack into a straight-out brawl that will position the extremes to both sides and probably create an impasse in Congress."[26]

On Friday, May 17, Marshall, Katzenbach, Guthman, and Oberdorfer accompanied Robert Kennedy on a flight to Asheville, North Carolina, where the attorney general was scheduled to address a seminar on the Cold War. They brought up the idea of a new civil rights bill, and they found, to varying levels of surprise, that the attorney general was wholly on board with their thoughts. Legislation was needed, he agreed. The question was what, and how to do it constitutionally. They returned that evening, and over the weekend they began to hash out the framework for an administration-sponsored omnibus civil rights act.[27]

On Saturday, the group, along with Schlei and Ramsey Clark of the Lands Division, huddled in Robert Kennedy's office to develop an outline for a bill. The focus, everyone agreed, had to be on public accommodations and school desegregation, the two issues that seemed to matter most to the Southern protesters. Issues like job discrimination, let alone job creation, would have to wait until later. Late in the afternoon, Kennedy and Katzenbach ordered Schlei to form a team and have a draft ready for the president by Monday afternoon.[28]

Marshall and his colleagues did not need a meeting to tell them action was necessary—everyone else was saying it, too. On May 19 the NAACP announced a campaign against de facto segregation in twenty-five states across the North, particularly in schools. More pressing, in early May a group of GOP senators threatened to attach a version of Title III to an administration-supported farm bill. Together, the restiveness among black activists and the receptiveness among Republicans to their concerns set up a painful paradox for the national Democrats: if the Southern Democrats posed a political challenge for any proposal, the nation's black population stood ready to exact an equal price at the polls for inaction. "The political stakes in the approaching civil rights battle are particularly high and the Republicans are spoiling for a fight," wrote the columnist team of Rowland Evans and Robert Novak. "From the wings, millions of Negro voters are watching closely."[29]

Monday afternoon, Robert Kennedy and Marshall sat down with the president and several men from his staff—White, congressional liaison Larry O'Brien, speechwriter Ted Sorensen, and appointments secretary Kenneth O'Donnell—to work through the details and politics of the emerging proposal. The Justice Department men had drawn up a short memo with the key elements to a possible proposal. First, they wanted a bill to outlaw segregation in public accommodations like restaurants and movie theaters—not only because "this is an issue that affects all Negroes, even in the North," but also because the constitutionality of Jim Crow laws was currently before the Supreme Court; should the court decide in favor of the laws (and against civil rights protesters), a provision like this would respond to "the wide frustrations and anger which such a decision would create."[30]

There were two ways to go about banning discrimination in public places under the Constitution. They could either go with the Commerce Clause in Article I, Section 8—giving Congress the power "to regulate commerce . . . among the several states"—which would allow the federal government to ban segregation in any public accommodation that touched interstate commerce in any way; or the Equal Protection Clause of the Fourteenth Amendment, which banned discrimination by governments or government-sponsored or -licensed activities. Because the Commerce Clause had been used to justify much of the New Deal, Democrats had a soft spot for its application. Moreover, the Justice Department men, particularly Marshall and OLC head Norbert Schlei, were reluctant to rely on the Fourteenth Amendment. It had been used to justify a brace of Reconstruction-era civil rights laws, which were passed by Republican Congresses and were therefore favored by pro-civil-rights Republicans. The problem was that those laws were subsequently struck down by the Supreme Court. While much had changed since the late nineteenth century, and there was little chance that the liberal Warren Court would rule the same way, Marshall, Schlei, and others thought the risk was not worth it. The Commerce Clause was the safer route.[31]

Additionally, they considered legislation to protect the right to demonstrate, giving the Justice Department the power to sue local officials who were interfering with protesters. The concern here was the same as the one expressed at the May 12 meeting over whether to deploy troops in Birmingham: such a law could give the local authorities an excuse to pull back, putting the federal government "in the business of police protection." At the same time, it would force the government to pick and choose which protests were worth defending, creating a de facto system of federal endorsement of certain acts of free speech, but not others.[32]

Finally, they agreed that legislation was needed on school desegregation, including a requirement that districts develop desegregation plans and the "power for the Department of Justice to bring suit upon the recommendation of the educational authorities charged with administration of the bill in the event that schools districts were completely uncooperative in the development of the plan." This title, they noted, would not have any timelines.[33]

The president had just returned from a spin through the South, where he had addressed a warm crowd at Vanderbilt University, in Nashville—"I got better applause there than any place else in the South, I'll tell you that," he said, rocking back proudly in his chair—and then flew on to Muscle Shoals, Alabama, where he politely butted heads with Governor Wallace. From conversations he had on the trip, the president seemed convinced that it would be relatively easy to get Southern whites to accept a ban on segregation, if Southern blacks did not "push this thing too far." To keep that from happening, Kennedy floated the idea of limiting the right to demonstrate, but pulled back immediately when Marshall balked.[34]

Marshall then brought up the demands for a broad Title III provision, and at the very least a robust public accommodations law. It was a civil rights proposal that the president found self-evidently necessary, but that his brother, for once, was the more reticent about. Since many drug stores in the South allowed blacks to buy food but not sit down, he reasoned, they were not being denied service per se. "They can stand at the lunch counters," the attorney general retorted bluntly. Nevertheless, when the men began to hash out a wish list of proposals, Robert Kennedy included a public accommodations law alongside voting rights and school desegregation. He also floated the idea of sitting down with the owners of chain businesses such as theaters and department stores to see what it would take for them to "meet with Negroes and try to work it out on a community basis." He suggested bringing in black leaders, including King, but the president wanted to hold off; "otherwise the meetings will look like they got me to do it," he said. Instead, he wanted to meet with a delegation of mayors and governors first.[35]

As a measure of the president's seriousness on the bill, he talked about bringing the Republicans into the fold, something he had never done before on civil rights. "I think it's possible that as the mood of the country gets uglier and uglier, the Republicans are going to say we can't play the Southern Democratic game anymore," he said, and predicted that "they'll join us in cloture and something will get by."

Both O'Donnell and O'Brien were pragmatic partisans of the president, having known him since the beginning of his political career (O'Donnell's relationship with the family went even further back—he had played varsity football with Robert at Harvard), and they both expressed deep reservations about the legislation. As O'Donnell later recalled thinking, "It's very east for Nick Katzenbach to sit over there and say we should send a piece of legislation up to the Hill, but we're the ones who have to get it through."[36]

O'Brien, who had staved off presidential endorsement of the 1962 legislation, feared that a close alignment with the civil rights movement would hurt Kennedy among the Southern Democrats at a time when he needed their support for his tax cut. But for once, the pair—along with Sorensen, another holdout on the bill—were overwhelmed by the moment. Realizing the bill was inevitable, they insisted that they at least be allowed to begin with the hard work of smoothing the bill's entry into congressional waters.[37]

Though the details of the meeting remained secret, news of the president's emerging proposal quickly leaked to the media. On May 21, Hubert Humphrey told a Baltimore *Sun* reporter that Kennedy was considering an omnibus bill, in part as a response to "increasing restiveness" among senators. Just a few days before, the bipartisan team of Thomas Dodd, a Democratic senator from Connecticut, and Senator John Sherman Cooper of Kentucky introduced their own public accommodations proposal. "Neither bill," wrote the *Sun*, "under present conditions in Congress, would have much chance of passage, since both would be opposed to the limit—including filibusters—by Southerners." The next day, the president told reporters that "we are considering whether any additional proposals will be made to the Congress. And the final decision should be made in the next few days."[38]

WHILE IN BIRMINGHAM, Marshall had spent some time talking with Dick Gregory, a black comedian and outspoken civil rights activist. Gregory said that part of the administration's problem was that the Kennedys never actually talked with black people. Marshall relayed the suggestion to Robert Kennedy. The attorney general asked if Marshall could set up a meeting with the author James Baldwin, whose essay "Letter from a Region of My Mind" he had read in the *New Yorker*. Marshall got in touch with Baldwin, who agreed to come to Washington to meet Kennedy on May 23.[39]

When the day arrived, though, Baldwin's plane was delayed, and by the time he got to Kennedy's northern Virginia home, the attorney general had only twenty minutes to talk. Kennedy began by admitting that the proposals under consideration were focused on issues facing Southern blacks and would do little to help those in the Northern cities. What, he asked Baldwin, should be done? Baldwin offered to assemble a group of black activists and intellectuals for Kennedy to meet with. By chance, Kennedy said, he was going to be in New York the next day—why not set up a get-together that afternoon?[40]

The next morning, Kennedy, Marshall, and Oberdorfer flew to New York for a meeting with the heads of several major five and dimes, theaters, and department stores—Woolworth's, Kress, J. C. Penney, McCrory, Sears—to discuss what they could do to desegregate their branches in the South. Kennedy came away with noncommittal responses, assurances that the chains would do the best they could but that they could not promise anything that would undermine their profits, which in the South, they insisted, meant acceding to customers' demands that they remain segregated.[41]

Kennedy and his aides then headed to his father's apartment at 24 Central Park West for the meeting with Baldwin's hastily assembled focus group. If not a who's who of the black community in New York, it was a good cross-section: Kenneth Clark, the eminent psychologist from the City College of New York; the singers Harry Belafonte and Lena Horne; the playwright Lorraine Hansberry; Jerome Smith, a twenty-four-year-old veteran of the Freedom Rides; Baldwin's brother David and a friend of his, Thais Aubrey; Martin Luther King Jr.'s lawyer, Clarence Jones; and the Urban League activist Edwin C. Berry. (The white actor Rip Torn, who was active in civil rights, was also there.)[42]

Clark and Berry were supposed to set an intellectual, measured tone for the meeting, but it derailed almost immediately. "In that moment, with the situation in Birmingham the way it was," said Horne later, "none of us wanted to hear figures and percentages and all that stuff. Nobody even cared about expressions of goodwill."[43]

Smith, a passionate man with a pronounced stammer, began by saying, "Mr. Kennedy, I want you to understand I don't care anything about you or your brother." He said it was obvious that the Kennedys did not care about Southern protesters. In fact, he said, just being in the same room as the attorney general made him sick to his stomach.[44]

Kennedy was visibly offended, but rather than engage with Smith, he tried to ignore him. He began addressing Baldwin, but Hansberry cut him off. "You've got a great many very, very accomplished people in this room, Mr. Attorney General. But the only man who should be listened to is that man over there," she said, pointing at Smith. The young Freedom Rider began explaining what he had lived through in the South, emphasizing how little the federal government had done to help him.

Eventually Kennedy interrupted him. "Just let me say something," he said.

"Okay," said Smith, "but this time say something that means something. So far you haven't said a thing!"

Kennedy tried to explain the bills, but Smith just scoffed. The situation was far too dire. He was a nonviolent man, he said, but he was unsure for how long. "When I pull the trigger, kiss it goodbye!"

Trying to inject some balance to the conversation, Baldwin asked Smith if he would ever fight for his country. "Never!" Smith said.

That drove Kennedy over the edge. He had been just a few years too young to fight in World War II, the war that had killed one of his brothers and made a hero of another. "How could you say that?" he demanded. "Bobby got redder and redder and redder, and in a sense accused Jerome of treason," recalled Clark.[45]

Kennedy asked for ideas. Baldwin said the president should personally escort students into the University of Alabama who were being blocked by Governor Wallace. He should get rid of J. Edgar Hoover at the FBI. The Department of Justice should be more aggressive in Birmingham. The attorney general insisted that he was working closely with King, which brought forth peals of cynical laughter.

Eventually Kennedy ran out of the energy to both respond to the attacks and keep his anger in check, and he just sat there quietly as Baldwin's panel took turns berating him, his brother, and the federal government. "It became really one of the most violent, emotional, verbal assaults that I had ever witnessed before or since," said Clark. Finally, after three hours, the meeting broke up.

The encounter had a profound effect on Kennedy. At first he was just angry. When Belafonte apologized afterward for the group's hostility and said he agreed with Kennedy, the attorney general glared at him and said, "How could you just sit there and not say anything?" After returning to Washington, he sat down for a debriefing with Schlesinger. "They don't know anything," he said. "They don't know what the laws are—they don't know what the facts are. They don't know what we've been doing or what we're trying to do. You couldn't talk to them as you can to Roy Wilkins or Martin Luther King. They didn't want to talk that way. It was all emotion. Hysteria. They stood up and orated. They accused. Some of them wept and walked out of the room."[46]

But over the next several days and weeks, Kennedy began to change. As his own anger faded, he found that the evident passion and stinging sense of injustice he has witnessed in Baldwin's group had left an impression on him. "The more I saw him after this," Belafonte recalled, "the more he no longer had questions that were just about the specifics of federal government intervention, or the civil rights strategy of the moment. He began to move to broader philosophical areas, began to know more about cause and effect and why." Asked later to illustrate Kennedy's education in civil rights, Marshall shot his hand straight up. Ed Guthman saw it, too. "After a day or two, Bob's attitude about the meeting began to shift. He had never heard an American citizen say he would not defend the country and it troubled him. Instead of repeating, as he had, 'Imagine anyone saying that,' he said, 'I guess if I were in his shoes, if I had gone through what he's gone through, I might feel differently about this country.'"[47]

On May 29, Robert Kennedy paid a surprise visit to Johnson's Committee on Equal Employment Opportunity. Kennedy sat quietly for a few minutes as

NASA administrator James Webb gave a presentation of his agency's progress. Then Kennedy began to cross-examine Webb, quickly establishing that NASA, which handled billions of dollars in contracts annually, had just two people— or one and a half, since one of them was Webb, who had other duties—making sure that the companies it did business with did not discriminate. "I don't think this gentleman over here that spent a year and a half on this program—if he has, evidently, some other responsibilities, I don't think he is going to get that job done," Kennedy said. "He has got $3.9 billion worth of contracts."[48]

Webb meekly tried to defend himself. "I would like to have you take enough time to see precisely what we do."

But Kennedy blew past him. "I am trying to ask some questions. I don't think I am able to get the answers, to tell you the truth."

At that point Johnson stepped in to defend Webb. "Do you have any other questions?" he asked Kennedy.

"That is all for me," said the attorney general, and he stalked from the room.

Kennedy's performance served many purposes, including venting steam from his encounter in New York as well as getting in some sucker punches against his nemesis, Lyndon Johnson. But it was also typical of the way Kennedy came to a new passion—intensely, with something to prove, enemies to make, and battles to be won. "Racial justice was no longer an issue in the middle distance," wrote Schlesinger. "Robert Kennedy now saw it face to face, and he was on fire."[49]

JOHNSON WAS HUMILIATED by Kennedy's attack on Webb, but the next day he redeemed himself with a rousing speech at Gettysburg, Pennsylvania, part of the Civil War centennial commemorations going on throughout the early 1960s. The events had so far been tightly scripted to avoid any mention of race or slavery, except in the most abstract terms; the theme, if there was one, centered on regional reconciliation and the folly of brothers fighting brothers—as if the issue motivating the Civil War was just a misunderstanding, not the question of whether a nation founded on liberty could countenance slavery.

Johnson had initially tried to get out of delivering the speech, telling one of his secretaries to decline the invitation for him (she did not). Like his boss, the vice president had spent the late 1940s and 1950s in an ambivalent relationship with the issue of civil rights: to him it was another chip in a game of political poker. He opposed changing Rule 22, and he oversaw the evisceration of the 1957 and 1960 civil rights acts. That is not to say he didn't value civil rights; after all, he took risks to make sure both acts passed. But since entering the vice presidency, and particularly since the start of 1963, Johnson had been taking an increasingly unalloyed stance on the issue, including a rousing pro-civil-rights speech on January 7, 1963, at Wayne State University.

It is hard to say why Johnson turned so resolutely on race. His own explanation, and one supported by many of his biographers, is that he had long supported civil rights, but as a senator from Texas he was bound to represent the attitudes—including the prejudices—of his state. Now, as vice president, he could cast those strictures aside. But Johnson also had a political calculus in mind: he was well aware that the white South was beginning to slip, slowly, out of the Democratic Party's sleeper hold and into the more natural grasp of conservative Republicanism. His own vacated seat had been won, in a special election, by the right-wing Republican John Tower, and he had seen his good friend and Alabama senator Lister Hill almost lose to a Republican in the 1962 midterms. The Democrats needed a new base, and African Americans could provide it—if the party could give them a reason.

Johnson ended up going to Gettysburg, and he was glad he did. He let loose that day with a fiery denunciation of the country's racial status quo. The vice president was not a gifted speaker; for much of his career, Johnson was a master of the backroom deal, the compromise, the arm twist. Aside from his canned campaign speeches, he had never had to convince, to win over an audience. And yet as he found civil rights, he also found a speaking style that suited him; the operator was becoming the orator, and nowhere were his newfound gifts more evident than on that day in south central Pennsylvania.[50]

After a few introductory words about the site's hallowed ground and the sacrifice made by men on both sides, Johnson got to his main theme. "One hundred years ago, the slave was freed," he said. "One hundred years later, the Negro remains in bondage to the color of his skin. The Negro today asks justice. We do not answer him—we do not answer those who lie beneath this soil—when we reply to the Negro by asking, 'Patience.' It is empty to plead that the solution to the dilemmas of the present rests on the hands of the clock." Without saying as much, Johnson was aligning himself hand in glove with Martin Luther King Jr. and attacking, in all but name, his own president and his strategy of gradualism and nonintervention.[51]

"The solution is in our hands," Johnson went on. "Unless we are willing to yield up our destiny of greatness among the civilizations of history, Americans—white and Negro together—must be about the business of resolving the challenge which confronts us now." But Johnson also warned blacks not to lose faith in the law, or the possibility of change through it. "The Negro says, 'Now.' Others say, 'Never.' The voice of responsible Americans—the voice of those who died here and the great man who spoke here—their voices say,

'Together.' There is no other way." The speech was duly noted in newspapers the next day, but few reporters paid close attention to it. If they had, they would have seen that yet another member of the White House inner circle had come around forcefully to the idea of major federal action on civil rights.[52]

Two days after Johnson returned, he was invited to a meeting at the White House to discuss the evolving civil rights bill. The president and attorney general were there, as was half the cabinet, not to mention the usual Justice Department and White House advisers: Marshall, Sorensen, White, O'Brien, Martin. The drafting process had been a whirlwind: since the first meeting about the bill in Robert Kennedy's office, almost two weeks prior, Schlei and his team—including two twenty-year department veterans, Leon Ulman and Harold Greene, who had fled Nazi Germany as a young man and went on to serve as a federal district court judge—had been working nonstop as ideas and revisions to the draft poured in from various corners of the White House, the Justice Department, and the president's allies on the Hill. "Whenever anybody had a suggestion, I'd go racing off and implement the suggestion," Schlei recalled."[53]

Still, very little of substance changed between the initial draft and the one on hand at the end of the month. The biggest alteration, Schlei said, was the addition of what he called "judicial words," including a long-winded preamble full of legal jargon and posturing. The fear was that the bill's reliance on the Commerce Clause would mean that it would end up in the House Committee on Interstate and Foreign Commerce, which was chaired by the segregationist Southern Democrat Oren Harris of Arkansas (who had had a brief turn in the limelight in 1959 as the head of the "quiz show" hearings, in which a number of TV game shows were accused of fixing their results). If it went to Harris's committee, the drafters feared, it might never come out. To prevent that, Schlei said, "I rewrote the preamble of our bill so as to include as many terms as possible suggestive of the idea that the bill would fall within the Judiciary Committee's territory," where it would be shepherded by the liberal Democrat and civil rights partisan Emanuel Celler of Brooklyn.[54]

The draft had three main elements. First was a public accommodations law, rooted in the Commerce Clause, which banned segregation in non-owner-occupied hotels and motels, movie and stage theaters, and restaurants that did at least $150,000 in annual business or were located near a major highway—the key element for each establishment being that they had a firm connection to interstate business, either through the goods and services they offered or the clientele they served.

Second, the bill offered technical assistance to school districts to devise desegregation plans and offered financial aid to those with plans already in place; it also allowed the attorney general to intervene in lawsuits against schools or individuals that interfered with desegregation—essentially, this was Title III for schools.

And third, it created a statutory basis for the President's Committee on Equal Employment Opportunity, which would allow it access to more resources. (Thanks to a 1944 amendment by Richard Russell, committees created by the executive branch, like the PCEEO, had limited access to funds.) The bill would also roll in the voting rights and Civil Rights Commission planks from the president's February legislation, which was languishing on Capitol Hill.[55]

The conversation on June 1 focused on specifics. Was it better to set an annual income test for restaurants, or should it be based on the number of tables? What criteria should determine whether the attorney general intervened in a school desegregation lawsuit: Should it be based on whether the plaintiffs had the financial resources to sue themselves, or whether such an intervention would "materially advance" desegregation in the district? Or both?

What became clear in the course of the meeting was how much of the urgency to act came from the immediate politics of civil rights, and Birmingham in particular. At the outset, Robert Kennedy praised the legislation because "what this will do is get them into the courts and off the streets"—and "off the front pages of the paper." The same went for the schools provision: "The reason we're doing schools," the attorney general said, "is because something negroes feel strongly about is education."[56]

At one point President Kennedy turned to Johnson and asked for his input. "I don't know," Johnson said sheepishly. "I haven't read the bill, I haven't seen it." A few minutes later, though, the vice president let loose with a lengthy critique of the bill, both as a policy and political matter. Though he agreed that "if we don't do this, they'll be out in the streets," he felt the bill did not do nearly enough to address long-term problems, particularly black educational attainment and employment. He also cautioned the president to consider "how much of this can you chew." It would take two to three months of Democrat versus Democrat combat, potentially damaging the party at the outset of a presidential campaign. "Nine out of ten people talking are going to be Democrats, and they'll keep talking dictatorship and freedom and states rights."

This was too much reality for Kennedy, who wondered aloud whether this was even worth it. "What is going to be the result if we don't have any further legislation?" asked the president. "Will we just have these riots?"

"I don't think we really have an alternative. You couldn't go on and not have legislation," interrupted Marshall. "You'd have a major fight in Congress, you'd have a lot of Republicans and a lot of Democrats putting legislation in. Everybody would be saying 'where is your legislation?' I couldn't possibly defend that position. I think it's absolutely essential that you have legislation."

That seemed to snap the president out of his momentary doubt, and he dived back into the discussion. What about doing something on job discrimination, he said, like the FEPC proposal that liberals had been hawking since the end of World War II? Here Johnson, despite his earlier call to swing for the fences, recommended pragmatism. "I think you ought to try to get what you send up there," he said. "FEPC never made much progress in the House." In the end, Kennedy decided to merely endorse the idea of an FEPC, which had been included in several Republican and Democratic bills already under consideration in Congress.

Kennedy still wanted to do something on employment. Though his efforts to pitch the tax cut as a quasi-civil-rights measure that spring had come across as maladroit marketing, he did believe that helping blacks could not stop at civil rights laws alone. He was already quietly developing ideas for a more direct assault on long-term unemployment and poverty, ideas that would only reach fruition long after his death, as Lyndon Johnson's War on Poverty. But he also recognized that the country was in no mood for civil rights legislation, a major tax cut, *and* a massive antipoverty measure. At one point he turned to Louis Martin and asked, "What's the mood of the country and what should we do about it?"[57]

As Martin recalled, "I told them that they were concentrating on Birmingham and what was happening there but they also had to worry about the possibility of riots in Chicago, Detroit, Pittsburgh, and New York."

To his surprise, Vice President Johnson nodded his approval. "Louis is right," he said. Martin, feeling the wind at his back, said the president should include a Works Progress Administration for the cities, to the tune of $1 billion. "We've got a tremendous number of young unemployed kids who have no hope for the future," he said.

The attorney general laughed. "Well, we might think about a half a billion," he said.[58]

Instead, Kennedy settled for a pair of measures proposed by Secretary of Labor Willard Wirtz that he could take unilaterally—mandating that unions involved in government contract work desegregate their apprenticeship programs, and conducting a thorough search of the laws on federal employment to make sure they did not contain discriminatory measures. The meeting wrapped up, and the consensus was to announce the bill on June 4.

But Johnson had much more to say. On the Saturday before the meeting he had asked O'Donnell for a fifteen-minute meeting with the president, but the appointments secretary, O'Donnell—who hated Johnson, and whom Johnson both despised and feared as the sort of Ivy League elite he had battled his entire career—had said no.[59]

Instead, over the next several days Johnson spoke to as many of Kennedy's inner circle as he could about his concerns on the bill. On June 3 he got Ted Sorensen on the phone. Johnson was worried that Kennedy was diving into the fight without a plan of attack. "He's already tried out this literacy bill by this shooting-from-the-hip business," he said. "Hell, they messed around there four or five days, had a little perfunctory vote and said it was hypocritical and disgraceful. Didn't you think so?"[60]

"Last year?" Sorensen asked.

"Yeah."

"Well, I think we could have done better."

"Sure we could have, sure we could have." This time had to be different. The president needed to start with a "Gettysburg" speech somewhere in the South—Johnson suggested San Antonio or Jackson, Mississippi—that would make the moral case for legislation; doing so might win over some Southern whites, and it would let the nation's blacks know he was firmly on their side. "We got a little pop gun, and I want to pull out the cannon. The president is the cannon." Kennedy also needed to force Republicans to back his bill by threatening to tar them as anti-civil-rights in the next election. With the GOP in his pocket, Kennedy could go to the Southern Democrats and say, "Now here we got to do it either in the streets or in the courts. And they're going to do it in the streets. I can't sit idly by, and what do you recommend, senator?"

Of equal importance was making a moral commitment to blacks, especially because, in Johnson's eyes, the bill faced a rough path toward passage, and might not pass at all. If it failed, blacks needed to know the president had tried his best. In any case, "I don't think the Negroes' goals are going to be achieved through legislation," he said—"what Negroes are really seeking is moral force."

For Johnson, it was a matter of timing, of waiting until the situation was right for the bill. Sorensen said he was worried that the South was "hot enough" and felt immediate action was needed. But Johnson disagreed. The tax bill had to pass first, for one thing, or else it would become hostage to the Southern Democrats' delay tactics. In his typical folksy idiom, Johnson said, "I'd move my children on through the line and get them down in the storm cellar and get it under lock and key, and then I'd make my attack."

Moreover, the administration needed to get a firm sense of how many votes it had behind the bill, "and we can get them a whole lot better before the message than we do afterwards." Just as important as getting favorable senators on board was sitting down with Richard Russell to find out the Southern

Democrats' game plan, and what Russell thought of the bill. "I would make them show every card they got," he said.

When the bill hit the Senate, Johnson said he would employ the same hard-ball tactics he had used with the 1957 and 1960 bills, particularly round-the-clock sessions. "This crowd, they're experts at fighting this thing and we're not prepared for them," he said.

The call with Sorensen was also a chance for Johnson to air personal griev-ances against the rest of the administration. He did not like being cut out of the planning process so far—"I don't know who drafted it," he said, "I got it from the *New York Times*"—and he particularly resented Robert Kennedy's commando raids into the PCEEO: "Bobby came in the other day to out Equal Employment Committee and I was humiliated."

But Johnson ended on a positive note. "I don't want to spend a week telling these newspaper reporters why I disagree, and I never do," he assured Sorensen. "So whenever he wants" my advice, "why, I'm available."

Sorensen had barely said a word, and it's not clear from the transcript that he was really listening. "Well, I'll pass all this on to him, you can be sure," Sorensen said, hanging up.

Johnson also tried to get an audience with Robert Kennedy, but the attor-ney general brushed him off by sending Schlei in his place. The two met on June 4 in the vice president's office on Capitol Hill, a palatial suite that he had secured from his successor as Senate majority leader, Mike Mansfield. "He was undoubtedly somewhat unhappy that he was talking to me instead of to some-body else," recalled Schlei. Nevertheless, the pair spoke for forty minutes—or, rather, Johnson did; Schlei listened and tried to get in an occasional word, almost wholly without success. "He certainly did talk," Schlei recalled later. "To this day I couldn't tell you whether he had hold of my lapels or not. He may have. He absolutely poured out his soul. He really—he must have been four inches away from me really telling it to me like he thought."[61]

Johnson's main concern, Schlei reported, was timing. The Kennedys had done a good job developing the bill, but they had not given enough thought into the basic mechanics of getting it passed. "He said that the legislative proposal would be disastrous for the president's program and would not be enacted if submitted now," Schlei wrote afterward in a memo to Robert Kennedy. Johnson emphasized that he was not against the bill, but that he thought the White House needed a better plan. Critical to any effort, he said, was getting the Republicans on board, particularly the Senate minority leader, Everett Dirksen. He should run the bill by Richard Russell, who would oppose it but give his honest assessment of its flaws, and the House parliamentarian, to make absolutely sure it would go to the Judiciary

Committee. Finally, Kennedy should take his campaign to the South by making a major speech in each of the states on the moral importance of non-discrimination. He even had a place in mind to start: a new NASA facility in Mississippi, where Kennedy should declare that anyone willing to send black soldiers to fight "for this flag"—at which point, Schlei recalled, Johnson grabbed the small American flag standing on his desk—should be willing to support the civil rights bill. Then, and only then, should the legislation go to Capitol Hill.

While it is unclear whether all of Johnson's advice made it to the Oval Office, the president was willing to act on some of his vice president's recommendations. In a memo to Labor Secretary Wirtz and Anthony Celebrezze, the secretary of health, education and welfare, he reported that "the vice president feels, on the basis of his experience with the Committee on Equal Employment Opportunity, that the Federal Government should and could be doing much more to relieve Negro unemployment by additional and intensive job training programs for the unskilled the illiterate and those on public welfare." To that end, Kennedy instructed the two to review existing programs and proposals to see if more could be done. Kennedy also met several times with congressional leaders, from both sides of the aisle, to sound out their feelings on civil rights legislation. Moreover, while the exact reasons were never explained, the president decided to put off announcing his proposal for several days—a decision that may well have reflected Johnson's advice to spend more time preparing the political groundwork.[62]

At the same time, there were attempts by different White House staffers to pare back the bill. On June 8, Martin arrived at the attorney general's office to learn that a movement was afoot to pull the public accommodations title from the bill. Martin went ballistic. "Listen, you are worried about unrest," shouted the tall, bespectacled, usually jovial Martin. "You're worried about civil anarchy. But what's the trigger? One of the triggers is this business about public accommodations. That was the thing in North Carolina when the students sit in whenever blacks are refused service. That immediately causes anger and there is absolutely nothing we can do with a civil rights bill if we don't address it." Robert Kennedy and the other men in the room were speechless. But Martin was not finished. "I have a daughter, and there is an Italian restaurant not too far from my house. I understand they don't want any black customers. If my daughter is turned down by that guy, I'm going to take a gun and shoot him. And as old as I am, if I feel that way about it, what do you think about young blacks?" The public accommodations title stayed in the bill.[63]

*

MARTIN'S IRE WAS reflected in the headlines, which were reporting daily on the latest flare-up in the South, this time in Jackson, Mississippi. The state capital was a boomtown, having gone from just 22,000 people in 1920 to 144,000 in 1960, thanks in part to a profitable but ultimately misbegotten effort to find oil under its loamy soil. Like Birmingham, Jackson also had a large and woefully oppressed black population, one that by the spring of 1963 was pushing hard against the strictures of Jim Crow. Unlike Birmingham, though, Jackson was largely an NAACP town, thanks to the work of Medgar Evers, the head of the state chapter. A varsity college football player, Army veteran, and insurance salesman, Evers had been haunted by the violent power of Jim Crow racism ever since, as a child, he saw the mutilated body of a friend of his father's left to lie limp after he was murdered by a white mob. Evers managed to knit together a delicate alliance of NAACP moderates, old-line ministers, and action-oriented students, a potent mix that his bosses in New York hoped to use to their advantage in their turf war with the SCLC.[64]

The NAACP national leadership had watched with envy as King took over and then took national the Birmingham movement; the association had spent the previous fifteen years assiduously building a robust Southern membership, and it worried that King was poised to co-opt it, with Jackson being an obvious next target. Gloster Current, the NAACP's director of branches, had told Evers to "hit hard" in Jackson as soon as the crisis in Birmingham was over, and the Mississippian had spent much of May leading a boycott of downtown stores and in negotiations with the mayor, Allen Thompson. The mayor eventually agreed to a tentative partial desegregation deal at the end of May, then quickly disowned it on May 28.[65]

That same day the first sit-ins began. Four black students and a white professor from nearby Tougaloo College sat down at a Woolworth's lunch counter. A white mob set upon the protesters, insulting them, pouring condiments on them, and eventually beating three of them, including the professor, in the face. The police stood by and did nothing, though one of the beaten protesters was later charged with disturbing the peace. A photo of the assault appeared on the front page of the New York Times the next day.[66]

Evers announced a "massive offensive" in response. Over the next several days Jackson became a reprise of the Birmingham action. Nineteen picketers were arrested on May 29. The next day hundreds of black students poured out of Lanier Junior and Senior High School carrying flags and singing, "We want freedom." A line of sixty police officers stopped them and said they were parading without a license. When the demonstrators refused to move, a cop hit one of them in the thighs with his nightstick, crumpling him to the ground. They were then led to trucks and hauled off to a hastily erected hogpen of a prison. In all, some five hundred were arrested that day; the next day, another hundred were taken in, including NAACP president Roy Wilkins, who had flown in to advertise his organization's leadership in the Jackson movement. In the melee Thelton Henderson, a black Department of Justice official, there to observe, was arrested as well. A few days later someone threw a gasoline bomb into Evers's carport, but it did not explode.[67]

On May 30, King requested a meeting with the president and the attorney general to press his case for an executive order against segregation. But Lee White, instructed to keep the civil rights leader at bay, said no. That night, speaking with his advisers Stanley Levison and Clarence Jones (in a conversation picked up by FBI wiretaps placed on Levison's phone), King said that the best way to follow up the success in Birmingham was to stage an enormous demonstration in Washington, one that would induce Kennedy to "really push" legislation.[68]

Jackson was not the only place on edge. Protests of varying size were erupting across the South. On May 29, approximately three hundred blacks, including the Olympian Wilma Rudolph, sought service at a Clarksville, Tennessee, restaurant. On June 6 alone, 257 people were arrested in Tallahassee, Florida, and 278 in Greensboro, North Carolina. It was all the Department of Justice could do just to keep track of them: on May 27, Robert Kennedy sent a memo to Southern district attorneys asking them to note "any places where racial demonstrations are expected within the next 30 days."[69]

And John Kennedy had other parts of the civil rights picture to deal with. Since May 29 he had been meeting with a string of interest groups—governors, mayors, business leaders, women's associations, clergy, lawyers—to convince them of the need for significant change on the racial front, not only in terms of immediate legislation but also on long-term problems like youth delinquency, school dropouts, and black employment. The president, the attorney general, and the vice president were present at most of the meetings, along with relevant cabinet members. By all accounts, Johnson was the star of the meetings. "Kennedy had made an intellectual appeal for the lawyers' duty and so forth," Morris Abram, a New York lawyer and civil rights activist, recalled. "There was no passion in any of it until LBJ took the podium. And he gave an impassioned speech about what kind of a country is this that a man can go die in a foxhole and can't get a hamburger in a public restaurant. I would say he was by far the most effective fellow there. I was impressed by him."[70]

Each meeting was tightly tailored by Lee White to speak to the particular group's concerns, but also to draw out of them ways they could contribute to civil rights progress. To the governors, Kennedy pitched the importance of local and state biracial committees. He told labor leaders that expanding black employment opportunities was the best way to reduce the risk of further violence. To the 250 clergy who gathered on June 17, he appealed to them to "recognize the conflict between racial bigotry and the Holy Word." All told, between May 29 and June 22, Kennedy met with 1,558 people.[71]

Though Kennedy's and Johnson's speeches at the meetings were more hortatory than concrete, and some of the participants later derided the meetings as trumped-up, pointless affairs, they got many of the attendees talking with each other, and within a month had spun off a half dozen advocacy groups and affinity networks that would play a critical role in organizing public support for the civil rights bill. Kennedy asked J. Irwin Miller, an Indiana industrialist and the first lay president of the National Council of Churches, to organize both a religious advisory group on civil rights and a committee of business leaders to push for the bill among the corporate community.[72]

Kennedy was also pressing his case with Capitol Hill Republicans. On June 5 he met with Senate Minority Leader Everett Dirksen, House Minority Leader Charles Halleck, and House Republican Whip Leslie Arends. Dirksen, to Kennedy's surprise, was supportive; though he expressed reservations about certain aspects of the bill—most notably the public accommodations provision—he gave Kennedy his assurance that he would take the administration's side against a likely Southern Democratic filibuster. That same day, the Senate Republican Conference released a statement announcing that it would "support further appropriate legislation required to help solve the problems of our Nation in the field of civil rights."[73]

Republicans in the House were less quick to rally to the Kennedy bill. Many members—and not just the liberals—supported legislation, and had been pushing for it since the beginning of the session. But the White House and congressional Democrats had largely ignored them, calculating that there were too few Republicans to pass the bill themselves and that there were enough Democrats to pass their own bill with minimal GOP involvement. At the same time, House Republicans doubted the administration's resolve, especially when it came to omnibus legislation—many were still smarting from the experience of 1957, when they passed an expansive civil rights bill only to see Lyndon Johnson water it down in the Senate.

House Republicans were also pressing forward with their own legislation. Two days before Johnson's meeting with the three GOP leaders, thirty House Republicans had introduced a civil rights bill that included a strong Title III provision, precisely the element that Kennedy was so averse to including in his own legislation. Yet on June 4, when they tried to explain their bill on the House floor, Democrats had churlishly and repeatedly interrupted them;

eventually two leading liberals, James Roosevelt and John Bell Williams, moved to adjourn before the Republicans could finish (the motion lost by an overwhelming vote).[74]

Nevertheless, the Republicans used their bill to attack the administration, and to call attention to the lack of bipartisan cooperation on civil rights. "There has been no legislative submission on the Birmingham question, and on the question of public facilities as yet by the administration," said Representative John Lindsay of New York during a June 6 *Today* show interview. "I've sent word to a highly respected member of the Democratic side in the House that on the bill [Clark] MacGregor, [William] Cahill, and [Charles] Mathias, myself, others have been pressing for, we'd like the administration to help us get it through the House of Representatives."

"Did you get a response?" the reporter asked.

"We haven't gotten any response as yet," Lindsay said.[75]

But the biggest challenge facing Kennedy that early June was in Tuscaloosa, Alabama, where Governor Wallace had declared that he would block two black students, Vivian Jones and James Hood, from registering for admission to the University of Alabama, despite a May 21 court order commanding him to allow them in. Indeed, one of the reasons Kennedy had delayed introducing the bill was that Marshall and John Doar had to pull out of drafting sessions to go to Alabama on June 1 to start preparing for the showdown with Wallace, which was set for June 11.[76]

The White House had known of Wallace's plans as early as November 1962, when Frank Rose, the president of the university, had called Marshall to tell him about the impending court order and Wallace's intentions. He appeared serious: Wallace had told the state's education leaders that if they dared integrate their schools, "there won't be enough state troopers to protect you" and that he would even cut off state financing to them. Wallace continued to stand firm through the spring; on June 2, despite the court order, he went on *Meet the Press* to reaffirm his intention to "stand at the door," though he promised "the confrontation will be handled peacefully and without violence."[77]

As the day of the students' admission approached, White House and Justice Department officials debated how best to ensure they got safely into the school. Some proposed a rehash of Ole Miss, with federal troops escorting them bodily into the registrar's office. But Katzenbach, having learned more than a few lessons during the Mississippi crisis, had a better idea. Wallace, he realized, was all bluster, a man who might believe his racist convictions, but acted on them mostly to appease voters. Katzenbach would go to Tuscaloosa himself, he decided, and let Wallace have his show, then insist on escorting the students to register. Wallace, through a back channel provided by Alabama senator Lister Hill, told Kennedy he would comply, and he brought in 825 state troopers to keep order.[78]

On the afternoon before the confrontation, Ted Sorensen suggested to Kennedy that the next day, fresh from his presumed victory over Wallace, he should go on TV to mark the occasion. The idea for some sort of presidential address—a "fireside chat," in Rooseveltian parlance—had been bouncing around the White House for months. It had been suggested at the president's meeting with the ADA on May 4, at the height of the Birmingham crisis. Soon after a reporter had asked whether it would help for the president to give a national speech on race relations. "If I thought it would, I would give one," the president demurred. "I made a speech the night of Mississippi at Oxford to the citizens of Mississippi and others that did not seem to do much good." At a meeting in the Oval Office on June 10, Kennedy expressed skepticism, saying, "It just really depends on whether we have trouble at the university, then I would; but otherwise, I don't think we would at this point." But his brother replied forcefully: "I think it would be helpful. I think we have reason to do it, you don't talk about the legislation, you talk about unemployment, talk about education, you do it for 15 minutes, I think it would alleviate a lot of problems."

"Well, I suppose I could do it," Kennedy replied.[79]

By the morning of the eleventh, Katzenbach had been awake for thirty-six hours. He had spent the previous day at a nearby Army Reserve facility, walking through every possible contingency—he even found a soldier roughly Wallace's height and build so that soldiers could practice picking him up and moving him out of the way, should the governor prove recalcitrant. It was an odd role in which to find this former University of Chicago law professor; then again, it was the second such crisis Katzenbach had managed in nine months, and he did so with a steely insouciance. On a phone call that morning, Robert Kennedy had put his daughter Kerry on the line. "Do you know what temperature it is?" Katzenbach asked her. "It is 98 degrees—you tell your father that we're all going to get hardship pay."[80]

Later, on the way to the university at the head of an Army convoy, Katzenbach got a message that Robert Kennedy wanted to speak with him. When the radio in the truck went on the fritz, he stopped at a shopping mall and found a pay phone. Kennedy stood in his office, three of his children playing at his feet, his walls decked with maps of the campus and Tuscaloosa area. His last instructions for dealing with Wallace were brief. "The president wants you to make him look foolish," Kennedy said.[81]

That was the easy part. Wallace had scripted the event carefully. For the point of confrontation he chose an auditorium with a classical colonnade out front that he thought would look great on TV. He had a wooden lectern set up from which to deliver his speech, even drawing lines and circles on the ground in front of him to show Katzenbach and his aides where to stand for the cameras. But Katzenbach understood the power of the visual media, too; ignoring the lines, he got close enough to the five-foot-seven governor so that his own six-foot-two frame towered over him (though Katzenbach later said he was also trying to get out of the sun).[82]

Katzenbach, his hands crossed under his armpits, told Wallace to step aside. By agreement, Wallace then gave a seven-minute speech in which he denounced the federal government and refused to budge. "The unwelcome, unwanted, unwarranted, and forced induced intrusion on the campus of the University of Alabama today of the might of the central government offers a frightful example of the oppression of the rights, privileges, and sovereignty of this state by officers of central government," Wallace said.

Katzenbach waited patiently, his arms still folded, his gaze condescending. "Governor, I am not interested in a show, and I don't know what the purpose of this show is," he said when Wallace had finished. "From the outset, governor, all of us have known that the final chapter of this history will be the admission of these students." Wallace was silent.[83]

"Very well," said Katzenbach. He returned to the truck for the students, then walked them to their dormitories and lunch. Meanwhile, Kennedy ordered the Alabama National Guard federalized. At three o'clock, with Katzenbach and Wallace back in position and a hundred troops, now under Kennedy's control, ringing the scene, Wallace gave one last, short statement and backed off. When Robert Kennedy got word, back in Washington, he lit a cigar.[84]

The crisis over, John Kennedy decided to go ahead with the speech anyway. Tuscaloosa may have ended peacefully, but that morning's newspapers carried reports of mass arrests in Cambridge, Maryland. Earlier that day a telegram had come in from King urging the president to find a "just and moral solution" in Danville, Virginia, where police had attacked a group of civil rights protesters.[85]

The president called each of the three networks to reserve fifteen minutes at the 8:00 P.M. time slot, but it was not until less than an hour before he was to go on air that the president's aides started in on the text. In one room, Sorensen and White talked their way through a draft using notes from Kennedy and Martin; as they talked, Gloria Sitrin, one of Kennedy's secretaries, simultaneously typed up a draft. Meanwhile, in the next room, the Kennedy brothers scratched down random notes that the president could draw on if he had to slide into extemporaneous speaking.[86]

As the hour approached, the speech still was not ready. The cameras were being set up in the Oval Office; the president paced the Cabinet Room, starting to panic. He looked at Marshall. "Come on Burke," he said, "you must have some ideas." Sorensen came in with a draft, but Kennedy thought it was stilted. With no time to rewrite, the president grabbed the assortment of sheets, scratch pads, and scraps of paper and walked next door. He slid behind the desk, and the cameras started to roll.[87]

"Good evening, my fellow citizens," Kennedy began. "This afternoon, following a series of threats and defiant statements, the presence of Alabama National Guardsmen was required on the University of Alabama to carry out the final and unequivocal order of the United States District Court of the Northern District of Alabama." He praised the university community for remaining calm, then shuffled through several minutes of his standard patter on civil rights—that America was founded on principles of equality, that the country was "committed to a worldwide struggle to promote and protect the rights of all who wish to be free," that troops abroad were sent to Vietnam and West Berlin "regardless of color."[88]

But then Kennedy hit his stride. "We are confronted primarily with a moral issue. It is as old as the scriptures and is as clear as the American Constitution," he said. This was not about sectional or party politics, not about pitting one race against the other. Rather, it was about bringing all Americans together behind a set of principles upon which everyone, as Americans, should be able to agree.

"The heart of the question is whether all Americans are to be afforded equal rights and equal opportunities, whether we are going to treat our fellow Americans as we want to be treated. If an American, because his skin is dark, cannot eat lunch in a restaurant open to the public, if he cannot send his children to the best public school available, if he cannot vote for the public officials who represent him, if, in short, he cannot enjoy the full and free life which all of us want, then who among us would be content to have the color of his skin changed and stand in his place? Who among us would then be content with the counsels of patience and delay?"

The ugly facts of racism in America undermined the values the country stood for. "We preach freedom around the world, and we mean it, and we cherish our freedom here at home. But are we to say to the world, and much more importantly, to each other that this is a land of the free except for the Negroes; that we have no second-class citizens except Negroes; that we have no class or cast system, no ghettoes, no master race except with respect to Negroes?"

These were sentiments drawn straight from the movement he had kept at arm's length for so long, and from a vice president he had so often relegated, on purpose or not, to an embarrassingly marginal role in the administration. More than that, it was an expression of not just sympathy with the movement, but empathy for black Americans as Americans—not as charity cases, or as political problems, but as fellow citizens. "The fires of frustration and discord are burning in every city, North and South, where legal remedies are not at hand. Redress is sought in the streets, in demonstrations, parades, and protests which create tensions and threaten violence and threaten lives."

The answer, he said, could no longer come through repression—nor could it come through demonstrations alone. It must come through legislative action, first and foremost in the United States Congress. "I am, therefore, asking the Congress to enact legislation giving all Americans the right to be served in facilities which are open to the public—hotels, restaurants, theaters, retail stores, and similar establishments," he said. "This seems to me to be an elementary right. Its denial is an arbitrary indignity that no American in 1963 should have to endure, but many do."

The last four minutes of Kennedy's speech were completely unscripted, and it showed. He repeated himself, circled back. "As I have said before, not every child has an equal talent or an equal ability or an equal motivation, but they should have the equal right to develop their talent and their ability and their motivation, to make something of themselves," he said. At the point where he should have been plumbing his oratorical depths for a moving conclusion, he tossed a bone to the moderates and conservatives, who feared black violence was the driving force behind Washington's sudden attention to civil rights. "We have a right to expect that the Negro community will be responsible, will uphold the law," he said—but then added, "but they have a right to expect that the law will be fair, that the Constitution will be color blind, as Justice Harlan said at the turn of the century. This is what we are talking about and this is a matter which concerns this country and what it stands for, and in meeting it I ask the support of all our citizens."

Rhetorically, it was not Kennedy's best speech; his delivery was awkward at times, rushed, halting, his peroration rambling. But in its content, it rivaled his most historic addresses. No president had ever taken on race as squarely as he did in those fifteen minutes. He both accused the country of moral hypocrisy and gave a rousing call to unity. He put himself behind transformative legislation, but also challenged the country to effect the sort of moral change that government action alone cannot realize.

Millions watched the speech. From Atlanta, King sent a telegram to the president lauding it as "one of the most eloquent, profound and unequivocal pleas for justice and freedom by any President." Wilkins did likewise, calling it "a clear, resolute exposition of basic Americanism."[89]

The Southern Democrats, naturally, were none too happy with it. In a statement the next day, Richard Russell attacked the bill, saying if passed it would usher in "a socialistic or communist state." Strom Thurmond proposed a general strike among Southern Democrats in order to block all of Kennedy's agenda unless he gave up on civil rights.[90]

Historians would later call Kennedy's June 11 speech the beginning of the "Second Reconstruction." At least within Congress, it certainly unleashed forces that Kennedy had a hard time controlling, let alone comprehending. Though the Southern Democrats declined to go in with Thurmond on a general strike, they did put the president on notice by defeating a routine bill to finance the Area Redevelopment Administration, which many of the House Southerners had backed when it passed in 1961. Later that day, Kennedy commiserated over the loss with House Majority Leader Carl Albert. "It's just in everything, I mean, this has become everything."

"It's overwhelming the whole, the whole program," Albert said. "I couldn't do a damn thing with them, you know."

"Civil rights did it," the president sighed.[91]

IN JACKSON, MEDGAR EVERS had been at an NAACP meeting and had missed the speech, but his wife, Myrlie, had stayed up with their children to watch it. They were still awake at midnight when their father pulled into the driveway, his Oldsmobile packed with T-shirts reading "Jim Crow Must Go."[92]

As Evers mounted the porch, a shot rang out. Hit in the back, Evers crumpled. "Turn me loose!" Evers cried. He died less than an hour later.[93]

The impact of Kennedy's speech cannot be separated from the national shock at Evers's murder. Though he was hardly a household name, the assassination of the highest-ranking NAACP official in Mississippi brought the urgency of the civil rights question into a focus that no presidential speech could ever achieve.

The ripples from Evers's death even reached the White House. A few days later, Kennedy was talking with Schlesinger, his in-house intellectual and an on-again, off-again professor in Harvard's history department, where Kennedy had first developed the anti-Reconstruction, anti–Radical Republican views that permeated his Pulitzer Prize–winning book *Profiles in Courage*. The South, he had believed and written, was at war with itself and best left alone, so that in time men of wisdom and honor could bring their homeland into the modern era. The worst thing that could happen would be for intolerant moralists to force change upon the region.

Now, finally—after Oxford, after Birmingham, after Tuscaloosa, and now

Jackson—he told Schlesinger that his old views were crumbling. "I don't understand the South," he confided. "I'm coming to believe that Thaddeus Stevens"—a hardline abolitionist and architect of Reconstruction—"was right. I had always been taught to regard him as a man of vicious bias. But when I see this sort of thing, I begin to wonder how else you can treat them."[94]

CHAPTER 3

AN IDEA BECOMES A BILL

THE EIGHT DAYS BETWEEN KENNEDY'S speech and his submission of the civil rights bill to Congress on June 19 was an almost constant blur of activity at both ends of Pennsylvania Avenue, with frequent stops midway at the Department of Justice. On June 12, the day after the president's speech, three aides to Senate Majority Leader Mansfield—Harry McPherson, Bobby Baker, and Ken Teasdale—sat down to think through the first of many conundrums facing the bill's supporters: how to introduce it.[1]

The trio knew that White House strategists had already decided that the inevitability of a long filibuster by Southern senators meant the bill should start out in the more liberal House of Representatives, where it could gather momentum before hitting the Senate. But there was no guarantee the bill would emerge from the House, let alone emerge in an acceptable shape—liberals might overload it with politically untenable planks, like a universal Title III, or Southern Democrats might find a way to gut it. As a backup, McPherson, Baker, and Teasdale decided Mansfield should introduce the bill simultaneously in the Senate.

But here was another problem. On an uncontroversial matter, the process would be fairly straightforward: assuming the president's party is in control of Congress, he would get the chairman of the relevant committee to sponsor the bill. But in this case, that man was James Eastland of Mississippi, the head of the Judiciary Committee and an implacable segregationist. So Mansfield would have to do it himself.

Mansfield, however, had already decided that his best position was one of nonpartisan impartiality, the better to win over Republicans and, perhaps, a bravely errant Southerner (Ted Sorensen, in a June 14 memo to the president, had wondered if "any Southerner be persuaded to be a 'Vandenberg'?"—a reference to the Michigan Republican senator who had broken ranks with his party's isolationist wing to help create the United Nations). Therefore,

Mansfield, through McPherson, insisted that he introduce the bill in conjunc-
tion with Everett Dirksen, the Senate minority leader.[2]

This presented a third problem. Dirksen supported civil rights legislation—except Title II, the public accommodations provision and the heart of
the bill. He had said as much at a bipartisan leadership meeting at the White
House on June 13.

The solution, Mansfield and his lieutenants decided, was to split the bill
into two parts, one containing everything except Title II and another
comprised solely of Title II. Mansfield was so sensitive to Dirksen's position,
and so convinced that Dirksen held the key to the bill's success, that he refused
White House entreaties to sponsor the Title II bill himself. "My sponsorship of
the public accommodations portion of the legislation may well jeopardize
passage of the remainder of the legislation, which, even in itself, is not by any
means assured of 67 votes at this point," Mansfield wrote in a pointed memo
to the president. In the end, the majority leader and the president compromised. Mansfield introduced the administration's bill, then cosponsored a
version of the same bill, minus Title II, with Dirksen. Finally, Mansfield
enlisted Washington's Warren Magnuson, who had risen from an itinerant
farmhand to become one of the Senate's most respected liberals, to introduce
the Title II–only bill.[3]

While the three Senate staffers hashed out Mansfield's strategy, a mile away
at the White House the Kennedy team kept busy with the president's intermi-
nable series of interest group meetings. On June 13 he met with some two
hundred labor leaders. On June 17 he met with an equally large number of
religious leaders, drawn from an ecumenical roster—rabbis, Catholic priests,
Southern Baptists, black preachers. The latter meeting took an awkward turn
when Kennedy asked for comments and was confronted by the Reverend
Albert Garner of Lakeland, Florida, the president of the ultraconservative
American Baptist Association. "Our people religiously feel with moral convictions that racial integration that would lead to intermarriage is against the will
of their creator," Garner said. Kennedy was caught by surprise; rather than
push back, he dodged, saying, "I think the question of intermarriage is really a
question removed from what we are concerned with. That is a matter for the
individuals involved." Still, the meeting was a success, if only because Kennedy
used the occasion to announce the creation of a religious advisory committee,
under the leadership of J. Irwin Miller, the Indiana industrialist and National
Council of Churches chairman.[4]

Meanwhile, halfway between the White House and Capitol Hill, the Justice
Department drafting team was continuing to rework the bill. Though its core
parts were in place, two more titles were added after Kennedy's June 11 speech.

The first was an idea that had been floating around Congress since the late 1950s: a federal civil rights mediation service, which would parachute into nascent trouble spots before they got out of hand. The addition was partly political. It was thought that Southern Democrats would support a plank that put voluntary, nonbinding mediation between Jim Crow businesses and the hard force of federal law.[5]

The other plank was equally political but aimed at the other end of the spectrum. For years now, Representative Adam Clayton Powell Jr. of Harlem, a fiery and controversial black politician, had appended "Powell amendments"—requirements that whatever the program was, it could not be implemented in a discriminatory manner—to various pieces of domestic legislation, in essence turning otherwise innocuous bills into civil rights proposals, which Southern Democrats would then turn on. The amendments made for good protest theater, but the consequence was a lot of very angry, otherwise pro-civil-rights legislators, who saw their bills sandbagged—and there was little they could say in response, lest they be tarred as anti-civil-rights. Several of them came to Robert Kennedy and Norbert Schlei demanding that they add a universal Powell amendment to the bill, applying a nondiscrimination requirement to all federal programs, so that Powell would finally shut up.[6]

At first Kennedy, afraid of overloading the bill, was resistant, even when Representative James O'Hara of Missouri, a liberal ally, passed him a bill that he had already drafted to create just such a requirement. But on the weekend before the bill was introduced, Kennedy called O'Hara at home and asked him to draft a Powell plank to add to the bill. O'Hara called his secretary and had her meet him at his office, where he dictated a new version and had it in the attorney general's hands by 1:00 P.M. This new plank, which came to be known as Title VI, gave the president the power to cut off funds to a state or local program that used them in a discriminatory manner.[7]

There was also an extensive discussion over whether to add something about jobs—an FEPC, or else a training and public works title. But the sense inside the drafting room was that such a title would be a step too far for a bill that was already an enormous gamble. If the Republicans were wary of a bill banning discrimination in public accommodations—a law that was limited to the South, where the Democrats held sway—how would they feel about a bill that reached into the offices of their corporate allies and told them how to run their hiring practices? And yet fair employment had been a central demand of the civil rights movement for decades; it was impossible not to do *something*. "We were all conscious of the fact that some kind of provisions with respect to fair employment were terribly important and also in the almost, I think actually unanimous opinion of everyone who was involved in this, impossible to enact," recalled Nicholas Katzenbach. And so, at the last minute, another compromise was reached: Kennedy would explicitly endorse FEPC legislation that was about to be taken up by the House Education and Labor Committee and sponsored by James Roosevelt, a liberal California representative (and son of Franklin Roosevelt). The drafters hoped such a gesture would pacify civil rights groups, though as Katzenbach admitted, "it was window dressing."[8]

There was a more contentious debate over whether to include a program of vocational training and, even, public jobs for millions of unemployed African Americans. Blacks had been by and large excluded from the public works programs of the New Deal, and many veteran New Deal liberals—Lyndon Johnson, for one—saw both a chance to right that wrong and an opportunity to take otherwise idle workers off the street. One such advocate was G. Mennen Williams, a former Michigan governor who was now the assistant secretary of state for African affairs (an heir to the Mennen personal care products fortune, Williams was known to friends and reporters as Soapy). In a memo to Sorensen on June 15, Williams predicted a wave of violence that summer without the "immediate institution of public works and, if necessary, work relief measures, to help absorb the unemployed and school leavers."[9]

Williams's memo keyed into a complex discussion that had been going on for months within the administration. Kennedy was not a New Deal liberal; he preferred expansionary tax and trade policies over blunter, more direct tools such as public works as the best way to boost long-term employment. Privately, though, Kennedy recognized that efforts to boost economic growth would not do much to help the most marginalized workers, at least in the next few years. In September 1961 he had won passage of the Juvenile Delinquency and Youth Offenses Control Act, which included money to develop training programs for at-risk youth. And he already had Walter Heller, the head of his Council of Economic Advisers, working on plans for a major antipoverty bill, which he hoped to introduce in early 1964.[10]

As Heller's research was demonstrating—and as several high-profile books at the time, such as Michael Harrington's *The Other America*, were documenting—the poverty and jobs problem was much too large to address in an already enormous civil rights bill. Still, as late as June 18, the day before the president was to submit his bill, O'Brien and Sorensen wrote a memo to Kennedy urging him, during a final review of the bill with congressional leaders, to discuss the possibility of Senators Mansfield and Dirksen cosponsoring a jobs program to be considered parallel to the civil rights bill. News of such conversations leaked to the press, who reported that Kennedy was planning a "'huge' job training and vocational education to his civil rights legislative request"—according to Senator Hubert Humphrey, with a price tag of up to $1 billion.[11]

Even as the drafting process advanced, the Department of Justice team was plotting its strategy for getting the bill through Congress. The need to win over Republicans was clear—but so, too, was the need to mollify liberals, who were likely to push back hard on a bill that left out both Title III and FEPC. On June 14, Burke Marshall sat down with members of the Democratic Study Group, a collection of liberal congressmen created in 1959 to organize and amplify their often-marginalized voices in an institution run by hardheaded realists like Lyndon Johnson and Sam Rayburn. Marshall was only partly successful in persuading them to back the bill; they agreed to support the newly added Title VI, the withholding of funds, but the only leader to come out in support of the bill in its entirety was Representative Richard Bolling of Missouri.[12]

Robert Kennedy, at a later meeting with the group, was no more successful. The DSG wanted to pursue the "strong-weak" strategy that had produced successful legislation in 1957 and 1960: load up a bill in the House with all sorts of seemingly valuable planks, then use all but a few of them as trading chips as it passes through the two chambers, picking off key votes along the way by agreeing to drop or water down particular planks. But the administration did not trust the liberals; it worried that liberals, especially among Republicans, would allow the bill to sink, then blame the administration. Katzenbach, who was at the meeting with Kennedy, told the DSG members: "We needed a law with a workable public accommodations section, not a Christmas tree that would never become law." Again Bolling came around, but otherwise, Katzenbach said, it was a "long, somewhat inconclusive conversation."[13]

When Soapy Williams sat down to write his memo about impending urban violence to Sorensen, he was not speculating—in the days after Medgar Evers's murder, nearly forty cities saw major demonstrations. Indeed, the slaying caught the nation's attention like no single civil rights murder since the lynching of Emmett Till eight years earlier. Whites were terrified, blacks were galvanized. On June 12, nearly four hundred people marched against segregation in Savannah, Georgia, telling the mayor he had forty-four hours "to give us our freedom." Five were injured that same day during a riot in Cambridge, Maryland, while three were hurt at a protest at a hospital construction site in Harlem. In Boston on June 11, forty protesters packed into a school board meeting room to call for an end to de facto school segregation in the city, while in Los Angeles on June 12, a burning pot of oil was thrown through a store window during the third day of protests against discrimination in that city.[14]

Things were particularly tumultuous in Washington. On June 14, thousands of marchers, backed by the NAACP, crowded in Lafayette Square, just north of the White House, holding signs reading "Whose Side Are You On?" and "Freedom Now!" Then they marched down Pennsylvania Avenue, heckled along the way by Nazis wearing gorilla suits. The marchers ignored them. Outside the District of Columbia building, city commissioner Walter Tobriner promised a crowd of hundreds that the city would enact a fair housing law "no later than this session." He also promised to pursue a fair employment law. "Waiting as long as you have," he said, "I, too, would be out there with you and not where I stand." The crowd cheered.[15]

Crowds then gathered at the Department of Justice building, where protesters demanded to meet with the attorney general. After twenty minutes, Robert Kennedy appeared, met by boos, a few cheers, and signs reading "Let Negroes Work in the Justice Department," "Don't Play Politics with Human Rights," and "Why an Almost Lily White Justice Department? It's not Easter." Kennedy, whom the *New York Times*, in its coverage of the protest, described as "smiling" but "obviously irritated," told the crowd that there was no discrimination at the department—even though, as he well knew, only a tiny fraction of the department's attorneys were black. "Any individual can come in here and get a job if he is qualified." Diffidently, but bravely, he added, "I'm not going out and hire a Negro just because he's not white."[16]

The most dangerous confrontations occurred in Jackson, in the wake of Evers's assassination. During a hundred-person march on June 13—in violation of a county court injunction against demonstrating—some eighty people were arrested and three injured, including a white professor from nearby Tougaloo College (John Salter, the same one who had been beaten by a white mob on May 28) and a fifteen-year-old girl. That afternoon Marshall received a frantic call from Thelton Henderson in Jackson. The black community was about to boil over. He told Marshall that he spoke with three black men with guns, one of whom said, "If they come up to me, I'll shoot their brains out."[17]

The next day the city granted black leaders their request for a parade permit, and on June 15 thousands attended a funeral service for Evers at the city's Masonic temple, including Martin Luther King Jr., Roy Wilkins, and the Nobel Peace Prize laureate Ralph Bunche. Afterward, though, some five hundred people braved three-digit heat to march through downtown, surrounded by police, chanting "Shoot, shoot!" Rocks were thrown, arrests were made. It seemed that a riot could break out any minute. Just then a voice shouted, "My

name is John Doar, and I am from the Department of Justice." Out stepped the
lanky Department of Justice lawyer, in shirtsleeves and a skinny black tie.
Doar, who had made a specialty of dropping into racial hot spots around the
Deep South, appeared seemingly from out of nowhere. "Medgar Evers would
not have wanted it this way," he shouted. Miraculously, the crowd and the
police backed down.[18]

Evers was a veteran, and he was buried on June 19 in Arlington National
Cemetery, across the Potomac River from Washington. Robert Kennedy was
one of the two thousand people in attendance, but his brother stayed at the
White House. President Kennedy did, however, invite Myrlie Evers and her
children to the Oval Office afterward, where he posed for a photograph and
gave the boys PT-109 tie clasps.[19]

AMERICANS AWOKE ON June 20 to headlines in their local newspapers
announcing President Kennedy's civil rights bill. He had submitted it, along
with a lengthy message, to Congress the day before, after one last Justice
Department drafting session that had Schlei, Harold Reis, and Sol
Lindenbaum making last-minute adjustments until two in the morning. The
message both echoed and amplified the urgency of his TV address eight days
earlier. "I am proposing that Congress stay in session this year until it has
enacted—preferably as a single, omnibus bill—the most responsible, reasonable and urgently needed solution" to the civil rights issue. "It will go far
toward providing reasonable men with the reasonable means of meeting
these problems, and it will thus help end the kind of racial strife which this
nation can hardly afford."[20]

But while Kennedy's June 11 speech focused on the moral imperative of
action, his message to Congress was couched in a concern over racial violence
and disorder—reflecting the Evers murder, the nationwide protests, and the
general fear that things would only get worse in the summer months. Tellingly,
the bill did the same: despite extensive debate during the drafting period, there
was nothing about employment, nothing about job training; the bill's planks
focused exclusively on the pressing demands of demonstrators, and Southern
demonstrators in particular. It was designed to have an immediate, concrete
impact on the issues of the moment in the South, and leave for later the long-
term problems facing black Americans in the rest of the country.

Kennedy's bill, which became known as H.R. 7152, had seven titles. Three
of them were holdovers from his earlier civil rights bill: a provision on voting,
including federal referees, expedited lawsuits, uniform registration standards,
and an assumption that anyone with a sixth-grade education was literate

enough to vote; technical and financial assistance for school desegregation; and renewal of the Civil Rights Commission.

The most significant new title was the ban on discrimination in public accommodations, which it specified as hotels, restaurants, "places of amusement," and retail stores. Most notably, the bill did not include a business size cutoff, an idea that had been bandied about in the early planning sessions as a way to draw in conservative Republicans. Enforcement of the title would depend on the aggrieved individual, who could file for a court order against an establishment if he or she felt discriminated against; if the owner refused to abide by the order, and a further step involving a government mediator failed, the complainant could file a lawsuit, which the attorney general could join. Equal access, Kennedy said in his message, "seems to me to be an elementary right. Its denial is an arbitrary indignity that no American in 1963 should have to endure."

The bill also added to the education title by creating a "Title III for schools," which allowed the attorney general to initiate or intervene in suits against school segregation. Until then, the cost of such suits had to be borne completely by individuals—a daunting task for the average black family in the South. The bill would also predicate technical and financial assistance on the existence of desegregation plans; in other words, it created a financial incentive for school districts that might otherwise be on the fence about desegregation to take the plunge.

Finally, the bill would allow the president to cut off federal funds to local or state programs that practiced discrimination, create a statutory basis for the President's Committee on Equal Employment Opportunity, and establish a federal mediation program, the Community Relations Service.

Kennedy's message did not ignore the jobs question entirely. He claimed that his pro-growth program, centered on tax cuts and free trade, would boost black employment numbers, and he called on Congress to enact a forthcoming, unspecified education bill. He also requested that Congress put more money into vocational training programs, and he announced that he had directed Secretary of Labor Willard Wirtz to ensure that federal apprenticeship programs were administered equally for all races. "Finally," he wrote, "I renew my support of Federal Fair Employment Practices legislation"— which was news, since he had never publicly, directly endorsed such legislation, but was still small beer for those in and outside the government who had hoped for much more.

Joe Rauh, among others, was dismayed that the bill "contained the administration's best estimates of what could be enacted, rather than what was needed." James Farmer, the national director of CORE, called the bill weak and, like Rauh, demanded the addition of a robust Title III plank. At its national convention in Chicago in early July, the NAACP issued a statement that the bill was "inadequate to meet the minimum demands of the existing situation," a point that Roy Wilkins tried to soften—but ultimately endorsed—on *Meet the Press* the following month. "It is incumbent upon the Negro population to keep asking for more," he said. Indeed, that was the inspiration for the controversial upcoming "march on Washington," in which tens or even hundreds of thousands of people would come to the capital for a day of protests and speeches—a plan that both the White House and Congress, not to mention the local District government, viewed with trepidation.[21]

But if many on the president's left were unhappy with the bill, so were many on his right. The Southerners, aware of the public attention already focused on the issue, were careful to avoid explicit defenses of Jim Crow segregation, let alone white supremacy. To hear them tell it, the question was wholly a constitutional one; the bill was an invasion of property and states' rights, and a dangerous power grab by the federal government. Discrimination, they typically conceded, was a bad thing. But people should be allowed to do whatever they want with their property, including discriminate against blacks. Any law that infringed on that right was tantamount to communism—or, as the Southern Democrats never tired of repeating, slavery itself.

Many of their initial reactions telegraphed clearly the arguments they would be making throughout the bill's long journey through Congress. Senator Eastland called it "the greatest single grasp for power by the Executive department that the nation has ever known." Echoing accusations that liberals were merely playing on black frustrations to win votes—historically, not an entirely unfair charge—Senator Lister Hill of Alabama said, "Many of our most sacred rights, including the right to own and use private property have been laid on the altar of political expediency." Senator Richard Russell of Georgia, the dean of the Southern Democrats, went further and tried to use Kennedy's concern over easing tensions in the black community against him. "The president of the United States, instead of having offered his support to the local authorities, who were overwhelmed by these mass movements, has in essence offered aid and comfort to them by saying, 'If you do not immediately pass a law, the situation will become much worse.'" And if the Southerners' strategy was not clear enough already, Eastland tipped his hand on the inevitable filibuster by saying that Congress needed to allow "time for the implications of this program to soak in on the American people."[22]

Not everyone was critical of the bill. It drew significant praise from establishment media outlets as a breakthrough piece of social legislation. The editorial board of the *New York Times* praised "the scope of the President's program and its gravity of tone," which "bespoke a sense of urgency and of high purpose that should help moderate the sectionalism and the partisanship that unfortunately are to be expected in the debate over his specific proposals."[23]

And not all black leaders were critical of the bill. The editors of the *Atlanta Daily World* hailed the bill and called for a moratorium on "continued demonstrations, provocative incidents, inflammatory statements, threats and actions, which could be viewed as tools of force, in an area where we are trying to win the united action of so many purposeful segments of the nation."[24]

Perhaps the most significant signs of support came from the Republican leadership in Congress. House Minority Leader Charles Halleck, despite pressure from many Republicans to play hardball with the president, said that his party "will move expeditiously and in a spirit of cooperation to get hearings started in the House Judiciary Committee on the civil rights proposals offered by the President today." The Republican record on civil rights, he said, "has been unmatched for 100 years and as always our attitude on this issue is constructive." Even Senator Barry Goldwater, a libertarian stalwart and likely contender for the 1964 presidential ticket, offered his qualified support, endorsing most of the bill but calling Title II "really objectionable." Goldwater also criticized the president for not going further on Title VI, saying that funds should be automatically cut off to discriminatory programs, not just left to the president's discretion.[25]

Praise for the bill was matched by skepticism over whether it could pass. E. W. Kenworthy of the *New York Times*, one of the better-connected reporters on the beat, wrote that while congressional leaders predicted that Kennedy's bill would survive in some form, "they also agreed that he had virtually no chance of getting the authority he seeks to enforce desegregation of privately owned public accommodations," thanks largely to the opposition from Senate Republicans. Even Jacob Javits, a professional optimist when it came to civil rights bills and their prospects on the Hill, predicted a "long, tough, hard fight ahead."[26]

From the beginning, Kennedy understood that that fight would be fought as much outside Congress as within it. As he and his staff were putting the finishing touches on the bill, they also invited a group of about thirty civil rights leaders—including King, Rauh, Wilkins, Farmer, Walter Reuther, Whitney Young, Dorothy Height, and A. Philip Randolph—to the White House to discuss the legislation on June 22. Robert Kennedy, Lyndon Johnson, and Arthur Schlesinger were also in attendance. Before the meeting, Marshall and the Kennedys met with King sequentially and alone. They demanded that he cut all ties with two of his advisers whom the FBI—thanks to wiretaps on the men's phones—suspected of being Communists. "I assume you know you're under very close surveillance," the president told him. King parried, asking for evidence. The president indicated that he would get it to him soon, then led King to the Cabinet Room.[27]

As Rauh later told the historian Taylor Branch, while the president and King were outside, the civil rights leaders had been maneuvering for the choice seats closest to the president, knowing that a good impression made that day could cement someone's role as the movement's point person at the White House. Wilkins and Reuther both wanted that job—but so did King, who had his lieutenant Walter Fauntroy save him one of the seats next to the president's.[28]

King and Kennedy soon joined them, and the president began by talking strategy: the committees, the filibuster, the key players. To succeed, he said, the bill needed to draw in people outside the traditional civil rights supporters, including Midwestern, small-town Republicans, as well as filibuster-friendly senators from the newer, sparsely populated mountain and southwest states. To win them over, he said, would take careful calibration of the civil rights message—a not so subtle criticism of the planned march on Washington.[29]

At this point Young asked if it was true that Kennedy was opposed to the upcoming march, which had been officially announced just the day before. "We want success in Congress, not just a big show at the Capitol," Kennedy said, tilting in his rocking chair. "Some of these people are looking for an excuse to be against us; and I don't want to give any of them a chance to say, 'Yes I'm for the bill, but I am damned if I will vote for it at the point of a gun.' It seemed to be a great mistake to announce a March on Washington before the bill was even in committee. The only effect is to create an atmosphere of intimidation—and this may give some members of Congress an out."

This was not what Kennedy's guests wanted to hear, but they were hardly surprised—the president was already on record opposing the march. The first to respond was Randolph, the wise old man of the movement who had organized the first March on Washington, in 1941, then called it off after President Roosevelt agreed to create an FEPC for government contractors (the office was shuttered in 1946). Randolph had frequently gone back to the idea in the years since, and was the driving force behind the current plans. "The Negroes are already in the streets," he said. "It is very likely impossible to get them off. If they are bound to be in the streets in any case, is it not better that they be led by organizations dedicated to civil rights and disciplined by struggles rather than to leave them to other leaders who care neither about civil rights or about nonviolence?"

Kennedy nodded. "This is true," he said. "But now we are in a new phase, the legislative phase, and results are essential. The wrong kind of demonstration at the wrong time will give those fellows a chance to say that they have to prove their courage by voting against us. To get the necessary votes we have, first, to oppose demonstrations which lead to violence and, second, to give Congress a fair chance to work its will."

Then Johnson chimed in to correct what he saw as a gross misunderstanding of Washington politics. It was not about protests in the streets, he said, or about pressure from lobbyists. "Not many votes are converted in the corridors," Johnson said. "Most fellows vote for what they think is right and for what they think their states want. We have about 50 votes for us in the Senate and about 22 against us. What counts is the 26 or so votes that remain."

Farmer, despite his public position against the bill, tried to take a middle ground. "We understand your political problem in getting the legislation through, and we want to help in that as best we can," he said. "But the civil rights forces have their problems too. We would be in a difficult if not untenable position if we called the street demonstrations off and then were defeated in the legislative battle."

King saw a chance to regain his hand after the president's private scolding. "It is not a matter of either/or," he said, "but of both/and. Take the question of the March on Washington. This could serve as a means through which people with legitimate discontents could channel their grievances under disciplined, non-violent leadership. It could also serve as a means of dramatizing the issue and mobilizing support in parts of the country which don't know the problem at first hand. I think it will serve a purpose. It may seem ill-timed. Frankly, I have never engaged in a direct-action movement which did not seem ill-timed. Some people thought Birmingham ill-timed."

"Including the attorney general," joked the president.

Someone in the group brought up the need for the president's bill to go further and include a Title III, to offer federal protection for demonstrators against local police brutality. But the president stonewalled. "Yes, but I know what Southern mayors and police chiefs will say," replied Kennedy. "They will say that all they are doing is trying to maintain law and order. In any case, I don't think you should all be totally harsh on Bull Connor. After all, he has done more for civil rights than almost anybody else." Whether anyone laughed at the president's gallows humor went unrecorded.

Kennedy shifted tone. "This is a very serious fight," the president said. "The vice president and I know what it will mean if we fail. I have just seen the new Gallup Poll: national approval of the administration has fallen from 60 to 47 percent. We're in this up to our neck." It was bad enough to have to advocate for the bill in the first place; losing, after a long fight, would be a disaster. "A good many programs I care about may go down the drain as a result of this— so we are putting a lot on the line."

The critical thing was to maintain good faith and communication between the civil rights movement and the White House and pro-civil-rights members of Congress. "I have my problems with the Congress; you have yours with your own groups," Kennedy said. "We will undoubtedly disagree from time to time on tactics. But the important thing is to keep in touch."

Kennedy then announced that he had to leave to get ready for a trip to Europe. Before he left, he said, "What seems to me terribly important is to get, and keep, as many Negro children as possible in schools this fall. It is too late to get equality for their parents, but we still can get it for the children—if they can go to school and take advantage of what educational opportunity is open to them. I urge to you get every Negro family to do this at whatever sacrifice."

The men came away impressed with the president's commitment. Rauh was struck by the contrast between the Kennedy he had just seen and the one he had dueled with at the ADA meeting two and a half years before. "It was a totally different attitude than he'd had in February of 1961," he said. "He was prepared if necessary to sacrifice everything for the fight. It was a moral issue. It was a great speech he made to us. I felt from that moment he was terribly committed." In fact, to put a finer point on his commitment, that same day the president issued an executive order giving the government the power to pull out funding from construction projects that discriminated against blacks, and he asked the Pentagon to consider closing military facilities near towns that practiced Jim Crow segregation.[30]

King, on the other hand, gave a statement afterward saying that the president had tried to get them to call off the march but that he and others had refused. "If there is a filibuster in Congress, we will have a nonviolent peaceful demonstration in Washington," he said—in other words, a Birmingham-style campaign in Washington. "We feel a demonstration would help the president's civil rights legislation, would help dramatize the issue." King's comments drew a distancing rebuke from Wilkins, who said the NAACP would have nothing to do with sit-ins in the capital. "I am not involved at the present moment" with the march plans, he said, a statement that was only technically accurate, and only for the time being.[31]

The civil rights leaders then repaired for lunch at Reuther's suite at the Statler Hilton, where they pressured King to back off his plan for another Birmingham. Wilkins and Reuther wanted no demonstration at all, but "quiet, patient" lobbying. Eventually they persuaded King to agree tentatively on a straightforward, one-day march of the kind Randolph had long been advocating. But the lunch ended without a firm commitment from anyone.[32]

Still, the meeting with Kennedy bore significant fruit. It convinced the civil rights leaders, long and justifiably skeptical of the president's intentions, that his drive for civil rights legislation was for real. It brought them together behind a specific, practical plan for the March on Washington. But above all, it generated a momentum to work together on pushing the civil rights bill, and to set aside, for the moment, the differences that had plagued them up until now—Reuther and Wilkins tacitly agreed to overlook ongoing tensions between labor unions and the NAACP, while the establishment civil rights groups agreed to work with King's upstart SCLC to make the march a success. Forces both inside and outside the government were now aligned behind the civil rights bill; the question was whether they could agree on just how strong that bill should be.

AFTER A BRIEF stop at Camp David, Kennedy flew to Europe, where on June 26 he stood before the Rathaus Schöneberg in West Berlin and declared "Ich bin ein Berliner." That same day, his brother was making his own important appearance—as the opening witness in the House Judiciary Committee's hearings on the civil rights bill.

The House Judiciary Committee was the province of Emanuel Celler, a House veteran from northeast Brooklyn who had taken office during the Harding administration. Manny, as he was known to his friends, was born in 1888 in Brooklyn, the grandson of two sets of German immigrants and the son of a whiskey rectifier (that is, someone who buys and redistills raw whiskey). He went to Columbia for his undergraduate and law degrees, then ran his own law practice until he won election to the House in 1922. As a young man he was renowned for his endlessly energetic ambition, but by the early 1960s he had aged into an avuncular, genial politician. He was beloved by children in his district for his magic tricks, particularly ones involving rabbits. He had other extracurricular avocations as well. At the time it was acceptable for a sitting member of Congress to hold an outside job, and many members of the Judiciary Committee maintained law practices back in their districts. Celler was no exception—a fact that brought him under harsh criticism toward the end of his career from the columnist Jack Anderson, who accused him of using his political position to push the interests of one of his clients, a power plant construction firm.[33]

Having Celler officially in charge of the bill in the House was a double-edged sword. He was a fiercely loyal Democrat, with a deep admiration for John F. Kennedy. But Celler was also much more liberal than the administration, and he was pulled further left by the growing number of black voters moving into his district, which had once been a bastion of white ethnic voters.[34]

And while Celler was known for his tight, partisan control of the Judiciary Committee, by 1963, age had loosened some of his grip. At times he was little more than a figurehead, with much of the substantive work being done by the committee's staff director, Bess Dick, and its general counsel, Bill Foley. Still, Celler had enough power over the committee to shunt the civil rights bill into Subcommittee 5, ostensibly focused on antitrust—Celler's legal specialty—but really a catchall spot for legislation in which Celler had particular interest. Alongside Celler were six decidedly liberal Democrats, including Robert Kastenmeier of Wisconsin, Peter Rodino of New Jersey, and Jack Brooks, a maverick from Texas (the Republicans were all conservatives, including one of the few Southern Republicans in the House, Florida's William Cramer).[35]

Seated to Celler's right on the committee dais was the ranking Republican, William M. McCulloch of Ohio. The two were close friends, but aside from their abiding interest in the law—McCulloch, like Celler, had a healthy legal practice back home—they had almost nothing in common. Celler was the product of New York's working-class, immigrant cosmopolitanism; McCulloch was born in 1901 on a farm outside the central Ohio hamlet of Holmesville, the descendant of abolitionists who had settled the area in the decades before the Civil War.[36]

After college, McCulloch moved to Jacksonville, Florida, to practice law. In rural Ohio, he had lived in a monochromatic world where he rarely saw blacks; in Florida he saw the awfulness of racism in its most mundane yet hideously arbitrary forms—one department store might forbid blacks from using a dressing room, while another might bar them from coming in at all. McCulloch had been raised to believe that racism was the product of ignorance and that intelligent, educated people like himself would know better than to traffic in prejudice. Yet here he was, mixing with local lawyers and businessmen who proved often to be the most vicious defenders of Jim Crow racism. "It's amazing how persons of good education and good business experience are so personally prejudiced," he told an interviewer years later.[37]

McCulloch returned to Piqua, Ohio, where he opened a law practice. But he also grew active in local civil rights politics, acting as an adviser to the Piqua branch of the NAACP in its push to desegregate the city's restaurants. He won election to the House of Representatives as part of the Republican landslide of 1946—even though, as one reporter later wrote, "his personality was so cold many observers classed him as an arrogant stuffed-shirt individual."[38]

McCulloch's early years in the House were defined by the clash between his strict adherence to small-government, balanced-budget conservatism and his quiet, rock-hard commitment to civil rights—all the more surprising given that only 2.7 percent of his voters were black. He continued to support efforts to end government-sponsored segregation, but he was wary of laws that intruded on private property, like FEPCs, a position that drew the ire of the *Cleveland Call and Post*, the state's largest black newspaper. Yet in 1956 and 1957, he led the House Republicans in not only supporting Eisenhower's civil rights bill, but defending it against efforts by Senate Majority Leader Johnson to weaken it—a campaign that led the *Call and Post* to revise its previous assessment. "Red-haired mustached Bill McCulloch has proved our judgment of him was a gross mistake," wrote John Combs, one of the paper's political columnists.[39]

McCulloch sponsored Eisenhower's 1959 civil rights bill, which required the retention of voting records, extended the Civil Rights Commission, and gave courts the power to appoint election referees where rights violations were known to occur—a small bill, to be sure, but McCulloch put the best spin he could on it. When House Rules committee chairman Howard Smith claimed that the bill would put manacles on the South, McCulloch retorted, "We have no intention of putting manacles on anyone. On the other hand, I would like to break the chains that have held others in bondage and denied them their constitutional rights."[40]

Yet like many Republican civil rights advocates, McCulloch's relationship with pro-civil-rights Democrats, and the movement, was strained. To him, liberals were either inept idealists or crass opportunists, who saw civil rights as a tool for grandstanding and gaining black votes—but not, in his mind, achieving the sort of incremental results that he felt were the only realistic way forward. He called out the Department of Justice's 1962 literacy test bill, which would declare anyone with a sixth-grade education as literate enough to vote, as "very limited," noting that millions of black adults lacked such qualification and even Abraham Lincoln would not have made the cut.[41]

McCulloch was particularly incensed over the way Johnson and the congressional Democrats had conspired to pare back the 1957 civil rights bill after so many Republicans, under McCulloch's direction, had risked their political standing at home to support it in the House. That betrayal still grated at him in June 1963, when the administration asked him to cosponsor, with Celler, H.R. 7152—a request that he swiftly rejected, not wanting to tie himself too closely to a piece of legislation that the Democrats might well drop or water down in the future, or, should the two parties manage to get it safely to passage, claim as their own.[42]

And, after all, the Republicans had their own bills on the table. By mid-June 1963, more than a hundred major civil rights bills sat before the House, many of them Republican-sponsored, and many of them in the Judiciary Committee.

Even at this early point, national attention was focused on how the bill would fare before a Senate filibuster. But how the two parties—and these two powerful representatives—navigated the partisan politics in the House would determine whether the bill made it to the Senate in the first place.

On May 8, while the Birmingham crisis reached its highest pitch, Celler had opened hearings in Subcommittee No. 5 on 89 of those bills—41 from Democrats, 49 from Republicans. The nation, Celler said in his opening statement, was on the brink of disaster. "The deprivation of civil rights to a class of our citizens has, we must admit, led to smoldering resentment by the dispossessed and this smoldering resentment has to explode," he said. McCulloch endorsed Celler's statement, and extended the committee's view from the South to the rest of the country. "What is happening in Little Rock and New Rochelle, in Oxford and Chicago, in Birmingham and Rapid City, is convincing truth that tension exists and resistance remains." The country, he said in an echo of some of the most liberal commentators on the race crisis, was undergoing a sea change "in the state of minorities from that of master-servant to that of brother-to-brother."[43]

The hearings, however, drew almost no public attention, and even the subcommittee members paid only passing notice. Then, shortly before 10:00 A.M. on June 26, Robert Kennedy, with Marshall in tow, marched through the French doors of Room 346 of the Old House Office Building to address Subcommittee 5. Suddenly, the civil rights hearings were the hot ticket on Capitol Hill. The subcommittee had eleven members, and all were present. Another fourteen members from the full committee had been allowed to join the committee behind its horseshoe-shaped dais. There was space for just seventy seats in the audience, and the room was packed to standing room only with reporters.[44]

Kennedy had a difficult task: he had to defend the administration's previous efforts, explain why circumstances merited a more robust approach, beat back the liberal Republicans' own legislation—and yet also portray the bill as a moderate, pragmatic solution that conservative Republicans could endorse.

He did this by inverting the history of the last two and a half years: rather than using the federal government's circumscribed powers on civil rights as a cover for doing nothing, as his department had done, he claimed that the administration had done the most it could with the limited tools at its disposal. "We have made significant progress in enforcing the Civil Rights Acts of 1957 and 1960," he said. But the past several months had demonstrated that the federal government needed the power to do more. "The events that have occurred since the President's first message—in Birmingham, in Jackson, in nearby Cambridge, in Philadelphia and in many other cities—make it clear that the attack upon these problems must be accelerated."[45]

Kennedy also defined the core of the bill: Title II, rooted in the Commerce Clause, a discussion that took up a third of his twenty-five-page statement. "Discrimination in public accommodations not only contradicts our basic concepts of liberty and equality, but such discrimination interferes with interstate commerce and the development of unobstructed national markets," he said. He also tried to preempt what had already become the leading Southern Democrat talking point against the title: that it violated property rights by forcing business owners to serve everyone equally, regardless of race. "Some of those who complain most loudly about interference with private property rights, ironically, are often those who most stoutly defend the laws, enforced by a number of states, which forbid Negroes to be served," he said (an echo of Samuel Johnson's 1775 quip, "How is it that we hear the loudest yelps for liberty among the drivers of negroes?").[46]

His statement over, the attorney general began to take questions from the committee, and immediately ran into problems in the form of hostile questions from his critics, cold shoulders from his allies, and a surprising ignorance of the bill's mechanics on his own part. In response to a query about the limits of the title, Kennedy said that the key criterion was how involved a business was in interstate commerce. "As far as the department store, retail shop, market, drugstore, gasoline station, and lunch room are concerned, the establishment must be involved to a substantial degree with interstate commerce," he said. "So that takes it out of the category of just the very small."[47]

"What is meant by substantial?" asked Celler.

"It is more than just minimal."

"I take it the legal phrase de minimis is used."

"I translated it, Mr. Chairman," Kennedy said testily.

None of this was very satisfactory to the rest of the panel, especially the liberal Republicans from the main committee who were sitting in for the day. The bill did, after all, include language connecting it to the Equal Protection Clause of the Fourteenth Amendment, which would ban discrimination by a business licensed in any way by the government, down to the smallest barbershop. But it pointedly did not rely on the Equal Protection Clause, and instead made the Commerce Clause its primary justification. According to the administration, the Fourteenth Amendment had been rendered so narrowly applicable by the Supreme Court in the post-Reconstruction era that even with the changing times, the administration did not want to take an unnecessary constitutional risk. But the other obvious, but unstated, reason was political: the Fourteenth Amendment was a "Republican" tool, passed by a Republican Congress after the Civil War, while Franklin Roosevelt had used the Commerce Clause to greatly expand the power of the federal government during the Depression. This was a slight that many liberal Republicans could not abide.

By midafternoon, the questions still had not moved off Title II. At one point Kennedy let himself get trapped into admitting that "it is very possible that you could have an establishment, for instance, in a city or community that didn't have anything to do with interstate commerce"—and thus untouchable by the bill. And he agreed that "Mrs. Murphy," a hypothetical widowed owner of a small boardinghouse, should not be covered. Though this limit was always part of the administration's plan, the next day newspapers depicted Kennedy's answer as a major concession, and evidence that the administration planned to jettison much of the bill as it made its way across Capitol Hill.[48]

As the day drew on, Kennedy grew more testy and dismissive in his answers. George Meader, a Michigan Republican, asked Kennedy if he was familiar with the Republican bills. "I am not," Kennedy said, with impolitic insouciance. "I think the chairman said, there are 165 bills, or 365. I have not read them all."[49]

Meader seemed to find the attorney general's answer acceptable, but his colleague from the full committee, John Lindsay of New York, did not. As Meader was rambling on about the Fourteenth Amendment, Lindsay interjected, "Would you yield to me?"

Meader gladly gave Lindsay the floor.

"I am quite deeply disturbed, Mr. Attorney General," Lindsay began, "that you have never bothered to read this very important legislation that was carefully drafted and introduced by four of us on the minority side of this committee and many additional Republican members, long before the administration saw fit to take any position on this subject at all." Lindsay had recently introduced his own public accommodations law, to complement the raft of bills introduced by Republicans introduced since the first of the year. What is more, Lindsay said, his bill relied on the Equal Protection Clause, which would sidestep the need to analyze the size of each business to see if it met the interstate commerce test. And, he said, this being 1963, eighty years after the Supreme Court's disastrous ruling on the Equal Protection Clause, there was little chance the title would be found unconstitutional.[50]

"Congressman, I am sorry I have not read all of these bills and I am sorry I have not read your bill," Kennedy snapped. "I personally think, I join with you, that the Supreme Court probably would uphold it. But the fact is that there is a Supreme Court decision on the books at the present time which declares it unconstitutional. That is the law of the land at the present time."

That set Lindsay off. "In view of the fact that you apparently did not consider these bills at all I can't help but ask the question as to whether or not you really want public accommodations legislation or not." Then he turned up the heat a little more. "Let us be frank about it. The rumor is all over the cloakrooms and corridors of Capitol Hill that the administration has made a deal with the leadership to scuttle the accommodations" title.

Celler jolted up. "If I am part of the leadership I have not heard of it."

"I am not referring to the chairman," Lindsay said.

"Let us confine ourselves to specifics and withdraw all rumors," Celler said. But he had lost hold of the reins.

"My question is," continued Lindsay, "is the administration prepared to press for public accommodations legislation even though the Congress has to stay here until New Years to get it through? Will you settle, if necessary, for the Fourteenth Amendment approach, the Lindsay approach, in order to get a maximum number of votes to get a bill through? I am not sure that you can get a bill through which is based on the Interstate Commerce Clause."

Kennedy struggled to contain himself. "There were an awful lot of statements made, Congressman. I am surprised by this, but maybe I shouldn't be, that you would come out here in this open hearing and say that you heard these rumors and have nothing more to substantiate them than the fact that you have heard rumors in the cloakroom. I think it has been made clear, and I don't think that the President nor I have to defend our good faith in our efforts here to you or to really anyone else."

Lindsay pulled back. "I think we can agree on one thing which is that we want a bill," he said. "I am not sure that you have the votes or can get the votes if you insist on just the one method and this is what troubles me."

A few minutes later, he leaned back to his aide Robert Kimball, his point person on civil rights and the author of several of the Republican bills. "Do you think I was too hard on him?" Lindsay asked.

"Well maybe a little," Kimball said. "But I can understand why you were." Lindsay was serious about civil rights as a Republican issue and had been working hard on his own bill for months—only to see the attorney general ignore it. "I thought somebody should say something," Lindsay said. But there was a personal element to the attack: Katzenbach later recalled that the two men had once had a shouting match during a party at the Manhattan home of George C. Lodge, the son the Massachusetts Republican senator Henry Cabot Lodge Jr., and had carried a mutual grudge ever since; it is also possible that Lindsay foresaw the day when Kennedy would decide to run for office himself and turn to New York City—Lindsay's territory—to establish his base.[51]

Personal politics aside, Kennedy had clearly made a gaffe by dismissing Lindsay's proposal so summarily. It insulted not only a leading liberal Republican, but by extension the entire Republican Party, the support of which the White House desperately needed. But there was good reason to be wary of the Fourteenth Amendment, aside from the constitutional question. If enforcement relied on licensure, then all a recalcitrant state needed to do to get out from under the law was to amend or even dissolve its licensing system. That might be a bad thing for public health—without it, anyone could be a barber, or a doctor—but it would keep the federal government from enforcing desegregation.

There was another significant exchange that day. At one point William Miller, a Republican from western New York who was serving as the chairman of the Republican National Committee (and would be Barry Goldwater's running mate in 1964), asked whether Title III, which dealt with school desegregation, also mandated school integration—in other words, whether districts with schools that were legally open to all, but were overwhelmingly white or black thanks to housing patterns, were required to take active steps to achieve racial balance. In New York, he said, "it would necessitate the cost of hundreds of thousands of dollars just to create a racial balance and would possibly require white students to spend two or three hours on a bus just to get to another school to comply with racial balance." Miller's was not an idle question—on June 18, James Allen Jr., New York's state education commissioner, said that it was not enough to ban segregation, but that the state also had to eliminate "racial imbalance." De facto school segregation was, beside fair housing, the hottest racial topic in Northern communities; just a few weeks earlier, nearly a hundred people had crammed into a school board meeting in Boston to demand that the city begin bussing students to achieve racial balance.[52]

The question caught Kennedy off guard; he was so focused on addressing Southern civil rights issues that he had given scant thought to the concerns of the rest of the country. "It is not our objective to try to get balance because perhaps that is not the best way to proceed," he said. "But at least we felt it should start to be explored and communities which are dealing with this problem should have the benefit of expert advice and perhaps some economic incentive to try to deal with it." Still, Miller's question hinted at a whole new front of opposition to the bill, and another area where it failed to address the concerns of blacks living outside the South.[53]

The day ended with a whimper; Kennedy had made his appearance and defended the bill as best he could, but he had proved a poor advocate—unprepared on the details, unwilling to sit through the frustrating but predictable hail of pinprick questions from the dais. The next day's headlines said it all: ROBERT KENNEDY OFFERS TO MODIFY CIVIL RIGHTS BILL, said the *New York Times*; R.F. KENNEDY O.K.'S RACE BILL LIMITS, said the Baltimore *Sun*—hardly the bold opening the administration was looking for. Nor did the bad press stop. Lindsay was not alone in hearing rumors of a possible compromise. "It is believed in some quarters," reported the *Los Angeles Times*, "that the actions of the Southerners indicate that a filibuster can be avoided, and a watered down, but meaningful, civil rights program can be enacted."[54]

More critically, though, Kennedy revealed how poorly the White House and the Department of Justice were prepared to work with Republicans. Lindsay in particular was key. Though he was too liberal to have much influence among the rank-and-file Republicans, the administration needed him on its team; otherwise, he could align with liberal Democrats, who could then claim their own unwieldy (in the administration's eyes) alternative had bipartisan support.

THREE DAYS LATER, Katzenbach sat down to write an extensive memo to Robert Kennedy detailing his strategy for getting the bill out of Congress and to the president's desk. Katzenbach was not a born politician—he had spent most of his career in academia, most recently at the University of Chicago. But he was a quick study and proved to have a sharp tactical mind; he also spent hours that summer quizzing old congressional hands like Lawrence O'Brien on the intricacies of House and Senate procedure and, more importantly, the unwritten rules that dictated whether a bill would live or die on Capitol Hill.

He began his memo by working backward: if the goal was to get the bill intact through the Senate, then a filibuster was inevitable—which meant they needed 67 votes to stop debate and bring the bill to a vote, which meant winning 19 of the 34 Republican votes (assuming all 48 non-Southern Democrats voted for the bill). The only way to do that, he wrote, was to get Dirksen on board, as early as possible. Why so early? Because Katzenbach could then take Dirksen's support for the bill to House Republicans, who were open to civil rights but wary of siding with legislation that might get pared back in the Senate. Dirksen, of course, did not support Title II, but Katzenbach hoped that his support on everything else could give momentum to the bill in the House, and that by the time it reached the Senate, Dirksen would have to choose between agreeing to the entire bill or standing in the way of historic legislation. Given Dirksen's enormous self-regard and well-known reputation as a dealmaker, Katzenbach told Kennedy he was confident it would work out.[55]

But that still left the House. Though Katzenbach did not say it explicitly in the memo, everyone in the administration knew that Kennedy's testimony had been a disaster, insulting potential Republican crossovers and giving the impression that, once again, the White House was not as supportive of civil rights legislation as the president had said on TV. They needed a strategy, not just an assumption that they could offer a moderate bill and watch the Republicans fall in line. And the first step in that direction was to woo McCulloch—in person, and with a gesture that underlined the White House's awareness of the critical role he would play.

The next week Congress was in recess for the Fourth of July holiday, and most members went back to their home districts, including McCulloch. On July 2, Burke Marshall followed him.

McCulloch's son-in-law, David Carver, met Marshall at the Dayton airport and drove him to Piqua. The two took an extended tour of the town, as McCulloch was giving a speech that morning to the local Rotary Club. Finally, early in the afternoon Marshall climbed the stairs to the second-floor offices of McCulloch, Felger, Fite, and Gutmann, located in the handsome neoclassical Piqua National Bank Building, not far from the Miami River.[56]

Marshall's mission that day was to get McCulloch behind the bill. Most congressmen would have scoffed: here was a representative from the other party, just 16 months before a presidential election, asking him to drop his own legislation on a potentially decisive issue and back the administration's. McCulloch, though, agreed almost immediately—contingent on Marshall's promise that the bill would not get trimmed in the Senate, and that Kennedy would give the Republicans equal credit. The first demand was already part of the administration's strategy, and the second was a small price to pay for coop-eration. Marshall's trip was a breakthrough—with McCulloch on board, House Republican buy-in was almost guaranteed. The two men shook on it, and Marshall caught a late flight back to Washington.

Robert Kennedy was elated. Not only had Marshall brought back great news from Ohio, but representatives from around the country returned to Washington to report that their constituents were strongly behind Title II. As the president said in a statement after a July 9 breakfast with the congres-sional leadership, "Even though the public accommodations section is causing controversy, it is clear to most Americans that when the basic consti-tutional rights of an individual to be treated as a free and equal human being come into conflict with the preferences of those who operate public accom-modations, then the elementary rights to equal citizenship and equal treatment must prevail."[57]

*

WHILE KENNEDY WAS wrangling with Congress over the civil rights bill, movement leaders were wrangling over the planned march on Washington. The June 22 lunch in Walter Reuther's Washington hotel suite had resolved nothing; though King had agreed in theory to a march—a rally, really, perhaps around one of the monuments on the Mall—instead of a moving, shouting, singing, provoking demonstration, there was no formal agreement, and both the NAACP and the United Auto Workers refused to back the project.

The day after the meeting at the White House, King flew to Detroit for a "Walk to Freedom" rally that would provide a preview of the March on Washington. Organized by local labor activists and church leaders in the face of opposition from the local NAACP, the event was a massive success: 125,000 people, including Mayor Jerome Cavanaugh, marched down Woodward Avenue, Detroit's main thoroughfare, to Cobo Hall, where King tested out some of the lines he would later polish to a historic high gloss in Washington: "I have a dream this afternoon that one day, right here in Detroit, Negroes will be able to buy a house or rent a house anywhere that their money will carry them."[58]

On July 2, the same day that Marshall sealed the administration's plan with McCulloch, the leaders of the major civil rights groups, along with representatives from labor and the leading religious organizations, met at the Roosevelt Hotel in New York to discuss the bill, the march, and how they could coordinate what many worried had become redundant and often competitive efforts.

The meeting also had a significant subtext: at the June 22 lunch, Reuther had called for the creation of a "coalition of conscience," a clearinghouse operation to coordinate civil rights lobbying efforts across the dozens of groups active on the issue—with, of course, himself at its head. This struck not only the black civil rights leaders but many white activists as politically inept: Reuther was letting his ego blind himself to the awkwardness of a white union boss asserting control over an issue centered on the rights of millions of blacks, many of whom had mixed feelings about the labor movement. Reuther's white skin aside, many did not like the idea of having a single person in charge, officially or putatively, at all—there was too much difference between, say, the NAACP and the SCLC to make a hierarchical structure work.[59]

Fortunately, there was an alternative already in place: the Leadership Conference on Civil Rights, an umbrella organization that was created in 1950 to lobby for a permanent FEPC. By 1963 it included some sixty organizations, from unions to church groups. Though it was an ad hoc operation, existing more on paper than in practice, the LCCR received significant financial support from the UAW, and had a proven record of coordinating lobbying efforts across a wide variety of groups on issues like Rule 22.[60]

After the June 22 lunch ended, Reuther had asked Arnold Aronson, the executive director of the National Community Relations Advisory Council (later renamed the Jewish Council for Public Affairs), to lead his proposed coalition. Aronson was a longtime civil rights activist and an ally of A. Philip Randolph, so Reuther may have been hoping to coopt the black labor leader by choosing him. His move backfired: Aronson turned down the offer, then told Randolph and Roy Wilkins about it. They agreed that the only way to block the UAW president was to show why his proposed organization was unnecessary. They arranged it so one of the first items of business at the July 2 meeting was a proposal to move the LCCR into a higher gear, with a staff and offices in Washington and with Wilkins as the titular head; as a consolation, they agreed to ask the UAW to pay for it.[61]

Reuther, to their surprise, agreed, and within a week, the LCCR Washington office was open, in empty space on Connecticut Avenue owned by the Industrial Unions Department of the AFL-CIO. Aronson was named to head it, with the journalist Marvin Kaplan and the veteran ADA organizer Violet Gunther as his deputies. The office would coordinate lobbying efforts on the bill, but the actual work plodding the halls of Congress would be done by the organizations themselves.[62]

The discussion at the Roosevelt then moved to the march. The Detroit rally had proven to Wilkins and Reuther that the momentum existed for the march to happen, with or without the NAACP and UAW, and that it could be done peacefully. Reuther had also come under pressure from the White House and Louis Martin, who likewise realized the march was inevitable—and that the UAW, with its deep pockets, could exert a moderating influence on the event. And so both leaders agreed to endorse the march, and to contribute money, manpower, and political influence. With just eight weeks to go, the planners were going to need it.[63]

SEATED ALONGSIDE THE civil rights and labor leaders at the July 2 meeting was James Hamilton, who ran the Washington office of the National Council of Churches. The NCC represented many of the country's mainline protestant denominations, including some African American churches, but until recently had been quiet on civil rights. Through the 1950s its leaders had issued statements and vague directives promoting racial equality, but it had refused to take a stand on specific civil rights issues, even those within the churches themselves, like segregated congregations. When the Emmett Till murder trial ended in acquittal in September 1955, the general board of the council refused to make a statement, saying it "did not want to criticize the verdict of a jury."[64]

But a new generation of socially conscious church leaders was coming to the fore, both in the NCC and in the denominations themselves. In 1957, Will D. Campbell, a World War II veteran who had been driven from his job as the director of religious life at the University of Mississippi for his opposition to segregation, organized the "Southern Project" under the NCC's Department of Racial and Cultural Relations. The project, which was really just Campbell, a car, and a few part-time assistants, put on training seminars and outreach programs for Southern whites interested in integrating their communities.[65]

The rate of change at the NCC accelerated rapidly in 1960 with the election of J. Irwin Miller as president, the first layperson selected for the post. Miller was the chairman of Cummins Engine, one of the country's largest diesel engine manufacturers, based in the small Indiana town of Columbus. A graduate of Yale and Oxford and an accomplished violinist, Miller was the archetype of the enlightened industrialist: through a special fund at Cummins, he had commissioned world-renowned architects including Eero Saarinen and John Carl Warnecke to design schools, churches, and other civic structures around his hometown, the better to keep top-flight managers from fleeing for jobs in larger cities. Miller also took positions uncharacteristic of a successful capitalist, like supporting unionization and calling for higher taxes on the wealthy.[66]

Miller brought that same progressive attitude to the NCC. At the first general board meeting after his election, he gave a rousing speech explaining his vision for the council over his three-year term. "We are changing," he said, "from the simple to the complex, from the familiar to the strange, with a speed which exceeds all experience, and in a direction which we do not yet seem to have calculated." Too often, the NCC, and protestant churches in general, had refused to recognize progress. That had to change—or else the churches would begin to lose their relevance. "By following such a path, we may somehow miss serving the clear need of our time."[67]

Central to Miller's vision for a socially engaged Christianity was civil rights. Along with like-minded, socially active church leaders like Robert Spike and Eugene Carson Blake, Miller believed that civil rights activism was part of the NCC's dual role of bearing witness to the work of God on earth and to facilitating the direct communication between God and individuals. Under Miller's aegis, in May 1963 the NCC created the Commission on Race and Religion, which reported directly to the general board and had an annual budget of over $100,000. Over the coming year the commission would use that money to send ministers into the Deep South, to bail out civil rights protesters, and to make thousands of sack lunches for the March on Washington. Miller also volunteered, at the June 17 meeting of religious leaders at the White House, to organize an ecumenical committee to coordinate lobbying by Catholic, Protestant, and Jewish organizations on the civil rights bill.[68]

Like Miller, leaders from across the mainline Protestant world saw the civil rights bill as their chance to become more involved in bringing about concrete improvements in race relations and the lives of African Americans—to answer what many in the younger generation, inspired by Christian existentialist philosophers, referred to as the *kairos*, or opportunity created by God, that they saw inherent in the civil rights movement. Still others saw a more earthly crisis at hand: "If we don't get strong federal civil rights legislation through this time I fully expect blood to flow in almost every street in the nation," wrote Jon Regier, the NCC's director of home missions, to Robert Spike, the head of the Commission on Religion and Race. "I honestly believe that this is priority number one and am prepared to risk the ire of every home mission board in America by throwing our staff behind it."[69]

A week later Regier and Spike convened a top secret meeting at New York's University Club between religious leaders—including Father John Cronin of the National Catholic Welfare Conference and Rabbi Philip Hiatt of the Synagogue Council of America—and Louis Oberdorfer of the Justice Department to "develop working relationships between the major religious bodies of the nation with the federal government in the matter of the present civil rights crisis," according to a confidential NCC memo.[70]

Activating the churches was critical to the White House strategy. In a memo to Robert Kennedy at the end of June, Katzenbach argued that winning "conservative and middle of the road sentiment in favor of our bill" among the public was essential to putting pressure on the conservative Midwestern Republicans who could well hold the balance of the votes between the liberals and the Southern Democrats. "It is important to organize private sentiment in such a way that it has as its immediate target particular Congressmen from particular districts." In most cases, those congressmen were untouchable by unions, civil rights groups, and other traditional liberal pressure groups. The churches, though, had enormous sway.[71]

Central to that effort was Hamilton. A respected but unassuming church operative, Hamilton had been a Capitol Hill habitué since his law school days at George Washington University, where he had made pocket money as a doorkeeper for the House of Representatives. At the July 2 meeting in New York, he pledged $5,000 to the LCCR's Washington efforts. But more importantly, he immediately began to bring the full weight of the American religious community to bear on the bill. On July 25, thanks to Hamilton's organizing, for the first time ever representatives from the country's three main religious confessions—Catholicism, Judaism, and Protestantism—gave joint testimony before the Senate. Hamilton's real genius, though, was to recognize the impact that grassroots organizing by churches far away from the District of Columbia could have on countless senators and congressmen—a strategy that would bear immense fruit in the coming months.[72]

JUST AS THE Leadership Conference was settling in to its new Washington office, another group interested in civil rights was getting started across town. This one, though, came from the opposite side: the sole purpose of the innocuously named Coordinating Committee for Fundamental American Freedoms was to kill the civil rights bill.

The committee was the brainchild of John Satterfield, a lawyer from Yazoo City, Mississippi. Satterfield was, according to *Time* magazine, "the most prominent segregationist lawyer in the country": he had spent over a decade doing legal work for segregationists and other right-wing causes, even as he commanded mainstream respect as a leading member of the American Bar Association; he even served as its president from 1961 to 1962. In late 1962 he defended Mississippi governor Ross Barnett against federal obstruction charges during the Ole Miss integration crisis, and he served as counsel for the Mississippi State Sovereignty Commission, which funneled public money to various segregationist causes, including the White Citizens Councils that had sprung up across the South in response to the Supreme Court's *Brown* decision. The commission also operated a unique national PR effort: working on the premise that the rest of the country would be less supportive of civil rights if it understood the reality of race relations in the South, it sent some 180 teams on "informational" trips into Northern states from 1961 to 1963.[73]

In a similar vein, Satterfield believed that the civil rights bill was simply the product of emotion over reason, that many of its supporters were both moved by the passions of Birmingham and afraid of seeing similar protests spring up elsewhere. If the bill could be delayed, those passions might cool; at the same time, an aggressive campaign to educate the public about what he saw as the bill's hidden threats—to private property, to freedom of speech—could put significant pressure on enough senators to defeat the bill. (Satterfield assumed that the House, dominated by liberals, was a lost cause.)

On July 17, Satterfield wrote a long memo explaining his vision for CCFAF—and what it would take to make it happen. It needed office space close to Capitol Hill and a research staff. It needed a list of senators vulnerable to the committee's message, and background files on each of them. It needed to line up expert witnesses to testify at congressional hearings. It needed to prepare pamphlets and ads attacking the bill, as well as "slogans or cartoons or posters available to be placed in all forms of businesses." It needed to hire a ghostwriting service to tailor its message to different constituencies— pamphlets that depicted the bill as a threat to unions would go out to labor leaders, while pamphlets focused on its unconstitutionality would go to lawyers. It needed mailing lists, which it could get by drawing on Satterfield's extensive network of contacts in the legal, business, and right-wing communities. And finally, the committee needed lists of newspaper editorial pages around the country—but particularly outside the South, and above all in the Midwestern and mountain states. All he needed to make it happen, Satterfield wrote, was $100,000 for the next six months.[74]

Beginning in July, Satterfield held a series of off-the-record breakfasts in Washington and Chicago to raise support for CCFAF. The first, on July 11, took place at the Mayflower Hotel. Likely out of respect for Satterfield, seventy-five representatives from the Chamber of Commerce, the American Bar Association, and other interest groups were represented, but none agreed to join the effort (the meeting in Chicago, according to John Synon, CCFAF's staff director, was an even bigger flop—intended to address the region's leading lawyers, it was attended only by a handful of far-right-wingers).[75]

Fortunately for Satterfield, he had a few deep-pocketed and influential friends, many of them outside the South. William Loeb III, the publisher of the Manchester, New Hampshire, *Union-Leader* and an outspoken supporter of various right-wing causes, agreed to chair the committee, with James Kilpatrick, the editor of the Richmond, Virginia, *News Leader* and a frequent contributor to *National Review*, as vice chairman. And while CCFAF was officially funded by the Mississippi State Sovereignty Commission, that agency was primarily a conduit for business interests eager to defeat the bill but wary of drawing attention to themselves. Chief among them was Wickliffe Preston Draper, a reclusive New York industrialist deeply involved in the eugenics movement. Over the course of the next year, Draper provided $215,000 of the committee's total $300,000 budget, sent through anonymous transfers from his bank account in Manhattan to the Mississippi state treasury; the sovereignty commission then drew on treasury funds to pay for Satterfield's work. Thanks to Draper, while the bill's supporters may have greatly outnumbered its opponents on Capitol Hill, Satterfield's group suddenly had a sizable war chest to do real damage to it.[76]

THOUGH PRESIDENT KENNEDY, Celler, and Mansfield all promised publicly that the subcommittee hearings would go quickly and that the bill would be in the Senate by the end of the year, internally the president had started to apply the brakes.

Kennedy had other priorities in Congress besides civil rights, after all, most notably the tax cut, and early on he and his team made the strategic decision to get the tax cut out of the way before the civil rights bill got to the Senate. The reasoning was simple: if civil rights came first, the Southern Democrats could essentially hold the tax cut hostage by filibustering until the 1964 election loomed, forcing the White House into making concessions; moreover, even if the civil rights bill did get through in time, the fight would likely have soured so many Southerners on the administration that they might oppose the tax cut just to spite the president. It could even be a problem for the bill in the House, should the president begin to push hard for civil rights too early.

In a phone call with the president soon after the tax bill was introduced, Wilbur Mills of Arkansas, the Southern Democrat overseeing the bill as chair of the House Ways and Means Committee, warned, "If we are not careful we can get traded out of house and home on most any kind of legislation that comes up between now and the time the House acts on civil rights."

Kennedy, trying to play off Mills's suspicion, replied, "I'm not worried about civil rights in the House. If it doesn't pass, it doesn't pass." By mid-July, Celler had agreed to the administration's demand that he slow down the pace of his committee's hearings, and not make any enemies with the Republicans in the process.[77]

Around the same time, Hubert Humphrey came to Celler with yet another reason to go slow: given that Senator Eastland chaired the Senate Judiciary Committee, it was unlikely that he would be inviting the bill's supporters to testify on the Senate versions of the bill. Therefore, Humphrey hoped that Celler could do the next best thing and hold thorough hearings in the House. Doing so would also preempt what everyone knew would be the Southerners' first line of attack: to have the bill sent to Eastland's committee, where it could be held indefinitely, at the chairman's discretion. With an extensive hearing in the House, the bill's backers in the Senate could argue that it did not need yet another spin in a committee.[78]

Despite the administration's strategy of backing the version of the bill introduced in the House, the Senate still conducted its own hearings, in two different committees: the president's bill, sponsored by Mansfield and Warren Magnuson, went to the Commerce Committee, chaired by Magnuson himself, while the other two bills—the Dirksen-Mansfield alternative, with Title II removed, and the Title II–only version—went to Eastland's Judiciary Committee.

The administration's bill was off to a bad start. Despite predictions by Senate civil rights leaders that it would immediately garner 50 cosponsors, by mid-July it had only 47—just three short of the goal, but in a game of inches, where each vote up to 67 was critical, those three made an immense, and dispiriting, difference. On June 27, Bobby Baker, the secretary of the Senate and a man second only to Lyndon Johnson in his grasp of the upper chamber, wrote a frightening memo that concluded: "It is virtually impossible to secure 51 Senators who will vote for the President's Bill"—let alone 67. He did offer a slight hope, saying that the odds of passage were fifty-fifty if the bill's supporters could win over Dirksen and two other key conservative Republicans, Bourke Hickenlooper of Iowa and George Aiken of Vermont. If they could not, though, the result would be disaster, not just for the bill but for Kennedy, too. "The president could very easily lose the election if we fail to secure passage of the bill."[79]

Meanwhile, in public opinion polls taken after the bill was announced, Kennedy's popularity ratings had dipped below 50 percent for the first time since he came into office, a coincidence that many read as a sign of national public aversion to civil rights. To the White House, such polls made the Senate hearings all the more important: since they were much higher-profile than those in the House, they might feed positive coverage for the bill in the press.[80]

The Commerce Committee hearings opened on July 1, and Robert Kennedy took the stand the next day. This time he was prepared, and it was a good thing: Senator Winston Prouty, a conservative Republican from Vermont, asked him such extensive and detailed questions into the constitutional background of the bill that at one point Kennedy quipped, "I feel like I'm taking my bar exams." Strom Thurmond then grilled him for two more hours, during which the senator gave the attorney general a pocket-size Constitution and suggested he read it. "Bobby didn't know whether to laugh or cry," said a Justice Department aide later.[81]

The next two weeks of hearings passed uneventfully, though the newspapers trumpeted a tense exchange on July 10 between two sons of the South: Thurmond, a former South Carolina governor and one of the bill's most adamant opponents, and Secretary of State Dean Rusk, a Georgia farm boy who had gone on to a Rhodes Scholarship and an illustrious diplomatic career. Thurmond accused Rusk of endangering American foreign policy by testifying on behalf of a bill tinged with communist ideas and asked him what he thought of the demonstrations around the country. "If I were denied what the Negro citizen is denied," Rusk said, "I would demonstrate."[82]

Such testimony, though, was relegated to the inside pages of most newspapers; rhetorical fireworks aside, it meant little to the substance of the bill. But the papers could not ignore the committee's July 15 witness, Alabama governor George Wallace. Despite overseeing the crackdown on demonstrators in Birmingham and standing on the losing side of the schoolhouse door in Tuscaloosa, Wallace was enjoying a moment of national celebrity. To some he was a grotesque joke; to others he was merely a curiosity, an articulate, obviously intelligent defender of an immoral social order. To a growing number of Americans, though, he spoke to an inchoate fear of government overreach—a fear he played with great skill that day.

"We daily see our government go to ridiculous extremes and take unheard of actions to appease the minority bloc vote leaders of this country," Wallace charged in his opening remarks. "I resent the fawning and pawing over such people as Martin Luther King and his pro-communist friends and associates." In the name of advancing blacks' rights, he said, the bill "places upon all businessmen and professional people the yoke of involuntary servitude—it should be called the involuntary servitude act of 1963." And while the bill was being hastily pushed through Congress in response to black-inspired violence, he said, if passed it would put the country "on the brink of civil warfare." Like John Kennedy, Wallace was seemingly born for the TV camera, and he ended with one of his many memorable sound bites: "If you intend to pass this bill, you should make preparations to withdraw all our troops from Berlin, Vietnam, and the rest of the world because they will be needed to police America."

The committee, stunned into silence, asked him a few pro forma questions, then broke for recess. But he had made quite an impression; Clair Engle, a liberal California senator, said, "You have to admire the way he presents his case. He's smart." Wallace then joined Thurmond for lunch in the Senate cafeteria, where they made a point of chatting with the black waitstaff for the cameras.[83]

Similar press attention was lavished on Robert Kennedy, who appeared before the Senate Judiciary Committee on July 20. This time he was better prepared. Eastland deputized Sam Ervin of North Carolina, a former state supreme court judge and a constitutional law expert, with examining the attorney general, which he did over the course of several days. Ervin promised to conduct his questioning "on the intellectual plane and not on the emotional plane," but made clear from the outset that his real intention was grandstanding. Because this was the version of the bill with Title II removed, the focus of the discussion fell on Title I—the voting rights provisions—which Ervin charged was a gross invasion of each state's power to determine its own electoral process.[84]

After detailing examples of voting rights violations in the South, only to have Ervin fall back to states' rights principles, Kennedy suggested that if Ervin would only take a tour through the region, he would see how routinely blacks' voting rights are violated. "I do not have even 48 hours to spare from my fight to preserve constitutional principles and the individual rights of all citizens of the United States," Ervin said indignantly. As it became clear that Kennedy was too well versed in the bill to be caught out in a mistake, Ervin fell back to a strategy of attrition, poking at minutiae in the hopes of catching Kennedy in some sort of trap. It was fruitless, but also exhausting. At one point during the multiday testimony Kennedy's wife, Ethel, saw Ervin at a White House dinner. "What have you been doing to Bobby?" she asked. "He came home and went straight to bed."[85]

WHILE THE ADMINISTRATION defended its bill in Congress, it was also trying to get ahead of the March on Washington. On July 17, President Kennedy, under pressure from his brother, reversed his earlier position and endorsed the event, figuring that it was better to try to influence it than to let it blow up literally on his doorstep. Robert Kennedy immediately assigned John Douglas, the head of the Civil Division, to oversee the administration's involvement—including the development of contingency plans should things go wrong, from pulling the sound system plug in the event of an unexpectedly heated speech to calling in the police if violence broke out.[86]

Though the march was originally planned to address "jobs and freedom," to focus on both the civil rights bill and the knottier questions of black unemployment, as the summer progressed that second emphasis was increasingly forgotten. King, the standard-bearer for the Southern civil rights movement that was pushing so hard for the measures embraced by the Civil Rights Act, nevertheless remained adamant that the march remain centered on economic justice, "to arouse the conscience of the nation over the economic plight of the negro." But Wilkins and Young, among others, who were more focused on the movement's short-term goals, promoted the march as an "all-inclusive demonstration of our belief in the President's program," leaving aside the fact that the president's program eschewed questions of economic justice. At the same time, they joined with Reuther in convincing Randolph and his deputy, the organizing genius Bayard Rustin, to move the events from the Capitol to the Lincoln Memorial and to ditch plans for thousands of protesters to flock to Capitol Hill on the morning of the march to request meetings with their congressmen.[87]

Wilkins and Young may have also been trying to moderate the march's image in response to unceasing criticism and fear coming from Congress and the white public. The media, having helped spin the vicious police response to the Birmingham demonstrations as somehow a product of the black protesters' own aggressive tactics, now bought their own hype about the risks involved in letting thousands of blacks march through the capital. Absent police violence, there was no reason to believe the event might get out of control. And yet, four days after the march was announced, the *Washington Post* editorial board, citing the events that spring in Birmingham, wrote with more than a touch of racial condescension that "leaders of the negro groups participating in the marches and demonstrations planned for Washington must be acquitted of any intention to introduce this sort of mobocracy. Nevertheless, it will greatly challenge their control and ingenuity to assemble a great crowd of some 100,000 people." Speaking for many wary members of Congress, Robert McClory, a Republican from Illinois, said that the march "held little hope for accomplishing any substantial legislative ends," and it "could even have quite the opposite effect." The administration was hearing the same thing: after surveying dozens of House members in mid-July, Joe Dolan wrote to Robert Kennedy that "the presence in Washington, at any time prior to final action on the civil rights bills, of any substantial number of individuals lobbying for the bills will lose a goodly number of votes."[88]

Meanwhile, in the weeks leading up to the march, leading newspapers carried "man on the street" interviews with whites around the country, expressing general support for civil rights but overwhelming opposition to the march itself. "A lot of the sympathy I had before is being whittled away," one schoolteacher in Pennsylvania told the *Wall Street Journal*. "I've always pushed for equal rights, but I don't approve of this mass and mob thing."[89]

Washington more or less shut down on the day of the march. A baseball doubleheader that day between the Washington Senators and the Minnesota Twins was postponed. Hundreds of businesses closed shop, and thousands of white suburbanites stayed home from work (Congress, however, decided to stay in session). "At ten o'clock the city was so empty that it looked as if a plague had struck it," wrote the *Washington Post* the next day. The city had 2,934 police officers on hand, as well as 303 police reserves, 335 firemen, and 1,735 National Guardsmen at the ready. Across the Potomac, 4,000 Army soldiers stood on alert in Virginia. Douglas had strong-armed labor leaders, who provided the sound system, to arrange a kill switch; during the speeches a Justice Department official stood at the side with a 78 of Mahalia Jackson singing "Got the Whole World in His Hands," ready to switch off a rabble-rousing speaker.[90]

And yet nothing of the sort happened. On the contrary, the march was the apogee of the civil rights movement. More than two hundred thousand people, twice as many as expected, came to Washington, from as far away as Los Angeles. Primarily African American, the crowd also included rabbis, white union leaders, and more than sixty-five members of Congress. All three TV networks covered it, with CBS showing it in its entirety, with field reports from correspondent Roger Mudd. As throngs of people came into town on buses and trains—one man arrived on roller skates from Chicago—civil rights leaders visited, by appointment, with Mansfield, Dirksen, Halleck, Speaker John McCormack, and House Majority Leader Carl Albert. They pressed for a strengthened civil rights bill, especially one with an FEPC added, but the lawmakers remained noncommittal.[91]

Despite the promotional emphasis, in the weeks leading up to the march, on the civil rights bill, many of the speeches at the Lincoln Memorial focused on economic justice. "We know that we have no future in a society in which six million black and white people are unemployed and millions more live in poverty," Randolph said. Reuther, speaking later, said the civil rights bill was a "meaningful first step" but one that needed to go further and address "the job question." The bill will fail in its intentions, he said, "as long as millions of American Negroes are treated as second-class citizens and denied jobs." And even Wilkins declared: "We want employment and with it we want the pride and responsibility and self-respect that goes along with jobs."[92]

The crux of these speeches—a call for jobs and economic justice, and a critique of the civil rights bill for failing to address them—was overshadowed by King's historic address near the end of the program. Yet that speech, aside from its rhetorical might, served a different purpose: though ending on a hopeful vision—a "dream that all men are created equal"—and full of praise for "the magnificent words of the Constitution and the Declaration of Independence," its substance was much more critical. A century after Abraham Lincoln signed a "promissory note" with the Emancipation Proclamation, King declared, "the life of the Negro is still sadly crippled by the manacles of segregation and the chains of discrimination. One hundred years later, the Negro lives on a lonely island of poverty in the midst of a vast ocean of material prosperity. One hundred years later, the Negro is still languishing in the corners of American society and finds himself an exile in his own land." The march, he said, represented blacks' demand that the country make good on that note.[93]

King's speech was the last major address of the day. The event ended at five o'clock with a benediction from Benjamin Mays of Morehouse College, King's alma mater, and hundreds of thousands of feet moved back to their buses, cars, and trains. Cleve Howell, a butcher from New York, rested on the grass south of Union Station, waiting for his train. "I hope those guys over there got the message," he said, motioning toward the Capitol.[94]

While the crowds headed home, the march's leaders made their way to the White House for an hour-long meeting with the president. Though Kennedy had endorsed the event more than a month before, he had refused requests to meet with the leaders beforehand, not wanting to get too close to an event that he still feared could blow up in the administration's face. Kennedy greeted them heartily—"I have a dream!" he said, arms open, as they entered—and then dived into an update on the bill's progress. At one point Randolph asked for a glass of milk; the president, remembering his manners, ordered sandwiches for his tired guests. Randolph then pressed the president to strengthen the civil rights bill by adding an FEPC, playing on many of the concerns Kennedy had been playing on all summer: youth unemployment, delinquency, school dropouts. Reuther, speaking next, asked for Title III—a big request, he admitted, but then the march demonstrated just how big the movement for civil rights change was. "We've put together the broadest working legislating coalition we've ever had," he said. Kennedy demurred, saying he was already fighting a tough battle over his current bill. Strangely out of tune with the moment, he recommended that blacks follow "the Jewish example" of community self-improvement rather than relying on the government.[95]

Ignoring that last comment, Wilkins and Randolph insisted that things in Congress were better than the president assumed, and that he was underestimating his own moral power. "Nobody can lead this crusade but you," Randolph said. But Kennedy's mind was in a different place; he was concerned that Republican support would collapse, since the party was intent on making inroads in the South. And where was the business community, which he had hoped would rally behind the bill? King suggested the president invite Dwight D. Eisenhower to endorse the bill, which the president agreed to do—but through a panel of religious leaders, not himself. The meeting ended shortly after six, the leaders going away with nothing save a few nice group photographs.[96]

The immediate coverage of the march fell into two categories: acclaim for the speeches and the orderly beauty of the crowd, and hard-nosed analysis of its impact on the civil rights bill. RALLY IMPACT ON CONGRESS STILL DOUBTFUL, read a typical headline, in the *Washington Post*. The march was wonderful, the article said, "but, on the record anyway, the limited commitments they brought back from the Capitol were substantially those they had already had." *Time* magazine was even harsher: "From the Capitol Hill leaders, and from the President and the Vice President, the visitors got polite words— and polite refusals. And as they left Washington they knew that there would be no FEPC, no authority for the Justice Department to step into every sort of civil rights case. Most frustrating of all, they knew that the public accommodations section of the administration's package was quite unlikely to pass the Senate." Even years later, key figures in the bill's journey, including Nicholas Katzenbach, said they didn't believe the march made a difference.[97]

This was more than a matter of jaundiced memory; a sense of frustration with the march's legislative payoff pervaded the movement as well. In an after-action report, the LCCR wrote: "In their round of morning meetings with the heads of Congress and their late afternoon meeting with the President, the leaders of the March occasionally had the frustrating sense of traveling in circles. The meetings were cordial and helpful. But the feeling remains no one is ready to follow the splendid example set by more than 200,000 marchers and take the first bold step toward strengthening the measure."[98]

Such pessimism, though understandable, missed the larger point of the march. As a spectacle captured magnificently by TV, it demonstrated to the countless millions of white Americans who knew the movement solely by the images from Birmingham that the nation's blacks came in peace. Very few of those viewers then turned immediately to their writing desks to pen a letter to Congress supporting the bill. But in the months to come, they would be more open to the follow-up appeals delivered by their ministers, less interested in the anti-civil-rights propaganda spilling forth from CCFAF, and more likely to sign a petition or even, eventually, to write a letter in support of the bill. The march, in other words, set a tone of moral optimism, a context that drove the politics of the bill long after the event had faded into history.

The march had other knock-on effects. Above all, it helped unify a still-fractured civil rights coalition. Though Reuther himself had never wavered in his support of civil rights or the groups leading the fight, many in the UAW and AFL-CIO, including its president, George Meany, did. Thanks in part to the bitter fight with the NAACP over discrimination within the garment and building trades unions, Meany had refused to endorse the march, and he stonewalled Reuther when the UAW president tried to press his case. Before the march, with Meany on the sidelines, it was an open question as to how much support Reuther could command from other member unions, let alone the rest of his leadership and the rank and file. Afterward, the flood of good-will for King and the civil rights cause effectively isolated Meany and gave Reuther a veritable blank check for pushing the bill with union resources over the coming year.

The march also spurred groups that were already involved to go further. Victor Reuther, one of Walter's brothers and the UAW's liaison to the NCC and other religious groups, was inspired by the march and created a planning committee to organize lobbying teams to spread across the Midwest, advocating for the bill. A few days after the march, a conference on the bill sponsored by the NCC opened in Lincoln, Nebraska, drawing 110 people from thirteen states; on September 12, another 900 people met in Des Moines, Iowa, to kick off a months-long multistate campaign for the bill. From there, four-person teams—composed of a theologian, a legislative expert, a representative from SNCC or SCLC, and a coordinator—spread out across the Midwest, organizing letter-writing campaigns, recruiting ministers to advocate for the bill in their sermons, and visiting representatives and senators home from Washington. According to Hamilton, between June and December 1963, the NCC's Committee on Race and Religion spent $185,000 on lobbying for the bill and on efforts to desegregate churches—or $1.4 million in 2013 dollars.[99]

IN FACT, LOBBYING for a stronger bill had begun well before the first marchers arrived in Washington that August morning. On June 7, even before the bill was introduced, the AFL-CIO's head lobbyist, Andrew Biemiller, sent the White House a memo outlining labor's position on it, focused primarily on the need for an FEPC. "The package is inadequate," the memo read. The bill "is a patent compromise in a no-compromise situation. All-out fights are made on all-out measures. How is the public to understand that the Administration is going to make an all-out fight when it starts with a half-way measure?"[100]

The memo landed at the White House like a bomb. "That afternoon I get a call from Meany in Italy," Biemiller recalled. "He said, 'What kind of a memo did you leave with Jack Kennedy today?'" Meany told him Kennedy wanted to see Biemiller immediately. Biemiller hurried to the White House, and soon found himself face-to-face with the president. "It was one of the most painful meetings I've ever been in in my life," he said. "Jack Kennedy insisted we were going to kill the bill. He said, 'Now mind me, I'm not opposed to it as a separate piece of legislation. But I don't see it's important as these other things are. And I can't go with you.'"[101]

The administration continued to resist as the summer progressed. "F.E.P. continues to be a major problem," reported Katzenbach to Robert Kennedy on August 19. "Larry O'Brien is meeting with Biemiller this morning and asking him to show us that the necessary Republican votes to pass F.E.P. as part of the omnibus bill are finally committed as a condition for administration support."[102]

The White House was doing more than sticking to its bipartisan strategy: it was also increasingly concerned that the white public was turning against the bill. Despite the warm fuzzy feelings around the March on Washington, polls showed that many, sometimes even most, whites thought Kennedy was moving too fast on the bill. More disturbing were the reports of a nascent white backlash against civil rights in general among the Northern white working class. Wayne Hays, a Democrat who represented the industrial Steubenville, Ohio, area, told Justice Department lawyer William Geoghegan that his mail was running nearly 100 percent against the legislation. The issue, he reported, was jobs. "Many of them seemed to have the impression that the legislation has something to do with providing more job opportunities for Negroes, and since unemployment is still high in the Steubenville area this causes some alarm among White voters who are unemployed or whose job future is precarious," Geoghegan wrote. Another aide, John Bartlow Martin, returned from visiting his family in the middle-class Chicago suburb of Oak Park with a similar report, though this time focused on housing—and beliefs that the White House wanted to make it possible for blacks to move into white neighborhoods.[103]

On top of all of that, the White House was playing defense on a recent Pentagon order to restrict soldiers' access to segregated facilities off-base and to permit them to march in civil rights demonstrations—moves Kennedy agreed with, but which were handled ineptly and gave the Southern Democrats a platform from which to accuse the president of politicizing national defense. With a looming election the next year, it is no wonder the administration held back—and in some cases, like a Justice Department indictment of nine protesters in Albany, Georgia, seemed to be working against any faint pro-civil-rights image it might have acquired.[104]

Fortunately for labor and its allies, the White House was not the only avenue through to the bill. Several members of the liberal majority on the subcommittee stood ready to strengthen the bill, including adding an FEPC; the only question was whether Celler would let them. All through July, the LCCR and its constituent groups had been pressuring Celler to open the bill to amendments in Subcommittee No. 5. He had signaled his openness to additions during hearings on July 24, when he said, "Don't misunderstand me. I want to put everything I can in the bill." Celler was always likely to let them have what they wanted—not only was he more liberal than the administration thought, but while he remained a Kennedy loyalist he seemed to chafe a bit at being treated like a "Daley Democrat," a machine pol with no conviction of his own. "The impression downtown, at the Department of Justice, was that Emanuel Celler would do what he was told to do," said his former aide Ben Zelenko. "He had been through a lot, and he bucked them." Finally, at a meeting with Biemiller, Rauh, and several other LCCR representatives on July 31, Celler said he would agree to almost every item on the LCCR wish list: an FEPC, a robust Title III, a mandatory Title VI funds cutoff, and an unchallengeable presumption—not just a debatable assumption—that a sixth-grade education meant someone was literate enough to vote. He reiterated that commitment on August 7 in a speech to the NAACP, promising to include both FEPC and Title III in the bill.[105]

Despite its aggressive push for a bigger bill, the LCCR did appreciate the limits of its advocacy. At a July 24 meeting, aides to Adam Clayton Powell Jr. urged them to try to push Representative James Roosevelt's own FEPC bill, H.R. 405, to the House floor, bypassing the Rules Committee by means of an aggressive, risky tactic called "Calendar Wednesday." Rauh, speaking for the rest of the LCCR representatives, said absolutely not—the risk was too great, and a failure could hurt Kennedy's bill. Powell later said he would ignore them, and was only placated once Celler promised he would make sure H.R. 405 got added to the main bill.[106]

By late August, with the likelihood of a stronger bill increasing, Rauh ordered the rest of the LCCR lobbyists to ease up. It was time to play nice with the administration, because the subcommittee vote was only the first of many to come. "I recommend that the organizations of the Leadership Conference on Civil Rights and the additional cooperating groups accept the Justice position and its good faith as well," he wrote in an August 30 memo.[107]

AFTER MORE THAN a hundred witnesses and twenty-six hundred pages of testimony, Subcommittee No. 5 finished its public hearings in early August, and on the fourteenth it went into executive session. There, away from the public, the members would debate and amend the bill before voting on whether to send it to the full committee—and, eventually, to the House floor.[108]

In keeping with his promise to President Kennedy to hold off on the bill until the tax cut was safe, Celler dragged out the first several weeks of executive session meetings, allowing long-winded and somewhat pointless debate. Usually either Marshall or Katzenbach was present, and at the end of the day they would return to the Department of Justice and assign someone from Schlei's drafting team to rework the bill accordingly—though most of the changes, especially those submitted by Republicans, were inconsequential. "They would often pursue at great length the meaning of a particular word or phrase searing for ambiguities, trying to point up poor draftsmanship," David Filvaroff, one of the team members, recalled. "The burden which fell to the Department was to respond to these by memoranda or arguments which adequately met the arguments made or by coming up with new language which avoided the asserted, if often unreal, difficulties."[109]

Celler waited until September 10, when the tax cut was on the House floor, to begin marking up the bill—reading the bill line by line, with committee members adding amendments, sometimes just single words, as they went along. By then the Department of Justice men, whose attendance at the executive sessions required the unanimous consent of the members, had been kicked out, after Representative Meader of Michigan raised an objection.[110]

Then they started to debate additions to the bill. Since the liberals dominated the subcommittee, the conservative Republicans could do little more than raise objections, but Celler did not want word to leak out that the bill was gaining strength before he was ready to announce it. And so he promised McCulloch and others that the votes were only tentative, that they would go back through at the end and reassess each addition before making the bill final. They raised little objection as the subcommittee approved Byron Rogers's amendment to grant the attorney general the power to sue over denial of access to any public facility, including parks and pools. Nor did they object to Robert Kastenmeier's expansion of Title II to cover all public accommodations, save for small rooming houses (even though it was an affront to McCulloch, who had just finished working on compromise Title II language with Katzenbach). And they raised hardly a hand against Celler's addition of a new title that would allow federal appeals courts to review cases that segregationist federal judges on the district level had passed down to a state court, which presumably was even more hostile to civil rights.[111]

But the bill was weakened in other ways. McCulloch objected to the findings that prefaced the bill—and since they had been added primarily to ensure the bill went to the Judiciary Committee, they had served their purpose, and were duly dropped. But he also wanted to tighten the rules on voting in Title I. The way the bill was written, a voter who sued to get onto the rolls could vote immediately—even though the enhanced legal mechanisms that made such a suit possible, including intervention by the Justice Department, could only be summoned if evidence of widespread voter intimidation was found. But because such a determination could take months to complete, McCulloch feared the bill was putting the cart before the horse—that it made it easier for people to vote, including, potentially, those who should not be permitted, before the grounds for admitting them were established. He therefore proposed quarantining such votes until a three-judge panel could reach a conclusion.[112]

McCulloch also demanded that the words "and racial imbalance" be removed from Title III, which meant that technical and financial assistance could not go to school districts trying to correct for de facto segregation—in effect limiting the bill's education plank to Southern schools. Though the change significantly limited the bill, it was readily accepted by even the pro-civil-rights members, who knew well the growing political challenges that de facto segregation posed in their districts. (The revision echoed a change made by Justice Department attorneys in early August, when they had rewritten Title VI to explicitly exclude federal funds used to guarantee home loans, removing the threat of substantive federal action against housing discrimination.)[113]

As they proceeded, racial tensions continued to heat up as students went back to school. On September 5 a bomb went off at the Birmingham home of a local black leader, Arthur Shores; one man was killed and sixteen injured in the riot that ensued. That same day Governor Wallace, who had said he would not interfere with federal court orders to desegregate schools in his state, ordered state troopers to block black students from entering schools in Birmingham, Mobile, and Tuskegee. When a federal judge issued an injunction against the troopers, Wallace sent out the Alabama National Guard—which Kennedy then, for the third time that year, federalized. Finally, on September 10, Wallace gave in, saying, "I can't fight bayonets with my bare hands."[114]

Five days later, a bomb went off in the basement of the 16th Street Baptist Church in Birmingham, killing four young girls and injuring a fifth. In the violence that followed, a police officer shot a black teenager in the back, killing him, and a pair of white Boy Scouts shot and killed another black boy riding his bicycle. Like Medgar Evers's murder three months earlier, the bombing shocked the world. Kennedy placed the blame squarely on Wallace: "It is regrettable that public disparagement of law and order has encouraged violence which has fallen on the innocent." Still, he waited several days to meet with civil rights leaders, and even then was noncommittal on whether he would take steps to strengthen the civil rights bill.[115]

The bombing pushed the LCCR organizations to lobby even harder for a stronger civil rights bill. "In the face of these murders it is obscene to talk about the compromise necessary to obtain a rule or to achieve cloture or to argue the need to protect the right of the small businessman or the bowling alley proprietor to discriminate," said Wilkins. Robert Spike, speaking for the NCC, said: "Out of this dark night of violence a new dawn of racial justice must come, and the churches have the clear and unmistakable duty urging it. The first step which must be taken, and take at once in Birmingham is not to be repeated, is the immediate passage of a strengthened civil rights bill." When Kennedy dragged his feet on his response, the LCCR lashed out. "The administration itself, almost as if Birmingham hadn't happened, shows no inclination to work for the kind of amendments that would improve the bill, and that is a cause for keep disappointment," the group said in its September 20 newsletter. "Administration officials have not been content to remain passive. They have been arguing against some of the most meaningful amendments being proposed—an FEPC provision, for instance."[116]

The bombing, and the heavy movement pressure that followed, dramatically altered the dynamics of the subcommittee. On September 25, the same day the House voted to pass the tax cut bill, Rogers offered a Title III amendment, empowering the attorney general to sue, or join suits, that alleged discrimination by public officials. Almost immediately after, Peter Rodino offered a title that would ban employment discrimination based on race, religion, color, or national origin, enforced by a fair employment practices committee with cease-and-desist powers. Taken together, these two amendments represented the Holy Grail of the civil rights forces; now all they had to do was keep them in the bill.[117]

A fuming McCulloch told the reporters gathered outside the committee room that the new Title II and FEPC planks "may strangle" the bill altogether. Kastenmeier's public accommodations additions in particular, he told a reporter for the *Dayton Daily News*, were "so severe they threaten passage of civil rights legislation, not only in the Senate but even in the House. I am opposed to these unbelievably severe powers that would cover every business in Ohio that carries goods and services to the public." Still, he held out hope that "compromise, moderation and understanding" could bring the bill back into shape before the final vote.[118]

But McCulloch hoped in vain. On October 2, Celler moved the subcommittee through votes on the "tentative" amendments, with each getting easy approval by the Democratic majority as the Republicans looked on helplessly. Even the liberal Republicans were apoplectic: Lindsay had offered an amendment to add a Fourteenth Amendment justification to Title II, much like Kastenmeier's, but it had been shot down by Democrats—and now he watched as the Democrats roundly approved an identical amendment by one of their own. The voting over, the Republicans, conservative and liberal, stormed out of the committee room.[119]

The bill, and Celler, drew immediate praise from civil rights groups and liberal media outlets. The *New York Times* editorial board said the chairman "has demonstrated that Congress can supply initiative and intelligence in a great cause on the rare occasions when it is so moved." Even before the bill was publicly reported, the LCCR demanded that Kennedy immediately endorse the new draft. "The administration should embrace the subcommittee version and support it vigorously," the group said in a statement. "When it does it will find enough Republicans to join." If the president did not, warned Wilkins, black America would explode. The reaction "will differ according to degree and the part of the country and will consist of rallies, petitions—and maybe marches."[120]

Others were less enamored. McCulloch called the amended bill "a pail of garbage," and said he did not know if he could even work with the Democrats in the full committee. Charles Bartlett, a political columnist said that the liberals had failed the bill by letting the political optics of their home districts get in the way of a meaningful bill. "Celler has endangered the measure by approaching it in a candidly political way," Bartlett wrote. [121]

Katzenbach had been away for three days on a Justice Department mission to Nicaragua, and he only found out about the new draft when he returned. "Our worst fears had been realized," he later wrote. When he challenged Celler, the chairman said that it was all going according to plan, and that the bill would be put back in order in the full committee. "He did not say how." [122]

CHAPTER 4

THE OCTOBER CRISIS

A FEW HOURS AFTER CELLER announced the subcommittee draft of H.R.
7152, Katzenbach practically hauled him bodily into a meeting with
Marshall, O'Brien, and Celler's Judiciary Committee counsels, Ben Zelenko
and Bill Foley. The deputy attorney general was apoplectic; the last he
had known, before being booted from the executive sessions by Meader,
was that Celler was on track to deliver the president's bill, modified to
fit McCulloch's specifications. The bill that emerged, he said, was
unrecognizable.[1]

Did Celler not understand, Katzenbach demanded to know, that McCulloch
was the key to the whole enterprise? Don't worry, said Celler. Everything was
going according to his plan. He had passed the loaded bill to appease the liberals; the Republicans on the full committee would now pare back the bill.
Katzenbach was hardly convinced. In measured but heated words, he explained
that the last thing McCulloch wanted was to be seen as the one forcing a
compromise on civil rights. The Ohio Republican would rather let the bill die
at Celler's hands than take responsibility for watering it down. In any case,
what was Celler's plan? The chairman wilted. "I do not believe he has any idea
how this can be accomplished," Katzenbach wrote in a memo to Robert
Kennedy after the meeting. "What a mess!"

With Katzenbach's memo in hand, Robert Kennedy sat down with Celler
the next morning. Celler, he practically screamed, had failed the administration, and failed the bill. From here on, the Department of Justice would handle
the bill. "It was unpleasant," Kennedy recalled understatedly. The only solution
was for Celler to step aside and let Katzenbach and Marshall negotiate a
compromise directly with McCulloch.[2]

Celler was unhappy with the way he was being treated by the executive
branch, but he was also aware of how badly he had erred in letting the liberals
load up the bill. "He thought that he was being scolded. And he was being

scolded," said Marshall. "He did resent it at the time. But then, I think, he finally came around and accepted it."[3]

The proposal to let Katzenbach take the reins of the bill in negotiations with McCulloch was unprecedented, and a clear violation of the traditions of the separation of powers. Once a bill was before Congress, the White House was supposed to step aside and let the legislative branch do its job. Instead, Kennedy demanded that an unelected official, and not even a cabinet-level official at that, go around the Judiciary Committee chair and work out a deal with a member of the minority party. And for this to happen on an issue like civil rights, an issue that Celler had been so committed to for so many years, must have burned especially hot. It is a testament to his fealty to the Kennedys and the party, and perhaps his own waning rigor, that Celler agreed to let them proceed—and not only that, but he called McCulloch and gave him his blessing to go meet with Katzenbach directly.[4]

The Justice Department wasted no time. That afternoon, Katzenbach and Marshall went to McCulloch's office. The Judiciary Committee Republicans had already had their own meeting, just hours after the bill was announced, joined by Minority Leader Halleck. They were furious, and, as Katzenbach expected, they refused to help Kennedy pare back the bill to make it palatable for the Senate, Celler's ostensible strategy. McCulloch relayed that anger, with a dollop of his own, to the two Justice men next day. This was an exact replay of 1957 and 1960, he told Katzenbach, and he wouldn't go along. The original bill would have already been a hard sell to conservative Republicans—this new version would be impossible. "It would be cut to pieces, nothing would be left, and he would not lift a finger to stop the debacle," recalled David Filvaroff.[5]

But, McCulloch said, he was not giving up. The bill—even in its souped-up version—could survive the House if it looked as if it was being pared back significantly. McCulloch knew what it would take to appease his colleagues, but with the national election just over a year away, he did not want to be responsible for his party's acquiring an anti-civil-rights image. So McCulloch proposed a deal: the White House would take the public responsibility for exacting cuts to the bill, and he would win over Charles Halleck, and the two of them would then win over enough Republicans in the Judiciary Committee to pass the bill.[6]

With McCulloch on board and Celler sidelined, Katzenbach had one more group of stakeholders to win over: the LCCR. The administration had long been wary of the civil rights lobbyists, whom they saw as a cross between starry-eyed idealists and interest-group opportunists, playing on the ever-dashed hopes of American blacks to gain office, money, and prestige. But Kennedy and his men also recognized that any successful bill required their efforts to drum up popular support. Katzenbach and Marshall had done all they could that summer to keep them on board without letting them steer the ship, but the subcommittee bill ruined everything. Seeing the possibility of a strong bill making it out of the Judiciary Committee, the civil rights groups were going to go all out to keep it intact.

Katzenbach made some perfunctory efforts to win them over. That Sunday he sat down in Larry O'Brien's office with a klatch of the LCCR's leaders to lay out his case for compromise—most significantly, ditching Title III powers and paring back, if not discarding, the FEPC. It was an ugly meeting. One LCCR representative, a protestant pastor, told Katzenbach he was as guilty of murder as whoever had planted the bomb at 16th Street Baptist.[7]

A few days later, Katzenbach had a similarly frustrating conversation with Walter Reuther, who insisted that the subcommittee bill could survive—that the country was at a unique moment where dramatic change was not only necessary but possible. When Katzenbach demurred, Reuther accused him of being too much a professor. Katzenbach demanded that Reuther tell him where the votes would come from. "I said, 'Alright, I can count up votes in the committee and I can count up votes in the House of Representatives. What have you got?'" Katzenbach recalled saying. Reuther responded, "I haven't been into the specifics but I know the mood of this country."[8]

Of course, on one level Reuther and the LCCR were simply being strategic—though they might settle for a compromise in the end, they had no incentive to stop pushing for something better. And the White House was not as angry at them as it might have seemed: after all, the further left that the liberals staked their position, the more the White House could leave in the bill and still call it a compromise. And yet the pastor's comment to Katzenbach makes clear that this was not all just posturing: many liberals had never forgiven Kennedy's earlier quiescence on civil rights, and they really did believe that to compromise on Title III and a robust FEPC was to gut the bill. The exchanges underlined the surprisingly wide gap between two groups that should have been closely united, a division that could well have destroyed the bill.

The liberals continued to play hardball through October. As rumors about secret negotiations between the Justice Department and the Republicans leaked out, groups like the ADA lashed at the White House. "The ink had hardly dried from the print of the excellent House Judiciary Subcommittee civil rights bill before the Administration supported efforts to weaken it," the ADA wrote in its October 11 newsletter, which went out to thousands of leading Democrats around the country. And the group heavily lobbied individual representatives, particularly the liberal Republicans now torn in three ways by a desire to see a strong bill, anger with liberal Democrats for not sharing the bill with them, and a fealty to the party leadership. As Clarence Mitchell pleaded in an October 8 letter to one of them, Representative Charles Mathias Jr. of Maryland, "the principal reason" for paring back the bill "is the Republicans on the full committee will not support a strong bill. I vehemently disagree with this reasoning." Later in the month King went after Kennedy directly, saying, "No president can be great or even fit for office if he attempts to accommodate political expediency with human rights."[9]

President Kennedy was just as disappointed, though in his case it was with the subcommittee bill. "I don't think it's going to pass," he told the Reverend Eugene Carson Blake on September 30, after he had learned of the amended bill. To Marshall and Robert Kennedy, he even entertained the idea of letting the liberals run away with the bill, then blaming the Republicans for killing the legislation and reaping the benefits in November 1964. The president, Marshall recalled, mused over "whether we should just accept the fact that we were going to lose the bill and have the President, therefore, just get on the Democratic side of it and accept the liberals' position and throw the bill away."[10]

But Kennedy was too committed to the bill—and, more importantly, he could already see a way through the morass. The thirty-fifth president is often criticized for his lack of feel for Congress, a charge given weight by the number of landmark bills still floating around Capitol Hill at his death. But while Kennedy may not have had the legislative deftness of Lyndon Johnson, he was far from inept. Kennedy was the first president since Roosevelt to regularly lobby for bills personally or through dedicated liaisons, and he was the first to have a reporting system for each bit of legislation—who talked to which representative, where each senator stood on a bill—so that the White House could coordinate its lobbying efforts with precision. And whereas previous presidents had worked solely with the congressional leadership, Kennedy reached deep into the rank and file. Drawing on his wealth of charisma and genius grasp of the symbolic power of the presidency, Kennedy held regular coffee and breakfast meetings, as well as frequent after-work cruises along the Potomac on the presidential yacht, the *Sequoia*. And it worked: in 1961 the White House sent 53 major bills to Congress and won 33 of them, a better record than Eisenhower had achieved in six years.[11]

At no time was Kennedy's underappreciated legislative skill more apparent than on civil rights that fall. For Kennedy, as for his aides, the questions were purely mathematical ones: How strong a bill could they write and still win the sixty Republican votes they believed they needed to pass the bill on the House floor? And before that, how strong could a bill be and still win the three Republican votes necessary to ally with the liberal Democrats to overcome the

Southern Democrats who stocked the Rules Committee, where the bill would go after Judiciary? And, before getting to either of those votes, what must they do to win at least five Republicans in the Judiciary Committee? Kennedy was less concerned about the Judiciary Committee, where he felt the bill had a good chance of surviving, than the House as a whole. "They'll vote for the bill," he complained to Blake about the House Republicans, "but you wouldn't get even 60 votes. That's a lot of votes for them." But he also understood the symbolic importance of getting a strong bipartisan vote out of the committee. If it passed on the strength of a few liberal Republicans alone, but lost McCulloch and the conservatives, then Kennedy and his team would have a hard time selling it as a truly bipartisan product on the floor of the House.[12]

Once McCulloch's demands became clear, Kennedy decided on a three-track strategy. First, Katzenbach would work with McCulloch, in secret, to hammer out a compromise. Second, as the vote in the committee grew closer, he would personally lobby both McCulloch and Halleck to make sure they could deliver the votes. And third, he would send his brother back to Capitol Hill to explain why the administration opposed the subcommittee bill. (Actually, Kennedy did not oppose all of the subcommittee bill—he was personally delighted that the liberals had inserted an FEPC title, telling Blake that he would rather sacrifice other sections of the bill than lose it, because "at least with FEPC, you get something dramatically important. And that would be a tremendous breakthrough.")[13]

Early in the negotiation process, the bipartisan leadership met with Katzenbach in the office of John McCormack, the Speaker of the House. McCormack was the son of Irish immigrants, and although he became a successful Boston lawyer and then a renowned politician, McCormack never forgot the anti-Irish sentiment that had been at least as large an obstacle to success as his lack of formal education. Like several men in the Democratic leadership at the time—Larry O'Brien, Mike Mansfield, the Kennedys—McCormack drew on fresh family memories of discrimination signs in his approach to civil rights. As he told Andrew Biemiller, the congressman turned labor lobbyist, "I know about discrimination. When I was a kid trying to get my first job, 'no Irish need apply.' I've never forgotten it. I'm against discrimination." One evening, the historian and former congressman D. B. Hardeman recalled, McCormack was at a dinner meeting with a group of bankers in Boston. As McCormack was leaving, one of the men approached him in the lobby. "Tell me John, why do you always have a lot of Jews around you?" the man asked. McCormack turned and screamed, "You goddamn son of a bitch, you're one of those haters!" and pushed him hard in the chest, sending him sprawling across the floor.[14]

That same passion came out in the bipartisan leadership meeting. Though the administration was on record supporting the new FEPC title, and although Kennedy privately wanted it to remain, Katzenbach himself was hoping to persuade the leadership to undermine it so that it could be easily traded away later. Instead, McCormack delivered a moving speech about how much an FEPC would have helped his father get out from under the yoke of anti-Catholic, anti-Irish Boston. And in any case, he told Katzenbach, "I know the president didn't ask for it, but a lot of water has gone over the dam since then." It was one thing for Clarence Mitchell to insist on an FEPC; without McCormack's support, no amount of Republican support could save it.[15]

At the same time, Halleck refused to back the FEPC plank, and he stormed out of the room. "Larry and I thought the meeting had been a disaster," said Katzenbach. "I think this was the low point."[16]

After several more days of backroom negotiating, McCulloch and Celler agreed to invite Robert Kennedy to appear before the full Judiciary Committee on October 15, for what turned out to be two days of testimony (an objection by wily Southern Democrats on the committee to holding the hearing in the afternoon, while the House was in session, forced the attorney general to return the next day).

This time Kennedy was ready. He appeared in the committee's chamber in the Cannon House Office Building promptly at 10:00 A.M., with both Katzenbach and Marshall in tow. He began by emphasizing the underlying bipartisan goal of the civil rights bill. "Differences as to approach and emphasis must not be permitted to be escalated into the arena of politics—or the country will be the loser," he said. He then walked through the administration's "edits" of the subcommittee bill. On Title I, he agreed with McCulloch that the impoundment amendments were "unnecessary and objectionable"—that by setting aside registered ballots until a judge determined whether there had been widespread voter discrimination in the district, the amendment essentially "destroys the basic purpose" of the title. He did not, however, oppose the inclusion of state elections in the bill; as he and Katzenbach had decided earlier, whether or not they were explicitly included in the bill did not matter, since a mandate that federal elections conform to the law would still force state procedures to conform as well, unless states wanted to undertake the high cost of running their own elections on different days, without federal assistance. And Kennedy guardedly endorsed the new FEPC, though he warned that "it will take the highest statesmanship to avoid the morass of partisan politics which could only result in the failure to enact legislation at this session of Congress."[17]

But he opened fire on the new, universal Title III. It was, first of all, an ineffective measure. A ban on violating someone's civil rights would not have prevented the 16th Street church bombing, for example, since "injunctions cannot prevent crimes by unknown persons." Moreover, it went much further than the 1957 version. Whereas that title dealt only with violations of voting rights, this one dealt with violations of any civil right: freedom of speech, freedom of assembly, freedom of religion—rights that the drafters clearly did not intend to protect with the legislation. And it would not do much against a police officer who hit a protester in the heat of the moment. Moreover, the bill would be a nightmare to enforce: What constitutes a civil right, and who decides? But most important, Kennedy feared that the creation of a federal mandate to protect individual rights would give state and local authorities an excuse to "abdicate their law enforcement responsibilities, thereby creating a vacuum in authority which could be filled only by federal force. This in turn— if it is to be faced squarely, Mr. Chairman—would require creation of a national police force. This is a step which is historically, and with good reason, abhorrent to our federal system." In short, Kennedy told the committee that he was being offered powers that he did not want—and did not want any other attorney general to have, either.[18]

After his first day of testifying, Kennedy held a press conference where he was asked whether the bill could come together on a bipartisan basis. He struck a pessimistic note. "I think it is at a very tough and critical and crucial point. I think it is very tough," he said. And though he kept his criticism ostensibly bipartisan, no one needed to be told where it was aimed. "I think the problem at the present time is that you haven't reached a consensus after four months of people who are interested in obtaining passage of a civil rights bill. Some Republicans and Democrats in my judgment are going to have to really have some courage and statesmanship and also be willing to work some of these matters out and arrive at a consensus which would be acceptable, and that has not been done."[19]

But if Kennedy showed his tough side on the first day, on the second he revealed a side that most Americans were not yet familiar with but that his brother and his inner circle had been seeing more and more of that summer: deeply empathetic, passionate, and morally driven. At one point Representative Elijah "Tic" Forrester, from rural Georgia's Third Congressional District, asked how Kennedy could defend appeasing the demands of unruly civil rights protesters.

"If you were a Negro in Albany, Georgia, you would be protesting, Congressman," Kennedy replied. "You wouldn't accept it, you couldn't accept it as a human being, the situation in Albany, Georgia."[20]

"I would say this, Mr. Attorney General," Forrester said, "if I were a Negro, I might do that, but a white man couldn't do it. That is a right that the Negro has that a white man doesn't have. You wouldn't permit the white man to go down the street like that, would you?"

Kennedy kept hitting the basic point: the bill was not about white versus black, or North versus South, but about the government empathizing with a part of its citizenry that had been systematically denied its rights under the Constitution. "Congressman," Kennedy said, "if I were treated by the white population as the Negro has been treated by the white population, I would take to the streets. And that is why I can't understand your opposition to this legislation. You say they shouldn't demonstrate and they shouldn't protest, and yet you won't support something that will remedy some of these problems. And that is what it comes down to basically."

Kennedy and Forrester weren't the only pair to illustrate the role of empathy, and its absence, in motivating the two sides of the civil rights issue that day. While defending Kennedy's testimony, James Corman, a Democrat from Van Nuys, California, said, "I do not think anyone can get a feeling of the problem from the testimony. I think one day in Jackson, Mississippi and one day in Yazoo would do more to gain support for this legislation than six months of hearings"—at which point Edwin Willis, a relatively liberal Southerner from the Louisiana bayou, snapped: "I have spent 59 years, and you sort of get a different evaluation of the depth of it and perhaps a different impression." Willis's inability to grasp Corman's point explains much about how Southern Democrats could dedicate so much of their lives to oppressing millions of black men and women.[21]

Nevertheless, Kennedy's performance drew the predictable criticisms from the left. The black media was particularly incensed. The *Chicago Daily Defender* wrote that "Kennedy bowed to racist pressure in an appearance Tuesday before the House Judiciary Committee," while the *Los Angeles Sentinel* urged readers to send telegrams to the committee liberals demanding that they stand fast with the subcommittee bill. "There is no reason for this kind of sellout," said Clarence Mitchell. "The administration should be in there fighting for the subcommittee bill." The LCCR sent Celler a three-page memo demanding that he remain committed to the subcommittee bill, while the American Jewish Congress, a strongly pro-civil-rights group that Celler had long championed, sent a letter to him demanding that he oppose all "administration proposals to soften the civil rights bill."[22]

The mainstream press was more divided; while the *Chicago Tribune* blasted its criticism of his performance with the headline EASE HOUSE RIGHTS BILL, BOB KENNEDY ASKS: ATTORNEY GENERAL SAYS MEASURE GOES TOO FAR, the *New York Times* took the administration's side, declaring, ROBERT KENNEDY TRIES TO PREVENT GRIDLOCK.[23]

But Kennedy's testimony had its intended effect. McCulloch praised him for making "very useful, very constructive suggestions, some that I would make and have been making," and even Lindsay set aside his personal grievances to note, "I think that it was helpful that he came up." And Kennedy's testimony gave cover for Celler to issue his own face-saving message soon after, telling reporters that he would "put aside my own feelings" and "exert every effort toward advancing a bill along the lines recommended by the Administration."[24]

With Celler and McCulloch on record behind the administration, Robert Kennedy then sought out the non-Southern Democrats on the Judiciary Committee, many of whom were still unaware of the secret negotiations between Katzenbach and McCulloch. The morning after his appearance before the committee, Kennedy, along with Katzenbach, Marshall, and O'Brien, met with most of them in Celler's office. Kennedy explained the deal: that without Republican support, the bill was dead, but that by making a few cuts McCulloch and his crew would get back on board. Title III had to go, and the voting rights, public accommodations, and FEPC titles would have to be pared back—though McCulloch in principle supported all three.[25]

If Kennedy was expecting intransigence, he was shocked to find agreement—though salted with a large dash of skepticism. "They simply could not accept that Halleck would ever agree to a bill as good as this, and therefore they thought they were being conned," recalled Katzenbach. Suddenly, what looked like a lost cause just weeks before was on the verge of rescue—and in a better shape than anyone could have imagined. That afternoon Celler met with McCulloch, then announced that the committee would move toward a vote on the entire bill within a week.[26]

Lindsay continued to press for the subcommittee bill, asserting, without proof, that a majority of the Republicans on the full committee supported it. And Celler now had to find non-Southern Democrats willing to take a political risk and offer amendments to whittle back the bill per McCulloch's demands: limiting Title I to federal elections, dropping Title II coverage for retail and personal service businesses, and ditching Title III altogether.[27]

Celler had found a willing accomplice on the amendment on Title I: Roland Libonati, a Chicago Democrat. Libonati was famous around the halls of Congress for having worked as Al Capone's lawyer, though he denied any illicit ties to organized crime. (He was also known for his wonderfully quotable malapropisms; among his gems was the observation that fall was the time when "the moss was on the pumpkin.") It is unclear why he agreed to offer the amendment: Libonati was a committed labor liberal who resented Robert Kennedy's aggressive investigations into union-mob ties in the 1950s. Perhaps the answer is that he was simply a cog in the Chicago political machine, and more or less obliged to do whatever Mayor Richard Daley told him to do. Though no record exists, it is likely that someone in the White House went to the mayor and explained what they needed done, and Daley gave Libonati his marching orders.[28]

Libonati introduced his amendment on October 10. But rather than plaudits, he drew condemnation: protesters picketed his Chicago office, while his fellow Chicagoland representative (and one of the few blacks in Congress) William Dawson harassed him endlessly to change his vote. But the breaking point came when Libonati caught Celler in an interview on CBS News. As he related the story to a *Time* magazine reporter, "So then I'm sitting down, just like you and me are sitting here now, and I'm watching television and who do I see on the television but my chairman. And he's telling 'em up there in his district that he's for a strong bill, and that he doesn't have anything to do with any motion to cut the bill down. So when I hear that, I says to myself, 'Lib, where are we at here, anyway?' And I think that if they're gonna get some Republican votes anyway, and if the chairman says he doesn't have anything to do with my motion, then certain representations that were made to me is out the window."[29]

On October 21, toward the end of a late-afternoon meeting with a group of Harvard undergraduates who were visiting Capitol Hill to lobby for the bill, Libonati told the students that he was going to withdraw his amendment—a scoop duly reported in the next day's edition of the *Harvard Crimson*. Word of Libonati's plan quickly made it to McCulloch, who called Robert Kennedy's office.[30]

Kennedy was out, so McCulloch left a message—which Kennedy later swore he never received. In any event, Libonati's about-face the next morning came as a complete surprise to the rest of the committee. Celler opened the meeting by saying they had two amendments to vote on, Libonati's and a move by William Tuck of Virginia to send the bill back to the subcommittee. Suddenly Libonati rose and declared, "Mr. Chairman, I move to withdraw my amendment!"[31]

Confusion coursed through the room. Someone shouted, "Who paid him off?" Before Celler could get control of the proceedings, Libonati's motion was approved by a voice vote. Tuck then withdrew his motion, though a group of eight Southerners offered their own motion to remit the bill to the subcommittee, which lost by a vote of 9–21. Then Arch Moore, a moderate Republican from West Virginia, went in the opposite direction and moved to approve the bill, sending it to certain death before the Rules Committee—and if not there, then on the House floor.[32]

Within minutes, the administration's carefully choreographed compromise had collapsed. Worse, the Moore motion had enough support to pass. The liberals and the Southern Democrats were happy to send an overloaded bill to the House, where even the most moderate Republicans would have a hard time swallowing it.

Moore's motion required a roll call vote. But just as the clerk began reading through the committee members' names, the noon bell rang, announcing the opening of the day's House session. Thinking quickly, Texas Democrat Jack Brooks, a maverick liberal and close ally of the administration, raised a point of order that the committee had to come to a halt. Celler, relieved, adjourned for the day, leaving the Moore motion as the committee's pending business.[33]

The next morning, Katzenbach went to see McCulloch, hat in hand, yet again. And yet again, McCulloch was furious that the administration could not control its party's rank-and-file members, particularly on such an important vote. His old suspicion of a double-cross started to sneak up—after all, he had known the day before that Libonati was going to withdraw his amendment. How could the attorney general not have?[34]

Finally, Katzenbach convinced him that Libonati had gone off the reservation and that both Celler and the president were still committed to a deal. But McCulloch said that after the latest incident, there was no way their current deal would garner more than seven Republican votes—not enough for the bill to pass safely, and far too few to justify calling it a bipartisan vote with a straight face. A new deal would have to be struck, one that cut even further into the subcommittee draft, starting with the FEPC.[35]

Given his druthers, Katzenbach might have been fine ditching the FEPC; under the administration's playbook, everything outside the original bill was just ballast that could be jettisoned in a legislative storm. But both the president and the Speaker had told him over the previous weeks that they wanted the title to remain, and so he was in a bind with McCulloch—or would have been, if not for a fortuitous conversation the previous afternoon in the office of an old friend, the New Jersey Democrat Frank Thompson. Katzenbach was desperate for ideas that might placate McCulloch, particularly compromise measures that would not concede too much of the meat of the bill.[36]

What about the Griffin bill? Thompson asked.

Katzenbach pleaded ignorance. The Griffin bill, Thompson explained, was a piece of FEPC legislation from a few years back—but instead of giving the commission cease-and-desist powers, it was required to sue in federal court. The agency would still have power, but the role of the courts would provide a built-in check on it. Better yet, Griffin was a Republican, whereas the version currently attached to the civil rights bill came from the office of the ultraliberal

James Roosevelt. Republicans had rejoiced when the Griffin bill was voted out of the House Labor and Education Committee, and they had been crestfallen when it did not survive the Southern-dominated Rules Committee. Swapping Griffin for Roosevelt would achieve several things at once: it would soften the bill; it would give the Republicans a trophy in their mission to shape, and win credit for, the bill; and, most importantly, it would raise the price for opposing the bill. How could Republicans oppose a title that they had championed just a few years before?

Katzenbach thought it was a brilliant idea. He cleared the idea with Robert Kennedy and O'Brien, then took it to his next meeting with McCulloch. The Ohio Republican was for it, and thought it would help the bill get through the Judiciary Committee. But he did not think Halleck would go for it—and without Halleck, they would never get the sixty rank-and-file votes they needed in the full House.

Over the next few days Katzenbach and McCulloch met constantly—including once at McCulloch's apartment, to avoid being seen—and hammered out the rest of their new deal. McCulloch, perhaps impressed by the bipartisan gesture on the Griffin bill additon, did not ask for much else; his primary demand was the elimination of the Community Relations Service from the bill, a request Katzenbach gladly conceded.[37]

With a new compromise starting to gel, on the evening of October 23, Kennedy called the bipartisan House leadership to the Cabinet Room of the White House. The men entered through the Diplomatic Reception Room off the South Portico, away from the prying eyes of journalists in the West Wing. Along with Halleck and McCormack were Majority Leader Carl Albert of Oklahoma, Minority Whip Leslie Arends of Illinois, McCulloch, and Celler, as well as Vice President Johnson, Robert Kennedy, Katzenbach, and Marshall.[38]

The meeting began with Halleck's report on a meeting of the GOP leadership that morning, which he had rushed back from Indiana to attend, only to hear that many of his members wanted to ditch the bill entirely. "I think it's only fair to say that this damned thing has gotten all fizzled up and fouled up," he said. "I must say that Bill McCulloch and Les Arends and I kind of got our ears beat down a little bit this morning. Isn't that a fair statement?"

"That is a fair statement," McCulloch concurred.

After letting the two men vent a bit more, President Kennedy stepped in. The bill could still work, he said—everyone in the room wanted it to pass, and getting it there was just a matter of making the right concessions to bring in just enough support from each side. "I think that if we both do our job, we ought to be able to put together a majority."

McCulloch agreed: "I don't think we're too far apart," he said. But then, on the verge of agreement, the two sides drifted apart over a detail regarding the ballot impoundment provisions under Title I. For another hour, this was the pattern: Kennedy, or Halleck, or McCulloch would take the lead in urging unity, suggesting that compromise was right around the corner, only to have things collapse a moment later.

It became clear that the nub of the issue was how to sell the agreement to their respective parties without knowing for sure that the men across the aisle were on board first. Kennedy pleaded with McCulloch to get together with Katzenbach and work out a preliminary deal. "Then I can say to the Democrats, 'Here's the best we can do, and my judgment is, we ought to try to do it,'" he said. "Then if I can get them to agree, the numbers it requires, I'm confident we can get the Republicans."

Halleck was not quite convinced—at which point Kennedy put the screws on. It did not matter to him, politically, if the subcommittee bill or a compromise went to the House floor. If Halleck did not play ball, Kennedy would just endorse the subcommittee bill, let it go down in flames, and reap the political windfall of having supported a strong civil rights proposal only to have the Republicans and Southern Democrats kill it.[39]

"I'm in a pretty good position," Kennedy said. But, he added, "I think we're both better off, if we got together." He suggested that Katzenbach sit down with Celler and McCulloch the next day and work out a rough draft. "Then I will ask the Democrats to come down to the house, down here, and I'll ask them if they'll go for it. If I can then get enough of them to go for it, I will call you."

Still, Halleck was uncomfortable. "Our principle trouble over there has been the conviction that got abroad, after Manny's subcommittee blew this thing up to be hell, that the whole purpose of that was to put the Republicans in the position of emasculating the bill," he said. What he did not mention was that he was under particular criticism from young-gun members of his party, particularly Griffin and Gerald Ford, for what they said was Halleck's imperious, self-interested leadership style. His history of meetings like this one, with Halleck and McCulloch essentially deciding policy for the entire House delegation, had led in January to a coup against Charles Hoeven, a close ally of Halleck and the chair of the House Republican Conference, replacing him with Ford and putting the minority leader on notice. It was bad enough that Halleck was once again unilaterally reaching a compromise with the president; if the bill failed, he would be run out on a rail.[40]

Eventually, though, he gave in to Kennedy's wheedling and deputized McCulloch to reach a deal with Katzenbach. Asked later why he conceded, he said in part it was because he figured civil rights legislation was inevitable, and he did not want to set his party up to be on the wrong side of history. Celler offered to host the meeting in his office, but McCulloch demurred. "As Charlie says, you have your arm around me too much now," he said. They decided to meet in Katzenbach's office instead.[41]

With the meeting ended, John Kennedy headed upstairs, where he met Jackie and their friends Ben and Tony Bradlee for dinner. Ben Bradlee, then the Washington bureau chief for *Newsweek*, recalled that Kennedy was in a foul mood after going toe-to-toe with Halleck. "Trying to touch Charlie is like trying to pick up a greased pig," the president said. To boot, "it's a lousy bill as it now stands"—in part because of the concessions on Title I, which included giving districts the right to appeal judicial findings of discrimination, opening up the possibility of endless legal wrangling before a single black voter could go to the polls. Still, over the next week Kennedy fought for the bill with a skill and tenacity that gave the lie to the notion that he was out of touch with Congress and unwilling to get his hands dirty in legislative power politics—he was, after all, Joe Kennedy's son, the scion of a tough line of Boston Irish operators.[42]

The next day Halleck and Everett Dirksen held one of their regular joint conferences, referred to by the press, with mild disdain, as "the Ev and Charlie Show." The two would crack lame jokes, go on endless tangents, and rarely say anything of consequence—one political cartoonist had a reporter ask Dirksen, "In a thousand words or less, are you verbose?" But this event was a bit different. Though both expressed skepticism that the bill could get to the Senate by the end of the year, Halleck put himself squarely behind passage of the bill in the Judiciary Committee. "I must say that some things were written in [the subcommittee bill] that would make it very difficult for me to support the bill, and I guess that's pretty much the attitude of the administration," he said. Still, he said in his typical loquacious style, if the Democrats were willing to set aside the subcommittee draft and negotiate a compromise, "I can see no reason why the Republican members of the Judiciary Committee would not in the future as they have very evidently done in the past do their level best to try to write good legislation."[43]

Afterward, Halleck and McCulloch sat down with the Republican Judiciary Committee members to discuss compromise. Halleck told them he was getting "a lot of heat from the president. You'd better make up your minds. When you guys decide what you want, I'll take it down to the White House." Then McCulloch pressed his own angle. "If you have one iota of compassion in your heart, and if you support the Constitution, you know there's only one thing to do," he said. One or both tactics worked, and the majority agreed at least to oppose the Moore motion, if not vote for the bill itself.[44]

Around the same time, Kennedy called a meeting in the White House's Yellow Room of the Northern Democrats on the Judiciary Committee. The president, recalled representative Don Edwards of California, was in a convivial mood, laughing and smoking a cigar. "He was wearing a beautiful blue shirt," Edwards said. Kennedy began by explaining the rough outlines of the compromise, then asked the men to give up on the subcommittee draft and support the compromise instead. "We want to pass something," he said. "We sympathize with what you've done but we can't pass the bill in its present form."[45]

George Senner, a representative from Arizona, spoke up first. "We're with you, Mr. President." But the rest remained muted, shifting uncomfortably in their chairs to indicate their dissent from Senner's hasty exclamation. Their unresponsiveness did not faze Kennedy, though. He still had a few days to win them over; the important thing was that they not make promises in the meantime to the LCCR. He told them to stay loose, not to commit to anything too early, and that the bill was still being worked out.[46]

The meeting over, Kennedy twiddled his thumbs waiting for Halleck to call to tell him how many Republicans would get behind him. The minority leader had promised he would call by noon, and Kennedy began to worry as the clock ticked into the afternoon hours. "The thought crossed our minds that we had been had, that the crafty Republican leader had only been pulling our legs with his promise of cooperation," recalled O'Brien, who sat nervously in the room with the president. A few minutes before one o'clock, Kennedy decided to call Halleck. "It was a measure of his anxiety about the civil rights bill that he was willing to call a Republican leader who had failed to make a promised call to the President and who, for all we knew, was sitting in his office with a few cronies having the laugh of his life," O'Brien said.

When he did get Halleck on the phone, though, the news was better than he could have expected. "Mr. President, I'm terribly sorry, I had a hard time catching a couple of my fellows and I just talked to the last one," Halleck said. "But I was just about to call you with good news—I've got you the vote[s] to get your bill out of the committee." Kennedy, O'Brien said, "was overjoyed."[47]

Things were not quite as rosy as Halleck made them out to be. Ironically, he had commitments from most of the conservative Republicans, but he still faced a potential problem with the liberals, particularly John Lindsay, who might throw roadblocks in front of the compromise out of sheer petulance for being excluded from the negotiations. So Halleck sent McCulloch to appease him.

McCulloch first sent one of his Judiciary staff aides, William Copenhaver, to speak with Robert Kimball, Lindsay's closest staff adviser and point man on civil rights. Kimball said he did not think Lindsay would vote for the bill.

"Lindsay simply doesn't trust the administration to keep any kind of commitment," he said. Still, Copenhaver said, it would be worth trying to win him over. "I'll go to Lindsay if you think this time there's a chance" of the compromise bill happening, Kimball said. "I'll try to help, but only if that is the case."[48]

While most of McCulloch's colleagues left town for the weekend—Halleck was in Indiana, Lindsay at a wedding in Virginia—he stayed in his office, working the phones, trying to rope in the remaining dissidents. "McCulloch never left his desk except to sleep," recalled Kimball. On the morning of Saturday, October 26, he had a long talk with Lindsay, telling him that it was he, not the Democrats, who was coming around, and that he was willing to accept a bill with just minor edits. But to go out on a limb like that, he had to have Lindsay in his corner. To stroke Lindsay's ego even further, McCulloch asked if he would sit down with Katzenbach at a secret one-on-one meeting Monday morning to give his input and blessing to the compromise. Elated to be finally included in the negotiating process, Lindsay said yes—and that if he liked what he saw, he would support the new draft. When Lindsay returned to Washington, he told Kimball, "I'm so proud that Bill has come so far. I can't desert him now. He has made a tremendous step forward a stronger bill."[49]

Monday, October 28, the day before the Judiciary Committee was set to meet on the bill, was a near-constant flurry of activity. Though there was now significant support in both parties for the compromise, that support varied: some were willing to vote against the Moore motion, but not for the new bill; others had offered only a vague commitment and could still be swayed by the roaming packs of LCCR lobbyists circulating through the House office buildings trying to pick off errant liberals. Though the civil rights lobbyists knew the subcommittee bill was probably lost, they figured they could still extract concessions from the White House if they attracted enough support.[50]

The day was a delicate dance. Halleck was refusing to endorse the bill officially until the Democrats were in line. But to round them up, Katzenbach had to show that the votes were there from the Republicans. The morning began with Lindsay, now fully on board with the compromise, having breakfast with the liberal Republicans on the committee and trying to get them to follow him. Lindsay then carried their support to his meeting with Katzenbach at the Congressional Hotel, just south of the House office buildings on Capitol Hill.[51]

After Lindsay left the hotel, Katzenbach was joined by Marshall, McCulloch, Copenhaver, and Kimball to work out the final details of the compromise. Marshall would occasionally step out to call Robert Kennedy for approval of a particular change, but for the most part they worked quickly, and by lunch they had a draft in place.[52]

The major changes included limiting Title I, on voting rights, to federal elections; excluding shopping and "personal service"—barbershops, nail salons—from the public accommodations coverage; prohibiting judges from requiring that school districts achieve racial balance; eliminating the Community Relations Service; making the Civil Rights Commission permanent; and changing the FEPC's enforcement power from cease-and-desist orders to filing suit in federal court. To win over individual members, a few other changes, small but significant, were made, like giving the Civil Rights Commission the power to investigate voter fraud—a key demand of Representative William Cramer, a Florida Republican.[53]

McCulloch then called Halleck, who with Arends got together the rest of the GOP House leadership: Gerald Ford; George Miller; Clarence Brown, the ranking Republican on the powerful Rules Committee; John Byrnes, the ranking Republican on the equally powerful Ways and Means Committee; and Melvin Laird, who had helped engineer the Ford coup against Charles Hoeven earlier that year. Halleck had left all of them out of the negotiations; in fact, none had more than an inkling that talks were even under way. The men groused about being excluded but agreed to back Halleck. Meanwhile McCulloch continued to work the phones to sew up the Republican votes on the committee. He also tried to get Moore, the West Virginia Republican, to withdraw his motion, but to no avail.[54]

With the Republicans falling into line that afternoon, John Kennedy called back the thirteen Northern Democrats from the Judiciary Committee. Katzenbach's best guess was that Halleck and McCulloch could deliver no more than six or seven votes, which meant that Kennedy had to get at least ten of the thirteen to back him. So far, only three—Celler, Senner of Arizona, and Harold Donahue of Massachusetts—had announced support for the compromise. Two others—Jack Brooks of Texas, a loyal Kennedy man, and William St. Onge of Connecticut, who had given Celler his proxy before going into the hospital—were undeclared but considered sure things.[55]

For the rest, Kennedy had already deployed his aides to soften them up; in the case of Herman Toll, a liberal from Philadelphia, the president had even threatened to withdraw from a scheduled fund-raising parade and dinner for him on October 30. Others required a softer approach: Peter Rodino, of New Jersey, said that he did not think the compromise FEPC plank was strong enough and that he would consider amending it on the House floor. Kennedy, knowing that the representative would never do anything that would endanger the bill, said that would be fine.[56]

Kennedy had one last sit-down that evening with Halleck. Each of them lowballed the number of votes he had in hand, hoping to pressure the other to get more over the next twelve hours or so. Halleck, impressed by Kennedy's pursuit of the deal, said he would do his best. With that, Kennedy gave the signal, and by prior agreement copies of the new bill went out by courier to the allied Judiciary Committee members that night. It was going to be close, and the president wanted his side to have every possible advantage. During the night, Kimball got a call from William Higgs, one of Robert Kastenmeier's aides. "It could go either way," Higgs said, "by one or two votes."[57]

The next morning Katzenbach gave McCulloch one more call before going in to brief the president. They walked through the new draft, line by line, to make sure nothing was in disagreement. At the end of the call, Katzenbach asked McCulloch where Halleck stood on the FEPC. McCulloch said he wasn't sure, but he wasn't optimistic.[58]

Katzenbach then called Kennedy, who was getting ready for his own final meeting with Halleck. Everything was set, he told the president. Halleck had come around to supporting the bill—even, he said by mistake, the FEPC—and so the committee vote was in the bag. Kennedy thanked him and went to meet the minority leader, Arends, and McCulloch.

Halleck had come bearing even better news than the day before. That morning the Judiciary Committee Republicans had met in Arends's office, where they had counted eight votes in favor of the compromise, plus George Meader's vote against the Moore motion (he refused to say how he would vote on the bill itself). Kennedy and Halleck then went over the basics of the bill, conversing like two chummy boxers after an inconclusive prizefight. Each had won something, and each could share in the glory of watching a civil rights act with their imprint pass the Judiciary Committee. But as Halleck stood to leave, he said, "You do understand, don't you, that my commitment does not extend to FEP. I'm not at all sure about that."

Kennedy was stunned. Katzenbach had said the opposite. But he did not skip a beat. His arm around the minority leader, he said, "Charlie, we need a bill that will pass the House. It's almost time for the vote. Let's get the votes and get this thing out of the committee. And I'm grateful for your help."

After Halleck left, Kennedy wheeled on Katzenbach. "I thought you told me he was committed on FEP?"

"I did, and he is," said Katzenbach. "Don't worry about it. He will support it. It would be a mistake to pressure him." According to Katzenbach, it was an honest error—in a rare moment of confusion, he had misremembered what McCulloch had told him about Halleck's support. It was not until a year later, when he was preparing for an oral history interview with the journalist Anthony Lewis, that Katzenbach was digging through his papers and found a scribble from his call with McCulloch. It said, clearly, that Halleck opposed a fair employment practices title. "If I had looked at my notes, we might never have [had] an FEP, I guess," he said.[59]

Emanuel Celler called the Judiciary Committee to order at 10:45. Before him sat minutely detailed instructions from Katzenbach, with Brooks looking over his shoulder to make sure he followed them. First, he called up the Moore motion for a vote. It failed 15 to 19. Libonati, who had vowed to back the White House after getting a tongue-lashing from Mayor Daley, had switched his position again, and he voted to support Moore. Interestingly, one Southern Democrat also voted against the Moore motion, Ed Willis of Louisiana, a relatively moderate Southerner and close social friend of Celler and McCulloch.[60]

Celler then called up the compromise bill and had Foley read all of its fifty-six pages. Foley was a well-known alcoholic, and his energy flagged repeatedly as he worked through the bill, getting closer and closer to noon, when the committee would have to recess. His mouth ran dry, he tripped over words. "He was not a fast reader," recalled Zelenko flatly.[61]

When he finally finished, at 11:52 A.M., Celler said a few words, then passed the floor to McCulloch. "It is important at this point not to yield for anything but a question, particularly not an amendment of any kind whatsoever," Katzenbach had instructed, and Celler did not. On cue, as soon as McCulloch finished, Rodino offered a motion to close the debate and move to a vote. Celler recognized him; several members offered to second the motion, and it went to a vote. The clock ticked; as soon as the noon bell rang to announce the opening of the House floor, the opposition forces would surely call a point of order to end the session. The clerk tore through the names, finishing just as the bell rang. The bill passed 20 votes to 14, with the Southern Democrats and a smattering of liberals in the minority.[62]

WHEN KENNEDY GOT the news a little while later, he cheered. But not everyone agreed with his jubilation. "Today's events are no cause for rejoicing but are a challenge to work to strengthen the bill," said Roy Wilkins. James Farmer, of CORE, called it "a slight improvement on the original Administration package, still it is not acceptable." Others were less welcoming. The *Washington Post* sent a reporter to a showing of *Lilies of the Field*, the Sidney Poitier star vehicle, at the Tivoli Theater in north central Washington, D.C. Several members of the black elite were there, and all had an opinion about the just-passed bill. "I don't think very much of the new bill," said Julius Hobson, a local civil rights activist. "I didn't think much of the original bill, and this is just a watered down version of that." Walter Reuther was incensed; he had the UAW issue a scathing analysis of the new draft. "The public accommodations section of the compromise bill draws a morally indefensible distinction between places that are and are not covered," it read. "Under its provisions, it would appear that an American citizen, simply because of color, could be denied the right to try on a suit or dress in a department store, get a haircut or beauty treatment or a shoeshine or go swimming or bowling." The harshest words came from the LCCR: "We deplore the actions of the administration and the Republican House leadership in securing the defeat of the Subcommittee bill on civil rights."[63]

The next day Kennedy went to Philadelphia to stump for Mayor James Tate, who was running a tough reelection campaign. But he found the streets half empty, save for protesters bearing signs with messages such as "Kennedy—why compromise on civil rights?" (The compromise was not the only reason for the protesters' ire: Tate had been vilified by the civil rights community for not fighting harder against job discrimination.)[64]

Kennedy's temporary woes were nothing compared with the more lasting scars left on Halleck. A few hours after the vote, Kennedy called the minority leader to thank him. "I got a lot of mad people up here," Halleck said. "A lot of guys bitching, I'm not sure they'll make me leader again, but I don't give a damn."[65]

Halleck's imperiousness won him few supporters among the liberals, while his leadership mistakes, compared with his support for a too-liberal bill, touched off a near civil war within the House GOP. On October 30, about sixty House Republicans met at a Washington hotel to hash out their grievances and propose a coup—this time against the minority leader himself. Halleck had ignored them, they groused; worse, he had embarrassed them by forcing his rank and file to support a draft version of the bill that many were already on the record opposing. Worse, though, was the fact that the Republican House leader was holding secret meetings with the White House, appearing to accede to Kennedy's every demand. How could they disagree with Democratic senator Richard Russell, who said that Halleck was now "adorned in the leather shirt and tasseled moccasins of the New Frontier"?[66]

A petition went around, calling for Halleck's resignation. Clarence Brown, the ranking minority member of the Rules Committee and no friend of Halleck, nevertheless saw the danger in setting off a war with the party leadership and urged calm. After a heated debate, Brown won the day, and the members filtered back to the Hill—though they were hardly pacified. A few days later one of them, reportedly Durward G. "Doc" Hall of Missouri, left a folded black umbrella on Halleck's desk, a pointed reference to that infamous compromiser Neville Chamberlain, who was seen carrying just such an accessory during his negotiations with Adolf Hitler before World War II. After the 1964 elections, Halleck was defeated by Gerald Ford in the minority leader vote, thanks undoubtedly to his actions on the civil rights bill.[67]

The bill was now ready to go to the Rules Committee, pending the final majority and minority reports. For reasons that can only be chalked up to Celler's poor control over his committee, the minority report was not ready until November 20, some three weeks after the bill passed. The minority reports, penned by Moore, Meader, and others, were a litany of purple-prosed complaints against both the bill and the suspect manner in which Celler had moved it to a vote. "Where it came from is a deep, dark secret," wrote Moore. "The bill reported was conceived in segregation, born in intolerance, and nurtured in discrimination."[68]

Though the minority reports would later provide rich fodder for the mailing campaigns of the Coordinating Committee for Fundamental American Freedoms and other anti-civil-rights groups, they made no difference to the course of the bill. With the reports filed, Celler could officially hand off the bill to the Rules Committee—and the next great challenge. Howard Smith, the Southern Democratic chair, was on record saying that the bill would take weeks, if not months, to consider fully—a bald attempt to delay its almost inevitable passage in the House.

While the committee dawdled, the lobbyists swarmed. All that month, armies of activists from across the LCCR had been trooping through the House office buildings, meeting with representatives and urging action on the bill. On November 13, dozens of members of the United Steel Workers of America came to town for a three-day stint; two days after they left, 315 college students and advisers from 86 campuses, jointly sponsored by Jewish, Protestant, and Catholic organizations, came for their own three-day campaign.[69]

The delay gave Halleck and Dirksen an opportunity to distance themselves from the administration. "There is a faltering effort now underway by apologists for the White House to blame the Congress because President Kennedy's legislative program is in a mess," Dirksen said at the next "Ev and Charlie Show," on November 21. "The president, who had promised major civil rights legislation in 1961, failed to live up to his promise... Then he expected Congress to act in a few months on a program he had delayed for two and one half years."[70]

The next day, President Kennedy was in Dallas. By early afternoon on November 22, 1963, the country had lost its thirty-fifth president. A few hours later, its thirty-sixth, Lyndon Baines Johnson, was sworn in—and a new chapter in the story of the civil rights bill began.

CHAPTER 5

"LET US CONTINUE"

LYNDON JOHNSON, THAT MOST ENIGMATIC of modern presidents, was never more of a puzzle than on the afternoon of November 22, 1963, when Air Force One touched down at Andrews Air Force Base bearing both him and the body of his slain predecessor. Kennedy had always seemed more than just a man; he was, for many Americans, the embodiment of an idea, a hope for the new. Even Richard Russell cried when he learned of the assassination.

Now that brash youthfulness had been replaced by a man most Americans knew only slightly, and then only by his taglines: the masterful Senate majority leader, the vice president chosen mainly as a sop to the South, the Dixie Democrat who had pushed through two civil rights bills. Had Kennedy gone with one of his other top choices in 1960—young New Frontier poster boys like Governor Orville Freeman of Minnesota or Senator Henry Jackson of Washington—the country might have been more at ease in its mourning. It would have continued in Kennedy's brisk footsteps. But no one knew where Johnson would take the country, because no one knew Johnson.

Almost no one, that is. Within the White House, and particularly within the vice president's inner circle, it was common, if often unspoken, knowledge that Johnson had been evolving rapidly, particularly on matters of race. Histories of the Johnson era often look to his senatorial experience for insight into his approach to the presidency. But while his time on Capitol Hill no doubt helped him in the White House, the differences between Senator and President Johnson are more telling than the similarities. It is the thousand days in between that explain the most. Lyndon Johnson's time in the vice president's office might be compared to the period a butterfly (or a moth) spends in a chrysalis. Before it, he was driven by the accumulation and deployment of power as its own end; as he sat in the vice president's office, or beside Kennedy at cabinet meetings, he thought deeply about what that power might be used *for*, what he would do with it if he ever had it. Not everyone around him noticed, but at critical moments—in his May 30 speech at Gettysburg, or in his comments to Sorensen and Schlei in June—one could glimpse a new Johnson, one passionately concerned about the welfare of the less privileged, the down-trodden, the oppressed, and one committed to throwing the entire weight of the federal government behind their uplift. Perhaps, as Johnson claimed in his memoir, that concern had always been there, ever since his days teaching poor Mexican American schoolchildren in Texas. But if it was, it had long been buried by ambition to scale the political heights, and it was only during his almost three years of static captivity—unable to legislate, unable to act—that he realized what the whole exercise was about in the first place.

Almost as soon as he landed at Andrews, Johnson began converting his pent-up energy into a kinetic frenzy. That night, after speaking by phone with former presidents Truman, Hoover, and Eisenhower, he decided to prepare an address to a joint session of Congress the following week. It would, above all, honor the fallen president—but it would also introduce the nation to his successor and assure them that he planned to follow Kennedy's agenda. And while the speech would range across the spectrum of President Kennedy's program, pride of place would go to the civil rights bill—as he told his aide Jack Valenti, "to get civil rights off its backside in the Congress and give it legs." Much of Johnson's first several months were shaped by his intense focus on the civil rights bill; it has even been suggested that one reason he opposed letting the FBI take the lead on the assassination investigation—instead letting Texas authorities, who had a jurisdictional claim over the case as a murder investiga-tion, take charge—was that he did not want anything to intimate the specter of federal power over states' rights while he was organizing for a massive push behind the bill.[1]

But while Johnson very much wanted to see the Civil Rights Act pass, even the bill was just a means to an end. Through the course of 1963, two lines of thinking had emerged within the pro-civil-rights forces inside the federal government. One, behind the Kennedys, believed that the issue was funda-mentally a question of political rights: give blacks the right to vote, the right to compete in the job market, the right to go to good schools, and equality will be realized. The other, which found its most forceful advocate in Lyndon Johnson, believed that political equality, though important, was inevitable, and that presidential and congressional energies were better spent on a wide-ranging, deep-pocketed program of material uplift, a second New Deal. But to get the political capital he needed to introduce such a plan, Johnson needed to shore up his base among the liberals. "I knew that if I didn't get out in front of this issue, they would get me. They'd throw up my background against me, they'd use it to prove that I was incapable of bringing unity to the land I loved so much," he said later. "I had to produce a civil rights bill that was even stronger than the one they'd have gotten if Kennedy had lived. Without this, I'd be dead before I could even begin."[2]

Over the weekend Johnson spoke with the congressional leadership, almost all of them in person, including his mentor and now, on civil rights, opponent, Senator Russell.

"Dick," he said, "I love you. I owe you. But I'm going to run over you if you challenge me or get in my way. I aim to pass the civil rights bill, only this time, Dick, there will be no caviling, no compromise, no falling back. This bill is going to pass."

Russell, who refused to call his old friend by anything besides his new title, replied, "You may do just that, Mr. President. Bu I am here to tell you that it will not only cost you the south, it will cost you the election."

"Dick, my old friend, if that's the price for this bill, then I will gladly pay it."[3]

Johnson also began reaching out to civil rights leaders: he asked Walter Reuther for ideas to put into his speech; he asked Roy Wilkins to meet with him at the White House the next week. "We're just beginning to fight," he told Whitney Young during a phone call on Sunday, November 24. The next day, he told King the same—and that he would push Congress to the wall to pass the items on Kennedy's agenda, including civil rights. "We just got to not let up on any of them and keep going," he said. "I'm going to ask the Congress Wednesday to just stay there until they pass them all. They won't do it. But we'll just keep them there next year until they do, and we just won't give up an inch."[4]

That night he talked on the phone with Hubert Humphrey from his mock French château home, known as the Elms, in Washington's hilly, forested Spring Valley neighborhood (it would be another decade before the Naval Observatory was designated the vice president's official residence). Humphrey had called to tell him about the defeat of a bill to block credits on sales behind the Iron Curtain. Johnson asked what the senator was doing for dinner.[5]

Humphrey, one of the hardest-working men in the Senate, declined Johnson's implicit invitation to dine with him, saying he had had a snack and needed to stay at the office.

"Well, come on over anyway and have something more to eat," Johnson said. "I want to talk to you."

When Humphrey arrived, he realized it was more than a social call: some of Johnson's closest aides, including Abe Fortas, Valenti, and Cliff Carter, were there, and over dinner—and into the next morning—the men edited the developing draft of Johnson's upcoming speech. Ted Sorensen had been working on it since Saturday, and Johnson had already gathered substantial input from a range of sources, from Reuther to Adlai Stevenson, on everything from jobs to the United Nations. But Johnson wanted these men, and Humphrey and Fortas in particular, to give it polish. Humphrey said it should be short and direct, and he suggested what became one of Johnson's most memorable lines: to answer Kennedy's inaugural call "Let us begin," Johnson should respond, "Let us continue." Humphrey and Fortas left around 2:30 A.M., and they worked on the draft for the next two days.[6]

DESPITE A FEW memorable addresses here and there through his career, Johnson was not much for speeches. So when he entered the House chambers on the evening of November 26, just a day after Kennedy's funeral, expectations for a great oration were not particularly high—and yet, paradoxically, both the audience in the Capitol and the millions of Americans watching on TV hoped desperately for a clear sign that, yes, everything was going to be all right.[7]

Johnson mounted the podium, expressionless behind his rimless glasses, peering out over the audience: the full complement of House and Senate members, the Supreme Court, the Joint Chiefs of Staff, the mayors of New York and Chicago. Robert Kennedy sat at the end of the front row, his body shrunken in mourning—"White with fatigue and grief, and he stared glassily ahead without a flicker of emotion," wrote Anthony Lewis in the *New York Times*.[8]

The president looked down at his speech, held in a black loose-leaf notebook, with text in large, spaced type and notes in between the lines. Just before he spoke, he looked up to the gallery, where his wife, Lady Bird, sat with Zephyr Wright, the family's longtime servant and the black woman whose daily humiliations under Jim Crow, Johnson often said, had inspired his pursuit of civil rights legislation.

Then, as if speaking directly to the grief-stricken attorney general, Johnson began. "All I have I would have given gladly not to be standing here today. The greatest leader of our time has been struck down by the foulest deed of our time."[9]

But he then immediately pivoted to the core of his speech, the point he would hammer again and again through the next several minutes. "Today John Fitzgerald Kennedy lives on in the immortal words and works that he left behind," he said. "No words are sad enough to express our sense of loss. No words are strong enough to express our determination to continue the thrust of America that he began."

And at the spear-tip of that thrust, he said, was civil rights. "Above all, the drama of equal rights for all Americans, whatever their race or color—these and other American dreams have been vitalized by his drive and by his dedication." The audience broke into a deafening roar. He went on to speak of the United Nations, military support for allies abroad, defense of a strong dollar—all of which were at the core of Kennedy's agenda, and all of which Johnson would continue. Kennedy, he said, had told America that its work would not be done "'in the first thousand days, nor in the life of this administration, nor even perhaps in our lifetimes on this planet. But let us begin.' Today," Johnson said, "in this moment of new resolve, I would say to all my fellow Americans, let us continue."

Johnson then turned to the civil rights bill itself, whose passage, he declared, would be a fitting tribute to its author. "No memorial oration or eulogy could more eloquently honor President Kennedy's memory than the earliest passage of the civil rights bill for which he fought so long. We have talked long enough in this country about equal rights. We have talked for one hundred years or more. It is time now to write the next chapter, and to write it in the books of law," Johnson said. "I urge you again, as I did in 1957 and again in 1960, to enact a civil rights law so that we can move forward to eliminate from this nation every trace of discrimination and oppression that is based upon race or color." As he spoke, he stuck out his chin, a point of physical pride, but he eschewed the finger-pointing and voice-raising that typified his stump speeches.

Johnson then ran through lesser items—the tax bill, the foreign aid bill— only to return, yet again, to civil rights. "The time has come for Americans of all races and creeds and political beliefs to understand and to respect one another."

And though he was interrupted by applause thirty-one times, no cheers were as loud as those that erupted each time he mentioned civil rights. "Everywhere you looked, people were crying," wrote the journalist Hugh Sidey.[10]

Johnson's genius was to tie the driving need for peace and tolerance in the wake of Kennedy's assassination to the push for racial progress. Though Kennedy's death had nothing to do with his push for civil rights, Johnson was able to link the two urges as part of the same whole—and to demand that achieving the former meant making progress on the latter. It was a theme he repeated less than twenty-four hours later, in his Thanksgiving Day address: "It is this work that I most want us to do: to banish rancor from our words and malice from our hearts; to close down the poison spring of hatred and intoler- ance and fanaticism; to perfect our unity north and south, east and west; to hasten the day when bias of race, religion, and region is no more; and to bring the day when our great energies and decencies and spirit will be free of the burdens that we have borne too long."[11]

The acclaim for Johnson's speech before Congress was overwhelming. The address "surprised even his admirers with its force, its eloquence, its mood of quiet confidence," wrote the *New York Times*. But the most surprised were the civil rights leaders who had long held a dim view of Johnson's commitment to the cause. Later that night Arnold Aronson of the LCCR sent Johnson a hastily compiled note full of praise. "At the conclusion, all of us were moved to applause," he wrote. "It was not alone because you called for swift enactment of civil rights legislation; but also because after the terrible violence of the past few days, it was reassuring to hear a voice speak of the need for tolerance and understanding." Dick Gregory, the black comedian and civil rights activist, quipped, "As soon as Lyndon Johnson finished his speech before Congress, twenty million of us unpacked."[12]

OVER THE HOLIDAY weekend Johnson continued to court civil rights leaders. That week Joe Rauh got a call from Kenneth O'Donnell to come to the White House and meet with Johnson. When he arrived, Johnson began entreating him with tough talk on winning civil rights, on pushing poverty programs— basically, the LCCR wish list. "I've got to laugh because it's so humorous," Rauh recalled. "There was the president I'd fought so long and hard talking to me and taking the attitude of 'it's very important, let's let bygones be bygones.' Over and over again he said, 'If I've done anything wrong in the past, I want you to know that's nothing now—we're going to work together.'"[13]

But it was one thing for Johnson to call for the bill's passage; it was another to actually do something about it. And at first, there was little Johnson could do besides play cheerleader and exhorter in chief. The bill was stuck in the House Rules Committee, which was led by the archsegregationist Howard W. "Judge" Smith of Virginia. Since taking control of the committee in 1955, the courtly representative had used its power over deciding which bills moved to the House floor to block virtually every piece of civil rights legislation. The bill seemed likely to face the same fate. "John Kennedy's bill was in real trouble when he died," said Rauh.[14]

Smith's delay tactics were part of the Southern Democrats' overall strategy for the bill. They realized that, especially with Kennedy's death, they had little chance of killing the bill outright. They had always leaned on public indifference and alliances with conservative Republicans to block bills in the past, but public sentiment and Capitol Hill politics were aligned too strongly, for once, in the other direction. Their best hope was to drag the bill into the next summer, when, they believed, increasing black militancy would create a backlash against the bill. Senator George Smathers, a moderate Southern Democrat and close friend of Johnson (and Kennedy), told the new president as much on December 29. "The more time that transpired between this talk about needing the civil rights bill, and the day that the civil rights bill was actually voted on, the stronger position the Southerners would be in."[15]

But inside Congress, work was under way to get the bill moving. For one thing, whereas in the past the House Republicans on the Rules Committee, who held the balance of power between the Southern and Northern Democrats, had joined with Smith to hold up civil rights bills, this time they made clear that their patience was thin. Clarence Brown, the ranking Republican on the committee and a recent convert to civil rights (thanks to an odd-fellows friendship with the NAACP's Clarence Mitchell), had said as much to Smith early on: after a short delay, if Smith did not let the bill go to the floor the Republicans would join with the Northern Democrats to force it out.[16]

Still, the Republicans and Northern Democrats could not agree on how to move the bill out of the committee—and each suspected the other of plotting to use the impasse to embarrass the other. Almost as soon as the bill arrived on Smith's desk, the Northern Democrats made it clear they would push for a discharge petition, a contentious procedure designed to force the hands of obstreperous committee chairmen. It begins with a member of a committee filing a motion with the clerk to, in the words of the House rules, "discharge the committee from further consideration of the bill" and move it to the House floor. Once a member files a discharge petition, it lies open on a table in the House chamber for members to sign; it goes into effect if a majority of the entire House signs it.[17]

But there are two complications regarding a discharge petition. For one, members can remove their names at any time—and often do. "If you started to approach" 218 names, said O'Brien, "all of a sudden you'd find names disappear." That meant that Republicans trying to court Southern Democrats but also keep their civil rights bona fides safe could sign the petition and thus claim to be for the bill at hand, but could also remove their signature if it looked as if the petition might be approved, thereby avoiding the wrath of Judge Smith.

Second, there is no time limit on how long a discharge petition can sit open—and as a result, the procedure itself, unless it has significant, immediate support, often has much less impact on the Rules Committee than its supporters hope. As the *Congressional Quarterly Weekly Report* noted at the time, discharge petitions are nearly impossible to win. Six had been filed in the 87th Congress, from 1961 to 1963, and not a single one passed.[18]

Still, both Johnson and the House Democratic leadership decided to go ahead with the discharge petition strategy. On November 29 the president got on the phone with David McDonald, the United Steelworkers president, who had just brought scores of his men to town to lobby Congress on the bill.

Johnson told him he needed the union men back on the Hill, this time to push Midwestern representatives to sign a discharge petition. "See that every man that you've got is up there next week talking to them—and I don't want it coming from me," he said. That same day, he urged A. Philip Randolph to focus his civil rights colleagues on a petition as the only way to make Republicans move off the fence. Civil rights representatives needed to tell the House Republicans that they were either with the bill or against it—and that they would pay at the polls for their opposition.[19]

On the morning of December 4, Johnson, who was living at the Elms to give the Kennedys time to leave the White House, had an aide find out where George Meany lived; he then had his limousine driver swing by the labor leader's house, and on the ride in to downtown Washington the president urged him to bring as much pressure as possible on House members to sign the discharge petition.[20]

The next morning he did the same with Charles Halleck, taking him to the White House for a breakfast of melon, fried eggs, coffee, and bacon—thick-cut bacon, Halleck noted later, "which I guess Lyndon knew a fellow from Indiana would like." All the while, Johnson was pressing Halleck on the discharge petition, asking him to release his members to sign it, or at the very least to agree to hold the House in session after the beginning of the congressional Christmas break on December 14. Halleck refused both demands. Then Johnson brought up the possibility of placing a $50 million NASA electronics center at Indiana's Purdue University. Halleck, who loved congressional pork as much as thick-cut bacon, said in that case he would think about it.[21]

The president moved into the White House on December 7 with a green-topped desk, four television sets, a bust of Franklin Roosevelt, and an eighteen-button phone—which he immediately put to heavy use. Two days later, Celler filed the motion to discharge the bill from the Rules Committee (Johnson had wanted Carl Albert to file the petition, but the majority leader demurred). Larry O'Brien recalled a meeting with Johnson soon after Celler's filing in which he told the president he had a list of 22 members he thought were vulnerable to pressure on the discharge petition. "He wanted to know who the 22 were, so I pulled it out of the inside pocket of my jacket and showed it to him," O'Brien said. "He promptly called the White House operator, the names were all given and the directive was to get them on the phone promptly wherever they could locate them. I don't know whether he went through the whole 22, but I suspect he did."[22]

Almost immediately, 131 members signed the petition—but the count stayed around there for the next several weeks, creeping up by just a couple of dozen by year's end. "That ain't many!" shouted Johnson when Albert called him on the night of the ninth to report the signatures. The signatories were almost all liberals and administration allies, but without sixty or so Republicans, the petition was worthless. Albert told Johnson he expected no more than twenty Republicans to sign.[23]

Johnson meant well, of course, but he was pursuing precisely the wrong tactics. Midwestern Republicans were unresponsive to big-city labor and civil rights lobbyists; if anything, these small-town men resented the implication that they should vote on anything other than their constituents' interests. That was why the only effective means of getting to such representatives was through the clergy—a fact, in late 1963, of which Johnson still seemed unaware. But it was also growing increasingly clear that the discharge petition was a losing tactic.

To be fair, Johnson was not alone in trying, and failing, to ratchet up the signatures (nor was civil rights his sole concern; he was also wooing Senator Harry Flood Byrd, the chair of the Finance Committee, to get the stalled tax bill moving). Just before Thanksgiving the NAACP sent a memo to all its branches urging them to visit their congressmen over the break and demand that they help move the bill forward. "Every name added to the petition puts pressure upon [Smith] to honor his commitment and hold hearings reasonable soon," the LCCR wrote in its December 16 newsletter. "Every name puts pressure on the other members of the Rules Committee to see that he does not delay consideration on the bill unduly."[24]

Johnson also took pains to hedge his bets. Though he publicly supported the civil rights bill, he did everything he could to hide his involvement in the politicking around its passage. Early on, he told O'Brien to make sure that Robert Kennedy personally agreed with his tactics, and he made it clear to the attorney general that he expected the Department of Justice to be the public face of the executive branch push. "I'll do on the bill what you think is best," Johnson told him. "We won't do anything that you don't want to do on the legislation, and I'll do everything you want me to do in order to obtain passage." This merely sounded deferential; in fact, Johnson wanted to make sure, if the bill failed, that the blame fell as far away from the Oval Office as possible—and, conveniently, as close to his archrival Robert Kennedy as he could arrange it. This is not to say that Johnson did not believe in civil rights as a goal—only that he was more skeptical of its chances than he let on.[25]

Indeed, contrary to what many of his biographers have claimed, Johnson's contribution to the bill's success was largely symbolic. Though he worked the phones and pressed the flesh in its favor, there is little evidence that he did much to sway many votes. His main focus was giving speeches and press conferences in which he emphasized his desire for the bill to survive Congress intact. And that symbolism was critical. It mattered immensely that Johnson placed civil rights at the beginning and end of his November 27 speech to Congress. It did not get the bill out of the Rules Committee, but it underlined the moral case for it and placed behind that case the immense prestige of the presidency—which, in the days after it was consecrated by Kennedy's death, had never been higher. Supporters of the bill could take risks, knowing that the will of the president was behind them.

Johnson repeated his commitment to the top civil rights leaders when they sat down with him at the White House—the men on a couch, the president in a rocking chair opposite and ever so slightly higher than his guests. James Farmer asked him why he supported civil rights, and Johnson reeled out his oft-told tale of the time he asked his black maid Zephyr Wright and her husband to drive his car from Washington back to Texas. As they traveled through the South, they found it hard just to locate a place to eat, or a hotel room for the night. That is why he wanted the bill.[26]

Johnson then told them about the present state of the legislation. "He said he was running into great difficulty," said Farmer, "but he's got to get that bill through, he's got to get it through, it's of vital importance." During the meeting he made a point of taking a call from Soapy Williams, one of the most high-profile white civil rights supporters in the president's inner circle. The men came away impressed. "LBJ is a man of great ego and great power," King told some of his aides after the meeting. "He is a pragmatist and a man of pragmatic compassion. It just may be that he's going to go where John Kennedy couldn't."[27]

WHILE JOHNSON AND the LCCR worked their separate campaigns to get the Rules Committee moving, the Committee for Fundamental American Freedoms was also shifting its operation into high gear. The committee had already decided to keep its powder dry on the House, where the liberal majority made passage almost inevitable, and instead focus on softening up public sentiment for the coming showdown in the Senate. In the October 12 issue of *National Review*, James Kilpatrick wrote an article that provided the basic intellectual playbook for the Southern Democrats' opposition to the bill; almost every argument that had or would emanate from the mouths of the anti-civil-rights legislators was expressed in his relatively brief piece. He attacked both the individual planks—Title I was an unnecessary infringement on states' rights to control their own elections, Title II was an invasion of private property, Title VI gave the president dictatorial power over the federal budget—and made general claims about the bill's appropriateness. Some were anodyne: "In a calmer climate," he wrote, "the bill's defects would be readily apparent." Others relied on painfully tortured logic. Discrimination is not bad, he claimed, because it happens all the time: "When a Virginian buys cigarettes made in Virginia, for that reason alone, as opposed to cigarettes made in Kentucky or North Carolina, he discriminates," Kilpatrick wrote. "Every one of these acts of 'discrimination' imposes some burden upon interstate commerce."[28]

By December, John Satterfield had secured funding for the committee into 1964, and he was lining up senators to deliver targeted speeches at the outset of the filibuster, a set of opening salvos that he hoped would knock the bill off its momentum. Lister Hill, an Alabama senator with a strong pro-labor record, had agreed to give a speech about how the bill would demolish union hiring and seniority practices. "Things are rocking along very well," Satterfield wrote in a December 3 letter to William Loeb.[29]

It did not help that dissension was growing among the fragile bipartisan coalition that had moved the bill out of the Judiciary Committee. The Republicans were afraid that the Democrats were maneuvering to embarrass them over the discharge petition, and that they would look like obstructionists if they did not do something to get the bill out of the Rules Committee. On December 11, Republicans on the House floor announced they would call up the civil rights bill using the Calendar Wednesday procedure, a rarely used—and even more rarely successful—process by which the House gives each committee the right to bring a bill directly to the floor without going through the Rules Committee; the bill is then debated for two hours and then voted on.[30]

Though the procedure is designed specifically to let committees bypass the Rules Committee, it is considered a nuclear option, and a Pyrrhic victory for a bill—with only two hours for debate, there is little opportunity to organize votes or win over wavering representatives. And it was not a practical option for the civil rights bill, since the committees would be called alphabetically, and the Judiciary Committee was the tenth out of eighteen—giving the Southern Democratic chairmen of preceding committees ample opportunity to hem and haw and draw out the procedure until the day ended.

Still, the Republicans announced their intention that morning to go ahead with the maneuver—if nothing else, it would force the Democrats, who were committed to the discharge petition route, to go on record opposing a maneuver to save the bill. "The Republicans who developed this civil rights bill" were now being shut out of managing it, charged John Lindsay on the House floor. The Democrats' position was "political demagoguery at its lowest level," said New York's Frank J. Becker and Washington's Thomas M. Pelly. A heated debate erupted. Richard Bolling, the liberal Judiciary Committee member from Missouri, denied that the Democrats were playing politics; rather, it was a pragmatic question. "Calendar Wednesday is an impractical, if not impossible way to consider the civil rights bill," he said. But it was also very easy for the Republicans to initiate: because Calendar Wednesday was a regular part of the House daily schedule, but was almost always done away with by unanimous agreement of all the members present, all the Republicans had to do was refuse to consent to skip that part of the agenda. To head off such a move, Albert offered a motion to adjourn the House early, which passed 214 to 166 on largely party lines. That may have saved the Democrats from voting against the civil rights bill, but it also deepened partisan hostility at a crucial time. And while McCulloch later insisted that he "did not think the partisan sparring would endanger the bill's bipartisan support," the discharge petition count remained frozen at 150.[31]

The year ended with no real public sense of when the bill would finally get moving. But privately, Clarence Brown had been slowly increasing pressure on Smith to act. Brown, like McCulloch and Halleck, was an unlikely civil rights champion. He was an acolyte of the isolationist, archconservative Ohio senator Robert Taft, and he tended to work closely with Smith to stymie liberal legislation that came through the Rules Committee. Like McCulloch, he was born in rural Ohio, and worked there until entering politics. And like McCulloch, as a young boy he had drunk deeply from the Midwestern abolitionist tradition; born less than thirty years after the end of the Civil War, it is likely that he knew more than a few proud Ohio veterans and antislavery activists. Brown's district was also home to a segment of the Underground Railroad, and later to Wilberforce University and Central State University, both historically black institutions. Finally, again like McCulloch, Brown spent time as a young man in the South—in his case, as a college student at Washington and Lee University in Lexington, Virginia. The town and the university were steeped in Southern history: Robert E. Lee had been president of the institution after the Civil War; across a broad parade ground stood the Virginia Military Institute, where many Confederate Army leaders had studied or taught, including its most famous professor, Thomas J. "Stonewall" Jackson. There can be little doubt that Brown saw Jim Crow racism up close, and like McCulloch was marked by it for life.[32]

As soon as the bill cleared the Judiciary Committee, Brown told Smith that he expected the Rules Committee to take it up in a timely manner. At first, Smith was diffident, though he knew well that without Brown and the conservative Republican committee members he controlled, he could not hold off consideration forever. Brown, in turn, was getting pressure from

Halleck and McCulloch. On December 4, five days before Celler introduced the petition, Brown met with Smith and told him that "the heat was getting so great"—and he made clear that with the committee's non-Southern Democrats lined up in favor of the bill, it would take just two or three Republicans to form a pro-bill majority that would, under the House rules, be able to force Smith to move the bill forward. "I don't want to run over you, but . . ." Brown told the chairman.[33]

In fact, underneath the partisan contretemps, Brown, Halleck, and McCulloch were working closely with John McCormack and Albert on a bipartisan plan to rescue the bill from Smith. Without informing Johnson, the Democrats agreed not to push the discharge petition too strongly, and it is telling that the signature of neither Democrat ever appeared on the sheet. In exchange, Brown said he would give Smith until the beginning of the next session of Congress to open hearings, and if he still refused, Brown and his fellow Rules Committee Republicans would join the liberals in a coup against the chairman to send the bill to the floor. Johnson must have eventually signed on to the deal, because, as Robert Loevy, a political scientist who was serving a Senate fellowship in the office of California's Thomas Kuchel that year, observed, White House pressure for a discharge petition petered out by the end of the year.[34]

But if the pressure in Washington was waning, a new, unprecedented source of pressure was waxing, far from the capital. In South Bend, Des Moines, Bismarck, and countless other Midwestern cities and towns, Protestant, Catholic, and Jewish religious leaders were organizing their own campaigns for progress on the bill. The National Council of Churches, under J. Irwin Miller, led the way. Since the council's September conference in Lincoln, Nebraska, hundreds and then thousands of civil-rights-minded church people had canvassed the region, delivering sermons, leading letter-writing campaigns, visiting congressmen, and organizing rallies, all in places where the sight of black skin was a rare occurrence and civil rights was a faraway concern. Much of the organizing was done by Victor Reuther, Walter Reuther's brother, who worked for the UAW as well as the NCC's Commission on Religion and Race. Reuther was a union man through and through, but he also understood that unions had little influence in the Republican Midwest—and yet that was where the survival of the bill might well be decided. Reuther organized the Lincoln conference, and in October he created a program in which teams of activists went from town to town drumming up support behind the bill, "like circuit-riding Methodist evangelists," in the words of historian James F. Findlay.[35]

As the year came to an end, the campaigns became increasingly sophisticated, leveraging the broad intelligence network provided by the LCCR's

constituent organizations. Lists of congressmen with their religious affilia-
tions and even home churches and synagogues circulated widely. The NCC
maintained an extensive reporting system, so that any time a member had
contact with a representative or senator, the information gleaned—would he
back the discharge petition, would he vote for the bill—could be analyzed
and used to fine-tune lobbying efforts. A half dozen religious groups, from
the Friends Committee for National Legislation—the lobbying arm of the
Quakers—to B'nai B'rith, sent regular newsletters with detailed, updated
information for letter writers and rally participants. One particular tactic
worked wonders: as soon as a representative boarded a plane at National
Airport in Washington to go back home, word would go out—oftentimes
from a sympathetic member of the representative's own staff—to his minister
or priest, who would then just happen to be at the airport when the representative landed. The minister would strike up a conversation, and quickly hit
on the pressing matter of civil rights. Miller had his own spin on that tactic:
whenever he was leaving Washington on his private plane, he would offer a
few Midwestern Republicans a flight home—and then lobby them relentlessly, twenty thousand feet in the air.[36]

Of particular effectiveness was James Hamilton's contact list of five thousand influential, activist church figures across the Midwest. He regularly sent
them detailed updates about the bill's progress; he also sent "immediate action
memos" to a smaller group of ministers when he needed, say, a flurry of phone
calls to a key representative just before a big vote.[37]

In the end, the church pressure worked where unions and civil rights
groups—and Democratic presidents—could not. Republican representatives
returned from their Christmas vacations complaining of the near-constant
visits, letters, and phone calls from their ministers and fellow congregants
urging them to support the bill. Nor could they ignore two pressing facts:
nearly two thirds of all Americans supported the bill, and nearly four out of
five approved of the job President Johnson was doing. The case for obstructing
civil rights legislation had never been thinner, and the case for getting it out of
the Rules Committee—if not voting for it—had never been stronger.[38]

As early as December 5, the day after Brown had first confronted Judge
Smith over the bill, Smith had said in a formal statement that while he thought
the bill was a monstrosity, "I realize the great national interest that has been
aroused on both sides of this controversy and it is my intent, with the approval
of the majority of the Rules Committee, to hold hearings on this bill reasona-
bly soon in January."[39]

Two weeks later, he went even further, virtually conceding defeat. "I know
something about the facts of life around here," he said, "and I know that many

members want this bill considered. They could take it away from me, and they can do it any minute they want to." Smith was not giving up, but he was recognizing reality: in the present political environment, he could slow the bill for a few weeks, but there was nothing he could do to stop it. As he told Robert Kimball in January, "You'll have to run over us; we know that, and we know we'll be run over."[40]

ON THE MORNING of January 9, 1964, Chairman Smith gaveled to order the Rules Committee hearings on the civil rights bill. It was a cold yet humid morning—a particularly enervating climatic combination that Washington seems to excel in—and some fifty reporters, along with assorted onlookers and scores of House staff, crammed sweatily into the forty-five-seat Room H-313. The room was at the northern end of the Cannon House Office Building, a stunning neoclassical pile designed by Carrère and Hastings, the same firm that built the New York Public Library. Out its windows, behind Smith, the audience could see the equally imposing Library of Congress.[41]

The room felt like a sauna, but the real heat was on Smith: the night before, Johnson, in his first State of the Union address, had reiterated his call for rapid action on the bill. "Let this session of Congress be known as the session which did more for civil rights than the last hundred sessions combined," the president had said at the very beginning of the speech.[42]

And yet Smith was not going to let the bill roll through his committee. He had opened the hearings as promised, but he did not say how long he would go before closing them. This was the man who had retreated to his 170-acre northern Virginia farm to delay hearings on the 1957 civil rights bill. He claimed a barn had caught fire, prompting Speaker Sam Rayburn to quip, "I knew Howard Smith would do most anything to block a civil rights bill, but I never knew would resort to arson." If anyone expected the bill to now sail through the Rules Committee, they did not know Howard Smith.[43]

Smith called Celler as his first witness. "Mr. Celler," he said, "there is a rumor around that you want to get a rule of H.R. 7152."[44]

"I confirm the rumor," Celler replied.

Smith, along with Brown, proceeded to grill Celler relentlessly for two days. It was not the Brooklynite's finest hour. He offered vague, contradictory answers to questions about arcane but important details of the bill. He denied, against all evidence, supporting the parts of the subcommittee bill "which I felt were too drastic," adding, "I personally did not agree to all terms of the subcommittee bill." At one point Katherine St. George, a Republican from New York, leaned over to Smith and said, "You've got him pretty well tangled up."

"I didn't tangle him up," Smith replied. "He tangled himself up. He just doesn't know what's in this bill."[45]

Celler's efforts at sympathy for the South came off as patronizing and careless. "I am not unaware of the price that must be paid for the advancement and the culmination of the cause of civil rights," he said. "It is easy for myself and other Northerners to demand that some change their mores, their customs, wrench away from tradition, but it is like asking one to sever hand from wrist. I wish, truly, it could be otherwise, but unfortunately it cannot. The die is cast."[46]

Most of Smith's and Brown's questions focused on the bill's last few days before Celler's committee. When pushed to explain why he and the Justice Department only sent copies of their final, compromise bill to their allies on the committee the night before the vote, Celler replied with mock amazement—there was no need to do so earlier, since the final version, he said, was substantively the same as the subcommittee draft. "The bill that was reported by the subcommittee practically contained every single subject that is in the bill before you now," he said, "so that if anyone says they had not seen that bill or its terms or its phrases, it is beyond my comprehension how they could say that."

Smith refused to let Celler's audacious historical revisionism stand. "I am astonished if the parliamentarian told you that you could railroad a bill through without giving members the opportunity to discuss it," he said.

Celler feigned offense. "That is a rather unusual word and sort of taboo—'railroad'—we do not railroad anything through."

"Would you prefer strong-arm?" Smith replied.[47]

Later Smith hit Celler with a surprise punch. "I have just received a letter this morning, which I was going to bring to your attention later, from the National Women's Party," he said. "They want to know why you did not include sex in this bill. Why did you not?"

Before Celler could respond, St. George chortled, "If I may be facetious, is that"—sex, that is—"another dim memory, Mr. Celler?"[48]

But Celler, who was never one to pass up a chance at shtick, played along. "It reminds me of the Frenchman who was going up the Empire State Building in New York. Somebody said, 'How do you like it?' He said, 'Well it reminds me of sex.' 'Reminds you of sex? Why is that?' The answer was, 'Everything reminds me of sex.'"

Smith was in no mood to play along. Despite his segregationist beliefs, he was also a longtime advocate for women's rights. He had sponsored repeated efforts to pass an Equal Rights Amendment, and he was a close friend of Alice Paul, the founder of the National Women's Party (NWP). "You did not answer my question," he told Celler.

"This is a civil rights bill," Celler said.

"Don't women have civil rights?"

"They have lots of them. They are supermen."

Smith pushed harder. "I have not found out yet why you did not put sex in."

"Do you want to put it in, Mr. Chairman?" Celler replied.

"I think I will offer an amendment. The National Women's Party were serious about it."

After Celler came McCulloch. Smith tried to pin him down on the bill's final few hours, to admit that it had, indeed, been railroaded. How had he managed to read the bill so quickly? Smith asked. "Because of my receding red hair," McCulloch joked. But he was just parrying; he had no intention of selling out Celler. "Really, I said so much about every item on this bill for months and months, more time for explanation would have been unnecessary." McCulloch's performance over the next day and a half was everything Celler's was not: serious, clear, impassioned, witty when necessary but always tacking back to the heart of the bill. "My interest in civil rights legislation is to give a governmental urge and help to a thing that is necessary if we are not indefinitely to have two classes in this country."[49]

McCulloch could hardly imagine it, he said, "if, by reason of my red hair, my darling daughter could not go to the municipal swimming pool in my town if she wanted to. I have great feelings, strong feelings, against any system which would prohibit my son from playing softball, basketball, or skiing in the public park which is financed by me as a negro."

Of all the obvious divisions between the supporters and opponents of the bill—race, region, religion—none was as stark as the mark of empathy. Men as different as McCulloch and Celler, who disagreed on almost everything else, still managed to come together behind government action on civil rights because they had the moral imagination to see themselves in the place of a black American. Those who did not have that capacity, or refused to exercise it, managed to utter such inanities as "If I were cutting corns, I would want to know whose feet I would have to be monkeying around with. I would want to know whether they smelled good or bad"—as Mississippi representative William Colmer said during the hearing.[50]

With Celler and McCulloch out of the way, Smith turned to the hearing's main event: more than a week of testimony from Southern Democratic representatives lambasting the bill, the Judiciary Committee, the Kennedy administration, and the civil rights movement itself. The speeches were mostly rehashes of the Southern Democrats' arguments from the summer—the 1883 Civil Rights Cases prevented the use of the Equal Protection Clause to bar discrimination; the states had the right to run their own elections—along with

Children being sprayed with fire hoses while demonstrating for civil rights in Birmingham, May 4, 1963. Photo by John Duprey/*New York Daily News* Archive via Getty Images

Alabama governor George Wallace confronts Deputy Attorney General Nicholas deB. Katzenbach at the University of Alabama, June 11, 1963. Library of Congress

President John F. Kennedy and Vice President Lyndon B. Johnson at a meeting on civil rights legislation with American business leaders, June 4, 1963. JOHN F. KENNEDY PRESIDENTIAL LIBRARY AND MUSEUM

President Kennedy discussing his forthcoming civil rights legislation in a nationally televised address, June 11, 1963. JOHN F. KENNEDY PRESIDENTIAL LIBRARY AND MUSEUM

Protesters demanding an end to employment discrimination at the March on Washington, August 28, 1963. LIBRARY OF CONGRESS

Leaders of the March on Washington meeting with President Kennedy after the event. From left: Whitney Young, Martin Luther King Jr., John Lewis, Joachim Prinz, Matthew Ahmann, A. Philip Randolph, Kennedy, Walter Reuther, Lyndon B. Johnson, Roy Wilkins. LIBRARY OF CONGRESS

Attorney General Robert F. Kennedy and Representative Emanuel Celler (N.Y.) during Kennedy's October 16, 1963, testimony on the Civil Rights Act before the House Judiciary Committee. ROGERS PHOTO ARCHIVE

President Johnson addresses a joint session of Congress on November 27, 1963. Behind him are House Speaker John McCormack (Mass.) and Senator Carl Hayden (Ariz.), the president pro tempore of the Senate. AP Photo

President Johnson meeting with civil rights leaders on January 18, 1964. From left: Martin Luther King Jr., Johnson, Whitney Young, James Farmer. LYNDON B. JOHNSON PRESIDENTIAL LIBRARY

Southern senators meet to discuss their historic filibuster against the Civil Rights Act. From left: Sam Ervin (N.C.), James Eastland (Miss.), John Stennis (Miss.), obscured, obscured, Richard Russell (Ga.), Spessard Holland (Fla.), Russell Long (La.), Allen Ellender (La.), Willis Robertson (Va.), Strom Thurmond (S.C.). TED RUSSELL/TIME & LIFE PICTURES/GETTY IMAGES

Theological students stand vigil in support of the Civil Rights Act in front of the Lincoln Memorial. Francis Miller/Time & Life Pictures/Getty Images

A meeting in a Denver church to discuss local activism in support of the Civil Rights Act, March 10, 1964. Meetings like this were common across the Midwest that year. Photo by George Crouter/ The Denver Post via Getty Images

Senators Mike Mansfield (Mont.) and Everett Dirksen (Ill.) during the Civil Rights Act filibuster.

Pro–civil rights senators celebrate the defeat of the Southern filibuster, June 10, 1964. From left: Kenneth Keating (N.Y.), Clifford Case (N.Y.), Everett Dirksen (Ill.), Jacob Javits (N.Y.), Leverett Saltonstall (Mass.), John Pastore (R.I.), Hubert Humphrey (Minn.), Warren Magnuson (Wash.), Hugh Scott (Penn.).

President Johnson signs the Civil Rights Act as senators and civil rights leaders look on, July 2, 1964. LYNDON B. JOHNSON PRESIDENTIAL LIBRARY

Some businesses, like Lester Maddox's cafeteria in Atlanta, closed shop rather than integrate after the passage of the Civil Rights Act, but most acquiesced quietly. ROGERS PHOTO ARCHIVE

money for better schools, money for better housing, money for job training, money for community development. The president "made it very clear that he feels the fight on poverty and illiteracy is a vital part of the fight on discrimination," said Farmer after the meeting.[53]

But Johnson also felt that too much pressure from the outside could derail the bill. On January 21, Johnson called Clarence Mitchell and Joe Rauh to the White House. He told them that he stood by his word from November and would continue to push for the civil rights bill without weakening amendments—but without any strengthening amendments, either. Katzenbach, he explained, had devised a precise but risky strategy that depended on keeping the bill as intact as possible, and changes in either direction would kill it. Surprisingly, Mitchell and Rauh agreed, and they told their LCCR colleagues to hold off pressing for a stronger bill.[54]

At the same time, the president renewed his pressure on Halleck to get the bill moving. Newspapers were reporting that even though the hearings had started, the timetable for the bill to reach the floor had slipped from early February to sometime in March. Some two dozen Southern Democrats were still scheduled to testify, and Smith was limiting sessions to just three days a week. And so, on January 18, with the discharge petition stuck at 178 signatures, Johnson called the minority leader into his office. The bill needed to get to the House floor soon, for Halleck's own sake. "If I were you, Charlie," he said, "I wouldn't dare . . . go out and try to make a Lincoln Birthday speech; they'll laugh you out of the goddamned park when Howard Smith's got his foot on Lincoln's neck." Johnson also reiterated his promise to try to land a science center at Purdue; with Halleck still there in the room he called James Webb, the NASA administrator, to see what could be done.[55]

It is unclear whether Johnson's pressure on Halleck had any effect, or whether it was Brown getting tired of Smith's antics, but over the next few days rumors began to circulate that Rules Committee Republicans were "increasingly restive," as the *New York Times* reported, and were working with Northern Democrats on a plan to take over control of the committee from Smith. At the same time, Speaker McCormack began his own pressure campaign, telling Smith that he wanted the bill out by the end of the month. And, of course, Halleck did not need Johnson to tell him about the importance of getting the bill out of the House before the Lincoln Day holiday, when Republicans traditionally headed home to trumpet their party's position on civil rights.[56]

The legislative agenda was not the only thing on Johnson's mind; the president was at the same time fighting off a nagging scandal involving Bobby Baker, a former protégé who had been named secretary of the Senate while Johnson was majority leader. Among other things, Johnson had taught him new attacks on the FEPC. They seemed to compete over who could draw the most grandiose, frightening caricatures of the bill. Representative William Tuck of Virginia claimed that "the right of homeowners to freely build, occupy, rent, lease, or sell their homes is destroyed under Title VI." (He also said, "We have lived in peace and harmony between the races for a period of more than 300 years, more than any other place in the Western hemisphere.") Not to be outdone, Alabama's George Huddleston Jr. said, "If this is a watered down version of the subcommittee's civil rights bill, as the chairman of the full committee has said, the water was saturated with hemlock." But the best line of the hearing was uttered by John Dowdy of Texas. Attacking the speed and support with which the bill had moved through the full Judiciary Committee, he said, "If you ran a skunk across the floor and had 'civil rights' written on the side of it, it would be the thing to vote for because it is called civil rights."[51]

WHILE THE RULES COMMITTEE prattled, Lyndon Johnson was doing his best to clear a path for the bill once it left the House. His first task was to get the tax cut bill out of the Senate Finance Committee, where it had been stalled by its chairman, Harry Byrd of Virginia. Byrd was a segregationist and enemy of the bill, but he was also a budget hawk. He held up the tax bill in part to derail the civil rights bill, but also to win spending concessions from the president. On December 4, Byrd had told Johnson that he would release the tax cut bill if the White House could trim its upcoming budget to $100 billion. Johnson then spent the next several weeks driving his advisers and budget experts to trim spending wherever they could.[52]

Johnson's efforts on the tax cut were not solely to benefit the civil rights bill. He needed to prove he could carry on Kennedy's legislative torch, he needed a quick win in Congress to solidify his political capital, and he believed, as Kennedy did, that the cut really would provide a shot in the arm to the economy. But all those things, including the tax cut—and even, in some ways, the civil rights bill itself—were but a prelude to Johnson's real goal: a massive antipoverty program. Hints of that vision began to dribble out around the first of the new year; even as Johnson was promising Byrd that government efficiency was of paramount importance, he was telling George Meany and Walter Reuther that the budget savings would go to new and enlarged social programs.

Then, on January 18, he summoned King, Wilkins, Young, and Farmer—all of whom he had kept in close touch with over the holidays—to the White House for a morning meeting. But instead of discussing the civil rights bill, Johnson unveiled a new project: a "war on poverty," one that would aim billions in federal dollars at the entire spectrum of the nation's social ills:

the importance of precise vote counting among senators. After Johnson left for the vice presidency, Baker had held the same position under Mike Mansfield, who followed Baker's advice closely. But in early October 1963 Baker resigned under a cloud of ethics charges stemming from his involvement with a series of companies that appeared to have benefited from government kickbacks. And while none of the specific accusations related to Baker's time working for Johnson, the Capitol Hill rumor mill declared the president guilty by association, and his enemies in the Senate began to circle, speculating about investigatory hearings to be held that spring.[57]

ON JANUARY 22, Richard Bolling informed Smith that the end was nigh: if he did not conclude the hearings within a week, a bipartisan group of representatives would take over the committee. The next day, after a closed-door meeting by the panel, Smith announced that he would indeed bring things to a close by January 30. "I've been around a long time," said the eighty-year-old chairman, "and I recognize the facts of life, and one of the facts of life is that this bill is going to the floor, and that it is going soon." Later that day, he announced the terms and schedule for the House debate, should his committee pass the bill. The House would take up the bill on January 31 and finish by February 11, just in time for the Lincoln Day recess. When he was finished, Clarence Brown congratulated him. "You have done everything, Mr. Chairman, which you have stated you would do."[58]

At noon on January 31, 1964, the Senate chaplain, Bernard Braskamp, opened the House debate on the civil rights bill with a short invocation. "As we have therefore opportunity, let us do good unto all men," he said, quoting from Galatians 6:10. Carl Albert then called quorum, and three short bells pealed through the House offices. As the members trickled in, the elaborate preliminary steps to get the debate going began. First, the House had to pass a resolution accepting the Rules Committee's guidelines for the debate—in this case, there would be ten hours of debate, with each member limited to five minutes of speech time.[59]

Moreover, the bill would be considered by the "Committee of the Whole," a common procedure whenever the House debates a bill. Though the composition of the House and the Committee of the Whole are the same, the latter operates under different rules: most importantly, there are no recorded votes, and no one in the galleries is allowed to take notes. The procedure originated in medieval England, and was used whenever Parliament wanted to discuss matters away from the king's purview—which is why, as part of the procedure, the ceremonial mace, a symbol of the executive branch, is removed. That was also why, after Braskamp's invocation, Speaker McCormack, who had authority over the entire House but not its committees, stepped down from the leadership dais, and Eugene Keogh, a New York Democrat, took his place.[60]

By the numbers, the debate seemed like a forgone conclusion: there were only a hundred or so reliable Southern Democratic votes, and as long as the Republican leadership stuck with the bill, they would combine with the unified Northern Democrats to produce an overwhelming affirmative vote. But there were still risks. In a memo to Celler on January 28, Judiciary Committee counsel Foley raised the possibility that the Southern Democrats could try to send the bill back to the Judiciary Committee—or another committee altogether—on procedural grounds. "The opponents of the bill will argue that the bill providing for an FEPC should have been referred to the Committee on Education and Labor, which had already reported a similar proposal." There were also any number of weakening amendments that opponents could bring up for a vote; all they had to do was wait for a moment when most of the bill's supporters were off the floor. And since individual votes were unrecorded, the Southern Democrats could also sway wavering supporters—say, people who were voting yes simply because Halleck told them to—to take a swipe at the bill. For such unrecorded, so-called teller votes, all members had to do was mark "yea" or "nay" on a card, then take it to a clerk at the back of the chamber. "It was easy for a congressman to slip into the line supporting a crippling amendment without being held responsible," recalled Katzenbach. "To keep the bill intact required votes, and that meant people one could count on into the small hours of the morning."[61]

With such risks in mind, Katzenbach and his team girded for battle. First, he had David Filvaroff and his drafting team compile a thick loose-leaf binder of information on the history and legal basis of each title. The "green book," as it was called, then went out to each friendly representative. At over a hundred pages it was incredibly thorough, and within days requests for copies of the book began arriving from outside groups, not just in Washington but around the country—so many that the department, which understood the benefit of having such a resource spread as widely as possible but was also quickly running out of copies, had to start rationing them. Filvaroff and his staff also took over a coat-closet-size office just off the chamber floor, where they provided technical assistance on the finer points of the bill to members and their staffs.[62]

To keep an eye on the proceedings, Katzenbach also set up a duty roster of Justice Department lawyers to sit in the gallery and watch for anything suspicious. Though House rules prohibited them from taking notes, they could keep track of how many "friendly" members were on the floor; if there were not enough, and a key vote was about to start, they would head for a pay phone and call Katzenbach, who would send his troops out to round up AWOL representatives. And while they were not supposed to communicate with anyone on the floor, they also developed a system of signals with Celler's Judiciary Committee staff so that Celler could get the department's approval on whether to order the Democrats to accept a particular amendment.[63]

The Justice Department was not the only group watching the proceedings on the floor. Along with the official whip systems run by the two parties' leadership, the liberal Democratic Study Group set up its own whip network: twenty-one of its members were each assigned five or six friendly representatives to keep track of; if one of their charges went missing during a key vote, they would send a staffer to fetch him. The system was run by Frank Thompson, who, as an added incentive, plied compliant representatives with booze. "Frank Thompson was one of the unsung and unnoticed heroes of the House Democrats," Katzenbach wrote.[64]

At the risk of overkill, the LCCR had yet another whip system of sorts. A small army of college students, organized by a twenty-five-year-old labor activist named Jane O'Grady, set up camp in Thompson's office; from there "O'Grady's Raiders" roamed the halls of the House office buildings looking for wayward congressmen. When they found one, they would gently harass him with reminders about how much his vote mattered on civil rights. At least, they thought they were being gentle; after several days House members began to complain to the LCCR leadership, which had set up a command post in a suite at the Congressional Hotel just south of the House buildings, and O'Grady's raids were scaled back.[65]

As the members were working their way through the bill on the floor, lobbying activity by LCCR groups heated up off of it. Busloads of foot soldiers rolled in daily from across the country—church groups from Iowa, union workers from Cleveland, civil rights activists from New York City. When they arrived, they received instructions from the LCCR on whom to visit and how to present themselves. Union members were told to avoid Republicans, while church groups were assigned to rural and Midwestern representatives. They also received helpful tips for navigating Congress: "When in a congressman's office, get a visitor's pass, so you can go to house gallery afterward," noted one helpful sheet from the Union of American Hebrew Congregations, one of the many LCCR affiliates active during the debate.[66]

Watching over everything were Rauh and Mitchell of the LCCR, who rarely left their circuit between the House gallery and their headquarters in the Congressional Hotel the entire debate. At one point Representative James A. Haley of Florida referred to the pair as the "vultures" in the gallery who had managed to steamroll the bill through the House. (This was not the first time they had been derisively nicknamed by a Southern Democrat: Senator Harry Byrd had long since taken to calling Mitchell and Rauh the "Gold Dust twins," after a pair of black children who graced the label of a popular scouring powder from the early twentieth century.)[67]

To the surprise of many Northern Democrats, the Southern Democrats were much less organized than they had expected. They held a single, closed-door strategy meeting on January 30, where about sixty of them agreed to focus their attacks on Titles II, VI, and VII—but also to limit their speeches and avoid delaying tactics, because they did not want to turn off wavering members who might otherwise support their crippling amendments. In practice, though, they approached the debate pell-mell, throwing up amendments with no apparent plan of how to get them passed. Their whip system, wrote the *New Republic* in a postdebate postmortem, "was in total disarray," with many Southern Democrats skipping the debate entirely. The whole exercise must have seemed beside the point to many, since it was going to pass in any case— and the stronger the bill they sent to the Senate, the easier it would be for their colleagues across the Capitol to filibuster it.[68]

From the outset of the debate, the Northern Democrats exerted almost complete control over the proceedings. They faced a barrage of amendments, some of them ridiculous attempts to excise entire titles, but many of them cleverly crafted to whittle back small pieces of the bill in ways that might bring over fence sitters. On February 3, they handily defeated an amendment by Louisiana representative Edwin Willis to remove the three-judge-panel provision from Title I—allowing plaintiffs in voting rights cases to have their cases heard by three judges, selected by a circuit court judge instead of just one assigned by roster—which he claimed encroached on states' rights, and which some observers feared had a good chance of garnering enough Republican sympathy to pass. The next day—the same day Johnson signed the Twenty-Fourth Amendment, banning poll taxes—the bill's backers shot down an amendment by Representative Meader to limit the public accommodations law to hotels that served interstate travelers. At one point Lindsay asked Meader how close to interstates a hotel or motel had to be to count. Meader said two and a half miles was fine, but three miles was too far—prompting Morris Udall of Arizona to utter a short poem: "Where the roads turn and twist, civil rights don't exist, but on Interstate 4, you can't bar the door."[69]

A few amendments did get through, though even those passed with the consent of the Democratic leadership. In one instance, Representative Willis, a relatively centrist Southern Democrat and a close ally of the White House who, as a member of the Judiciary Committee, had helped moderate some of the most vicious attacks on the bill, asked Celler to give him a vote on a small amendment, something he could take back to his voters to prove his segregationist standings. Helping Willis might not cost much, Celler and Katzenbach figured, and it might help limit Southern intransigence on other bills. And the change Willis requested was a relatively innocuous one: to prevent the Civil Rights Commission from investigating "bona fide" private clubs, leaving them more or less free to discriminate. Since the bill made clear in other titles that such clubs were already off-limits, Celler said yes to Willis's amendment. From the floor, Celler said, "I am a pragmatist. I believe it proper in order to get this matter expedited and get this bill passed and sent to the Senate, I would accept it and concur in the gentleman's wishes." Ben Zelenko, one of his counsels on the Judiciary Committee, was on the House floor with him, and Zelenko said he "almost quit on the spot." He went up to the gallery to find Burke Marshall, to see if the Department of Justice would intervene. Marshall, though, dismissed him with a dose of Solomonic wisdom. "We have to give away things," he said. "After all, we have to deal with the Southerners tomorrow."[70]

There were a few moments where the civil rights forces lost control of the proceedings. On February 7, Representative Oren Harris of Arkansas offered an amendment to cut back Title VI by removing judicial review and changing it from a mandatory cutoff of funds to a discretionary power—which, in the hands of a less progressive president, might not be used at all. So far, such amendments had been assiduously batted down by the leadership. But at that instance, with most of the Republicans off the floor, Majority Whip Hale Boggs of Louisiana unexpectedly seconded Harris's motion. The few Republicans who were on the floor, including John Lindsay, exploded in anger. Suspecting a plot by Democrats to weaken the bill for partisan advantage, Lindsay shouted that it was "the biggest mousetrap that has been offered since the debate on this bill began" and that it would "gut" the title. "I am appalled that this is being supported in the well of the House by the majority whip," he said. "Does this mean there is a cave-in in this important title?"[71]

McCulloch, who had been in the bathroom, rushed to the floor. His wife, Mabel, who was sitting next to Roy Wilkins in the gallery, leaned over to the NAACP president and whispered, "Look! Bill's face is red. He's mad!" When he had composed himself a little, the Ohio congressman took the microphone to announce: "If we pick up this old provision which does not provide for judicial review, I regret to say that my individual support of the legislation will come to an end."

Finally, Celler took his old friend aside and convinced him that there had been no conspiracy and that Boggs was simply talking out of class—a fact

Boggs readily conceded. Celler then announced that he and the Democratic leadership were "unalterably opposed to the amendment." A teller vote was taken, and the amendment lost 80 to 206.[72]

ON FEBRUARY 8, Howard Smith submitted the amendment he promised Celler he would add during the Rules Committee hearing: the inclusion of "sex" in the language of the FEPC. Smith's amendment caught no one by surprise—not only had he announced his plan during the Rules Committee hearing, but he had said as much during a January 26 appearance on *Meet the Press*. When May Craig, a correspondent for the Portland *Press Herald*, asked him if he was serious about submitting the amendment, he said, "Well, maybe I would. I am always strong for the women, you know."[73]

Smith's amendment was immediately opposed by Edith Green of Washington, one of just eleven women in the House at the time (there were also two in the Senate), who had been enlisted by the White House to offer the most compelling speech against it—she was, after all, a woman, and one with strong anti-sex-discrimination credentials. Green argued that whatever the merits of the amendment, Smith was simply trying to add a poison pill to the bill, one that would drive away support from otherwise liberal male representatives. "At the risk of being called an Aunt Jane, if not an Uncle Tom," she said, "let us not add any amendment that could get in the way of our primary objective." But her efforts were to no avail—despite a few minutes of wolfishly chauvinist joking by Celler, the amendment passed 168 to 133. When the vote was announced, a woman in the gallery shouted, "We've won, we've won!" Another yelled, "We made it, God bless America." Guards moved quickly to remove them.[74]

"Along with Betty Friedan," wrote Smith's biographer, Bruce Dierenfield, "Smith must be credited with giving the modern feminist movement a powerful, if unanticipated, push forward." The question remains, though: Was Smith sincere in his desire to help women—or was he just trying to throw a wrench into the proceedings? Representative Martha Griffiths of Michigan said that Smith later told her the amendment was "a joke." T. M. Carothers, the counsel for the Rules Committee, said, "The ladies give him credit for helping them, but he had another motive. I wouldn't say he was in favor of civil rights."[75]

Such speculation is undermined, to some extent, by Smith's decades of support for the Equal Rights Amendment, which had been unsuccessfully proposed in every congressional session since 1923, and the months-long record of Smith's negotiation with Alice Paul and the NWP over whether to introduce the amendment.

Whatever his motives, his move was anything but spur-of-the-moment trickery. Most likely, Smith acted with multiple goals in mind. Dierenfield speculates that he wanted to help Southern businesses by, in effect, striking down gender-specific labor laws that prevented them from taking advantage of cheap labor. And Smith may also have agreed with Paul—who, though a leader on women's rights, was rather retrograde in her views on race—that if black men and black women were going to win labor protections, and white men were already in control, the only people who would be left out would be white women.

To some extent, it is a moot question. Had Smith not introduced the NWP's amendment, the group would probably have found someone else to do it. But it remains a great irony of the civil rights story that one of the men most responsible for holding back the advancement of American blacks was also the man responsible for the single biggest advance in women's rights since the Nineteenth Amendment granted them suffrage.

ON THE SAME day that Smith introduced his amendment, Charlie Halleck answered the last question facing the bill when he called together the Republican leadership for a morning meeting to announce his support for Title VII—the first time he had done so, and a sign that the Republicans would now fall behind the bill as a bloc. Even a bit of partisan sparring that evening— Celler refused to grant Halleck's request to keep the session going late so that Republicans could get away for Lincoln Day—did not undo the minority leader's commitment to the bill.[76]

Finally, on Monday, February 10, the House gathered to finish the consideration of amendments and move to vote on the bill itself. Smith made two last-ditch amendments, one that would strike Title VII's requirement that employers retain their employment and hiring records, and another that would allow an individual to choose the conditions under which he would work—a symbolic gesture meant to underline the Southern Democrats' repeated assertion that Title II, by forbidding discrimination in many commercial accommodations, was tantamount to slavery. "I know you are not going to adopt this amendment," he said to the bill's supporters, "but I just want to see you squirm. I just want to see you feel ashamed of yourselves. I want to see you get up and argue against the 13th Amendment, which you placed on the books 100 years ago."[77]

Two more amendments were adopted that day: one specifying that Title VII protection did not extend to atheists or Communists, and one from Robert Ashmore of South Carolina to put the Community Relations Service back into the bill. The latter move—a strengthening amendment from a Southerner—was a bit of a surprise, but Ashmore was sincere. He said later that if the bill was going to pass, he wanted the CRS in there as a mediating buffer between private citizens and the federal government. In all, twenty-six amendments had been voted on during the debate, and only four had passed—all with Celler and McCulloch's approval.[78]

While Joe Rauh and Clarence Mitchell watched the final sputterings of the debate play out on the floor, a thirteen-year-old House page approached and said there was a phone call for them. Rauh stepped out of the gallery and into the phone booth—and found himself talking with the president. "What have you done to get the bill on the floor of the Senate?" Rauh recalled Johnson shouting at him. "Here it was just passing the House and he wanted to talk about the Senate."[79]

A little while later Representative Keogh, who was acting as chairman of the Committee of the Whole, asked, "Are there any further amendments to Title Eleven?" There was silence. He hammered the gavel. "If not, under the rule, the committee rises." Keogh stepped down, the mace was returned to its holder, and McCormack returned to his seat. The Committee of the Whole was no more.[80]

A few hours later H.R. 7152 was brought up for a vote. It passed by a predicted, lopsided tally, 290 to 130. Thanks to the hard work of the church groups, of the sixty-seven representatives they targeted from Ohio, Illinois, Indiana, Nebraska, and South Dakota—almost all of them conservative small-town Republicans with no constituent interest in civil rights—only five voted against the bill.[81]

As soon as the clerk announced the results, Celler rose. "I want to state that the result would not have been the way it was were it not for the wholehearted support and most earnest and dedicated cooperation of my distinguished colleague and counterpart on the Judiciary Committee, the gentleman from Ohio." McCulloch rose to thank Celler, and within a few hours he was on his way, with his wife, to Bermuda for a much-deserved vacation.[82]

THOUGH THE BILL'S passage in the House was rarely in doubt once it cleared the Judiciary Committee, its success—and that of the tax cut in the Senate soon after—was an immediate public boost to President Johnson's fledgling administration. Praise poured forth. Among other publications, *Time* enthused about "Johnson's masterful dealings with Congress that got both bills moving swiftly and both through without casualty."[83]

But Johnson's eyes were already on the Senate. Despite the bill's success in the House, he was less confident that it could clear a filibuster by the Southern

Democrats. On February 11, he pulled Katzenbach aside at a White House reception. Dragging together two chairs, he bade his deputy attorney general to sit down. "How do you plan to get this bill enacted in the Senate?"[84]

Katzenbach said they owed it to McCulloch to try for cloture, instead of negotiating away parts of the bill to reach a compromise. "I think we have to try for cloture. We may not get 67 votes, but we have to try."

Johnson was skeptical. "What makes you think you have a chance for cloture?"

But Katzenbach, ever the scholar, had done his homework. "I think we can get 57 to 60 votes for cloture fairly easily. We have 51 Democrats and some liberal Republicans from New York, California, Pennsylvania, and New England who will support the bill. But not all will vote for cloture. We need at least half the 33 Republicans. Based on the cloture vote on the Communications Satellite Act"—in 1962 a bipartisan coalition had defeated a liberal filibuster against a plan to encourage investment in space-based telecommunications—"there are 74 potential votes for cloture. We need at least seven more from 14 senators who have voted at least once for cloture. That should be possible."

Johnson asked for specific names. Katzenbach reached into his coat pocket and produced a list of senators, and the two hashed out the most likely converts. Finally satisfied, Johnson told him to go for it.

During the days before and after the vote, Johnson was on the phone constantly with Senate Democrats, barking orders about how they should bring the bill over from the House, how they should work with the Republicans, how they should deal with amendments. But most of what he said was cheerleading, and his advice was on questions that Mansfield and his deputy, Hubert Humphrey, had resolved months before.

In truth, Johnson was preparing to take a step back from the bill—he knew it was in good hands, but he was not sure that those hands, that any hands, were good enough to get the bill intact through the Senate, and he did not want to catch any blame if it imploded. Almost from the first of the year he was working to downplay expectations of his coming role. In a January 6 call with Wilkins, he said: "I'll help you, and I'll confer with you, and you can come in every day and talk to me about it. I'll do everything that I can, but I don't want anybody to get any illusions that I'm a magician, because I'm not." On a phone call with Robert Kennedy the morning after the vote, he made it clear that his role would be to provide public support and review strategy, but that the Department of Justice was running the show. "Now, you get together with Larry [O'Brien] and Mike Mansfield in the morning and work out a procedure," he said. "We're going up against a more difficult task. I've never been able to see my way through it and I want to do everything I possibly can, but I don't want anybody to think there's any disagreement among us or that there is any sabotaging taking place . . . You touch whatever bases your wisdom indicates and then get back to me with your ideas."[85]

While Johnson reaped public praise for the bill, he was at most a supporting actor in the drama. The real heroes in the House were Katzenbach and McCulloch, who crossed party lines to hammer out repeated deals, driven by their conviction that something had to be done for black America. But their commitment would not have been nearly as strong had the civil rights community and the LCCR not brought constant pressure to act; though Katzenbach then and later railed on the liberals, and though Robert Kennedy repeatedly referred to them as "sons of bitches," their work was absolutely vital in providing political cover for the administration to accept a stronger bill. If the Civil Rights Act is a landmark in the history of racial progress in America, it is also a testament to the power of ordinary citizens to band together and drive their government to move forward.

CHAPTER 6
A BATTLE IS LOST

ALTHOUGH THE SENATE DID NOT take up H.R. 7152 in earnest until it passed the House, expectation of a filibuster had been building for months. Behind the scenes and in front of the cameras, senators on both sides of the bill had been getting ready since the first rumors of its existence had trickled out of the Department of Justice planning sessions.

There was, of course, the trio of companion bills in the Senate: a mirror of the entire bill, a version of the bill without Title II, and a Title II–only version. The three served a fourfold purpose: they allowed Senate leaders to test out which parts of the bill had the most and least support, they helped focus the chamber's attention on the issue, they provided a written record of debate (which would come in handy when filibusterers claimed that the bill was being rushed through), and—most important—they provided a set of fallbacks in case the House bill failed along the way.

But the Senate leadership had also been working on a strategy in case everything went right—and the Southern Democrats launched their filibuster.

One of the enduring questions of the civil rights bill was why the Southerners, faced with an overwhelming tide of public support for the bill, refused to compromise to get a weaker bill. After all, they had compromised in 1957 and 1960, and the results were watered-down legislation that did little to move the ball on segregation. To understand why they went to the mat on this bill, one first has to understand who the Southern Democrats were and where they stood in 1964.

From the early twentieth century through the 1960s, the Southern Democrats operated as almost a third party within the national political system. Though many of them supported the New Deal, they were overwhelmingly anti-federal-government and anti-labor. They were united and driven by a single, overriding political value: the interlocking set of local and state laws, customs, and government programs that defined and enforced Jim Crow segregation. If a federal program promised to help blacks, the Southern Democrats were against it, no matter how much it might benefit their states. It was possible at times for a Southern politician to downplay race as an issue, but it was impossible for one ever to appear weak on the issue.

Even the political culture of the Southern Democrats differed from that of the national party. Lacking serious Republican challengers, if any at all, the Southerners focused on winning party primaries—which, until the Supreme Court invalidated the practice in 1944, were run in most states as all-white affairs. Southern voters also placed a much higher value on seniority and longevity than voters elsewhere, because they knew well that the more senior a politician, the more power he had, the more likely he was to run a commit- tee, and, therefore, the better positioned he was to block antisegregation legislation. They became masters of procedure and institutional memory; they honed tactics and strategies for delaying and destroying legislation. Frank Valeo, the secretary of the Senate under Mansfield, recalled: "I don't know how many times people like [Illinois senator] Paul Douglas and others would think they'd found an answer in the rules and they'd come forward and try to hit Russell head on, and then all of a sudden they'd find themselves flat on the legislative ground again."[1]

These were Democrats in name only. The affiliation with the national party was largely an artifact of history: it made more sense for the Southern Democrats to align with conservative Republicans, but the Republicans were the party of Lincoln, and as such they remained a dirty word across most of the South until well after World War II. And yet, despite the antipathy between the Southerners and an increasingly liberal national party, the two stuck together as a matter of convenience. The national Democrats could dominate Congress with the eight- een or so Southern-bloc Senate seats and one hundred or so House seats; without those, the party would be in a permanent minority. But the Southerners also understood that they needed the national party in order to be in the majority, and to hold committee chairmanships, and to better crush antisegregation legis- lation, working on the time-honored principle that one should keep his friends close, and his enemies closer.

Still, beginning in the 1930s, the ideological differences between the national and Southern Democrats began to manifest themselves politically. Though Franklin Roosevelt largely agreed to the Southerners' demand that blacks be excluded from most New Deal programs, he also worked to isolate the South where he could—for instance, by backing a motion at the 1936 Democratic National Convention to rescind a rule that a candidate, in order to secure the presidential nomination, had to win two thirds of the delegates, which gave the Southern bloc veto power. He and his successor,

Harry S. Truman, also pushed to expand opportunities for blacks and wear away at federal support for segregation; however insufficient Roosevelt's Fair Employment Practices Commission was, it and other, similar steps were symbolic acts that left little doubt in Southerners' minds about where the Democratic Party was headed.

At the same time, enterprising white Republicans began to make inroads in the South. Until the 1950s, the Southern GOP was microscopic. In most places it consisted of a post office box and a few part-time loyalists; in other places it was mostly a black-run affair, whose leaders worked mostly for the patronage that would trickle down to them from national Republicans when their party was in power. But after the war, the Southern economy—goosed by the influx of defense money plants and military bases—began to boom, and with it the demand for a pro-business political party. With that influx of business came new ideas, and new people, migrants from other parts of the country who did not feel a blind compulsion to vote for the Democrats. In 1957, Meade Alcorn, the Republican National Committee chairman, announced that Lee Potter, an Arlington, Virginia, party operative, would lead "Operation Dixie," an effort to make "substantial Republican gains in Congressional, state, and local elections throughout the South" over the next decade.[2]

Some pro-civil-rights Republicans saw this as a positive development; going back to Abraham Lincoln, there was a strand of the party that believed in a "Silent South" that supported civil rights and other Republican values but was cowed into submission by Democratic oppressors. Given the opportunity to express themselves, the thinking went, they would go Republican. But whether or not those voters existed (and they probably did not, at least in the numbers that liberal Republicans hoped), party strategists made the cynical decision to run to the right on race, pitching a pro-segregation, pro-business platform that rapidly won over the region's booming capitalist class.

The turn to the far right caused no end of hand-wringing in certain corners of the party. "The argument that civil rights as a Republican cause must be abandoned or watered down is both immoral, and, in light of the party's condition nationally, extremely foolish," wrote the editors of *Advance* magazine, a liberal Republican journal, in 1962. But the results spoke for themselves. By 1962 the Republicans were not only running viable candidates in statewide elections but turning in respectable, if not winning, results. Lister Hill, the Alabama Democrat, nearly lost to a race-baiting Republican that year, while W. D. Workman Jr. won a respectable 42.8 percent against Olin Johnston in the South Carolina Senate race. And in Texas, John Tower became the first Republican to win a Senate seat in the state since Reconstruction.[3]

These results terrified the Southern solons who had spent their careers in command of the political process. The Solid Democratic South, they feared, was rapidly disappearing—not because the civil rights revolution was demolishing their raison d'être (though it certainly was), but because the Republicans were able to vocalize a new, subtler, and more palatable but no less strident racial message, one that rejected overt appeals to racism in favor of code words in the language of anti-Washington and pro-big-business.

By the time the civil rights bill arrived on Capitol Hill, Southern Democrats faced three choices: they could ditch their party for the Republicans; move to the left and hope to ride the wave of an expanding, post–Jim Crow black electorate; or double down on segregation and white supremacy, hoping to save their own careers if not their party. All these tendencies existed in the Senate in early 1964, and it is telling that when the civil rights bill came over to the Senate in February, the Southern Democrats threw everything they had behind the last option, making it clear from the first day that they would filibuster until either they or the bill died. White supremacy and Jim Crow were more than ways of life for these men; they were ideologies, and like old Soviets who held on to Stalin long after the Berlin Wall fell, most Southern Democrats simply could not conceive of a world where whites and blacks did not live in carefully circumscribed, master-and-servant relationships.

That is not to say that there was complete cohesion among the Southerners. While some, like Strom Thurmond and Sam Ervin, were willing to go all out to fight the bill, others, particularly younger, more worldly members like George Smathers, Al Gore Sr., and William Fulbright, were less determined and even considered possible crossover votes for the bill. None of them ultimately did cross over, but they helped in less overt ways: voting for or against key amendments (or not at all), supporting quorum calls, and providing backchannel intelligence. Among other things, Fulbright provided valuable information about Southern planning sessions to the White House through one of his aides, John Yingling.[4]

Holding these differing factions together was the unofficial chairman of the Southern Democrats, Georgia senator Richard Brevard Russell. Since 1948 the wiry, nasal-voiced patrician had led his troops time after time against civil rights bills. Under his rule, the Southerners had filibustered all but one of the civil rights bills that reached the Senate floor, and that was only because that bill, the 1957 civil rights act, had already been gutted by his acolyte, the then majority leader Lyndon Johnson (technically, even that bill had been filibustered, though only by a single senator, Thurmond, who spoke for eighteen hours against it). All but one Southern filibuster had resulted in the targeted bill's defeat, and again, that bill, the 1960 civil rights act, squeaked through thanks to Johnson's willingness to negotiate away all but a few meaningless titles.

And yet by the early 1960s, Russell was coasting on reputation; he was considered an anachronism by many in the Senate, and even among the Southern Democrats. On January 23, 1964, the country approved the Twenty-Fourth Amendment, banning poll taxes, a step Russell called "an embarrassment to me." Unruffled, one Georgia state senator who supported the amendment said that despite whatever sway Senator Russell might have held in the past, the people of Georgia "are now going forward with a little different beat of the drum."[5]

Yet if Russell was an anachronism, he also recognized that the days of the old racial order were numbered. He simply wanted it to change at his own glacial pace. "I believe the Negro has been imposed upon," he told *Newsweek* in August 1963. "He has been subjected to indignities. But we shouldn't upset the whole scheme of constitutional government and expect people to swallow laws governing their most intimate social relations. The tempo of change is the crux of the whole matter. Any realist knows that the 'separate but equal' doctrine is finished."[6]

Russell had long been torn by two competing desires—to integrate the South into the American mainstream, but also to protect traditional Southern society, particularly its racial hierarchies. Now, suddenly, the region was slipping quickly toward his first goal but away from his second, and he did not know how to respond. At times he seemed ready to give up completely; in October 1963 he wrote on a desk pad, "As of today am completely disassociated from any leadership responsibility of our group . . . too many hearts are not in it who have same priority." As Johnson's close aide George Reedy reflected, "I think Russell realized that a civil rights bill was inevitable, and I think that he also thought it was better to get the thing over with."[7]

But as the debate on the bill neared, Russell showed no sign of giving up. "I shall oppose this misnamed civil rights proposal with all the power at my command," he wrote to a constituent in early December 1963. "I must say, however, that we are terribly handicapped in our opposition. The two major parties have been combined in bidding for the minority bloc vote to such an extent that they disregard states' rights and the opinion of Southern white people amounted to nothing in their sight." When asked whether he would compromise, he said there was as much a chance of his laying down his opposition as Stone Mountain, a rocky outcropping east of Atlanta held sacred by Confederate sympathizers, moving to Dalton, Georgia, a hundred miles north.[8]

And so, as the bill neared passage in the House, Russell pressed forward with his planned filibuster. The idea behind the maneuver is simple, deriving from the seemingly virtuous notion that the Senate is a deliberative body, which considers all aspects of a piece of legislation before approving it. Unlike in the House, debate on the Senate floor is unlimited, brought to an end only when at least two thirds (now three fifths) of the senators agree to end discussion and bring the bill to a vote, a step called "cloture." To prevent cloture, the Southerners needed to organize just thirty-four senators in opposition. There were not enough of them to do that alone, but in the past they had drawn the balance from conservative Republicans as well as small-state senators, who saw the filibuster as a critical tool in protecting their diminutive constituencies from the political power of larger states. Russell's hope—a Hail Mary pass, really—was that he could keep this coalition together through the middle of 1964, when, he predicted, renewed black protests and the ensuing violence would turn white America against the bill.

Russell organized his 21 men—19 Southern Democrats plus Tower and West Virginia senator Robert Byrd, who was not technically a Southerner but sided with the Southern faction in opposing civil rights legislation—into three platoons, led by Hill, Louisiana's Allen Ellender, and Mississippi's John Stennis. Each platoon was responsible for keeping the debate going for a day; the other two days they rested. Rest was important: youngsters like Fulbright (fifty-eight years old) and Gore (fifty-six) aside, the Southern Democrats were significantly older than the Senate average, and some, like the seventy-six-year-old Willis Robertson of Virginia, were so feeble they could speak for only a half hour at a time before growing winded. Still, like the Confederacy during the Civil War, they did not have to defeat their opponents outright; they just needed to draw out the fight long enough that the other side gave up.[9]

NONE OF THIS was a secret to the bill's supporters, led by Hubert Humphrey and his Republican comrade, California's Thomas Kuchel. They were devising their own strategies in response. The first order of business was to decide whether they would try to out-talk the Southerners, grinding them down until they stopped talking and simply conceded the debate was over, or whether they would try to shut off debate by rounding up the sixty-seven votes needed for cloture. Most senators and their staffs supported the second option; there was simply no telling how long the Southerners could hold out, and the longer they waited, the more the country might turn against the bill.

That, at least, was the view inside the Capitol. Those outside, like Mitchell, Rauh, and the other civil rights lobbyists, saw things differently: to them, the bigger risk was in the compromises that might be made to win over conservative Republicans—and in particular Everett Dirksen, the Senate minority leader. They had reason to be skeptical: since 1950, no cloture vote on civil rights had ever won even a simple majority of the senators present and voting, let alone two thirds.[10]

For all involved—the Southern Democrats, the pro-civil-rights faction, and the movement activists—the variable that would determine whether they got their way was the man who succeeded Johnson as Senate majority leader, Mike Mansfield. How far would Mansfield push the bill? The problem was, no one except Mansfield himself knew the answer.

Mansfield was in every way the opposite of his predecessor, Lyndon Johnson: quiet and mannerly where Johnson had been loud and often willfully rude, a stickler for rules and scrupulous honesty where Johnson had been willing to do just about anything in the name of a favored piece of legislation. "These fellows are about as similar as Winston Churchill and St. Francis of Assisi," a colleague told *Time* magazine. Johnson liked to spit and curse; Mansfield puffed serenely on his pipe, packed with his favorite Sir Walter Raleigh tobacco. Johnson had cobbled together a scattered empire of office space around the Capitol; after taking over in 1961, Mansfield relinquished much of it. His treatment of Johnson's favorite room, S-211, located just off the chamber floor, must have grated on Johnson the most: it was designed as the Senate library and decorated with ceiling frescoes by the artist Constantino Brumidi, but Johnson had given it a gaudy new paint job and hung fluorescent lights that obscured the art hidden above. Reporters took to calling it the Taj Mahal. When Johnson left, he made a bid to keep it as a base for when he sat as president of the Senate, but Mansfield denied the request. He then had Johnson's lights and other latter-day interventions removed and left the room empty, taking a much smaller office across the hall instead.[11]

Mansfield ran the Senate in much the same way: hands off, minimalist, letting senators go their own way—he called himself the "servant not the suzerain of the Senate," a new tack that most of his colleagues loved, except when it produced fits of anarchy in the chamber. He was quiet to the point of exasperation; TV interviewers said they had to prepare twice as many questions for him as usual, knowing his answers would be terse. And yet Mansfield was greatly admired among his colleagues, particularly the Southerners, for his respect for Senate tradition—something they no doubt thought they could abuse when necessary.[12]

None of this was surprising to those who knew something of Mansfield's biography. Few modern senators had as rough or varied a life. Born in Lower Manhattan to Irish immigrant parents, he had moved out to Great Falls, Montana, at age seven to live with relatives after his mother died. He was a hardworking troublemaker, who worked for his uncle's delivery business but also ran away from home twice, once ending up in jail. When he was fifteen, after the United States had joined World War I, he talked his way into the Navy; he later served in the Army and the Marines before receiving his discharge in 1922. He returned to Montana, where he worked in copper mines during the day and toward his high school equivalence and bachelor's degrees at night; he received both in 1932, then a master's in 1934, after which he became a professor of Latin American and Asian history at Montana State University (now the University of Montana). He won his first House race in 1942, and a decade later, a Senate seat.[13]

There may be other men whose careers before their fortieth birthday included stints in the Marines, the mines, and the college classroom, but not many. Partly as a result of those experiences, Mansfield as a politician acted like he had nothing to prove; he never craved attention or approval. He had fallen into the leadership after Johnson had chosen him as his deputy in 1957; after Johnson left, Mansfield was the one man in the Democratic leadership that all sides—South and North, liberal and conservative—could agree on. Mansfield always insisted it was a job he never asked for, and one he performed only out of his sense of duty to the Senate.

Still, for all the respect accorded Mansfield, more than a few people wondered if he was the best fit for the majority leader's hat. By 1963 the Senate, many complained, had lost the energy of the Johnson years. "Fewer and fewer senators showed up for the daily sessions," wrote Frank Valeo, the Senate secretary. "The flow of legislation from the committees to the floor slowed to a trickle." And it was one thing to have a laissez-faire leader during normal times—but during a time of heightened tension, like the civil rights bill debate, you wanted a gut fighter, someone like Johnson who would crack the whip, cut the deals, make the bill happen. Mansfield would not—could not, by his nature—do those things. And who knew if he could take the pressure of a lengthy filibuster?[14]

It did not help the skeptics that as early as July 1963, Mansfield chose a decidedly un-Johnsonian strategy for the bill. Johnson had taken the Senate into round-the-clock sessions to break the 1960 filibuster, but Mansfield refused to follow suit. He also refused to enforce the often-ignored Rule 19, which limited senators to two speeches in a legislative "day" (different from a calendar day, a legislative day continues until the Senate decides to adjourn, which might not happen for weeks at a time). Johnson fumed, but Mansfield stood his ground. When a group of rabbis pressed him to reconsider during a meeting on February 5, he replied, "When Johnson was majority leader, he ran things the way he wanted them. Now I am majority leader and will run things the way I want them."[15]

Instead, Mansfield's plan was to be an honest broker, keeping the Senate on a normal schedule and letting the Southerners know his plans in advance. Mansfield believed that keeping things aboveboard would make the Southern filibusterers look bad, shoring up public opinion and, hopefully, swaying some senatorial fence sitters. But he also feared that a contentious, drawn-out debate could cause lasting harm to the Senate's reputation. As he told the Senate on June 18, 1963, "The majority leader has no suave parliamentary tactics by which to bring legislation to a vote. He is no expert on the rules and he is fully aware that there are many tactics which can forestall a vote."[16]

Mansfield's initial plan was to go for cloture votes on the new bill as early as March or April, the better to get the tumult over quickly. But under pressure from Robert Kennedy, he agreed to wait until Katzenbach and Marshall could round up the requisite sixty-seven votes—which, they all knew, could mean well into the summer, if ever.[17]

Mansfield did, however, make two decisions that pleased civil rights supporters. One was his selection of Hubert Humphrey as the bill's floor manager. Normally a bill would be handled by the relevant committee chairman—but in this case, that meant Mississippi's James Eastland. Humphrey, though, was a perfect choice. As mayor of Minneapolis in 1948, he had given a stemwinder of a speech at the Democratic National Convention that beat back a Southern attempt to add an anti-civil-rights plank to the party platform; his speech was so successful, in fact, that the convention ended up adopting the strongest pro-civil-rights plank in party history. Johnson, who became majority leader in 1953, saw a pragmatic streak in Humphrey, and he brought him into the Democratic leadership in the hope that doing so could give him an avenue into the party's liberal corners. Thanks to Johnson, by the end of the decade, Humphrey was one of the most powerful men in the Senate.[18]

Selecting Humphrey gave Mansfield several advantages: the majority leader could remain above the fray, free to meet equally with Southerners, Northern Democrats, and Republicans; he could exploit Humphrey's close relationship with the White House; and he could turn loose this man of seemingly boundless political energy on a subject that demanded more hours each day than most mortal men have to give.

But before Humphrey could take charge, Mansfield had to make sure the bill did not slip into Eastland's hands. Normally when a bill comes over from the House, it is read twice and then immediately shuffled over to the relevant committee, where it receives the same marking-up treatment that it did in the lower body before it heads to the Senate floor for even more debate, followed by a vote. But this was no normal situation. Since taking over the Judiciary

Committee in 1955, Eastland had turned it into a graveyard for civil rights legislation. He had already scrapped one version of the bill—the hearings for which brought both George Wallace and Robert Kennedy to the witness table. Mansfield did not want to risk a repeat with the real bill.

There was an alternative. As soon as the bill arrived on the Senate floor, Mansfield could move to have it put directly on the legislative calendar, skipping the Judiciary Committee and teeing it up for debate by the entire Senate. It was an unconventional move, but hardly unprecedented: Johnson had used the same procedure to bypass Eastland during the debate over the 1957 civil rights act.

AND SO, A few minutes past noon on February 17, after the Senate had returned from the Lincoln Day recess, a clerk from the House entered the chamber to announce that the lower body had passed H.R. 7152 and that it was now ready for the Senate (Johnson had urged Mansfield not to wait until after the holiday to introduce the bill, but as usual, the majority leader ignored him). A page then took the bill from the clerk and carried it to the president pro tempore. Following normal procedure, Mansfield said, "Mr. President, I request that House bill 7152 be read the first time." A clerk then read the bill's titles, which sufficed for "reading" it in its entirety.[19]

Had the clerk read it a second time, as was usually the case, the bill would have immediately gone to Judiciary Committee purgatory. Instead, Mansfield rose again. "Mr. President," he said, "I object to the second reading of the bill today."[20]

No one was surprised by Mansfield's move; not only had he been planning it since the previous summer, but he had even contacted Eastland a few days earlier to make sure he knew what was coming. Still, the Southerners immediately began protesting.

Mansfield, still standing, conceded that his maneuver was unconventional. "The reasons for unusual procedures are too well known to require elaboration," he said. But desperate times required extraordinary measures. "We hope in vain if we hope that this issue can be put over safely to another tomorrow, to be dealt with by another generation of senators. The time is now. The crossroads is here in the Senate."[21]

Mansfield's words were then echoed by his Republican counterpart, Everett Dirksen—"the distinguished minority leader," as Mansfield called him, "whose patriotism has always taken precedence over his partisanship." Almost since the moment the bill was conceived, it was apparent to everyone involved that Dirksen would be the key to its survival in the Senate. No matter what strategy the civil rights forces chose, they would need moderate and conservative Republican support—and the only man who could deliver that was the portly, curly-haired Illinois senator. Even the lobbyists knew it: in the fall of 1963 both Blake and Miller, from the National Council of Churches, traveled to Dirksen's hometown of Pekin, Illinois, to press him personally on the bill.[22]

For the moment, at least, Dirksen played along. He would, he said, "cooperate in every possible way, consonant always with the duty to make an independent judgment." Then, forebodingly yet with seemingly casual élan, he added, "Already some amendments have occurred to me. I shall try to shape them. I shall try to put them in form. If I think they have merit, I shall offer them."

The speeches over, the bill went on the back burner so that the Senate could consider and pass the tax cut, which had finally emerged from Harry Byrd's Finance Committee. Strangely, after pressing so hard to get the tax cut bill moving, Johnson now urged Mansfield to hold off until after the civil rights bill had passed so as to bring pressure from business groups on the Southern Democrats to end the filibuster and move on. Mansfield quietly refused. The Senate set the civil rights bill aside and voted for the tax cut on February 26.[23]

Mansfield and Humphrey did not ignore civil rights while waiting on the other bill. As part of his commitment to transparency, on the morning of February 19, Mansfield sat down with Russell to talk through how each side would approach the bill. Mansfield began by telling Russell that he would not make any major moves without informing the Georgia senator first; he also explained his intention to bypass the Judiciary Committee and place the bill directly on the Senate calendar. Russell, obviously impressed with the majority leader's candor, said he would not delay the tax bill, and that he would not oppose letting committees meet during the debate, though he could not guarantee other Southerners would go along with him. Russell was not acting out of pure magnanimity—he recognized that pushing too hard against the bill could create a backlash among moderate senators, not to mention the public. It is why Russell also let slip a critical concession: Mansfield's plan to skip the Judiciary Committee and take up the bill immediately was a debatable move under the Senate's rules, and therefore open to its own filibuster—something Russell planned to do. But, he told Mansfield, he would drop the "mini-filibuster" after a few weeks. Though he did not say it at the time, he feared that if this first filibuster came to a cloture vote and he lost, a precedent of support for the bill would be set, and Russell might see the real filibuster fall to pieces quickly.[24]

The next day Mansfield's advisers prepared the results of an internal study, based on interviews with senators and their staffs, about the bill's chances. The news was not good. "The success of a cloture attempt is precarious at best even with the support of Senator Dirksen," it concluded. "Once cloture is attempted and support for it is shown to be insufficient it will encourage the Southerners all the more and will identify those Senators who are disposed not to vote for cloture. The trading power wielded by these Southern committee chairmen is prodigious and could be used to persuade uncommitted Senators to hold the line."[25]

Dirksen's centrality to the bill's success, once hypothetical, was becoming increasingly real—without his endorsement, it was unlikely that more than a handful of moderate and conservative Republicans would vote for cloture, and the bill needed almost all of them to clear the sixty-seven-vote hurdle. And yet Dirksen himself was growing enigmatic. At times he seemed to be open to almost everything in the bill, including Title II, which he had vilified the previous summer; at the same time, he hinted mischievously that he had several major amendments up his sleeve, pounds of flesh that he might demand be cut from the bill in order to grant his support.

Most civil rights supporters interpreted Dirksen's caginess as the mark of an operator, someone less interested in the substance of the bill than in the opportunity to leave his fingerprints on a piece of major legislation. Dirksen's vanity was well known; he loved to speak, and to tell people how well he spoke (to be fair, he was a gifted orator, and would win a Grammy for his spoken-word album *Gallant Men* in 1968). The White House and the bill's supporters set out to cultivate his ego, to win him over by underlining for any and all to see just how historical his vote for the bill would be. Humphrey, knowing how much Dirksen loved flowers, sent him a bunch of red tulips in early February to soften him up.[26]

Later, on an episode of *Meet the Press* on March 8, Humphrey said that "Senator Dirksen is not only a great senator, he is a great American." After watching the show, Johnson called Humphrey and said, "Boy, that was right. You're going just right now. You just keep at it. Don't let those bomb throwers talk you out of seeing Dirksen. You get in there to see Dirksen! You drink with Dirksen! You talk to Dirksen! You listen to Dirksen!" Still, the expectation as the debate in the Senate began was that Dirksen would exact a significant price for his support, and that the bill's supporters would just have to pay it.[27]

Yet those who saw Dirksen as an empty custom-tailored suit drastically underestimated him. He was vain and opportunistic, certainly. But he was also a man who had risen from humble origins into the seat of American power, and he had not forgotten it. Born to German immigrant parents in Pekin, Dirksen had tasted something of the sting of ethnic hatred during World War I and after, when anti-immigrant, and in particular anti-German, sentiment swept through the small-town Midwest. Dirksen was not without racial insensitivity—during a 1924 business trip through the Deep South, he wrote to his wife that "the energy and ambition of those who till the land must have flowed away and left a residue of indolent white trash and niggers"; from a hotel in Vicksburg, Mississippi, he wrote that "Jews control the business here." But he was also appalled by the immense support that the Ku Klux Klan drew in the Midwest that same decade, and it was that experience, more than his offhanded racism and anti-Semitism, that he brought with him as he moved up through the ranks in Congress, first as a representative and then in 1950, after taking a two-year leave from politics to deal with an inflamed retina, as a senator.[28]

Whatever his past trespasses, Senator Dirksen built a decent record as a civil rights supporter. He was no Bill McCulloch, but he regularly introduced legislation calling for a voluntary FEPC, a federal antilynching law, and an end to poll taxes; he also championed the cause of black women's associations in their campaign to win federal tax-exempt status. Window dressing for black voters back home, perhaps, but his record on civil rights was respectable enough to get him named chairman of the subcommittee on civil rights and immigration for the 1956 Republican National Convention.[29]

None of this meant that Dirksen was bound to support cloture, let alone the civil rights bill. His opposition to Title II as an invasion of private property rights was real and heartfelt. But it also meant that what Dirksen wanted out of the bill, and what people thought Dirksen wanted out of the bill, were two different things. Whether those mismatched expectations could be reconciled might be the question that decided whether the bill survived the filibuster.

DIRKSEN MAY HAVE been the leader of the Senate Republicans, but on civil rights he did not speak for all of them. The liberal Republicans largely spoke for themselves on the matter—though they found themselves in an increasingly tough spot. Men like Clifford Case of New Jersey, Kenneth Keating and Jacob Javits of New York, and Thomas Kuchel of California were well to the left of many Democrats on most issues, and they were stalwart in their support of strong federal action on civil rights. Yet they found themselves in a party moving slowly but surely to the right. As the election season approached, it became increasingly clear that the Republican nominee for president would be their colleague Barry Goldwater of Arizona, a man they had assiduously tried to alienate for years, to no avail; at the same time, they watched as grassroots activists and big-business interests in the GOP opened a campaign to win over Southern voters, even at the expense of their party's historical commitment to African Americans.

The liberal Republicans had a working yet uneasy relationship with the liberal Democrats. On the one hand, they all wanted the same thing—namely, a strong civil rights bill. From the beginning, they met regularly, either in person or through their staff, and they coordinated their speeches and press appearances. Yet they were also each jockeying for the better position on the issue going into the 1964 campaign, and each was willing to use the bill as a weapon. The Democrats drew the Republicans in at least in part so that if the bill failed, they could spread the blame to the other party. Meanwhile, the Republicans planned to push for amendments to strengthen the bill—not because they thought they could win them, or wanted to jeopardize the bill, but simply to be on record supporting a bigger civil rights act when they knew the Democrats, per their leadership's orders, would have to oppose them. On February 23, Kuchel got things rolling by calling for extending Title I to cover both federal and state elections, the first of many such grandstanding amendments that served only to inflame the Democratic leadership.[30]

John Satterfield and the Committee for Fundamental American Freedoms watched all of this unfold with eager anticipation. Like Russell and the Southern Democrats, Satterfield knew that defeating the bill was going to be tough. And yet he also saw the fissures, the potential breaking points where a well-placed lobbying campaign could chip away a senator's support for the bill. Not for nothing did he seed a series of editorials in the right-wing *Chicago Tribune*, which ran for over a week in late February. The *Tribune* was the biggest paper in the Midwest, and one of the most powerful voices in Dirksen's home state. Each day a pair of pieces—one a bylined analysis, the other an unsigned editorial—took apart one of the bill's titles. For anyone who had followed the debate in the House, the paper's positions were nothing new: they said, for example, that Title I, on voting rights, was unnecessary; Title II, on public accommodations, was unconstitutional. Title VII was said to raise the specter of affirmative action: "The effect of this section is to attempt to legislate discrimination in reverse through preferential hiring." And the entire bill represented a dangerously large step toward a socialist dictatorship. "If the *Tribune* had not exposed the civil rights bill I would not have known any of its frightening aspects," wrote a reader in one of the many fawning letters to the editor that ran during the series. "The provisions of this bill sound like the mandates laid down to a conquered enemy by the conqueror." (To its credit, the paper also ran a letter that took eloquent exception to the *Tribune*'s scare tactics: "Surely the American legal traditions will survive this assault, for a greater integrity will be served. A civil rights law, like stitches in a wound, will eventually dissolve invisibly into the body of our Republic.")[31]

Alongside the *Tribune* coverage, Satterfield targeted smaller newspapers across the Midwest, as well as trade and professional groups that might be able to bring pressure on their home-state senators. He also bought up mailing lists for tens of thousands of people across the region, to whom he sent form letters that they could personalize and then send to their congressmen. He also sent out a series of booklets against the bill to anyone who requested them, including one that featured the minority reports from the Judiciary Committee (reports that Satterfield had mostly written himself). Russell was a particularly active subscriber to the CCFAF's publications: he sent a copy of one of the committee's antibill pamphlets with every copy of the bill requested by constituents. Satterfield's highest-profile move was a full-page advertisement that ran in some two hundred non-Southern newspapers in March. The ad was dominated by the headline BILLION DOLLAR BLACKJACK—THE CIVIL RIGHTS BILL, denouncing the legislation as "socialist."[32]

And it worked: by early March, senators were reporting an inundation of mail against the bill, much of it written in the same language and drawing on the same arguments. There was little doubt that the letter writing had been organized by CCFAF: Mansfield received a stack of identical missives, all noting that "according to a Past President of the American Bar Association"—i.e., Satterfield—"this bill is unconstitutional." And yet, given the bill's chances in Congress and tenuous support among the public, such letters could not be dismissed easily. By mid-March, senators in places like New York and Idaho were reporting that their mail was running four to one against the bill, and in some parts of the Midwest as high as ten to one.[33]

IT WAS WITHIN this context of shaky coalitions and organized public opposition that Mansfield moved, on February 26, to have the civil rights bill read a second time. He then asked that the bill be placed directly on the Senate calendar, bypassing Eastland.[34]

Russell shot out of his chair to object—as did Wayne Morse, a maverick Democrat from Oregon. Morse had been a Republican, but switched parties in the early 1950s to protest the GOP's selection of Eisenhower and Nixon for the presidential ticket. In 1953 he set the record for a one-man filibuster, speaking for more than twenty-two hours against a bill to allow oil drilling in certain wetlands (a record broken four years later by Strom Thurmond's attack on the Civil Rights Act of 1957). The Democrats welcomed Morse into their fold but did not appreciate his maverick tendencies. Rowland Evans and Robert Novak called Morse "the Senate's one-man obstacle course."[35]

Morse was a civil rights man, but he also believed the bill would benefit from some time in the Judiciary Committee, where its supporters could build up an evidentiary case for it. To Mansfield's consternation, Dirksen fell in line with Russell and Morse, raising fears that the minority leader was being courted by the Southern Democrats. Yet in the end, Mansfield won his motion handily, 54–37, including twenty Republicans. Mansfield then asked unanimous consent to refer the bill to the Judiciary Committee for two weeks, after which it would return the bill without changes. He was hoping to win over the vote of Alaska senator Ernest Gruening, who had supported Morse's motion to send the bill to committee but who, unlike Morse, did not firmly support cloture. As the civil rights lobbyists in the gallery went wild, both Javits on the left and Eastland on the right objected; Eastland said that such constraints on his committee would make any hearing a demeaning waste of time. Since Mansfield had asked for unanimous consent, not a vote, their opposition was enough to quash it, and the day ended in confused relief. The first hurdle had been cleared.[36]

With the civil rights bill on the calendar, Humphrey began to organize his campaign in earnest. Two days later, at 11:00 A.M., he sat down with Katzenbach and Marshall in his whip office at the Capitol to coordinate the White House and Senate strategies. Humphrey loved that room; though it was uncomfortably long and narrow, it offered a view out on arriving visitors, and Humphrey would often stand at the window, "watching the tourists, parents with small children, holding hands, skipping up the broad stairs. Buses would disgorge troops of Girl Scouts and Boy Scouts in neat uniforms. There was a freedom and joy in their movements as they came to gawk and talk to their elected representatives."[37]

At the meeting, Katzenbach gave Humphrey his blessing to work closely with the Republicans, regardless of how it would look politically. The bill, Katzenbach said, depended for its survival on the appearance of a united front, one that would induce wavering senators to get on board. At the same time, he insisted that Humphrey use his prerogative as the bill's floor manager to arrange for all proposed amendments to be funneled through the two parties' leadership in order to be considered. In other words, if a senator had an amendment to the bill, they would have to submit it to Humphrey and Kuchel for approval.[38]

With the Justice Department's endorsement in hand, that afternoon Humphrey met for the first time with Kuchel, the minority whip and Dirksen's designee to run the Republicans' civil rights effort. The son of an Anaheim newspaper editor, Kuchel (pronounced KEE-kul) was a protégé of Earl Warren and a lifelong politician, entering the state assembly a few years after graduating from the University of Southern California's law school. In 1952, Warren, then governor, appointed him to fill the remainder of Richard Nixon's Senate term. As a senator, he had laid down a progressive voting record, particularly on civil rights. But he had made a name for himself nationally as a stalwart critic of the far right, which he often brushed up against during the course of his political career in California's bustling Orange County.[39]

Humphrey and Kuchel were well matched: energetic, popular, charismatic, and completely committed to civil rights. At the meeting, which included Rauh, Wilkins, and Mitchell, the two agreed to a set of principles for fighting the filibuster. First, they had to set a strategy to maintain quorum. Contrary to the image created by such films as *Advise & Consent*, most of the Senate is not on the floor at any one time, even during important debates, and even though the Senate rules require a majority of fifty-one members to operate. Often they are back in their offices, or not even in Washington at all. That is because the rule is only enforced when a senator suggests the absence of a quorum, at which point a clerk reads off the list of senators, calls go out to the senators' offices, and as long as at least fifty-one appear by the end of the clerk's reading, the quorum is met. If the count falls short, though, the Senate must adjourn.[40]

Under normal circumstances, senators rarely make quorum calls—they interrupt the day's schedule and inconvenience their colleagues. But during a filibuster, a quorum call becomes a powerful weapon. For one thing, quorum calls soak up time, often an hour or more, time that the filibustering senators do not have to spend speaking. It also wears out the other side, whose members have to trek back and forth to the Senate floor, often several times a day. In contrast, the filibusterers can take it easy and let all but a few of their number leave the floor, since it is in their interest to have the Senate adjourn as often as possible—not only does adjournment also soak up time, but it means that Rule 19 resets, giving each senator two new speeches to make. (Although Mansfield had said he would not enforce that rule this time, there was no guarantee.)

To counter quorum calls, Humphrey and Kuchel agreed to maintain duty rosters for each party, with firm commitments to keep enough senators nearby to make sure calls could be met. Humphrey went further, asking that each Democratic supporter give him their travel schedule for the coming months so that he knew in advance who would not be in town. And they agreed to publish every morning a "civil rights newsletter" for all the friendly senators, their staffs, and the civil rights groups, laying out the upcoming day's events.[41]

The pair also named "title captains": one senator from each party who would be in charge of advocating for a particular title, defending it against attacks, and consulting with the leadership on any amendments to it. They set a schedule of daily staff meetings and frequent meetings of the leading senators. They agreed to follow normal Senate rules for the time being, but if the filibuster dragged out, they would begin to steadily extend the hours in session each day and enforce the two-speech rule.[42]

Finally, and most importantly, Humphrey and Kuchel agreed not to attempt a cloture vote until they had firm commitments from sixty-seven senators to end debate. With only fifty sure votes for cloture at that point, neither man knew when that would be.[43]

WHILE HUMPHREY AND Katzenbach worked the Senate, Johnson was busy working the public. In almost every public address—press conferences, campaign speeches, talks with constituents—he emphasized the need for a strong civil rights act. On the evening of February 27, Johnson told an audience at a $100-a-plate fund-raiser at the Fontainebleau Hotel in Miami: "This Democratic administration believes that the Constitution applies to every American of every religion, of every race, of every region in our country. I pledge you tonight, and the people of this Nation, and the people of the world, that this administration is pledged to protect the full constitutional rights of every American. We intend to press forward with legislation and with education—and yes, with action—until we have eliminated the last barrier of intolerance." Two days later, back at the White House, a reporter at a press conference asked him about rumors that he was willing to compromise on Title II. "I have never discussed this with anyone, and I would suspect that those rumors which you talk about, which I have read about, are strictly Republican in origin," he said puckishly. "I will say that the civil rights bill which passed the House is the bill that this administration recommends. I am in favor of it passing the Senate exactly in its present form. I realize there will be some Senators who will want to strengthen it, some who will want to weaken it. But so far as this administration is concerned, its position is firm and we stand on the House bill." A month later, in a meeting with a hundred fifty members of the Southern Baptist Christian Leadership Seminar, he implored them to get behind the bill, saying that no one "has a greater responsibility in civil rights than Southern Baptists."[44]

If Johnson did nothing else to help the legislation, constantly reiterating his support—support backed by a nearly 80 percent approval rating—was an enormous boon. Richard Russell himself admitted as much the next day on *Face the Nation*, when he said that he believed Johnson would throw everything he had behind the bill: "I think President Johnson feels if he loses any substantial part of it, that it will cast all of his statements of support for it in doubt."[45]

Still, Johnson was making a calculated withdrawal from his close identification with the bill in the days and weeks after Kennedy's assassination. It is telling how carefully Johnson chose his words of support—always making clear that while he wanted to see it pass, it was the job of the Senate, not the White House or Justice Department, to make that happen. At times he sounded more like a sportscaster than a player. On March 7, two days before the bill was to be taken up, a reporter asked him how long the filibuster might last. "I think that the leadership can best assess that," he said. "I would not want to estimate. I don't think anyone really knows how long the matter will be discussed, but I believe that there are senators who feel very strongly, both pro and con, and they will be given adequate opportunity to express themselves. Then I believe the majority of the Senate will have an opportunity to work its will."[46]

Yet Johnson was also already growing frustrated with Humphrey and Mansfield's leadership. In a heated phone call with Larry O'Brien, the president lashed Mansfield in absentia for not agreeing to round-the-clock sessions immediately. "I just want to be sure the attorney general approves of this," he said. "Because I sure don't. And if they agree with him, all right. But my judgment is they ought to start right out going right around that clock until they get it."[47]

"Well," O'Brien said, "I have a feeling that he'll—"

"You be sure that you explain to him that's my judgment on the matter, but I want them to handle the bill, and I'll work with them any way I can. And if Hubert and them work it out, that's their business. They ain't going to damn sure put it in my lap because I'm for civil rights—period. Just as it passed the House—period."

Johnson was trapped by his own strategy. He desperately needed the bill to pass, but it was too risky for him to get involved any further; if he did, he would have no one to blame if it failed, as he still suspected it would. But he also could hardly abide Mansfield and Humphrey's refusal to follow in his footsteps. They were charting their own path, and only time would make clear whether it was the right one.

ON FRIDAY, MARCH 6, the Senate voted on the last major piece of legislation on its docket besides the Civil Rights Act: a bill to provide new subsidies for cotton and wheat farmers—legislation that farm-state senators from both parties, and in particular Humphrey, had desperately wanted. They were still hedging their bets: if the civil rights bill failed, or went to the end of the session, they needed something to take back to their largely white constituents. With that out of the way, Mansfield announced that the Senate would take up the civil rights bill the following Monday.[48]

The next morning Humphrey had another meeting with representatives from the Leadership Conference on Civil Rights, this time without Kuchel. The LCCR had been pushing for a Johnsonian strategy—all-night sessions, strictly enforced speech limits—as well as a raft of strengthening amendments. The point of the meeting was for Humphrey to explain why that was not the plan of action. He and Kuchel had already agreed to keep the civil rights lobbyists at arm's length, largely at the insistence of the Department of Justice. But clearly Humphrey did not want them around too often, either.

"The House bill is a good bill," Humphrey told them. "In fact, there is so much good with it that it is hard to tamper with it." But, he added, "if the Senate messes with it too much, there won't be any bill," since it would upset McCulloch and most likely force the House and Senate to negotiate the bill in a conference committee, which would add more time and risk to an already fraught process. At Clarence Mitchell's insistence, Humphrey agreed that he would not dismiss strengthening amendments out of hand—but he underlined that the bar for acceptance would be incredibly high.[49]

A few minutes after noon on Monday, March 9, Mansfield moved to dispense with the reading of the Senate journal, the compendium of the previous day's activity, an almost daily request that was almost always granted by unanimous consent. But not that day. "I trust that the clerk will read the journal slowly and clearly enough for all members of the Senate to understand it," Senator Russell said slyly after objecting to Mansfield's motion.[50]

Russell's objection was critical: motions to take up a bill, like the one Mansfield was planning to offer, were not open for debate if offered during the first two hours of a Senate day, known as the "morning hour." If Russell and the Southern Democrats could stall until two o'clock, then Mansfield's motion would be up for debate—that is, to a filibuster. When the clerk finished, Russell immediately went on an extended harangue against the bill, easily filling the remaining time, and then some, wrapping up around 3:15; a glass of water sat on his desk beside him, untouched. Is the morning hour complete? he asked the clerk with faux naïveté. Indeed it is, came the reply.

Mansfield then rose to offer his motion to take up the civil rights bill, but he knew he was too late. "The issue of civil rights can wait no longer in the Senate," he said. But the motion was debatable, and the first filibuster had begun.[51]

*

THOUGH THIS FIRST filibuster—sometimes called the "phony" or "mini" filibuster—received less attention than its later, much longer cousin, it was actually the much more substantive of the two.

There were two lines of discussion going on simultaneously. First, in an argument that would run past the end of the phony filibuster, came a continuation of the debate over whether to refer the bill to the Judiciary Committee. Again, Morse led the charge. His concern, he said, was that the bill needed a long and involved legislative history so that later, when the Supreme Court inevitably took up one or more challenges to it, the justices would have a rich body of material in which to discover the Senate's intentions behind each detail in the law. "It is my opinion that every single sentence of this act will be litigated," he said on the Senate floor. "I wish to give the Supreme Court the strongest possible base, so that the law can be sustained."[52]

These were legitimate points. But Humphrey and Mansfield had answers. For one thing, the majority whip noted, the Senate had sent 121 civil rights bills to the Judiciary Committee between 1953 and 1963, and received not a single one back with a report—most recently the Senate version of the bill now under discussion. Of course, the Senate could always instruct the Judiciary Committee to return the bill in fourteen days. But as Mansfield noted, that would just mean starting the whole process over again, with yet another phony filibuster, and time was wasting. Moreover, added Thomas Dodd of Connecticut, the collected committees in the House and Senate had already held 83 days of hearings, heard from 280 witnesses, and produced 6,438 pages of material, in eye-strainingly small print. "Further hearings could be only a repetition of what has already been said," he argued.[53]

As this procedural discussion ran on, another debate centered on the merits of the bill—particularly Titles I, II, and VI. As in previous debates, the arguments put forth by the Southern Democrats tended to reiterate arguments first proffered by segregationist and conservative legal scholars, including John Satterfield and Robert Bork, then a young professor at Yale Law School, who had written scathing critiques of the bill in both the *New Republic* and the *Chicago Tribune*.[54]

But they also brought new arguments to the table, arguments designed less to challenge the constitutionality of or need for the bill, but rather to foment racial animosity by whites. On March 16, Russell resurrected an old proposal to give Southern blacks $1.5 billion in incentives to relocate to parts of the country where few of them lived—the better, in Russell's mind, to show white America just what it was like to live near them. (The proposal was mostly a rhetorical prop on Russell's part, and it did not go anywhere.)[55]

In another instance, Allen Ellender of Louisiana argued that voting restrictions were justified because otherwise, blacks would take over the government and run it into the ground—a claim that spoke directly to Northern white fears of social integration.[56]

Humphrey was flabbergasted. "How does the Senator justify that under the Constitution?"

"Well . . ."

"The Constitution is rather explicit on that subject."

"I understand that. I am not saying they should not be registered, but I am giving the Senator the reason why," Ellender said. "If this happened in the State of Minnesota, the Senator from Minnesota would do the same thing."

"Not at all. Not at all," Humphrey replied.

"The Senator from Minnesota has not lived in the South," Ellender said—implying, of course, that once Northern whites understood what it was like to live near blacks, they, too, would support racial restrictions. (He was also wrong on that point, since Humphrey had attended Louisiana State University for his master's degree.)

Humphrey's energetic engagement with Ellender was part of a tactic, worked out with Kuchel, to respond immediately and fully to any Southern argument, the better to demonstrate to wavering senators the commitment to the bill and the wrongness of the Southern Democrats' position—even if it meant making their fellow party members look foolish. On the first day of discussion, Lister Hill claimed that Titles I and II would create special classes of citizens protected by the law, which would in turn limit the rights of everyone else. "History aptly demonstrates that special privileges for one group can but result in a limitation of liberty and a denial of the rights of others," he said. This was nonsense—if anything, inasmuch as blacks were treated differently because of the membership in a particular group, the bill actually banned special treatment for them.[57]

Humphrey immediately challenged Hill. "The senator from Alabama realizes, does he not, that the common law of England, ever since the thirteenth century, or even before then, provided, in relation to innkeepers, that if there was a vacancy in an inn, and if a person had the necessary rental money, the innkeeper had an obligation to provide accommodation for him, without regard to caste or person."

Hill replied, "Oh, there were all kinds of laws in England, and the people of America rebelled against and opposed many of the laws of England."

"But they never rebelled against the English common law. They rebelled against abuses of the English common law. At any rate, I thank the senator from Alabama."[58]

The debate was also marked by small instances of the old Senate comity coming through. There was an element of pragmatism in their day-to-day relations: an opponent on one bill might one day be an ally on another. They were something like major-league baseball players: opponents, but also professionals who could separate the competition from the people behind it.

All of which explains an episode between Virginia's Willis Robertson and Humphrey. At the end of a particularly grueling day of debate, Robertson approached Humphrey at the dais and offered him a Confederate battle flag lapel pin. Humphrey accepted it, then praised Robertson's "eloquence and his great knowledge of history and law" and thanked him "for his wonderful . . . gentlemanly qualities and his consideration to us at all times." Robertson then returned the compliment, saying, "If it had not been for the men from Wisconsin and Minnesota, when Grant finally came down into Virginia, we would have won." The two then left the floor for Humphrey's office to have a drink.[59]

While the phony filibuster spun out on the floor, the pro-civil-rights Democrats and Republicans were still getting used to working together behind the scenes. At a meeting of the Democratic floor leaders—Humphrey, along with Phil Hart of Michigan, Paul Douglas of Illinois, and others—the senators discussed indications that the Republicans were still planning to introduce strengthening amendments in order to embarrass the Democrats, who would have to vote against them to protect the bill. And one Senate staffer, reporting on a conversation the day before with Kuchel's senior aide Stephen Horn, said that the Republican whip remained uncommitted to funneling amendments through the leadership—which in turn could lead to a flood of unwanted amendments being voted on before the leadership could decide how to respond to them. At the same time, many Republican staffers were wary of Democratic entreaties. As Horn noted on March 18, rumors of an impending cloture vote "might be a Lyndon Johnson attempt to embarrass the Republicans since we would be shy the 25 votes the GOP needs to deliver cloture. Those votes will be available five or six weeks from now, but not if the vote is held now."[60]

FINALLY, ON MARCH 26, just before the Senate left for its Easter recess—and with, by coincidence, both Martin Luther King Jr. and Malcolm X, the Black Muslim leader, observing from the gallery—the Southern Democrats yielded. The phony filibuster had already lasted much longer than the four or five days Russell had promised Mansfield; on March 23, Humphrey had even kept the Senate in session until 10:15 P.M., a taste of what was in store for Southern

Democrats when the real filibuster began. Not all of the Southerners agreed to give in; in a meeting the next morning, only seven out of twelve voted to let the bill proceed. The rest wanted to force a cloture vote. But Russell knew they would probably lose that vote, setting a bad precedent to go into an even more stressful and much longer one. Though the names in each column were unrecorded, it is likely that the losing votes came from firebrands like Thurmond and Ervin, who opposed the bill with blind hatred and, more important, feared that any weakness on the bill would make them fodder for an attack from the segregationist right back home.[61]

Once the Southern Democrats announced they would stop what they euphemistically called their "extended debate," the Senate voted by 67 to 17 to take up the bill. It was both a victory and a warning. The Southern move had been rare and aggressive, and one might have expected at least a few fence sitters to join with the civil rights forces. After all, voting to take up the bill was not an endorsement of it, or even a vote for cloture on the main filibuster yet to come. But the bill's supporters won just 67 votes, the bare minimum they would need to beat the upcoming filibuster. If they could not do better, the bill was dead.[62]

As soon as the vote was finished, Morse moved again to take up the bill, supported, this time, by Dirksen. Again, the vote was closer than Humphrey and his team would have liked—50 to 34. The bill was moving forward, but it could well be headed for defeat. As Russell intoned after losing the vote to take up the bill, "A battle has been lost. We shall now begin to fight the war."[63]

CHAPTER 7

THE SOUTH TAKES
ITS STAND

THE MEMBERS OF THE United States Senate slogged their way to the Capitol on the morning of Monday, March 30, through a freak early spring blizzard that dropped five inches of snow on Washington. In the middle of the storm, just outside the massive edifice, stood CBS News correspondent Roger Mudd. A D.C. native and a rising star on CBS's national news reporting staff, Mudd had made a name for himself covering such seminal events as the March on Washington and the Kennedy state funeral. In early 1964, Fred Friendly, the new president of the network's news division, had suggested that Mudd cover the filibuster in a one-man, flood-the-zone campaign, "not only on the evening news with Walter Cronkite but also on each of the network's four other TV newscasts and on seven of the network's hourly radio newscasts," Mudd later recalled. "My initial reaction was less than enthusiastic. It sounded more like a flagpole-sitting stunt."[1]

Still, Mudd was a good soldier, which was how he ended up standing in the blowing snow on Capitol Hill that morning. "This is not what you'd call a typical Eastern Monday in Washington—the snow, the cold, the frozen forsythia and the chilled cherry blossom buds, and inside the Senate wing, we are about to embark on an historic civil rights debate," he began his broadcast, his dark hair poking above his winter coat. "Leading off today will be the generalissimo of the pro-civil-rights forces, Democratic senator Hubert Humphrey of Minnesota."

The camera then panned to the Senate majority whip, bareheaded in a thin 42-long raincoat that was several sizes too big for him, the sleeves all but covering his hands. When Humphrey had arrived at the Capitol, CBS News director Bill Smalls had asked him to step aside to speak with Mudd before he disappeared into the building. Humphrey demurred, saying he needed his jacket. Smalls, thinking fast, offered him his, even though he was much taller.

And so the senator about to lead the most important fight of his life, and one of the most important in the long history of the Senate, found himself on national television, shivering in the snow in an ill-fitting coat.[2]

Though he put on a brave face for the camera, Humphrey's uncomfortable appearance hinted at a growing concern among supporters over the civil rights bill's prospects. That same day, Humphrey sent a memo to his assistant John Stewart in which he worried that "we are beginning to lose the public relations battle on the civil rights issue." Among other things, he said, the CCFAF ads "are having their effect. I don't mean to say the public has swung over against civil rights, but we are losing some ground." He even mused darkly on the prospects for widespread racial violence in the coming summer: "There is a sense of bitterness and open rioting which is going to kick back and could very well precipitate small Algerias all around the country." The answer lay in getting the bill through as fast as possible, to demonstrate that change was possible through the system. But to do that, the civil rights bill needed a massive public relations campaign of its own, drawing in religious leaders, doctors, and business people. "I don't think we can wait another day."[3]

It is significant that Humphrey left out the civil rights groups and labor from his list. From his perspective—one shared by Katzenbach and the Department of Justice—those proponents were doing more harm than good to the bill. Martin Luther King Jr., for example, had been talking about mass protests against the filibuster and had called on the Democrats to scuttle the bill if the Republicans demanded weakening amendments. Humphrey worried about how such public pronouncements would play once the delicate negotiations with Dirksen began. Dirksen was no friend of the civil rights lobby: the previous autumn, he and Clarence Mitchell had had a famous falling-out in which Dirksen had kicked Mitchell out of his office for daring to challenge his civil rights bona fides. And liberal organizations would be no help when it came to winning over Midwestern Republicans. Humphrey, at Katzenbach's request, had already frozen out the LCCR from almost all the daily meetings held by the civil rights senators and their staffs, a move that infuriated Rauh and Mitchell.[4]

Meanwhile, Humphrey and Kuchel had put together a plan for the first several days of debate. They knew that the country's attention, thanks to Mudd, would be focused on the filibuster for a time and then taper off—and they intended to own that time, not cede it to the South or the civil rights groups. They assigned each of the major titles to a Democrat and a Republican, each of whom was to prepare an extended, point-by-point explanation of the title. The marathon of speeches would begin with lengthy addresses from Humphrey and Kuchel themselves. By the time the Southerners began to speak, they hoped, the country's focus would be elsewhere—after all, even a congressional debate as pivotal as the one about to begin was, in its day-to-day details, still a congressional debate. High drama it was not.

The Senate was scheduled to take up the civil rights bill as soon as the session opened. But there had been an earthquake in Alaska the previous Friday—the most severe ever recorded in American history, killing 143 people and flattening communities across the south central part of the state. President Johnson persuaded Humphrey and Mansfield to take up the question of disaster relief first, the better to win points with Western senators who felt a regional connection to the beleaguered state (Johnson also lent Alaska's two senators the use of Air Force Two to return home).[5]

Humphrey finally rose at 1:30. The gallery was filled with onlookers, but the chamber was close to empty. The bill, he said, was simply a matter of fulfilling the promises set out in the Constitution. He then set aside his speech, all fifty-five pages of it, and took up a Bible. He read from Matthew 7:12: "Therefore all things whatsoever ye would that men should do to you, do ye even so to them, for this is the law and the prophets." Setting down the book, he intoned, "It is to fulfill this great admonition—this is what we are trying to do in this bill."[6]

Humphrey announced that he would refuse to answer any questions, since "I want to keep this short." He then spoke for three hours and twenty-six minutes. Kuchel's speech was significantly shorter than Humphrey's—it went for just an hour and fifteen minutes. "No American can read the thousands of pages of testimony which have been taken in field hearings all over the our land by the U.S. Commission on Civil Rights without being greatly impressed with the work of law and of the heart which still remains to be accomplished," he said.[7]

By the time Kuchel finished, just a handful of senators sat in the chamber, most of them signing letters and doing other miscellaneous office tasks. Gallery gawkers must have felt their expectations rapidly deflate as the senators shifted around the floor: these were not the exciting theatrics of national politics they had come expecting. But this was the way of Senate politics—to a great extent, what happened on the floor was the least important part of the civil rights battle.

DESPITE THE BILL'S challenges in the Senate, its supporters knew that success would present its own set of problems. A decade earlier, the *Brown* decision had spurred "massive resistance" across the South, with some school districts shutting down entirely to avoid having to admit black children. Racial violence spiked, and the strictures of Jim Crow tightened. Politicians across the region encouraged defiance; in Little Rock, Arkansas, it took federal troops to force compliance.

And so on April 1, the day after the Senate took up the civil rights bill, several top officials at the Department of Justice gathered to plot out how to best ease the bill's implementation. Just as the Justice Department had coordinated with outside groups to generate support for the bill, it was now looking to those same groups to pave the way for its acceptance by Southern society. Louis Oberdorfer, the deputy attorney general for the tax division and a native of Birmingham, had spent the last nine months building an ad hoc network of concerned civic and business leaders in the South. They were grouped into interest and industry groups: lawyers, industrialists, motel owners—each had its own committee.

Julius Manger Jr., one of the nation's most powerful hotel magnates, took a particular interest in leading his industry on desegregation; afterward he wrote a moving personal account about his conversion from civil rights apathy to activism at one of President Kennedy's conferences during the summer of 1963. Manger spent countless days in the spring of 1964 traveling around the South, persuading local hotel and motel owners to accept desegregation. "In Charlotte and Savannah we had a larger investment in our hotel and motel properties than anyone else," he wrote. "In both of those cities, therefore, I was able to say to other hotel and motel owners that I was not just asking them to do something and then going to walk away, but that actually we had a bigger investment to lose than they did." Thanks to Manger's leadership, scores of Southern communities were ready to accept, if not welcome, the bill when it went into effect. Oberdorfer later called Manger "one of the unsung heroes of the civil rights era."[8]

Several outside groups had their own networks that they coordinated with the department. Irwin Miller and Robert Spike had agreed to create a network of clergy around the South to push for compliance, while the Potomac Institute, a liberal think tank in Washington, organized lists of Southern editorial writers, business organizations, and civic groups. The institute used those contacts to build local ad hoc organizations to generate positive press coverage and an accepting business climate for desegregation—a grassroots effort that proved critical in communities that were wary of direct federal pressure.[9]

In each case, the networks provided both a tool for pushing acceptance in local communities and a source of intelligence on potential hot spots—in early June, for example, Luther Holcomb, the executive director of the Greater Dallas Council of Churches, passed on word that two local restaurants, the Lucas B&B and the Piccadilly Cafeteria, had said they would not comply with Title II.[10]

The overriding message passed through the networks, the planners at the April 1 meeting agreed, would focus on the bill's inevitability. For one thing, they communicated that, unlike after *Brown*, the federal government was intent on enforcing the legislation. At the same time, by pressing the idea that desegregation was a fait accompli, the planners were also taking advantage of the fact that many business owners wanted to desegregate, but did not want to be the first to do it, for fear that white customers would shun them for other, still-segregated facilities. If the department, through its various networks, could spread the word that the region was going "all in" at once, then desegregation might go more smoothly.

ON THE SAME day the Senate took up the bill, just a few blocks away from the Justice Department at the Statler Hilton, some eighty leaders from seventy-four member organizations of the Leadership Council on Civil Rights met for their own all-day strategy session. Although they were largely shut out of the backroom negotiations, these groups had their own plans for the bill. They emerged with a long schedule of campaigns and events meant to raise public awareness and ratchet up pressure on the Senate. Each group had its own plan. Every morning, an hour before the Senate opened, a minister would lead a prayer service at the Lutheran Church of the Reformation, an art deco pile of a building just a block east of the Capitol. Other groups, like the B'nai B'rith Women, scheduled "adopt a senator" write-in campaigns to Southern Democrats. Still others announced plans to bring their members to Washington to meet with their senators: the NAACP would bring representatives from 190 chapters to Capitol Hill; the AFL-CIO announced an upcoming conference in Washington that would see two hundred members descend on the capital. Humphrey, not wanting to isolate the civil rights groups completely, put in an appearance that turned the meeting from a strategy session to a pep rally. "I am so conditioned morally, physically, psychologically, the fight can go on for ten years and I won't run out of steam," he told the crowd. Humphrey expected the same level of commitment from his fellow Democrats. When a staff member told him that Senator Dale McGee of Wyoming had to leave early one day to have dinner with his family, Humphrey replied, "He better make up his mind whether he wants to be a father or a senator—he can't be both."[11]

As it had done during the House debate, the LCCR also organized gallery watchers to remind the senators that the public was watching and to act as an early warning system in case the Southern Democrats announced a sudden quorum call. "The success in maintaining packed galleries during the House debate was an appreciable factor in the victory there," wrote Violet Gunther, one of the three paid LCCR staffers, in a memo to member organizations. "We must do the same in the Senate." She drew up a schedule and distributed it among the organizations, with each one responsible for supplying manpower for one- or two-hour increments during each session. And the LCCR brought back Jane O'Grady and her raiders, who acted as the tip of the civil rights whip system, rounding up errant senators to meet quorum calls.[12]

On the same day as the meeting at the Statler, Mary Parkman Peabody, the seventy-two-year-old patrician mother of the governor of Massachusetts, was one of several people arrested in St. Augustine, Florida, for trying to integrate the Ponce de Leon Motor Lodge. Peabody had arrived in town a few days before as part of a wave of activists, most of them much younger than she, who heeded the call by Robert Hayling, a local civil rights leader, to make the historic city the movement's next battleground. Tensions had been simmering in St. Augustine since sixteen protesters had been arrested during a sit-in at a Woolworth's lunch counter the previous year. In September 1963, Hayling was beaten by a mob of Ku Klux Klan members and then charged with assaulting them. Rather than shrink in retreat, he had redoubled his efforts, and by early the next year had become a national cause célèbre in the black media. Hayling had spent the latter part of February and on into March traveling up and down the East Coast trying to attract volunteers—above all, Martin Luther King Jr. At first King demurred, referring Hayling to the Southern Christian Leadership Conference's Florida operation. King knew from hard-won experience that poorly planned campaigns, no matter how heartfelt, could only sap the strength of his organization. Still, he recognized the value of the St. Augustine campaign for its potential impact on the civil rights debate in Congress, and he supplied Hayling with a steady stream of SCLC lieutenants to help organize demonstrations and sit-ins (and, this being an oceanfront community, "wade-ins" at segregated beaches, too).[13]

Still, it was the big three religious faiths that provided the most organizational heft during the filibuster. No one else could match their manpower, organizational cohesion, or passion. Beginning in March, students, seminarians, and congregations flowed into Washington, marching, attending services, writing letters, and meeting, when they could get a few minutes, with senators. "You couldn't turn around where there wasn't a clerical collar next to you," recalled Rauh.[14]

Under the ecumenical aegis of the National Council of Churches' Commission on Religion and Race, an intelligence network was established to monitor each senator who had yet to commit on the filibuster and to bring pressure on them when they least expected it. When Senator Roman Hruska, a Republican from Nebraska, flew home on weekends, he would encounter one or another of the state's prominent religious leaders at the airport—a coincidence made possible thanks to the help of Robert Kutak, his administrative assistant, who tipped off the LCCR whenever his boss headed home. Likewise, John Cronin, who was leading the National Catholic Welfare Conference's efforts on the bill, called a bishop in South Dakota to help lobby Karl Mundt; the senator soon found himself meeting with a local priest with whom he had been close friends in high school.[15]

Across the country, but particularly in the Midwest, the fight for the civil rights bill was transforming formerly quiet, ordinary people into vocal full-time activists for racial equality. Ministers would sermonize about the bill on a Sunday morning, then ask their congregants to stick around for a letter-writing session. Senate staffers began to expect a surge in mail on Tuesdays and Wednesdays as those letters, posted first thing Monday morning, arrived in Washington. At Purdue University in West Lafayette, Indiana, a campus minister named Ernest Reuter organized Project Leadership Organization, a clearinghouse for training and information about the bill that linked together churches, temples, and campus ministries. "We in the Middle Western and Rocky Mountain states will hold the balance of power in this matter," he wrote in a letter announcing the project. "Because the issue is not as critical for us as it is for the old South and the Eastern states we have a responsibility to take a stand on an issue which surely divides the nation." Reuter had already played a key, unheralded role in pushing Charles Halleck closer to the bill. By the time the filibuster was in full swing, he and countless others had created a spontaneous culture of civil rights, evanescent and fragmentary but powerful in its moment. Of all the forces and personalities that coalesced around the bill, perhaps none was more critical to its passage than the network of religious organizations and their army of adherents.[16]

IN EARLY APRIL, following Humphrey and Kuchel at the Senate lectern were the paired title captains from each party, who held forth with their own soup-to-nuts explanations for their assigned sections of the bill. Attendance in the Senate dwindled rapidly as the debate fell into a call-and-response pattern in which a Democrat would rise to explain a title, after which a Republican would give almost the exact same set of points in his own words. Occasionally a Southerner would cross-examine the speaker, like the time Sam Ervin, from his desk piled high with law books, questioned Kenneth Keating for two hours after the New York Republican gave his defense of Title I. But that was the extent of the excitement, such as it was. Vermont's Norris Cotton often could be spied sleeping at his desk. But at least he bothered to show up. "At no time were there more than six senators on the floor," noted the correspondent E. W.

Kenworthy in the *New York Times*. Mudd, who sat in the gallery between filing stories, recalled that "the scene was one of minor, routine floor speeches: the almost empty chamber, the solitary speaker with a stack of documents on his desk and the ever present legislative assistant at his elbow, the presiding officer signing his mail, and the dumbfounded tourists who filled and refilled the galleries every fifteen minutes."[17]

Almost as soon as the debate started, the bill's leaders began to worry what would happen once their speeches, and the Southern Democratic attacks on the bill, had run their course. By "the 20th of April we should be face to face with the question of where to go next," wrote the Senate secretary, Frank Valeo, to his boss on April 9. Valeo reported that thirty-eight senators, including Dirksen, were dead set against cloture, and another eleven were strongly leaning against it. If he was right, the pro-civil-rights senators had an enormous amount of convincing to do, and no real plan for accomplishing it.[18]

A bigger problem was simply meeting quorum calls. The Southerners raised the question constantly, often several times a day. On Wednesday, April 1, just two days after the debate began, it took an hour and a half for the civil rights forces to wrangle enough senators to the chamber to make a quorum—a success made possible in part by Arkansas senator William Fulbright, a moderate Southerner who opposed the bill for political reasons back home but did what he could to help out its supporters. "The civil rights quorum machine continues to creak and sputter along," noted the bipartisan civil rights newsletter on April 3. "It took 53 minutes to make one quorum call on Thursday and 44 minutes to make the other one. This doesn't break Wednesday's record for all deliberate speed, but it comes close."[19]

The next day the Southerners struck gold. On Saturday, April 4, the civil rights forces failed to muster a quorum; just 39 senators answered the call, including a mere 23 Democrats. Of those who did not appear, 44 backed the bill, including three Democratic title captains, Warren Magnuson of Washington, John Pastore of Rhode Island, and Edward Long of Missouri. Humphrey was furious. In an emergency meeting of Democratic senators after the Senate was forced to recess, Humphrey demanded to know where the missing members were, then sent each of them an angry telegram ordering them to return to the capital immediately.

Then, on the following Tuesday, he and Mansfield hauled thirty of the wayward senators into a meeting, where they were seated in rows facing a table with the two leaders, plus Magnuson and Phil Hart of Michigan. Mansfield and Humphrey proceeded to lecture their colleagues like scolding parents, with Mansfield playing the disappointed father. "May I say in all frankness that I do not relish the job to which you have elected me," he said. "I am not pleading or begging for cooperation or understanding. I am telling you that I cannot do the job unless you meet me halfway or more than halfway." Humphrey then took over, saying that from then on he was going to keep a quorum duty roster and that the senators had to report to him whenever they planned to be away from the Capitol.[20]

The quorum failure did more than anger Humphrey; it uncovered tensions among the senators and raised questions about whether they could hold together against the Southerners' near-millenarian filibuster. Senator Joseph Clark of Pennsylvania complained out loud, during a meeting of pro-civil-rights senators and staffers that morning, that Claiborne Pell of Rhode Island, one of the truants, "should be kicked in the ass for going off to the beach for two weeks."[21]

That same day brought a bombshell from Wisconsin: George Wallace, the bantamweight segregationist governor of Alabama who was running for the Democratic presidential nomination, had won a third of the vote in the state's primary, or some 266,000 ballots. Governor John Reynolds Jr. had said before the election that even a hundred thousand votes for Wallace would be a disaster. The national Democratic Party immediately went into crisis mode, spinning the vote as an aberration, a result of Republicans crossing over to skew the poll results. But the magnitude of Wallace's victorious nonvictory overwhelmed all excuses: the voters in what was assumed to be a safely moderate state had turned out in droves to endorse a racist demagogue for president.[22]

Wallace's victory was not a total shock to those who had watched him criss-cross Wisconsin in the months before. He had packed the auditoriums of urban, ethnic, working-class neighborhoods in Milwaukee. And yet he also drew on a less evident but very rapidly growing fear among middle-class whites, the very people who were supposed to form the bedrock of national support for the civil rights bill. "Despite the Alabamian's dramatically visible support in working-class 'ethnic' precincts," wrote Wallace's biographer Dan T. Carter, "the typical Wallace voter was just as likely to be a suburban member of the Rotary Club as a regular at the union hall." But the details of the vote mattered less than what it said about the public's support for the bill. If voters in early April were turning away from civil rights, what might happen if the expected summer of demonstrations and violence arrived and the filibuster was still on? President Johnson worried that Wallace's success gave Southern Democrats a shot in the arm, and the "will to keep on fighting the civil rights measure until the liberal ranks began to crumble." The bill's opponents made great hay of the Wallace win; the conservative commentator William F. Buckley Jr. wrote in *National Review* that "what the white North is awakening to is the danger to individual liberty of the new and radical plans breaking up traditional American patterns for racial assimilation and conciliation. For reasons that seem less and less coincidental, the proposals tend to be backed most conspicuously by a segment of the community which is far gone in a commitment to state socialism, which despises the American way of life and our civilization."[23]

In fact, no one had to look beyond the other story in the papers on the day after the primary to find evidence of renewed racial tensions across the country. As voters went to the polls in Wisconsin, a young Cleveland clergyman named Bruce Klunder joined a protest against a construction project that local activists said had shut out black workers. At one point Klunder, a big, bespectacled man, "a sort of Clark Kent of the pulpit," as *Time* called him, threw himself behind a bulldozer while three other protesters ran in front. The driver, who did not see him, put his six-ton vehicle in reverse to get away from the men; Klunder was caught under the treads and crushed to death. Shock turned to anger among the protesters, who attacked the driver, then other workers and the site itself. Cleveland police arrived and a two-hour street battle ensued.[24]

As THE MONTH dragged on, the energy behind the bill shifted rapidly to the back rooms, and the attention—within the Senate at least—shifted to Dirksen. And Dirksen knew it, had in fact known since before the bill was first introduced that its fate would come down to him, to his ability to lead enough conservative Republicans to back a significant expansion of federal power. And yet Dirksen was ready to play along. Since the early 1950s, he had acted as a bridge between the establishment and conservative elements in his own party, whether it was President Eisenhower's internationalist foreign policy, which he sold to a Republican Senate still in the throes of Taftian isolationism, or the 1957 and 1960 civil rights acts, which he sold to a wing of the party that highly prized its "conservative coalition" with the Southern Democrats. Dirksen's magic lay in his ability to remain at the head of the Republican senatorial caucus even as, time and again, he crossed ranks against his colleagues. Dirksen imagined himself a statesman, cobbling together grand compromises in the greater interest of the country. He was, in the eyes of Senator Carl Curtis, "a superb leader in getting divergent factions together to get something done." But other Republicans and observers were less enamored, and saw in Dirksen a man whose greatest interest lay in his own career. No one, wrote the columnist Kenneth Crawford, "gauges the political wind with a wetter finger."[25]

Whatever his motives, Dirksen decided early on that he would support the bill. In late October 1963, Kennedy had invited Dirksen to accompany him, Katzenbach, McCulloch, and Halleck on a trip to Chicago to see the annual Army-Navy game at Soldier Field. At the last minute, a new crisis in Vietnam forced the president to cancel, but he sent the rest of the delegation on to the Windy City. Katzenbach later recalled that while Dirksen refused to commit one way or the other on the bill's particulars, he left no doubt where he stood on it overall. "His final words to me then were, 'Don't worry. This bill will come to a vote in the Senate,'" Katzenbach wrote in his memoirs.[26]

Others in the Justice Department agreed that the minority leader would come along at the right time. Norbert Schlei, the Justice Department official who oversaw much of the early drafting of the bill, would regularly meet with Dirksen to discuss how the bill was coming along. Even as Dirksen railed against Title II in public, Schlei noted, "in private he was from the outset seemingly friendly to the bill and its purposes." And by February, Dirksen was indeed laying the groundwork for a switch; at a February 20 press conference, he told reporters, with his own inimitable wit, that he was no longer opposed to Titles II and VII. "Do me the justice of putting in whatever you write down that I've always had an open mind and I always feel free to come along with alternatives and substitutes that are infinitely more to my liking because I still take my freedom straight. I'm like little Johnny when the teacher said to him, 'Johnny, how do you spell "straight"?' 'S-t-r-a-i-g-h-t.' 'And what does it mean?' 'Without ginger ale.'"[27]

Dirksen knew that he could not simply order his colleagues to vote for the bill. Some would support it on their own volition. But the Senate was a different place from the House, where the leadership called the shots. In the Senate, members considered themselves independent, and persuasion and horse trading were more practical tools than force. And Dirksen had already frayed his connections with several leading conservatives, most notably Iowa's Bourke Hickenlooper, a man of lower stature but equal ego (and greater seniority), who bristled at Dirksen's support of the Kennedy administration on the 1963 Test Ban Treaty, which Hickenlooper and the conservative Republicans had opposed. It was not the first time the two were at odds, and such splits, wrote the journalist Elizabeth Drew in the *Reporter*, "often left Hickenlooper and his fellow conservatives standing in the shadows while Dirksen rode forth into glory, proclaimed a hero for rescuing the Kennedy administration from defeat." Even Dirksen's home state was starting to buck him. In 1963 the Illinois chapter of the National Federation of Republican Women passed a resolution criticizing Dirksen for crossing over too regularly to support the president.[28]

And so, as the bill wended its way through the House and into the Senate, Dirksen had to do two things. First, he needed to lay the groundwork for a plausible conversion from skeptic to supporter while remaining careful not to tip off his watchful conservative colleagues. On February 20, he told a press conference, "I have no assumption in mind at the present time" for whether the bill would win a cloture vote, but that he would keep an open mind about it.[29]

At the same time, he had to make it appear that he would exact a high price for his support. In late March, word leaked that he had prepared a long list of desired amendments, some of them quite significant. On March 26, he had given a long speech in which he criticized parts of Title VII, saying that it posed onerous record-keeping requirements on businesses and risked undermining the strong equal opportunity laws that already existed in some states—including, he pointed out, Illinois. Four days later, though, after drawing criticism for his speech, he went up into the press scrum in the Senate gallery to try to convince them that he did not want to "emasculate" or "water down" the title.[30]

But that was not the message that many of the bill's supporters were getting. On the night of March 31, Clarence Mitchell had brought Humphrey a copy of what he said were Dirksen's amendments; he would not say where he got it, and he would not let Humphrey keep it. The men were gobsmacked: as Raymond Wolfinger recalled, the amendments were aimed directly at Title VII. "He let us look at it long enough to get a clear idea that, far from being technical or trivial, Dirksen's amendments would completely destroy the title."[31]

The amendments, which Dirksen presented to the weekly Tuesday luncheon of the Senate Republican Policy Committee, included some forty changes to Title VII alone, a fact that pleased Hickenlooper, the committee chairman. Among other things, Dirksen wanted changes to spell out when federal law superseded state antidiscrimination law, to extend the title to cover federal and state employees, to require that discrimination be explicit and "willful," to strike the House's inclusion of sex discrimination, and to reinstate the provision banning discrimination against atheists. He would also bar whatever government agency was established to implement Title VII from filing suits itself, placing the onus on the complainant. After the meeting, Dirksen addressed reporters gathered outside. The amendments, he said, had broad Republican support, and he would present them to the full caucus at a meeting on Thursday.[32]

Whatever reception Dirksen thought he would get at that meeting, he was met with a hailstorm of invective from the Republican liberals and moderates. It did not help that he tacked on an additional Title VII amendment, one to delay enactment of the antidiscrimination regime for two years. GOP senators Clifford Case, Kenneth Keating, and Jacob Javits had already said that the Dirksen amendments were "unacceptable." Still, they represented just twelve of the thirty-three Senate Republicans, and they were unable to force Dirksen into rescinding any of his proposals. The meeting adjourned after two and a half hours with nothing decided.[33]

The participants in the regular bipartisan civil rights meeting, which was going on at the same time in Humphrey's office, struggled to make sense of Dirksen's actions. Joe Rauh, who had been invited to attend, said he was perplexed by Dirksen's atheism amendment, which strengthened the bill substantially. He suspected that something was up: "We can no longer assume that that is being constructive," he said. Halfway through, Kuchel came in to report on the fight that erupted during the Republican meeting. Humphrey advised caution. Dirksen was solidifying his support for the bill the only way he knew how, Humphrey said. "Let the Republicans argue it out with their own leader," he said. "Dirksen told me that if he did not get support, then he would retreat." Steve Horn, Kuchel's point man on civil rights, agreed. "Dirksen will go through his public acting process, take a licking, and then be with us," he said.[34]

April 9 did see one bright spot in the filibuster. Edward Kennedy, the youngest brother of the slain president, gave his maiden speech on the Senate floor that afternoon. The thirty-two-year-old, elected the previous November, said he had initially planned to speak on industry and commerce in Massachusetts. "But I could not follow this debate for the last four weeks—I could not see this issue envelop the emotions and the conscience of the nation—without changing my mind," he said. Drawing equally on his brother and Martin Luther King Jr., he said, "As a young man, I wanted to see an America where everyone can make his contribution, where a man will be measured not by the color of his skin but by the content of his character . . . My brother was the first president of the United States to state publicly that segregation was morally wrong. His heart and soul are in this bill." When Kennedy finished and returned to his desk at the back of the chamber, five of his colleagues huddled around to congratulate him.[35]

AFTER THE APRIL 4 debacle, the civil rights forces had gotten better at answering quorum calls, but that did not stop the Southern Democrats from making them. On the afternoon of April 13, Dirksen, Mansfield, Humphrey, Russell, and thirteen other senators joined President Johnson at D.C. Stadium (later RFK Stadium) for the opening day game between the Washington Senators and the Los Angeles Angels. Humphrey had warned his colleagues earlier that there might be a quorum call, but Dirksen had insisted to him that there was an informal agreement to eschew such procedural tricks that day. But around 2:30, after a lengthy attack on the bill from the floor of the chamber, Florida's Spessard Holland looked around, saw how few senators were present, and suggested the absence of a quorum. A few minutes later and three miles away, in the middle of the third inning, the loudspeaker at D.C. Stadium called out, "Attention please!

All senators must report back to the Senate for a quorum call." A dozen men in suits suddenly rose from their seats around the president and hurried up the aisles, while a handful of Southerners, including Russell, an ardent baseball fan, remained. The fleeing senators filed into waiting limousines and made it back to the Senate in eight minutes, easily answering the quorum call.[36]

The Southerners struck again that night, this time during a performance of *The Comedy of Errors* by the Royal Shakespeare Company at the National Theater, cohosted by Lady Bird Johnson and Interior Secretary Stewart Udall. Several senators were in attendance. But when the call came in to the theater office announcing the quorum call, Udall refused to interrupt the play. The show went on, and the quorum call was met by other members of the chamber.[37]

Still, such hardball tactics raised the question of how long the pro-civil-rights forces could hold out. The growing possibility that they might craft a deal with Dirksen drove the civil rights lobby to fits. On April 10, Clarence Mitchell sent a memo to NAACP chapters warning them that the Dirksen amendments could be the first step toward a drastically weakened bill. "Senator Dirksen's amendments are poison for the most part," he wrote. "We must work hard to make sure all senators oppose them."[38]

Three days later, at a meeting with the Senate leadership, Mitchell blew up over the proposed changes. "If we let the Dirksen amendments prevail, it will be a disaster," he declared. "There will be a Negro revolution around the country."[39]

Humphrey chuckled, trying to defuse the situation. "We don't plan on letting them pass," he said. "Don't break out in a sweat, Clarence. I believe we should analyze the Dirksen amendments and then move to table them."

Humphrey's jocularity notwithstanding, the rift between the civil rights forces in Congress and those outside it was widening. Encouraged by Johnson's insistence that the bill pass intact, no matter how long the filibuster ran, Rauh, Mitchell, and others refused to accept Humphrey and Kuchel's cloture strategy. "The Leadership Conference is united in thinking that a cloture discussion is unwise," Rauh said at a meeting with Humphrey and several Senate staffers on April 16. "Cloture means compromise. There should be no cloture until the votes are counted." Instead, they insisted that Humphrey and Mansfield start to get tough, extending the Senate's hours and enforcing the rules on speech times.[40]

"To date, the South has the advantage," Mitchell said at the same meeting. "We are not winning, not because we are not strong but because we are gentlemen."

Humphrey pushed back. "We will have to plan on cloture," he said. "Nobody won a war [by] starving the enemy. We must shoot them on the battlefield."

"You are shooting your friends if you trade with Dirksen," retorted Mitchell. Now it was Humphrey's turn to erupt. "Unless we are ready to move in our clothes and our shavers and turn the Senate into a dormitory—which Mansfield won't have—we have to do something else. The President grabbed me by my shoulder and damn near broke my arm. He said, 'I'd run the show around the clock.' That was three weeks ago. I told the president he is grabbing the wrong arm."

The pressure was clearly getting to the majority whip, who then segued into his own lament. "I have the Senate wives calling me right now asking, 'Why can't the senator be home now?' They add, 'The place isn't being run intelligently.' Sometimes I'm working for longer hours. The president says, 'What about the pay bill? What about poverty? What about food stamps?' Clarence, we aren't going to sell out. If we do, it will be for a hell of a price."

Then, before Mitchell or Rauh could respond, another quorum call was announced. "I'd better answer the quorum bell," Humphrey said, and shuffled off.

Through the middle and end of the month, a general malaise had set in over the bill's leadership. "The filibuster," wrote John Stewart, Humphrey's aide, "was beginning to erode the confidence and ethos of those supporting the bill." The filibuster meant no other Senate business could proceed, and even Northern liberal Democrats were beginning to tire of it. Some began to suggest that they should go ahead and take a vote on cloture, just to see what would happen—even though the most realistic vote counts showed that fewer than sixty senators would support ending the debate.[41]

At the same time, compromise with Dirksen seemed out of reach: though on April 11 he announced that he had whittled his list of amendments from seventy down to fifteen (and from forty on Title VII to just ten), he retained the biggest ones, including a rule allowing state FEPCs to supersede the federal body and to bar the commission from filing its own suits. He did, however, drop his demand for a two-year delay in implementing Title VII.

Dirksen finally introduced the proposed changes on the Senate floor on April 16, but as was the case with all the amendments to the bill, he did not "call it up" for a vote. He also promised an additional amendment on Title VII, to be revealed in a few days. But even with the pared-back sheaf of amendments, one unnamed "prominent Democrat" told Robert Albright of the *Washington Post*, "The big question remaining is whether the price is too high."[42]

Humphrey told the attendees at the daily strategy sessions in his office, surrounded by charts and calendars and duty rosters (as well as a mounted deer head, a gift from Johnson), that he was still hoping to go for a cloture vote by mid-May. "I will try to find the maximum number of votes we can get," he said. But to get there, he added, more noise from senators and outside groups alike was necessary: there needed to be "a barrage of propaganda" to demonstrate to the public "that the business of government is held back because some people cannot vote."[43]

Humphrey was also banking on the possibility that Johnson would yet arrive to work his legislative magic. "Knowing the president," he told the *Washington Post*, "I expect him to work miracles. He has a mystery kit of legislative remedies."[44]

But Johnson was having mixed success at best. His speeches and press conferences were as strong and clear as anyone could have hoped, giving a much-needed shot in the arm to weary senators. But his backroom arm twisting was going nowhere. On April 10 he called West Virginia's Robert Byrd, a longtime ally but a bitter civil rights opponent. He begged Byrd to support the bill, for Johnson's sake. "You're with me! You're with me! You've got to be with me," he implored.[45]

Byrd was not moved. "No, my convictions are against the bill."

Johnson tried a different tack. It was what he, the president, wanted, and wasn't that reason enough? After all, this was an election year. "It's going to be rougher if I don't pass that bill."

"No, it won't either."

"Yes it will. Are y'all going to beat it?" the president asked, referring to the Southern Democrats, with whom Byrd caucused on civil rights.

"I hope to hell we beat it," Byrd said. "We're going to do all we can for Lyndon Johnson. We don't need that bill. You know, you know I'll carry the weight where it's needed."

"Yeah, I know that."

"But not on this."

"I know that."

Johnson hung up in dismay.

FORTUNATELY, THE PRESIDENT was not the only one pushing the hard sell on the bill. Early in the debate, Humphrey had told Mitchell and Rauh that "the secret of passing the bill is the prayer groups." All through April they had been pouring into the city, a holy crusade of theology students, ministers, rabbis, and churchgoers of all ages, many coming not to lobby so much as to "bear witness," to add to the critical mass of people in the capital that in their sheer numbers insisted that the Senate act. "Washington has not seen such a gigantic and well-organized lobby since the legislative days of the Volstead Act and the Prohibition amendment," said Richard Russell, in a mix of frustration and awe. "Groups of ministers from all over the nation arrive in relays . . . As these people undertake to make a moral issue of the pending question, the politicians are having a field day sanctimoniously moralizing over what is essentially a political question." One veteran AFL-CIO lobbyist, impressed with the coordination and influence of the church groups, said as soon as he got home he would "go out and buy me a stand-up white collar."[46]

Perhaps the most impressive display of pious activism began on April 19, when three seminary students from New York—one Catholic, one Protestant, and one Jewish—gathered in front of the Lincoln Memorial and stood there for several hours. They held a banner that read, "Night and Day as witness to our common effort to help secure Justice and equal rights for all our citizens by passing the Civil Rights Bill as it came from the House." After a few hours, they were relieved by another trio, who stood for a few hours. And so on, for days, then weeks, on until the end of the filibuster.[47]

The effort, called the Theology Students' Vigil for Civil Rights, was the brain-child of three young clergymen: Brother Jude Molnar, a tall, blue-eyed Franciscan monk; Jonathan Levine, a student at the Jewish Theological Seminary in New York City; and Tom Leatherwood, a student at Union Theological Seminary, catty-cornered from JTS across Broadway. "The idea started in New York, among the future ministers at Union," Molnar told a reporter from the *New Yorker*. "They simply crossed the street and enlisted the future rabbis, and then they invited the candidates for the priesthood down here to join them."

Every few days a rented car picked up new students in New York and drove to the Church of the Holy Comforter in Washington. Soon young clergy from seventy-five schools around the country were arriving under their own steam, bunking on air mattresses in the basement of the church rectory. A sign on the wall gave simple instructions: "Students should stand in silence facing the monument. At midnight the group leaving the vigil should spend a few minutes standing directly before the statue of Lincoln. We are not promoting, debating, or pushing, only witnessing. This is basically a silent prayer vigil, conducted by theological students of all three faiths working together on civil rights."

Meanwhile, in the Sylvan Theater, off to the southeast corner of the Washington Monument grounds, more secularly oriented students held a five-day "filibuster" for civil rights, giving speeches in favor of the bill. Dozens of other pop-up demonstrations took place throughout the spring, almost all in favor of the bill (the American Nazi Party tried to counterprotest the vigil at the Lincoln Memorial, but they were largely ignored and soon left).

As the filibuster ground on, hundreds of individual citizens—alone, in small groups, or as parts of large organizations—poured into the capital to join the fight for the bill. Among them were Harry and Ruth Kingman, a couple from Berkeley, California, who had made civil rights lobbying something of a post-retirement career. Harry Kingman was born in China to missionary parents and later played a season as first baseman for the New York Yankees. He spent thirty years as coach of the University of California, Berkeley, junior varsity baseball team, taking time out during World War II to work for the Fair Employment Practices Commission. Even after he returned to Berkeley, he remained active in Bay Area civil rights causes, and once he retired, he and Ruth began to make trips to Washington to advocate for federal legislation. (They even registered as lobbyists, refiling their paperwork every six months.)

The Kingmans played small but important roles during the debates over the 1957 and 1960 civil rights acts, and by 1964 they were well known around Capitol Hill. They became something like den parents for newcomers to the expanding circle of citizen lobbyists, holding parties at their apartment and helping acclimate people to the Senate's arcane procedures. In an April 13, 1964, letter to Dean McHenry, the chancellor of the University of California, Santa Cruz, the Kingmans detailed the work they had done while the bill was before the House and later in the Senate when the filibuster began. They took turns sitting in the galleries, watching the activity on the House and Senate floors; they also ran their own personal whip system for the West Coast senators and congressmen, talking with them regularly to address concerns about the bill and keep tabs on any fence-sitters. And they added a personal touch to the organizing efforts: Ruth Kingman, an accomplished amateur painter, hung one of her works, a portrait of the March on Washington called ". . . Have a Dream," in the office of Berkeley representative Jeffery Cohelan, which activists were using as a base during the House debate, and another entitled "We Shall Overcome" in the office of Senator Clark.[48]

What emerged in the streets of Washington, in the church pews of the Midwest, in union halls and NAACP chapter offices that spring, was a biracial, robust culture of civil rights activism. As Levine told the *New Yorker* reporter, "I don't know how much this demonstration is going to accomplish for civil rights, but I know what it's doing for us." It was a culture of protest but also of civic engagement, one that brought together black and white, secular and religious, young and old, conservative and liberal—a culture that would reverberate, even as it fractured, through the 1960s and beyond.

ARRAYED ALONGSIDE THIS outpouring of civic unity was another, more radical side of the civil rights community. Radicalism had always had a place within the black activist community, whether through religious groups like the Black Muslims, through the Communist Party, or through groups arrayed under the umbrella of black nationalism. Located primarily in the North and West, they fixated on issues largely outside the realm of the Southern movement: not voting rights or public accommodations, but housing discrimination, de facto school segregation, and job discrimination—issues that Northern liberals, even as they denounced Jim Crow, were loath to touch.

One hot spot of radicalism was the Brooklyn chapter of the Congress of Racial Equality. CORE was a national, nonviolent organization that had pioneered sit-ins and later started the Freedom Rides through the South. It was one of the largest mainstream civil rights groups, and its president, James Farmer, was usually included in meetings of black leaders with presidents and congressmen. But the Brooklyn CORE chapter had long been an outlier; aggressive and sectarian, led by a fiery Southern transplant named Isaiah Brunson, it kept white activists at an arm's length while planning aggressive demonstrations meant to disrupt daily life around New York.[49]

In mid-April, the chapter released a bombshell announcement: unless the city introduced "a comprehensive program, by April 20th, which will end police brutality, abolish slum housing and provide integrated quality education for all—we will fully support and help organize a community backed plan to immobilize all traffic leading to the World's Fair on opening day Wednesday, April 22."[50]

The 1964 World's Fair, located in Flushing Meadows, Queens, was to be an extravaganza of high-tech utopianism, a "universal and international" exposition that promised "peace through understanding," achieved by scores of corporate-sponsored pavilions hawking a future paved with punch cards, mainframe computers, and CRT displays. The government was there, too: NASA came with its latest experimental aircraft, the X-15; closer to earth, the Johnson administration had a pavilion showcasing the past and future achievements of the Great Society. Towering over it all was the Unisphere, a twelve-story stainless steel model of the earth. Organizers expected 70 million visitors over the fair's six-month run.[51]

Brooklyn CORE's plan, distributed by leaflets in the week's leading up to April 22, was simple: thousands of protesters were to drive their cars onto the highways leading to the fair, stop, take their keys, and walk away. They would turn the roads into parking lots. Those coming by train were told to pull the emergency brakes. Separate from the "stall-in," people were told to turn on the taps in their apartments to drain the city's water supply.[52]

Mayor Robert Wagner accused the group of "holding a gun to the heart of the city." On April 20, he held a four-hour meeting at Gracie Mansion, the mayoral residence, on how to deal with this cataclysmic showdown. The national CORE offices reacted as well; James Farmer suspended the Brooklyn chapter's membership.[53]

Just as worried were the stewards of the civil rights bill in Congress. By late April, there was a feeling on Capitol Hill that even a single incident could sway the Senate one way or the other, pushing the bill to victory or killing it outright. A massively disruptive protest on opening day at the World's Fair would fall decidedly into the latter category—especially because President Johnson was planning to attend. In a joint statement issued April 15, Humphrey and Kuchel warned: "Unruly demonstrations and protests that bring hardship, and unnecessary inconvenience to others—even those who have long suffered indignities—are not helping the cause of civil rights. Indeed, they are hurting our efforts in Congress to pass an effective civil rights bill."[54]

On the morning of April 22, Police Chief Patrick V. Murphy, who would later serve as the Washington director of public safety during the riots that tore apart that city in 1968, put dozens of tow trucks along the Triborough Bridge leading from Manhattan and the Bronx into Queens; he set up three command posts around the city and had a small air wing of helicopters circling overhead, looking for trouble. Senator Jacob Javits himself boarded the 7 train in Manhattan, which went out to the Flushing Meadows site and was therefore a prime target for brake pullers.[55]

The whole city, the whole country, braced for a confrontation.

And then, nothing. A few drivers ditched their cars on the way to the fair, but not enough to disrupt traffic. No one pulled a train emergency brake; even the city's water supply remained at its normal level. A scrum of protesters did manage to slip into the fairgrounds and picket the president's welcome speech, but otherwise, the stall-in was a bust.

What happened? Brooklyn CORE's plan was not as simple as Brunson made it out to be. People did not in fact want to leave their cars by the side of the highway. Nor did it help that fair attendance was low that first day, around twenty thousand, thanks to both the weather and the fear of protesters.

When asked how he felt about the desultory scattering of protesters who showed up, President Johnson could afford to be magnanimous. What was his reaction? "Frankly, one of compassion," he said. "Somehow I think all of us must learn understanding. It is ideal, I think, for us to contemplate that it is easy. But even though it is difficult it is still possible."[56]

BACK ON THE Senate floor, the debate had proceeded at its newsless, lackadaisical pace until April 20, when Dirksen offered his latest amendment, a statute of limitations for how long the attorney general could wait before filing an employment discrimination suit under Title VII. As he did with his other amendments—and as other senators had done with twenty-four others—Dirksen simply presented the amendment to Humphrey and Kuchel, who accepted it and promised to "call it up" for a vote after cloture.[57]

They did this because, since there could be no debate on an amendment until it was called up, they could maintain control over the proceedings. But that calculus changed a few minutes after Dirksen finished his speech. Most of the other amendments had been beyond-the-pale proposals by Southerners to lop off entire titles. But that day, Senator Herman Talmadge of Georgia rose and presented an amendment that recast the entire debate. Asking that his proposal "be read and made the pending business"—that is, not placed in the sheaf of other amendments on Humphrey's desk—he suggested that anyone charged with violating a court decree to enforce the bill's antidiscrimination titles could demand a jury trial. If, say, a restaurant owner refused to allow blacks to dine at his establishment, even in the face of a judge's order to do so, he could not be punished until a jury had declared him guilty.[58]

On its surface, the idea of a jury trial made perfect sense: Why shouldn't people facing jail time be allowed a trial by their peers? After all, said Talmadge, jury trials are a "fundamental civil right" that "has been held to be a sacred privilege of personal liberty" since the signing of the Magna Carta in 1215. In the face of a sizable expansion of federal power, retaining some place for the public in the legal process seemed a reasonable, modest request.[59]

As the debate ran on through the day, the Georgian senator backed off his intention to call for a vote that day, satisfied that he had given the Southern position a new wind. But unbeknownst to Talmadge, it also gave time for Dirksen and Humphrey to have a quiet meeting at the minority leader's desk. In hushed tones, Dirksen underlined for Humphrey what he had been planning all along: he wanted the bill to pass, and he just needed some way to leave his mark on it so he could win over skeptical conservative Republicans, who might otherwise balk at supporting a bill so heavily identified with the liberals and Democrats. He had just one more amendment, he said, and it was to Title II. Whether Dirksen was truly trying to play the statesman, or just trying to get on board with a bill everyone knew would be a historic piece of legislation if it passed, was not on Humphrey's mind at the moment. When the conversation ended, Humphrey rushed off to tell his aides the good news. "It appears that Dirksen is beginning to swallow the great man hook and when it is full digested we will have ourselves a civil rights bill," wrote one of them, Raymond Wolfinger, in his diary the next day.[60]

On April 23, Dirksen got a call from Mansfield, who said he was sitting in his office with Humphrey, Kennedy, Katzenbach, Valeo, and White House Congressional Liason Mike Manatos and that they wanted to talk with him about the amendment. When he arrived, they laid out their case: Talmadge's amendment would probably pass, and it would do irreparable harm to the bill. Before they could talk about Dirksen's amendments, they needed to deal

with this one. They asked if Dirksen would sponsor an amendment to counter Talmadge's: jury trials would not be required, but if a defendant did not
receive one, the most he or she could receive as punishment was sixty days in
jail. At first Dirksen agreed, and he quickly persuaded Mansfield to go along
with him. But then the old Dirksen came out, and he began to bargain. Ten
days, he said—the most a defendant could face without a jury trial was ten
days. No, Humphrey replied—forty-five days. Eventually they settled on
thirty days, or a $300 fine, and shook on it. Dirksen offered the amendment
the next day and asked that it be considered immediately.[61]

The Southerners thus faced a dilemma. If they supported the Dirksen-
Mansfield amendment, they would come away with a much more favorable
bill, from their perspective. But they would also be ceding the momentum to
the civil rights forces and giving a stamp of approval, however narrow, to the
bill. At the same time, if they insisted on filibustering the amendment itself
and lost, they would have proven they could be beaten. In for a penny, in for a
pound, they figured, and they decided to oppose any effort at compromise.
John Stennis of Mississippi said that "it is merely a slight concession in name
but still denies all defendants the right to a jury trial." The amendment was
"just a mustard plaster on a cancer," Russell said, refusing any entreaty to
consider it separate from the bill itself.[62]

A new fissure then emerged between Dirksen and the civil rights forces.
Dirksen wanted a separate vote, to get cloture on just the amendment. But
Humphrey and his allies in and out of Congress, still not completely trusting
the minority leader, smelled a ruse: if they held a cloture vote on just the
amendment now, and lost, Dirksen's hand would be greatly strengthened—
which would explain why he wanted a vote as soon as possible.

They grew even more suspicious after they learned that Dirksen had set up
a meeting with Johnson for the afternoon of April 29. If he could lay the
groundwork with Johnson, convincing him that he had the best interests of
the bill in mind, then he would have virtually a free hand in demanding
changes from the bills' supporters.

Humphrey decided he needed to act decisively to head off Dirksen. On
April 28 he burst unannounced into the White House. He blew past National
Security Adviser McGeorge Bundy and Secretary of Defense Robert
McNamara, who were waiting outside the Oval Office, and barged in on the
president, who was in the process of getting ready for his day's meetings.
Humphrey warned the president of Dirksen's intentions, and demanded that
Johnson take a hard line with the majority leader. Johnson, who had been
purposely staying aloof from the daily give-and-take of the bill, listened
intently but said little.[63]

A few hours later, Humphrey got in a limousine and headed over to McDonough Hall at Georgetown University, where he joined Kuchel, Javits, Keating and about five thousand other people—plus dozens of reporters and TV crews—for an ecumenical service in support of the bill. A choir, which sang Mendelssohn and other holy music in between speeches, was composed of singers from Catholic University, Howard University, Georgetown, and Temple Sinai. Though the evening was billed as nonpartisan and apolitical, there was no hiding its targets. "Too many of our top leaders are pleasing the mob," said Bishop B. Julian Smith in his opening remarks. "What is organized religion saying to them, and what is it saying to the less prominent communicants who use cattle prodders, water hoses, and dogs on human beings?"[64]

The evening was punctuated by three sermons from leaders of each major faith—Lawrence J. Shehan, the archbishop of Baltimore; Rabbi Uri Miller, the president of the Synagogue Council of America; and Eugene Carson Blake of the National Council of Churches. In a speech that made headlines the next morning, Blake told his audience that the civil rights bill would only pass when people of good conscience but indifferent attitudes toward the plight of others realized what was at stake. The movement could never convert diehard segregationists, he said, but it could win over those "who are confused and fearful, some selfishly indifferent, content to sit on the sidelines, who see no clear moral or spiritual issue before the nation, who allow consideration of order, peace, or private profit, to neutralize their too general moral commitment to justice or freedom. These are the Americans we must win to our side of the contest." With high-profile events like the Georgetown gathering, and polls showing national support shifting back to the bill, that is exactly what the civil rights forces were doing.[65]

THE NEXT DAY Dirksen made his trip up Pennsylvania Avenue to meet with the president. The appointment was hardly a secret; Dirksen told reporters beforehand that he intended to give Johnson the tough-guy treatment: "You say you want the House bill without any change. Well, in my humble opinion, you are not going to get it. Now it's your play. What do you have to say?" Dirksen said he wanted the president to endorse his amendments, in exchange for a promise to bring twenty-two to twenty-five senators to the cloture vote. He even took along a gift: a commemorative clock from an Illinois company celebrating its centennial.[66]

But Dirksen had overplayed his hand. The Democrats were already indicating they would concede on certain amendments; the day before, Robert Kennedy had indicated that the Title VII changes might be acceptable.

"Obviously there had to be some give and take," he said. And the bill's leadership had agreed to go after cloture on just the jury trial amendment after all. Moreover, Johnson was incensed over Dirksen's pre-meeting comments. In a phone call with Mansfield just before the meeting, the president complained, "I don't know what's happening to him lately. He's acting like a shit ass." Dirksen left empty-handed—Johnson did, nevertheless, accept the clock— and afterward told reporters that the two had barely discussed civil rights.[67]

Dirksen was having more luck with Russell. The Republican leader had been imploring Russell to allow a vote on the jury trial amendment if he had any hope of influencing the overall bill; Russell's absolutism, he said, was pushing away potential allies.

Russell knew it. He had wanted to allow a vote for a while, in order to show that the Southern Democrats were not being simply obstructionist, and therefore buying time and patience with conservatives and the public. But Strom Thurmond and his fellow absolutists had refused. Eventually Russell wore them down, and on May 1, he said he would allow a vote on the Dirksen-Mansfield amendment in five days. Even better for Russell's purposes, earlier that day he had persuaded Senator Thruston Morton of Kentucky, a moderate Republican who leaned toward supporting the bill but was also friendly with the Southerners, to offer what was called a perfecting amendment to the Talmadge amendment. The Talmadge amendment technically applied to all criminal contempt cases, and Morton proposed a tweak that would limit it to just civil rights cases. That made Morton's amendment, not Dirksen-Mansfield, the first order of business when Congress convened on the sixth. If it passed, it would shift the momentum back to the Southerners.[68]

THAT AFTERNOON DIRKSEN called the bill's supporters and their staffs to his office, where he announced that he was willing to begin negotiations. It was not yet a breakthrough, but it was the opening that the bill's frustrated backers had been waiting for.[69]

Had Dirksen caved? Was he giving in to public opinion, which polls now showed was over two-thirds favorable toward the bill? Was he being won over by Humphrey's constant, wheedling praise? Or was this the reveal in his magic show, to be followed by a prestidigitation in which he "brought the souls" to the cloture vote, as he had promised Katzenbach he would do all the way back in November? It was, in the opinion of the journalist Murray Kempton, very much the latter. "He began by binding to him those Republican Senators who wanted the civil rights bill weakened and who trusted him to leech it. Now, having assembled his troops, he seems ready to deliver them over to the bipartisan civil rights command," Kempton wrote in the *New Republic*. "When Lyndon Johnson was majority leader of the Senate, there used to be complaints that he passed weak laws by bemusing the liberals into thinking them strong. Now Everett Dirksen seems to be moving toward the passage of a strong civil rights law by telling the conservatives that it is weak."[70]

Not everyone agreed with Kempton, especially at the time, and Dirksen did his best to keep the civil rights forces guessing about his motives. On May 4, Senator Joe Clark approached Dirksen in the well of the Senate and asked him about his last, unrevealed amendment, what Clark called his "hydrogen bomb on Title II." Dirksen replied, "Joe, it is not a hydrogen bomb. It is more like a firecracker that a twelve-year-old boy would set off."[71]

"Will it be set off by a nice boy or by a juvenile delinquent?" Clark retorted.

And so by early May tensions were high, in and out of the Senate, as the bill proceeded along its two tracks: on the floor, the careful dance around the three jury trial amendments; off the floor, in the back rooms of Senate offices, the slow negotiations with Dirksen. Emotions and optimism swung wildly day by day; on May 6, Humphrey's aide John Stewart wrote in his diary: "It will be somewhat of a major miracle if the pro-civil rights forces can get themselves back in order and push ahead with some degree of resolution and determination." A few pages later, though, he noted in a burst of optimism, "It appeared that Senator Dirksen has now fully thrown his weight behind passage of the bill and upon cloture." Anything, it seemed, could happen.[72]

As a precaution, Humphrey, Kuchel, and Katzenbach had agreed to continue to keep the civil rights groups as distant as possible; they held morning meetings with the groups on Tuesdays and Thursdays where staffers gave a sanitized "executive" summary of the previous day's negotiations. This was also the session most senators attended. But it was not where the actual work occurred—that did not happen until the afternoon meetings, which usually became evening and even late-night meetings. Over the next several weeks, a regular routine emerged: five afternoons during the first half of May, the negotiators—Dirksen, Katzenbach, Dirksen's drafting experts, and a host of senior staff representing Humphrey, Kuchel, and others—would meet in the bourbon-stocked back room of Dirksen's office (a popular senatorial retreat that Dirksen called the Twilight Lounge). There, Frank Valeo recalled, "serious discussions could take place in seclusion and where toasts to progress could be drunk discreetly." Sometimes the liquor was counterproductive. "Night after night Burke and I would go over the bill line by line in the senator's back-room office . . . The senator would provide drinks for all, and we would proceed section by section through the bill," Katzenbach recalled. "It behooved us to get agreement before too much bourbon had dulled the senator's recall of what he had okayed." Still, out away from the glare of media attention and lobbyist pressure, forward progress was possible, and day by day they got closer to an agreement.[73]

The civil rights community was alternately frustrated and bewildered; Mitchell and Rauh began to suspect they were being shunted aside and demanded they be briefed on the afternoon negotiations. The civil rights groups "have no idea what's going on and are more or less going nuts," noted Stewart in his diary. Perhaps in an effort to influence the proceedings, Mitchell stepped up pressure on Humphrey to go to round-the-clock sessions, and even demanded that the Senate sergeant at arms arrest wayward senators during quorum calls. "Who is Senator Russell that cannot be arrested, if by being arrested he'll save some lives in Mississippi this summer?" Mitchell demanded to know.[74]

In response, activists outside the inner political circles began to raise the temperature of public attention to the bill. On May 6 the UAW issued a state-ment denouncing the negotiations with Dirksen. "We reject both as unwise and unnecessary current suggestions that concessions must be made to Senator Dirksen in order to purchase his vote for cloture," it read. Two days earlier, on May 4, at a conference in Philadelphia, CORE had announced it would send protesters to both national conventions that summer. That after-noon in the Senate, with just a handful of senators on the floor, Kenneth Washington, a young black man in a trim hat and thin black tie, interrupted a pro-jury-trial speech by Florida's George Smathers, shouting, "How can you say you are protecting the black man when there are only five of you there? I thought this is America, the land of the free." He managed to go on for several minutes before three attendants hauled him away.[75]

Such pressure was no doubt heartfelt. But it also served a strategic purpose, which its more realistic proponents must have understood: the combination of broad public support for the bill, amplified by the LCCR's field operations, and the Capitol Hill tromping of men like Rauh and Mitchell, opened up space on the left of the bill for negotiation. Dirksen was not only under pressure himself, but he could see the sort of pressure his colleagues across the table were under.

At the same time, though, pressure was growing from the right as well. On May 5, George Wallace won 30 percent of the vote in the Indiana Democratic primary. It was less than some expected, and not as impressive as his Wisconsin showing. But sharp-eyed observers noted that he seemed to do best in the northwest corner of the state, near Gary, where both its black and blue-collar white populations were concentrated (he also did well in the middle of the state, home to the highest concentration of white funda-mentalist Christians). For some, it was also evidence that John Satterfield's

CCFAF was having some effect. On the theory that Wallace's supporters were mostly disgruntled white ethnics, the committee had taken out anti-civil-rights ads in publications like the *Polish Daily News* of Detroit, *Serbian Struggle* of Chicago, and the German-language *Wochenblatt* of Omaha. And it had contacted the major donors of vulnerable senators, hoping to find pressure points.

The primary's impact on the bill was obvious, and opponents rushed to translate it into pressure to pare back the legislation. Barry Goldwater, the conservative Republican senator from Arizona with a tightening grip on the party's presidential nomination, said the Wallace nonvictory "might take out two of the most objectionable features—the public accommodation section and FEPC, and it might delay passage until after the November election."[76]

THE FIRST NEGOTIATIONS with Dirksen took place in the late morning of May 5, in his office. Mansfield and Humphrey arrived in high spirits; they had just come from a leadership breakfast at the White House, where the president had told them he would begin to put the screws on Arizona senator Carl Hayden to vote for cloture. Hayden was a strong supporter of civil rights, but he was holding off from a commitment to cloture out of tradition: Arizonans looked fondly on the filibuster because in 1911, senators had used the tactic to prevent the Republicans from merging the Arizona territory with New Mexico. In a rare instance of explicit horse trading on the bill by the president, Johnson promised that in exchange for Hayden's support he would push for the Arizona Water Project, a massive program to bring water to the bustling cities of Phoenix and Tucson. And the move seemed to work, for once. Stewart Udall, who had been a representative from Arizona before becoming secretary of the interior, wrote the president a few days later: "The reports I get from Senator Hayden's staff indicate that your gambit on cloture with the Senator at out Tuesday meeting was very persuasive."[77]

Along with the two Democrats, the men seated around a long table in Dirksen's office included Kennedy and Katzenbach from the Justice Department; Warren Magnuson; the Republicans Kuchel, Hickenlooper, and George Aiken; and a platoon of staffers. Dirksen began by announcing his additional changes, which, if not exactly a hydrogen bomb, were much more dangerous than the firecracker he had promised: not one more amendment, but forty more, divided into three categories of relative substance. The men around the table took a deep breath. Dirksen could not be trusted after all. Even Kuchel was dismayed and angry. But rather than quit in disgust, they bore down, and by the end of the meeting they had dispensed with the first, mostly technical, group of changes. The rest would have to be dealt with later.

There was, however, a method to Dirksen's madness, and it was significant that Hickenlooper was at the meeting. Though Dirksen was often seen in the press as the man with the key to the conservative Republicans, it was really Hickenlooper, his jealous Midwestern rival, who held the most sway. And it was Hickenlooper who still demanded more give from the civil rights forces before he or his allies would concede to cloture.[78]

A major step forward occurred on May 6, when the Senate took up the Morton amendment. The leadership hoped to defeat the amendment handily, but the exercise almost ended in a debacle. The first vote, on whether to take up the bill at all, was split 45–45, the narrowest possible victory for the civil rights forces.

Just then Utah senator Frank Moss, a Democrat, ran into the chamber and demanded he be allowed to vote as well. When the clerk said the vote was over, Moss lit into Mansfield. He had been on a phone call just outside, Moss said, and the majority leader had promised to come get him when the vote came. When the Senate took up the next motion, to table—that is, kill—the Morton amendment, Moss sided against the leadership out of spite, and the motion was defeated.

The Senate went wild. Mansfield, gaveling the chamber to order, commanded everyone but the senators to leave the room. Outside, the Republican and Democratic staffs stood on opposite ends of the anteroom, "Like boys and girls at teenage dance," noted Wolfinger in his diary. Finally, the leadership placated Moss, and the staffers were let back in. The Senate voted on tabling the Morton amendment again, and this time, with Moss on board, the motion passed, killing the proposal.[79]

After narrowly defeating the Morton amendment, the leadership had planned to move directly to the Dirksen-Mansfield amendment. But Richard Russell objected, and the narrowness of the vote on the Morton amendment persuaded Humphrey not to press the case. It also pushed the civil rights lobbyists over the edge. Convinced that the slim margin on the Morton vote would give Dirksen an enormous chip in the negotiations, Mitchell demanded in a meeting the next day—his first one since the Dirksen talks began—to see the text of the minority leader's amendments. Katzenbach told him there was no text, which was true only in the strictest sense, since it was constantly being rewritten and tweaked. Mitchell then demanded that the negotiations be called off completely.[80]

Just then Humphrey walked in. When Mitchell confronted him, Humphrey let loose. "Whatever we are doing has but one purpose," he lectured the NAACP lobbyist. "And that is to secure a civil rights bill. Anybody who has an alternative, I'm glad to hear it. It is not pleasant for Tommy Kuchel and myself to have it appear that Dirksen is writing the ticket. I want the bill passed—the House-passed bill. We will not eliminate any title, purpose, or emasculate the bill. We aren't going to agree or negotiate anything which vitiates the House view ... I'd rather have no bill than the shell of a bill"—an echo of what civil rights leaders, particularly Martin Luther King Jr, had been telling reporters in recent weeks. Mitchell, for once caught speechless, backed down, but it was clear that the relationship between the bill's supporters in the Senate and the civil rights movement was fraying, and might even break, with disastrous consequences for the bill.[81]

That same day, though, came another incremental breakthrough in negotiations. One of the sticking points for Dirksen had been the provision in Title II that the Justice Department could sue local and state governments when it believed there was evidence they were supporting "massive resistance" of the public accommodations law. The problem, Dirksen foresaw, was that the term "massive resistance" was so vague that it provided no real check on when and where the Justice Department could jump in. After lunch, Clyde Flynn, one of Dirksen's aides, came in with a suggestion: What about replacing the phrase "massive resistance" with "pattern or practice"?

Charlie Ferris, one of Mansfield's negotiators, loved the idea. "Give us an hour to talk about this," he said. He rushed over to the Department of Justice and presented the idea to Katzenbach and Marshall. "Jump at it, Charlie," Marshall said. "That's marvelous."[82]

DESPITE THE SLOW but steady progress, President Johnson was getting antsy. On May 12 the Senate tied its record for the longest filibuster ever, and the next day would surpass the record set in 1846 on a bill to assume complete control of the Oregon Territory from Britain. The next morning, at the Tuesday leadership breakfast, Mansfield told the president, with his usual pessimistic prognosis, that "progress on the bill to date is nil."

Johnson erupted at both Mansfield and Humphrey, shouting that they were failing at their jobs and demanding that they do as he had long said and enforce round-the-clock sessions. The two refused, but that evening Mansfield did extend the session to 12:18 A.M. as a shot across the Southern Democrats' bow. "That doesn't scare us," said Russell. "We're ready for it."[83]

That same night, Humphrey took Dirksen out for dinner, hoping to hash through their remaining differences. Nothing was settled, but the two men came away believing a final resolution was in the offing. The next morning Humphrey told Johnson, "We've got a much better bill than anybody ever dreamed possible."

And, indeed, the May 13 negotiations proved the turning point they were all waiting for. The civil rights Democrats—along with Kennedy, who attended that day's meeting—had decided to hold Dirksen's feet to the fire, figuring that it was too late for him to back out of negotiations. When Dirksen asked that they vote on each title separately, Humphrey simply refused. Dirksen backed down, then agreed not only to drop his request for a new Title XII (which would have contained all the attorney general's powers for the rest of the bill), but also accepted Flynn's proposed "pattern or practice" language for both Title II and Title VII.[84]

Robert Kennedy then forced Dirksen to drop his opposition to the voting fraud provisions in Title I, which McCulloch had added and which Dirksen felt implicitly targeted his home state of Illinois, where voting irregularity was widespread and well known. Kennedy did not particularly care for the provision, either—ballot box corruption had allegedly won the state for his brother in 1960—but he insisted that they needed to placate McCulloch if they wanted the bill to get through. And again, Dirksen retreated. At this point a bit of prearranged drama from the liberal Joe Clark—who stormed out of the meeting in disgust, allowing Humphrey to show Dirksen the pressure he was under from the left—was overkill. Dirksen agreed to leave that part of Title I alone.[85]

After several hours, the negotiators emerged from the office, where they were greeted by inquisitive reporters. Sitting in a row—Dirksen, Kennedy, Humphrey—each rattled off his approval of the deal. "We have a good agreement," said Dirksen. "The bill is perfectly satisfactory to me," Kennedy said. "And it is to me," chimed Humphrey. "We have done nothing to injure the objectives of this bill." Dirksen was quick to note that the agreement was not yet binding on any other senators, and that each side would have to present it to their respective party conferences the next week. Unsaid, but understood, was the approval Humphrey would have to get from the civil rights groups.[86]

Aside from a raft of technical changes, the new agreement rested on two major alterations to the bill. On Title II, the attorney general could no longer sue in individual cases involving public accommodations discrimination, but instead could only file suits where there was a "pattern or practice" of discrimination in a particular town or region. Likewise, he could not file suits on behalf of individuals alleging employment discrimination under Title VII (though he could still intervene in them if he thought doing so would advance the government's interest); however, he could file a suit where there was evidence of a "pattern or practice" in an entire industry. To make up for the lack of federal legal support for plaintiffs, the bill offered to pay the legal fees of successful litigants—a measure that seemed a sop at the time but became immensely important later on.

There were other, less important but still significant changes that might still derail the bill—for example, an agreement that, for the purpose of the legisla-tion, union hiring halls would be treated as employment agencies, which were covered by Title VII. Labor representatives had already voiced unease about this plank, because it opened a new door for antilabor regulations.

Humphrey wasted no time in getting the agreement before Rauh, Mitchell, and the Leadership Conference. Mitchell worried that relying on the whims of the attorney general might be dangerous—what if a conservative took the post? But Humphrey was in luck: despite the bluster and criticism from the left over the preceding months, the conference proved more pragmatic than he had expected, and overall, the leaders of the conference were satisfied with the deal. "I thought it would be a lot worse," Joe Rauh said.[87]

On May 19, the Republican and Democratic Party conferences met to discuss the agreement. No one expected much to come of the Democrats' conclave in the old Supreme Court chamber, since the party was split into a large pro-bill majority and an angry, uncommunicative Southern minority. "Today is the 60th day of debate on the civil rights bill," Mansfield said in opening the meeting. "That is a long time, too long." He asked his colleagues to consider the debate in light of the upcoming elections—and the fate of the Senate itself. "In my judgment, the longer we rally with this measure, the worse it is going to be for the nation and for all incumbents."[88]

Then it was the Southerners' turn. Russell called the bill "a punitive expedition into the South. It is clearer than ever that this bill is directed at the South and no other part of the country." Sam Ervin, surrounded by his usual pile of law books—props, really—dug into particulars of the deal, probing for constitutional inaccuracies. "Ervin made a general ass of himself throughout the conference by raising nitpicking points and by carrying on in a generally ridiculous fashion," noted John Stewart. But Ervin's request for a week to study the deal was granted.

The Republicans had actually begun their meeting first, at 9:00 A.M., but their meeting went much longer. Dirksen walked through each title, discuss-ing his amendments as he went along. But he got significant pushback from Hickenlooper, who felt increasingly put out by the praise heaped on Dirksen. The Senate still had "monumental" work to do "to meet the real evils of this bill," he said to reporters afterward.[89]

That afternoon Dirksen summoned reporters for what he called "a little sermon." Dirksen was an orator of considerable gifts, but so far he had left his rhetorical tools in his office when speaking on the civil rights bill. Perhaps he had seen what the civil rights spirit could do for a good speech and wanted to try it out for himself. Or maybe he had planned on this all along. When a reporter asked him how he had decided to set aside his original criticisms of the bill, he said that "no army can withstand the strength of an idea whose time has come"—a refrain, which he claimed to have cribbed from Victor Hugo, that he would often repeat, in various versions, over the coming weeks. Civil rights, he said, fell into a long line of such ideas: the civil service merit system, women's suffrage, child labor bans. He talked about the millions of black World War I and II veterans who fought for freedom but returned home to oppression. "Today the challenge is here," he said. "It is inescapable, and the time has come to deal with it."[90]

Dirksen did not, of course, come away from the negotiations empty-handed. His two key amendments to Title VII—to bar the attorney general from filing suits and to give state FEPCs priority in pursuing discrimination cases—were in line with the strong recommendations made by his allies in the business lobby, particularly in the Chamber of Commerce and the National Association of Manufacturers.[91]

The business lobby had become particularly concerned in November after an Illinois state FEPC commissioner had ordered Motorola, the telecommunications company, to get rid of a hiring test that he said did not "lend itself to equal opportunity to qualify for the hitherto culturally deprived and disadvantaged groups." The Motorola case gained national news attention and became a brief cause célèbre among enemies of the bill, particularly John Satterfield and the CCFAF, who were looking for a way to revitalize their flagging fortunes in the capital.[92]

Pressure began to build on the national business lobbies from state and local chambers and chapters, especially from the South and Midwest. But the Chamber of Commerce, NAM, and other groups had stayed on the sidelines, both because they considered the civil rights issue too hot to touch and because they were dominated by large corporations that already had substantial nondiscrimination policies in place. Still, in the face of mounting concern from state-level chambers of commerce, the national chamber assembled a list of recommendations on Title VII, warning that the bill "could be seriously harmful to the conduct of American business," which it then submitted to friendly senators. Over the signature of its president, Walter Carey, the chamber asked that Title VII be stripped from the bill; if that was not possible, then it should be limited to a role of conciliation and persuasion. And if even that was not acceptable, then, as a last resort, Congress should at the very least prune Title VII by allowing only individuals to sue—not coincidentally, Dirksen's primary amendment to the title. James B. O'Shaughnessy, a representative of the Illinois Chamber of Commerce, later boasted about his group's successful lobbying on the bill: "We like to feel that we had a small role to play in the drafting of the final version of Title VII, for after four delegate trips to Washington and numerous conferences of our labor relations committee, we developed sixteen pages of suggested amendments to the section, and many of them found their way into the statute."[93]

But Dirksen was carrying less water for the business community than people then and later believed. Despite the chamber's explicit demand that Title VII be stricken or reduced to a voluntary effort, Dirksen never extended those proposals to the negotiations. He began with the bare minimum the chamber asked for. And he readily agreed that the bill should cover the legal fees of successful litigants, even though that might open the door to a wave of lawsuits. In the end, Dirksen was no doubt eager to curry favor with the business lobby. Like most politicians, he was protecting his interests. But he was also trying to do what he thought was right—in this case, pass an effective civil rights bill.

Whatever his motive, over the next two weeks Dirksen worked assiduously to win over the twenty-five or so Republican votes he needed to deliver to guarantee cloture. The day after his Victor Hugo speech, which wags took to calling the "Sermon on the Mount," he met with Republicans to discuss his changes to Title VII. Despite trying to incorporate his colleagues' disagreements, Dirksen faced growing headwinds from Hickenlooper, who told reporters he had "serious reservations" about the bill, even with the changes. Dirksen's intramural predicament got worse: on May 21, Norris Cotton of New Hampshire told Dirksen that Hickenlooper, Roman Hruska, and three or four other conservative Midwesterners had decided not to back cloture on account of their continued discomfort with Title VII. Still, Dirksen pressed on. One sticking point was how the amendments would be offered—the Republicans, wary of appearing anti-civil-rights, demanded that Dirksen pair with Mansfield and that they present a revised bill, known in technical terms as an "amendment in the nature of a substitute." Dirksen agreed to take it up with Mansfield.[94]

On May 19, Dirksen pressed the remaining GOP holdouts in two separate meetings—and came away with enough commitments, however tentative, to declare victory. As always, national politics influenced the course of events. That day also saw George Wallace come unexpectedly close to winning the Maryland Democratic primary, which gave some conservative Republicans who were leaning against the bill a shot of confidence that public opinion was turning against it. At the same time, conservatives allied with Barry Goldwater, who was now adamantly opposed to both cloture and the bill, did not want to alienate the presidential front-runner before the all-important California Republican primary on June 2.[95]

On the other hand, the bill got a big boost on May 25 when two hundred clergymen from the big three faiths knelt on the Supreme Court steps, across from the Capitol, for a prayer service. "Help all who consider legislation," intoned Robert Spike of the National Council of Churches, "to see the larger need, and to hear the voice of the oppressed rather than the complaints of the comfortable." That same day, former president Dwight D. Eisenhower, after a long meeting with Roy Wilkins at his home in Carlisle, Pennsylvania, published a rare front-page opinion piece in the *New York Times* and other national papers urging Senate Republicans to support the bill. Calling for a "responsible, forward-looking Republicanism," he insisted that "as the party of Lincoln, we Republicans have a particular obligation to be vigorous in the furtherance of civil rights"—as direct a shot as he could take against Goldwater, the man who would likely soon follow in his footsteps as the Republican presidential nominee. Whether the holdouts would heed the call of the clergy and the ex-president was a question hanging over the bill—that day a poll of all senators found that the bill still needed twelve more votes to win cloture.[96]

That morning staffers for the key senators on the bill sat down at the Department of Justice to iron out the remaining differences. Humphrey and Mansfield had readily agreed to Dirksen's insistence that his amendments be offered all at once in a joint substitute amendment. Most of the remaining changes were to accommodate minor demands from Republicans—for example, specific language saying that nothing in the bill could be used to justify minority hiring quotas. The provision to exclude atheists from Title VII protection was dropped, and the waiting period for voluntary compliance on Titles II and VII was dropped from sixty to thirty days.[97]

With the changes settled, Dirksen, Mansfield, Humphrey, and Kuchel strode into the Senate chamber the next day to present their compromise bill. "As a result of various conferences and by the process of give and take, we have at long last fashioned what we think is a workable bill," said Dirksen. "We have now reached the point where there must be action."[98]

Not everyone was enamored with the new version of the bill, or with Dirksen. Russell said the deal "puts Charles Sumner, Thaddeus Stevens, and Ben Wade"— three of the most radical Republicans during Reconstruction—"to shame." That Humphrey or Kuchel might be proud to be affiliated with the abolitionist spirit seems not to have crossed the mind of the Southern senator, who could see in them only a deep hatred of the South. But Russell reserved a special place in his own personal hell for Dirksen, who had cast aside the comforts of the conservative coalition to curry favor with liberals. In doing so, Russell warned, "He has killed off a rapidly growing Republican Party in the South"—evidence, again, of how out of touch Russell had become with the pulse of the region.[99]

Mansfield gave one last concession to Dirksen: that they not file for cloture, the first step toward voting on the jury trial amendments, the substitute amendment, and then the bill itself, until after the June 2 primaries, for fear that injecting civil rights into the Republican primaries could upset what was by now a coronation of Goldwater as the party's candidate. Because of the time required between filing for cloture and taking a vote, it would be June 9 at the earliest before the first stab at ending debate could be made.[100]

But in one last shot at the bill, Russell announced on June 1 that he was ready to allow votes on the jury trial amendments. The move was in part a way to win back filibuster-weary Republicans. But it was also a clever way of sabotaging the carefully orchestrated proceedings—the civil rights bill still needed time to lock down enough guaranteed votes. Early votes that went against the bill's leadership could disrupt their fragile momentum, leading to a cascade of recriminations that might sink the whole thing.[101]

And so, in response, the Democrats launched a filibuster of their own—a counterfilibuster to keep the original filibuster alive. Meanwhile, they did all they could to collect more votes. On June 4, Republican Jack Miller of Iowa agreed to support cloture after weeks of intense lobbying by the archbishop of Dubuque. When Senator Wayne Morse told Humphrey he could not be there for the June 9 vote because he was giving a commencement speech in a small town in Washington State, Humphrey offered to send a jet to get him. Morse countered that the local landing strip was too small for a jet. Well, Humphrey replied, then we'll send a helicopter to take you to the closest jet-accommodating airport. Eventually, Morse gave in to Humphrey's relentless wheedling and said he would skip the speech after all.[102]

Still, the carefully erected edifice began to teeter. Dirksen came down with a fever and retired to his northern Virginia farm to recuperate. While he was away, Hickenlooper struck. With as many as twenty senators behind him, the Iowan charged that Dirksen had failed to consult with them on all his changes and that he and his backers were no longer beholden to his leadership on the bill—and in fact would refuse to support it unless given the opportunity to present their own amendments.[103]

Humphrey and Kuchel went into a tailspin. Who knew what Hickenlooper might ask? Could he really muster enough votes to kill the bill? And if they gave in to him, and he won his amendments, would that kill the bill's chances in the Senate—or later, in the House?[104]

CHAPTER 8

BREAKING THE FILIBUSTER

HICKENLOOPER'S REBELLION MAY HAVE caught Dirksen in a bind, but Mansfield still had a move to make. On Saturday, June 6, he rose in the Senate chamber to present the motion for cloture—and then immediately offered to postpone it if his colleagues agreed to vote on Hickenlooper's amendments.[1]

This was a brilliant parry by Mansfield. It used the immediate, surmountable challenge presented by Hickenlooper to overcome the greater challenge presented by Richard Russell. In proposing to delay the vote until Hickenlooper had his moment in the spotlight, Mansfield was playing to the Iowa senator's great vanity, thus defusing the threat that he and his supporters posed to the bill. And it worked: that evening Humphrey managed to wangle cloture commitments from three of Hickenlooper's troops, Karl Mundt, Roman Hruska, and Norris Cotton. "I do believe this unanimous consent agreement," Humphrey wrote shortly after the vote, "brought us the extra votes that we needed for cloture." Hickelooper agreed to come along soon after.[2]

But Mansfield was also putting the Southern Democrats in a terrible position. If they opposed the vote, they would lose any chance of winning over Hickenlooper's faction. But if they allowed it, they would be giving in to Mansfield and allowing a demonstration of how strong the bloc was behind the bill. After some internal debate, the Southerners chose the second course, even though they knew they had been checkmated. "This whole thing has been a very graceful ballet . . . but I have not derived much pleasure from it," Russell said. "I have concluded there is very little chance of me winning anything out of this situation."[3]

Hickenlooper's amendments, which he offered Saturday afternoon for a vote on Tuesday, were anticlimactically small: a revised amendment, originally from Morton, which would offer all criminal contempt defendants the right to a jury trial except under Title I; a limit on Title VII to cover companies with one hundred or more employees, originated by Cotton; and Hickenlooper's own proposal to eliminate any plank of the bill dealing with aid for school desegregation.

On Monday, the Senate opened with Mansfield's cloture motion, signed by twenty-seven Democrats and eleven Republicans—intentionally far fewer than publicly supported it, since the leadership did not want to reveal precisely how many senators they had behind them. That set in motion a two-day waiting period, meaning that the Senate would vote on Hickenlooper's and Cotton's amendments on Tuesday and make its historic cloture vote on Wednesday.

Despite the momentous occasion, the minds of many senators were elsewhere. Over the weekend two Navy reconnaissance jets had been shot down by Communist rebels over Laos, which the Pentagon answered by ordering armed escorts for such flights—evidence, if anyone still needed it, of the country's inexorable slide toward greater involvement in Southeast Asia.[4]

The next day the Senate narrowly voted to approve the Morton amendment, 51–48, thanks to last-minute reversals by senators Stuart Symington, Edward Long, and Henry "Scoop" Jackson, liberal Democrats who otherwise supported the civil rights bill. But both the Hickenlooper and the Cotton proposals went down handily (40–56 and 34–63, respectively). The leadership also allowed one more amendment vote, on a proposal by Senator Ervin to scratch the entirety of Title VII—a move that was roundly defeated and thus helped underline the momentum behind the bill.[5]

THE WAY WAS now cleared for the cloture vote the next day. But Humphrey and the White House still were unsure whether they had the votes. On Monday, Mike Manatos had informed Larry O'Brien that they had 42 Democrats and 23 Republicans in hand, two short of the 67 they needed to end the debate (Humphrey was a bit more sanguine, counting 66 votes in favor). There was a small number of wild cards, some of them less likely than others—even after the vote on Hickenlooper's amendments, the Iowan had made it clear he was uncommitted on cloture (he eventually voted for it); on the other hand, Manatos ranked border-state senators Ralph Yarborough of Texas and Herbert Walters of Tennessee, along with Howard Edmondson of Oklahoma, as possible to likely supporters.[6]

At precisely 7:38 P.M. on June 9, Senator Robert Byrd of West Virginia took a final, lonely stand against cloture. With a black leather notebook filled with several hundred pieces of paper before him, he began reading a speech that would ultimately last fourteen hours and thirteen minutes, well into the next morning. As Byrd settled into his one-man filibuster, the Senate emptied. Humphrey went off to dinner with the journalist Andrew Glass from the *New York Herald Tribune* at the Monocle, a new restaurant set between the Senate office buildings and Union Station. Outwardly, Humphrey was confident. At 7:30, he told Johnson he had the votes in hand. Johnson, Humphrey recalled, "said he hoped so, but he said it would be difficult. I told him I was sure of it."[7]

Privately, though, Humphrey was worried. He knew that no civil rights cloture vote since 1950 had won even a simple majority of the senators present and voting. After dinner, he went back to the office and spent most of the night working the phones, trying to win over the remaining fence sitters. That night John Williams and Carl Curtis passed word that they would support cloture. But by 1:00 A.M., Humphrey still did not have commitments from the three outstanding senators he thought should have been the easiest to get— Edmondson, Yarborough, and Howard Cannon of Nevada.[8]

Humphrey finally went to sleep around three in the morning, but was awake by 7:30, when he called Johnson to reiterate that he had the votes. Again, he was less sure than he let on; after hanging up with the president, he called Edmondson, Yarborough, and Cannon. The first two, as expected, fell in line and said they would support cloture. But Cannon had been an ambivalent supporter of civil rights in the past, and he felt a vote to back cloture now might hurt him in his reelection bid that fall (he ended up winning by just 84 votes). However, Humphrey knew that Cannon was under heavy lobbying pressure from the United Steel Workers, who had given significant financial support to his 1958 race and promised to do so again—if he supported cloture. Cannon had also journeyed to the White House to meet with the president on May 27, where he presumably received the full "Johnson treatment"—with the Texan wheedling, pleading, and perhaps threatening his former Senate colleague to vote to end debate. By the time Humphrey got Cannon on the phone that morning, he was ready to concede—almost. He told Humphrey that he would wait in the cloakroom while the votes were called; if he was needed, he would come out and vote yea. (According to the union lobbyist Jack Biedler, Cannon was finally swayed by a White House promise to open a facility in Nevada to mint silver dollars.)[9]

As Humphrey made his final telephonic rounds, reporters began to filter into his outer office. Humphrey emerged to find a packed antechamber, where he spied his old friend Cecil E. Newman, a Minneapolis businessman and editor of the *Minneapolis Spokesman* and *St. Paul Recorder*, the state's two largest black newspapers. He and Newman toasted the upcoming vote with glasses of orange juice. Humphrey then left for the Senate chamber; along the way, he passed a note to Phil Hart that said they had 69 votes—two more than needed.[10]

Meanwhile, rumors swirled about additional votes turning up—Lee Williams, a staffer for Arkansas senator William Fulbright, sent word to the White House that his boss had decided to vote for cloture; others said Johnson had persuaded him to vote for it after promising him the secretary of state position after the fall election. (Johnson had done nothing of the kind, and in any case Fulbright voted against cloture.)[11]

Outside, the thermometer was climbing toward an oppressive 100 degrees, a drastic change from the blizzard conditions that had marked the beginning of the Senate debate. Just before 10:00 A.M., the Senate chamber began to fill—senators on the floor, surrounded by their staffs; onlookers and reporters in the gallery, peering down to catch a glimpse of history. Senator Byrd was still winding down his eight-hundred-page speech, which ended just nine minutes shy of the top of the hour, when Senate President Lee Metcalf gaveled the day to order.[12]

Before the vote came a cavalcade of final speeches. Mansfield, true to his role as arbiter, downplayed his support for the bill and instead invoked the need for the bill to receive a proper vote. "The Senate now stands at the crossroads of history," he said, "and the time for decision is at hand." He then read a letter from one of his constituents, a young mother in Montana. "I wish there was something I could do to help," she implored. "The only way I know how to start is to educate my children that justice and freedom and ambition are not merely privileges, but their birthrights." The majority leader then ceded the floor to Russell, who loosed one last attack on the bill. It would, he said in his thirty-minute speech, "destroy forever the doctrine of the separation of powers."[13]

Finally it was Dirksen's turn. The minority leader had spent the previous night at his farm in Broad Run, Virginia, writing what he intended to be a historic speech. He rose at 5:00 A.M., finished the final draft, clipped some flowers for his office, and rode in to the Capitol. He arrived just as Byrd was finishing.[14]

Dirksen stood at his desk and began by introducing the final amendment in the form of a substitute, essentially the Mansfield-Dirksen package, with the newly accepted Morton amendment attached. Looking pale from his recent illness and gulping pills as he spoke, Dirksen launched into a plea for his party to hew to its pro-civil-rights legacy. Equality was, he said, inevitable. Citing yet again his paraphrased quotation from Victor Hugo, he said, "Stronger than all the armies is an idea whose time has come. The time has come for equality of opportunity in sharing in government, in education, and in employment. It will not be stayed or denied. It is here."[15]

But just as Dirksen moved toward the end of his speech, Metcalf cut him off. "The time of the senator from Illinois has expired," he said. "All time has expired." It was a rude and unkind move, especially by an ally of the bill, but Metcalf likely figured he needed to take some shots at the pro-civil-rights senators first if he was going to beat back any underhanded Southern maneuvers later.[16]

Per the Senate rules, Metcalf then ordered the clerks and staffers to leave the floor. "The chair submits to the Senate, without debate, the question: Is it the sense of the Senate that the debate shall be brought to a close? The secretary will call the roll." All one hundred senators were on hand for the vote—a vanishingly rare occurrence.[17]

Outside, Roger Mudd stood in the muggy heat beside a big board constructed by the CBS art department, with the names of all the senators. At the insistence of the Southern Democrats, who did not appreciate Mudd's obvious preference for the civil rights bill, the Capitol Police had forced him to move off the Capitol grounds, so he was broadcasting from across the street. As the secretary of the Senate, Felton M. Johnston, called the roll, a runner inside the Senate gallery would step outside and whisper each senator's vote to a producer, who sat on the phone with Mudd's producer on the other end of the line. Whenever a new vote came in, Mudd would check yea or nay beside the senator's name on the chalkboard.[18]

A few moments before the clerk read the name of Clair Engle of California, a Navy corpsman wheeled the senator—by then horribly weakened by brain cancer—into the chamber. He wore a steel brace to support his head, and a black bandana held his right arm up to his face.[19]

The clerk called Engle's name. Silence. He called it again. Then Kuchel, his fellow California senator, walked over to the clerk. "I do not believe that the senior senator from California is able to speak," he said. "I am certain, however, that he is prepared to vote. Upon the last call of his name I believe that the senators present today noticed that he made a perceptible motion of the index finger of his right hand toward his eye, in a manner which indicates that he wishes to cast a 'yea' vote on the bill. If the clerk will call his name again and if the distinguished senator makes the same motion, I request that the Senate record a yea vote." The clerk called Engle's name, and the ailing senator slowly lifted his finger to his eye. His vote cast, Engle was wheeled from the chamber. He died on July 30, 1964.[20]

Watching from the wings was John Synon of CCFAF. The committee, despite all its money and effort, had failed to sustain the initial wave of anti-civil-rights sentiment it had captured early in the filibuster. It had been unable to co-opt business antipathy toward Title VII, unable to capitalize on Wallace's primary wins. And yet up to the day of the vote the committee thought it had thirty-four sure votes against cloture. But Synon turned out to be a poor vote counter, and it did not take him long to realize that many of the "sure" votes were anything but. Synon said that by the time Nebraska's Carl Curtis voted yea, he knew it was over.[21]

When Johnston got to Abraham Ribicoff of Connecticut, the vote was still five short, with nineteen votes left to go. Then came five Southern "nays" in a row—Robertson, Russell, Smathers, Sparkman, and Stennis—a list Mudd referred to, on air, as a "murderers' row." Stuart Symington's yea vote put the vote at sixty-six, just one away—but then came four nays: Talmadge, Thurmond, Tower, and Walters.

Finally came John J. Williams, a Republican from Delaware known around the capital as "Whispering Willie"—with some irony, because while soft-spoken, he was also a relentless partisan and a tireless advocate of small government and cutting federal waste. He had used the filibuster on many occasions to take personal stands against bills that he thought might add to the federal cash cow, and he had most recently taken the Johnson administration to the woodshed over the Bobby Baker scandal. None of that mattered now. "Yea," Williams said.

The room exhaled. What no one thought could happen had happened. For the first time in history, cloture had been invoked on a civil rights measure. The South had been broken. Humphrey looked up at the gallery and raised his arms in silent triumph.[22]

Johnston finished the roll, then read it again, a standard practice to make sure late-arriving senators had their chance to vote. This time Cannon emerged from the cloakroom and voted yea. When it got to Hayden's turn, Mansfield shouted, "It's all right, Carl. We've got the votes." The Arizona senator emerged and voted nay.[23]

When the roll call was finished, the clerk read the results: 71 yea, 29 nay—Humphrey's prediction, which some had thought overly optimistic, was short by two. Forty-four Democrats and twenty-seven Republicans supported cloture; on the losing side were twenty-three Democrats and six Republicans, including Barry Goldwater and John Tower.

The seventy-five-day filibuster—totaling 534 hours, 1 minute, and 51 seconds of debate, by far the longest in history—was over. The chamber erupted in cheers. Larry O'Brien said, "It was like the home team winning the Super Bowl."[24]

The path to cloture was never assured, nor was it easy. Contrary to the conventional storyline, it was not primarily about "beating" the Southerners.

Rather, it was about cobbling together a coalition of votes from the liberal and conservative Republicans to pair with the pro-civil-rights Democrats. This cobbling together was performed not by a single field marshal—Lyndon Johnson, or perhaps Hubert Humphrey—but by a loose and often unstable assortment of forces in Congress, the executive branch, and the civil rights movement. Senators who might never have backed the bill, such as Jack Miller of Iowa or Howard Cannon of Nevada, were brought into the yea column thanks to the persistent urging of religious and labor organizations, which had been deployed through a coordinated effort by the Justice Department and the Leadership Conference. The story of the civil rights bill is about the interplay between elected officials, government officials, lobbyists, and countless thousands of activists around the country, pushing and pulling each other toward their common goal. If the bill did not satisfy everyone, it was broadly acceptable—and as such it demonstrated, more than perhaps any single piece of legislation before or since, the messy political genius of American democracy.

THE BILL WAS NOT safe yet. As momentous as the cloture vote was, it only meant that the debate over the bill itself was over, and that a vote on the legislation would in fact take place. But before that vote, the senators had to consider the amendments to the bill—as many as six hundred of them.

Many of the amendments were beyond the pale of consideration—Southern-born bids to excise entire titles or add unworkably onerous obstacles to enforcement—while others proposed innocuous fiddling with arcane subtitles. But several were carefully crafted to look like the latter but have the effect of the former, particularly proposals from legislative wizards like Sam Ervin. In order to get to a vote on the bill quickly, Mansfield planned to run through the amendments in rapid succession, with dozens of votes a day, and there was every chance that a pernicious, purposely complex proposal could come up for a vote when no one was paying attention and pass. As the bipartisan newsletter noted the next morning, "Some of the amendments that may be offered are likely to have hidden dangers behind an appealing facade. Serious damage can be done to the bill if such amendments are accepted. Therefore all Senate supporters of the bill are urged to remain on the floor or in their offices while the Senate is in session."[25]

In fact, such trickery is exactly what happened, just moments after the cloture vote was announced. The body took up the first amendment, a proposal by Ervin to prevent a defendant from facing the same charge twice, once under state and then again under federal charges. Ervin presented his amendment, which was technically a "perfecting" tweak to Herman Talmadge's jury trial amendment, as a simple check on double jeopardy. But it was a Trojan horse: if an all-white Southern state or local jury tried and acquitted a white defendant of violating a black man's civil rights, Ervin's amendment would protect him from federal prosecution. The civil rights forces realized immediately what the amendment could mean for the bill, but in the confusion after the cloture vote, they were unable to rally opposition. The Senate took a roll call vote, and Ervin's amendment failed by the slimmest margin, 47 to 48. At that point Talmadge withdrew his own amendment.[26]

Then all hell broke loose. A recount showed that Ervin's amendment had in fact won, by 49 to 48. But since Talmadge had withdrawn his amendment, Ervin's was rendered moot. Order on the floor dissolved. Senators began shouting at each other, and at Mansfield. "The leadership seemed to be losing control of their forces," noted John Stewart. Mansfield, deciding everyone needed time to "regroup, rethink, and recollect," announced a recess just after noon.[27]

Russell, dejected, ambled back to his office. Along the way he was joined by Clarence Mitchell, his putative foe and, needless to say, a leading representative of the race of people targeted by the bill. Mitchell, ever the good sport, praised Russell for leading a spirited fight; Russell, ever the gentleman, congratulated the civil rights leader on his victory. He also predicted that, if nothing else, his opposition probably helped the bill in the long run: unlike the Supreme Court's *Brown* decision, which many in the South rejected as undemocratic, the civil rights bill would be accepted because the filibuster had demonstrated the extensive and rigorous democratic process.[28]

The civil rights forces retreated to Humphrey's office. The majority whip, after meeting with reporters and giving a brief on-air interview with NBC News, arrived feeling magnanimous toward Ervin—or at least pragmatic—and he urged that they find a way to accommodate his amendment without tearing the bill apart. The Department of Justice staffers present said they would see whether they could come up with compromise language, and departed. Senate protocol and notions of fair play toward Ervin aside, Humphrey's performance post-cloture was making his aides nervous. "He seemed to be going out of his way to make it up to the southerners, who had been stung so badly with this overwhelming defeat," Stewart noted. For the rest of the day, "he was giving sort of general promises that this or that amendment could be accepted, without checking the text of the amendments through, and put himself in several awkward positions."[29]

The next morning the civil rights forces regrouped in Humphrey's office to work out a final deal on Ervin's amendment. The Justice Department's proposed new language limited the double jeopardy provision to "the laws of the United States," thus cutting off the possibility of a racist state jury precluding federal action. They also decided to oppose all other major amendments unless the leadership of both parties agreed to put one to a vote.[30]

That morning the Senate accepted four minor perfecting amendments by Jack Miller of Iowa, but by the afternoon the anti-amendment momentum was apparent. Twelve roll call votes on Southern amendments were taken, and the twelve amendments went down in flames. "By the end of the day," Stewart noted, the Southerners "appeared to be quite dispirited and in a certain state of disarray." The day ended just before 6:00 P.M.[31]

The next several days devolved into a turkey shoot against Southern amendments. There was no order to the votes, and no sense of purpose to the proceedings—it was understood that the amendments would be defeated, and yet no one had the will, or the desire, to tell the Southerners to stop. Humphrey had decided to let them run out their rope, and that to stop them in the middle of their death throes would only damage his chances of repairing relations later on. "The best thing to do under the circumstances," Raymond Wolfinger noted, "was simply to defeat amendments as they were brought up." The result was a near-constant stream of roll call votes, with senators casting nay votes without even knowing what they were voting on. "The various Southerners would call up a particular amendment, yield themselves anywhere from 30 seconds to 2 minutes to explain the amendment, and then settle back for the vote," Wolfinger wrote. Most of them were grandiose and unrealistic. Russell proposed an amendment to put the entire bill to a national referendum: "I appeal to those in this body who call themselves liberals to let the people vote"—a ridiculous position coming from a man who otherwise claimed to hold the republican tenets of the Congress just below the Ten Commandments. In any case, the amendment lost.[32]

The dismal parade continued through the rest of the week, with eleven amendments going down on June 12 and nine more on Saturday, June 13. On Monday it was an even bigger rout, with fourteen amendments falling, and only one getting more than thirty votes. Robert Byrd offered an amendment to kill Title II, even as he admitted it would be "voted down just as indifferently, mechanically, and summarily as other amendments have been voted down, but that doesn't mean that senators should roll over and play dead." On Saturday afternoon, Ervin announced he was taking the rest of the day off to go catch a Senators game, where, he said acidly, "a man doesn't strike out before he comes to bat and the referee's decision is not made in advance."[33]

One amendment that was accepted, after some negotiation with the Department of Justice, was a proposal by Russell Long to strengthen the exemption for private clubs in Title II. It was a seemingly small change involving a handful of establishments, but one that would resonate through the next several decades across the Deep South as countless white-owned restaurants converted themselves into "private" establishments with nominal membership fees to keep blacks out.[34]

By June 14 the Senate had covered only fifty-one of the six hundred proposed amendments. The Senate, so enthusiastic about seeing the light at the end of the tunnel on June 10, now sank into the realization that, as Michigan's Pat McNamara said, "We are in another form of filibuster." For most senators, the process had become one of automatically voting no, since the amendments were poorly explained, often incoherently technical, and against the wishes of both parties' leadership. Most took the advice of Vermont Republican George Aiken, who said he voted against any amendment that a senator took thirty seconds or less to explain. "The Aiken rule is a wonderful one and I endorse it," said John Pastore of Rhode Island.[35]

Outside pressure was building, too; on June 15, in sweltering 95-degree temperatures, twelve hundred union and church demonstrators arrived from New York to urge an immediate end to the amendments and a vote on the bill. In a conscious reprise of the March on Washington, they listened to speeches at the Washington Monument, then passed through the offices on Capitol Hill, meeting with senators and presenting their demand that "no further crippling amendments dilute the civil rights bill as it is presently framed."[36]

The next morning, Russell brought the Southern Democrats together to try to force an end to the charade—it was, he said, embarrassing for the Senate, embarrassing for the South, and embarrassing for him, personally, as the faction's leader. But again, the zealots won out, and the meeting ended with no agreement.[37]

Hearing this, Mansfield decided, at long last, to press the button on his nuclear option. He had refused all entreaties from Johnson, his colleagues, and the civil rights community to go into extended days, in the hope that the goodwill generated by his restraint would bring the debate to an end faster. Now, he realized, he had no choice. "Harsher tactics" were necessary, he said, and on June 16 he launched the Senate on an epic run of thirty-four roll call votes in a single day.[38]

By late afternoon the senators, for whom five roll call votes would normally have been a long day, needed a steady stream of alcoholic lubrication to keep going. "Senators began to get rather well oiled by frequent visits to their respective hideaways around the Capitol," Stewart wrote in his notes at the end of the day. The scene, he wrote, "has been almost festive." Dirksen, a well-known imbiber of both whiskey and gin, appeared particularly deep in his cups. Around seven o'clock, Eastland moved to adjourn for the day, drawing the support of Republicans Peter Dominick of Colorado and Edwin Mechem of New Mexico. Dirksen ran over to Dominick, "stabbed him in the chest with his forefinger, and said in the very strongest possible way, that Dominick would do what the leadership wanted," Wolfinger observed. Then, seeing that Mechem had slunk out of the chamber, the minority leader sent a squad of pages to hunt him down. When the New Mexico senator returned, "Dirksen almost assaulted him," telling him that he had to follow the leadership on procedural matters. "Then he literally took Mechem by the arm, dragged him under the desk, and said to him quite fiercely, change your vote. Mechem, quite reluctantly, did so."[39]

As the evening progressed, the scene in the Senate became as much about Dirksen's energetic antics as it was about the bill itself. At one point Russell Long, who had promised the leadership that his amendment on private clubs would be his last, offered a sheaf of additional proposals. Dirksen exploded. Running over to Long, he yelled, "Goddammit, you broke our deal!" Dirksen inched closer to Long's face, pointing his finger at his chest. "We should have never taken your amendment. Goddammit Russell, you broke your faith with us!" Finally Mansfield pulled Dirksen away. A few minutes later Dirksen came back to Long and apologized. The two shook hands, then hugged and walked out, presumably for a make-up tipple in Dirksen's office.[40]

Mansfield finally called it a day at 12:01 A.M., ending a marathon thirteen-hour session. In all, thirty-four roll call votes were taken, more than double the sixteen-vote record set in 1951. Fourteen of them were proposed by Thurmond, eight by Ervin, and seven by Long. As the evening was winding down, Russell decided the Southerners had done enough damage, and he hatched a plot with Lister Hill to make Thurmond, Ervin, and Long stand down. John Stewart, Humphrey's aide, overheard the Georgian tell the Alabaman, "If you can handle that damn fool Strom, I'll take care of Ervin and Long. Those guys are disgracing all of us and creating a great deal of resentment against us."[41]

Russell's plan must have worked: the next day Humphrey sat down with Thurmond and Ervin and worked out a deal to bring the amendment roller coaster to an end that day, and move to a final vote on the nineteenth. But the agreement guaranteed another storm of amendments, and another long day: ten and a half hours, twenty-two amendments, with twenty-one defeats (one, a proposal by Long to protect fraternities from Title II, was accepted). When their amendments had run out, several of the most ardent Southerners burned the rest of their energy on long-winded speeches, including a forty-three-minute rant by Hill.[42]

When they were done, Thomas J. McIntyre of New Hampshire, the presiding officer for the day, called for a vote on the last amendment: the Dirksen-Mansfield substitute (though Mansfield, in his typical modesty, insisted it be called the "Dirksen-Humphrey" substitute). It passed 76 to 18. "Take it easy and go home and get a good night's sleep," Mansfield said—advice that, coming at 9:30 P.M. after another long day of legislating, could be a comfort only to men who had just come off the longest filibuster in Senate history.[43]

Though few knew it at the time, in the middle of the day Humphrey had received word that his son Robert, then back in Minnesota, had developed a malignant brain tumor and needed an immediate operation. Despite breaking down in tears before Joe Rauh and Clarence Mitchell, Humphrey decided to stay in Washington.[44]

The morning of the eighteenth, with Edward M. Kennedy presiding, saw the rest of the Southerners unload their remaining time in heated, vitriolic attacks on the bill. Russell's speech was mostly a postmortem of the Southern strategy against the bill, and an effort to take the high road after dropping so low during the filibuster. "We have sought to appeal to the sense of fairness and justice of the members of this body," he intoned. "We made no secret of the fact that we were undertaking to speak in detail and at length in an effort to get the message across to the American people. We did not deceive anyone as to our purposes—"[45]

"The time of the senator from Georgia has expired," rang out a voice from the dais. Kennedy, among the least experienced and youngest members of the august Senate, had just cut off one of its most venerable.

Russell turned and glared. "I express the hope that those who are keeping the time will apply the same rules to others which they have applied to me," he said, and asked whether Humphrey had been given extra time during a June 17 speech.

"The senator from Minnesota was charged with nine minutes," Kennedy replied.

"I am glad to hear that," Russell said venomously, and sank into his chair.

At one point an eighteen-year-old onlooker named Jerry Lester Cochran unfurled a flag with a swastika on it and shouted from the gallery, "We have betrayed the white majority! Only Rockwell can save us now"—a reference to George Lincoln Rockwell, the head of the American Nazi Party. He was quickly removed by attendants and, as protocol demanded, taken to a hospital for "observation."[46]

The biggest story of the day, however, was Barry Goldwater—now, after winning the California primary, the presumed Republican presidential candidate—and whether he would back the bill. "Rarely has one man's vote been watched so closely as Barry Goldwater's on the civil rights bill," wrote *Time* magazine. That afternoon he announced that he would vote nay. "I am unalterably opposed to discrimination or segregation on the basis of race, color, or creed, or on any other basis," Goldwater said. But he could not vote for the bill, because he believed that Titles II and VII represented "a grave threat to the very essence of our basic system of government." Enforcement would require "the development of an 'informer' psychology in great areas of our national life—neighbors spying on neighbors, workers spying on workers, businessmen spying on businessmen—where those citizens for selfish reasons will have ample inducement to do so."[47]

Goldwater's opposition came as little surprise to some, but others, particularly in his own party, had hoped that the pull of presidential politics would work magic on his misgivings. Up to the last minute, Jacob Javits had been lobbying Goldwater to support the bill, for the party's sake. According to the columnists Rowland Evans and Robert Novak, Javits sent reams of memos to Goldwater's office underlining the bill's constitutionality. "It is now clear," the New York Republican said on the Senate floor just before Goldwater rose to speak, "that the mainstream of my party is [in] support of this bill." Others took a hard-line approach, charging that right-wing opposition to the bill, grounded in allegedly race-neutral principles of civil liberties and states' rights, was no better than the open racism of the Southern Democrats. But Goldwater was unmoved. "If my vote is misconstrued, let it be, and let me suffer its consequences," he said unhelpfully. "Barry, this is a dreadful mistake," said Javits after Goldwater had finished.[48]

Of course, Goldwater may also have been playing to the Southern vote; he had deep ties with Southern businessmen and politicians, and he had been saying for years that the GOP should do all it could to win Southern votes. Many Southern Democrats, in turn, welcomed him. "If he opposes this bill he could carry most of the South," said Allen Ellender of Louisiana. "I have not thought Goldwater could beat President Johnson but if he votes against this bill he is going to give the president a tough battle."[49]

June 19 opened with a quick vote on a motion by Al Gore Sr. to send the bill to the Senate Judiciary Committee, on the grounds that it had not yet received a thorough, legal examination from the upper chamber. There was a time when Gore's motion might have gotten traction, if only because the leadership thought he was one of the Southern Democrats who might "go Vandenberg" and switch sides. But Gore was facing a tight reelection campaign, and there was little to be gained by currying his favor—especially since the bill was now safe. His motion failed overwhelmingly.[50]

Then it was simply a matter of final speeches from the leadership. Humphrey discussed the long, hard slog that brought them to that day. "I doubt whether any senator can recall a bill which so tested our attitudes of justice and equity," he said. Mansfield came next, praising Dirksen and Humphrey, but most poignantly, President Kennedy. "This, indeed, is his moment," the majority leader said. Finally, Dirksen rose to explain once more his transit from opponent to full-throated supporter of the bill. It must pass, he said, "if we are to honor the pledges we have made when we held up out hands to take an oath to defend the laws and carry out the Constitution of the United States." He concluded, "I am prepared to vote."[51]

Once again, all one hundred senators were present—including the bedridden Engle—and once again, the vote was overwhelming. Supporting the bill were seventy-three senators, including four Westerners—Wallace Bennett, Alan Bible, Carl Hayden, and Milton Young—who had opposed cloture. Of the twenty-seven who voted against it, two—Cotton and Hickenlooper—had voted for cloture.

The leadership gathered for photos, though Mansfield humbly refused to stand in with Humphrey, Dirksen, Kuchel, and the rest. Humphrey and his aides and colleagues then strode out onto the eastern steps of the Capitol, where they were greeted by thousands of civil rights well-wishers. "Freedom!" they shouted. "You gave us justice!" Humphrey just beamed. "I feel like a heavy load has been lifted from my shoulders—a wonderful sense of relief and quiet joy," he told the reporter James Reston. After a celebratory dinner with Stewart, Humphrey went home to rest before flying back to Minneapolis to see his son.[52]

THE BILL NOW went back to the House, where it faced one more hurdle: its old nemesis Howard Smith, whose committee had to approve the new version of the bill for it to go to the floor. Fortunately, Emanuel Celler and Bill McCulloch had ways of dealing with the obstreperous chairman. On the morning of Monday, June 22, Celler asked that the House grant unanimous consent to approve the Senate's version of the bill. Four Southern Democrats immediately shot out of their seats in objection. Anticipating this, Celler proposed a resolution for the House to make the Senate draft its next order of business—a resolution that had to then pass the Rules Committee. Predictably, Smith was nowhere to be seen on the Hill, and he had already made it clear that he would delay considering it for as long as he could. But Celler then had three liberal members of the Rules Committee submit letters to Smith by registered mail insisting that he schedule hearings—the first step toward a vote to take control of the committee (upon receipt of such a letter, the chairman must schedule a hearing within seven days, or a simple majority of the committee can vote to take it away from him). Smith, seeing himself in a corner, agreed to open hearings on June 30, the last possible day.[53]

That week was not entirely full of good news, though. Late at night on Sunday, June 21, three civil rights workers went missing in rural Mississippi. The state was the site of "Freedom Summer," a months-long campaign by students from around the country, in coordination with local civil rights workers, to register black voters and offer classes on protecting their constitutional rights. Their disappearance made national news. Daily updates on the search for the men, or their bodies, hung over the last weeks of the civil rights bill.

Then next day Speaker John McCormack told reporters he expected the bill to reach the president's desk by July 4. Charles Halleck, still trying to regain some of his lost credibility with the GOP rank and file, needlessly lashed out at his fellow congressman, saying that putting the bill in Johnson's hands on Independence Day would turn a bipartisan bill into a tool for presidential aggrandizement (as if Johnson needed it), and he insisted that it be signed no later than July 2. Johnson's people had already been thinking along the same lines, but in reverse. They wanted the bill signing televised, with maximum coverage in the papers. July 4, they realized, was a holiday, when all but the most serious followers of the bill would tune out for barbeque and fireworks. Better, said Johnson's aide Bill Moyers, to sign it on July 2.[54]

That is, of course, assuming the bill's backers on the Rules Committee managed to pry it out of Smith's hands. On the morning of June 30, they put their plan into action. As soon as Smith opened the hearing, Ray Madden, a liberal Democrat from Minnesota, announced that a majority of the committee wanted to finish testimony by 5:00 P.M., then vote by the end of the day. When Smith balked, the committee went into executive session—no reporters or observers allowed—and voted 7 to 4 against Smith. "The country wants action on this bill, not more discussion," Celler said afterward.[55]

At five o'clock, the committee went back into executive session and voted 10 to 5 to grant the bill a rule and send it to the House floor. Then Richard Bolling moved to have Madden, not Smith, craft the rules for debating the bill on the House floor, citing House bylaws that if a chairman opposed a bill, a majority of the committee could replace him. Smith, who had sat on the committee for decades, was crestfallen. "I have never in all that experience," he said, "had any member of this committee make the motion made by the gentleman from Missouri today."[56]

But his plaint went unanswered. The rule was granted, and two days later Madden called up the bill on the House floor. After a round of speeches—including two by McCulloch and Celler that drew standing ovations—Madden moved the bill to a vote. It passed 289 to 126. The Civil Rights Act of 1964 was off to the White House, about to become law.[57]

CHAPTER 9

A BILL BECOMES A LAW

ON THE EVENING OF JULY 2, 1964, just five hours after the House passed the final version of the Civil Rights Act, two hundred fifty people gathered in the East Room of the White House to watch Lyndon Johnson sign it into law.[1]

This was by far the biggest night of Johnson's presidency since he addressed Congress a few days after Kennedy's assassination, and he and his staff had spent the previous week cramming like college students to make it perfect—not just for the dignitaries inside the East Room, but for the millions of people who would watch the ceremony on television. It was the first signal accomplishment of the Johnson administration, and a promise of more to come if voters chose him in four months. In the course of a half dozen major revisions—and countless minor ones—speechwriters Horace Busby and Bill Moyers went back and forth over whether the address should come before or after the signing, over how much Johnson should mention God, over how sensitive he should be toward the South.[2]

While the White House staff debated, the bill moved through its final motions in the House. On the morning of the second, after the Reverend Bernard Braskamp had opened the session by reading an apt passage from Leviticus ("Proclaim liberty throughout the land, unto all the inhabitants thereof"), Smith had taken one last shot at slowing the bill. He began by declaring that the fifteen minutes of debate established by Madden's rule was unfair, given how much the bill had evolved. But he reserved his real ire for the changes that he had always feared the bill represented, changes that were now wholly evident in the host of students and civil rights workers arriving in Mississippi for Freedom Summer. "Hordes of beatniks, misfits, and agitators from the North, with the admitted aid of the Communists, are streaming into the Southland on mischief bent, backed and defended by other hordes of Federal marshals, Federal agents, and Federal power," he declared—a grossly insensitive comment, given the national attention focused on the three CORE workers who had recently disappeared in Mississippi. Nevertheless, when Smith finished, the Southern Democrats applauded, and Emanuel Celler came over to his desk to shake his hand.[3]

Not all Southern Democrats in the House opposed the bill this time around, though. Several had had an election-year change of heart. One, Charles Weltner of Atlanta, had voted nay when the bill first came through the House but announced on the floor that morning that he had decided to vote yea this time (three Republicans did as well). The thirty-six-year-old first-term member represented the New South that the region's liberals, black and white, hoped would emerge with the bill's passage: a native Georgian who had attended Columbia Law School and returned home with a worldview much more cosmopolitan than that of the average white Southern politician. Men like Weltner (Richard Fulton of Nashville was another) represented urban, biracial communities, and they were well positioned—and forward-looking enough—to respond to an upsurge in black voting power.

On the floor, Weltner said that he had always agreed with the bill's goals, but he had voted against it the first time because he had reservations about its means of enforcement. Still, he said, with the final version before him, he had to make a decision. "What then is the proper course? Is it to vote 'no,' with tradition, safety—and futility?" he asked. "Change, swift and certain, is upon us. And we in the South face some difficult decisions. We can offer resistance and defiance, with their harvest of strife and tumult . . . or we can acknowledge this measure as the law of the land." The Old South was crumbling, and a New South, so long proclaimed but never fulfilled, was finally here. "Finally, I would urge that we at home now move on to the unfinished business of building a New South. We must not remain forever bound to another lost cause." When he finished, Northern Democrats erupted in a standing ovation; his fellow Georgians sat in silence. After the session, Secretary of State Dean Rusk, a fellow liberal son of the Peach State, called Weltner with congratulations. (Weltner won his reelection bid that year, but withdrew from his 1966 race after the state Democratic Party insisted that he sign a "loyalty" oath to support the pro-segregationist Lester Maddox for governor.)[4]

In contrast, three Republicans—Charlotte Thompson Reid of Illinois, Bob Wilson of California, and Earl Wilson of Indiana—who had voted for the original bill voted against the substitute, saying that they had held their noses the first time in the hope that the Senate would improve the bill to their liking. Their reversals, however, were meaningless; just after 2:00 P.M., the House voted overwhelmingly to send the bill to the president.[5]

*

THAT EVENING THE White House brimmed with civil rights leaders, congressmen, their wives, and countless reporters, seated on gilt chairs waiting for Johnson to arrive. The only Southerners in the room were two liberal former governors, Luther Hodges of North Carolina, now the commerce secretary, and LeRoy Collins of Florida, whom the president was about to name as head of the new Community Relations Service.[6]

When Johnson strode into the room, Robert Kennedy was the first to rise in applause; Dirksen, to his left, and Humphrey beyond him, stood in turn. Under the soft glow of a baroque chandelier, Johnson coursed along the front row of the audience, shaking hands. He then sat at a desk, arranged perpendicular to the rows of seats to be directly in front of four TV cameras. Set in front of him on the desk were one hundred pens, standing upright in holders; behind him stood an American flag. In his hand Johnson held a single rumpled sheet of paper, which he smoothed several times on the desk before looking up at the camera.[7]

"I want to take this occasion to talk to you about what that law means to every American," he began. The camera frame sat tightly around Johnson's head—his brow, furrowed; his glasses, semi-rimless; his suit and tie, black. He spoke slowly, with a heavy helping of creamy Southern drawl. "One hundred and eighty-eight years ago this week a small band of valiant men began a long struggle for freedom," he said. "They pledged their lives, their fortunes, and their sacred honor not only to found a nation, but to forge an ideal of freedom—not only for political independence, but for personal liberty; not only to eliminate foreign rule, but to establish the rule of justice in the affairs of men."[8]

Johnson had rarely invoked foreign policy as a justification for civil rights progress, but he did so that night. "Today in far corners of distant continents," he intoned, "the ideals of those American patriots still shape the struggles of men who hunger for freedom." Indeed, the growing conflict in Southeast Asia loomed over the opening of the address: "Those who founded our country knew that freedom would be secure only if each generation fought to renew and enlarge its meaning. From the minutemen at Concord to the soldiers in Vietnam, each generation has been equal to that trust."

And yet, he went on, those generations of Americans fought for an ideal future in an imperfect and unjust present, when so many were denied the basic protections of the Constitution. "The reasons are deeply embedded in history and tradition and the nature of man," he said. "We can understand—without rancor or hatred—how this all happened. But it cannot continue. Our Constitution, the foundation of our Republic, forbids it. The principles of our freedom forbid it. Morality forbids it. And the law I will sign tonight forbids it."

Critically, before going into what the new law would do, he offered an extended defense. He rattled off the bill's long journey to his desk—passing through long debates in both houses, along the way winning the endorsement of "tens of thousands" of religious, labor, civic, and civil rights leaders. It was a clear play to the legislation's millions of opponents: like the bill or not, everyone could agree that it was the product of a thoroughly considered democratic process.

Johnson then went further, explaining what the bill did not do: "It does not restrict the freedom of any American, so long as he respects the rights of others. It does not give special treatment to any citizen. It does say the only limit to a man's hope for happiness, and for the future of his children, shall be his own ability." To that end, Johnson said he was nominating LeRoy Collins, a former governor of Florida, to head the Community Relations Service—a step that underlined the bill's primary reliance on "voluntary compliance" and "the efforts of local communities and states." The federal government would "step in only when others cannot or will not do the job." The audience roared in applause.

Johnson ended with a stirring peroration, one of his rhetorical specialties:

> My fellow citizens, we have come now to a time of testing. We must not fail. Let us close the springs of racial poison. Let us pray for wise and understanding hearts. Let us lay aside irrelevant differences and make our Nation whole. Let us hasten that day when our unmeasured strength and our unbounded spirit will be free to do the great works ordained for this Nation by the just and wise God who is the Father of us all. Thank you and good night.

The audience again exploded as people from the first few rows rushed to surround the president. Johnson immediately grabbed for the forest of pens before him, using each to draw a fraction of an inch of his signature before handing it off to a well-wisher. "The president seems to have mastered the art of just touching each pen to the paper," said the correspondent Ed Herlihy in a Universal newsreel. Johnson had additional gifts for Dirksen and Humphrey: autographed copies of his signing speech. Johnson gave out so many pens that an aide had to go get more.

At one point the Reuther brothers—Roy, Victor, and Walter—saw Kennedy lingering sullenly at the back of the room. "Surely no one had contributed more to the moment than he," Victor said later. Roy went over to the attorney general and dragged him by the arm to the president's desk. "Mr. President," he said, "I know you have reserved a pen for your attorney general." But the warmth of the moment could not melt the disdain each man felt for the other. Johnson unceremoniously grabbed a handful and shoved them at Kennedy. "Give this one to Burke Marshall. Give this one to John Doar. You got any more now?" Just to underline his indifference, he gave Kennedy another pen on top. Kennedy silently accepted the pens, with a despondency not lost on others around him. This was a bill he had conceived with his brother and pushed through Congress using their strategy—and now his nemesis was getting the glory. "Our enthusiasm—that of Dr. King and myself—was sort of dampened by the sadness that we saw in Bobby's eyes and the coldness with which the President obviously treated him," said Walter Fauntroy, the Washington representative for the Southern Christian Leadership Conference.[9]

At the back of the line stood Lady Bird. "Did you remember that nine years ago today, I had a heart attack?" Johnson asked her when she reached her husband.

"Happy anniversary," she said.

"You look mighty healthy to me," Humphrey butted in.

"Luci's seventeen and I'm nine," Johnson joked, referring to his younger daughter, whose birthday they had celebrated earlier that day in the same room. Johnson met briefly with some of the assembled civil rights leaders; the First Family then left the ceremony, and the next day the capital, for a long vacation in Texas.[10]

Slowly the room emptied. The Senate leadership on the bill went back down Pennsylvania Avenue to the Senate office building, where they gathered in Humphrey's suite for a toast. At one point Warren Magnuson piped up to say, "Enjoy the party, boys, because just wait until the professors of government descend. You'll describe this struggle hundreds of times. I wonder how many Ph.D. dissertations will be written about this bill." A few hours later, Humphrey and Stewart closed up the office and left the building. On the sidewalk outside they found hundreds of people, still waiting for one last glimpse of the senator from Minnesota on his day of triumph.[11]

THE NEXT MORNING, customers at Leb's Restaurant, a diner in downtown Atlanta, were met with a sign from its owner, Charles Lebedin. It read: "Dear Friends: the law forces me to serve Communist-led hoodlums."

Leb's, an Atlanta institution, had a history of resisting integration. In 1962 the singer Harry Belafonte, in town for a concert, had twice tried to eat at the diner but had been turned away each time. Lebedin claimed that he respected Belafonte but that he did not want to risk losing white customers by serving blacks. In January 1964, during a citywide sit-in campaign, the sidewalk in front of Leb's was the scene of clashes between civil rights protesters and, at different times, Lebedin's security staff, the police, and Ku Klux Klan vigilantes. The fighting began when one of Lebedin's bouncers tried to punch a protester. At one point during the melee, Lebedin himself used the swinging glass doors to hit protesters as they attempted to push their way in. Now, less than six months later, Leb's was open, grudgingly, to all.[12]

Similar scenes took place across the South. To an extent that surprised almost everyone, Southern merchants and politicians largely acceded to Title II's mandate, accepting "testers" from civil rights groups who had been denied service just days before. George Bess, an Atlanta Urban League staffer who had helped organize the sit-ins against Leb's and other establishments, went that day for a meal at the Henry Grady, a posh hotel (later demolished to make room for the tubular Westin Peachtree tower). "It was very nice," he reported afterward. "You wouldn't have known we were Negroes . . . We were looking for dirty silver, a special table off in a corner, lack of courtesy, a long waiting period . . . there was none of this."[13]

In Kansas City, a thirteen-year-old black boy named Eugene Young went into the barbershop at the Muehlebach Hotel, paid two dollars, and got his hair cut. The day before, he had been refused service. In Birmingham, a seventy-year-old black chauffeur named J. L. Meadows walked into the Town and Country restaurant at the Dinkle-Tutweiler Hotel, ordered a meal, and was served. "I've been driving white folks down here for thirty-two years, and now I'm going to eat where I've been taking these white folks," he told *Time* magazine.[14]

Not every establishment opened its doors. Some, like the Robert E. Lee Hotel in Jackson, simply closed rather than comply (the Lee later reopened as a private club, the sort that Russell Long had fought to protect with his late-stage amendment). Others filed legal challenges; within two hours of Johnson's signature, Moreton Rolleston, the owner of the 216-room Heart of Atlanta motel, filed suit against the federal government, a case that eventually rose to the Supreme Court. A few establishments offered outright resistance. Two bowling alleys in Beaumont, Texas, refused testers, as did several restaurants in Selma, Alabama. Most famously, the Atlanta fast-food restaurateur Lester Maddox, who had been agitating against the bill for months, chased three would-be black diners from his Pickrick Restaurant. Maddox carried a blade-less ax handle, and over the next few months, hundreds of whites around Atlanta could be seen with "Pickrick drumsticks," symbols of their opposition to the bill. Maddox's obstinacy did not save his restaurant, which he closed in early 1965, but it did launch his political career; he would serve as governor and then lieutenant governor from 1967 to 1975.[15]

A few cities also refused to comply, though none barred blacks outright from public accommodations. Some followed the lead of Greenwood, Mississippi, which drained its city pools rather than desegregate them.[16]

Nor was violence unheard of over the following week. On the evening of July 3, blacks integrated six restaurants in Cambridge, Maryland, but at one, the Dizzyland restaurant, the owner assaulted one of the aspiring diners. On July 9, the actor Jack Palance, who had supported civil rights activism in the past, was seen entering the Druid Theater in Tuscaloosa, Alabama, with his family. Word spread that at least one black person had gone in with them. Several hundred people gathered outside, and a group of men entered and sat behind Palance and his family while they tried to watch Peter Sellers and Angela Lansbury in *The World of Henry Orient*. The men began harassing the actor about being a paid "outside agitator." Palance spun around and yelled, "You are scaring my children!" and he and his family stormed out—only to be met with brickbats and catcalls from the mob outside. Eventually the police arrived, and they had to use tear gas to disperse the crowd. Palance and his family escaped unhurt.[17]

Still, such scenes were relatively rare. As a Department of Justice report concluded at the end of the month, "The general picture is one of large-scale compliance, but with considerable defiance in Alabama and Mississippi, and pockets of defiance in Georgia, Florida, and other states."[18]

Why did the South acquiesce so readily? It helped enormously that the majority of the region's leaders urged full, immediate compliance. Jackson, Mississippi, immediately desegregated its facilities, a move that its mayor said "demonstrated clearly the common sense and dedication to law and order of our citizens, white and black."[19]

Southern senators likewise called for immediate adherence to the new law. Herman Talmadge told Georgians that "there is no alternative but compliance," while his colleague Richard Russell said: "It is the understatement of the year to say that I do not like this statute. However, it is on the books and it becomes our duty as good citizens to learn to live with it as long as it is there." William Fulbright of Arkansas said: "Differences of opinion—no matter how deeply felt—must be subordinated to law and resolved in accord with it." Likewise, Louisiana's Allen Ellender told his constituents that "I cannot agree with those who advocate flagrant and perhaps violent opposition to any statute enacted by the Congress, if declared constitutional . . . The fact remains that, until changed or repealed by the Congress, or else declared unconstitutional, the laws enacted by the Congress must be respected."[20]

Not all politicians were so reasonable. Both George Wallace and Mississippi governor Paul Johnson called on businesses in their states to resist the act until it had been tested in court. Johnson also warned civil rights activists to "move with caution or we're going to have some chaotic days." But they were largely ignored, and aside from them, even the act's staunchest critics—Thurmond, Robert Byrd, Ervin—wisely held their tongues.[21]

Also crucial was the measured, organized, and strategic approach to desegregation taken by civil rights organizations. For months before the law went into effect, SCLC, CORE, the NAACP, and myriad local groups were in contact with chambers of commerce, city officials, and individual business owners to negotiate the process of desegregation. In the weeks leading up to the bill's passage, the NAACP leadership spoke out repeatedly against "adventurism" in testing the new law's effectiveness. Above all they promised that desegregation would be orderly; it was in no one's interest for a restaurant or theater to be swamped with black customers in a time of heightened tension. "We're not interested in forcing our rights down somebody's throat," said Andrew Young of the SCLC, whose post-act integration initiative was called Operation Dialogue.[22]

Such efforts would have come to naught had many Southern business communities not been eager to put Jim Crow behind them. The national public opinion, at least for the moment, seemed to be tilting decisively toward civil rights. Moreover, by the mid-1960s, particularly in the larger cities, attracting non-Southern investment and workers had become a key part of civic economic strategies. And yet, as the *Wall Street Journal* reported as early as May 1963, Southern businessmen feared "the economic growth of their region may be stunted for years, perhaps decades, unless some way is found to halt the spread of strife between whites and Negroes." After all, said a business leader in Birmingham, "would you take an industry into a place where Bull Connor was police commissioner?"[23]

As the bill went into effect, local chambers of commerce went into action. In Jackson, the chamber voted unanimously on July 3 to comply with all parts of the act. As the Department of Justice concluded, "In many localities the business community has shown a willingness to obey the law without conspicuous leadership from public officials—and even despite negative reaction from them."[24]

The chambers did not act spontaneously: much of their willingness to accept the act was made possible by the nearly year-long campaign by the Department of Justice to prepare local communities for the coming change. And the government was not the only one: the volunteer networks of lawyers, motel owners, theater chains, and civic groups made sure that as many businesses as possible across the South were ready for the day when Title II became law. "Where there has been conscientious planning and efforts to prepare for the transition, compliance has been good and trouble minimal," noted the department. And where there was resistance, the federal government stepped in swiftly. On July 29, the Department of Justice filed its first suits under Title II, against twenty-six establishments in Tuscaloosa.[25]

Underlying all of this was the willingness of the white South itself to accept the Civil Rights Act, and above all Titles II, III, and IV, which brought an immediate upheaval to its racially ordered life. Like the rest of the country, by early 1964 even the white South was caught up in the moral righteousness of the movement. According to polls by the Institute of Public Opinion, in June 1963 only 12 percent of Southern whites supported a public accommodations law; by February 1964 the number had risen to 20 percent—hardly an overwhelming number, but indicative of a clear trend. It helped, too, that Lyndon Johnson, always popular in the South, had tied himself so closely to the bill; when an April 1964 Harris poll asked Southerners whether they approved of the way he had handled the legislation, 67 percent said yes.[26]

But above all, the majority of Southern whites were simply glad to have the fight, and Jim Crow, over with. Invested in segregation though they were, most Southern whites were not racial ideologues, rallying behind the Klan or the White Citizens Councils. They were tired of the racial strife, tired of the protests and violence, tired of having their region tarred as backward and evil. Even if they did not like the Civil Rights Act—and to be clear, the vast majority did not; millions voted for Barry Goldwater that fall—they could at least take solace in the fact that it bore within it the possibility of social peace.[27]

It goes without saying that the surprisingly rapid, peaceful fall of Jim Crow did not mean that whites welcomed blacks as equals, or that they welcomed them into their social, economic, and political worlds. One reason why Southern whites accepted the changes wrought by civil rights legislation was that the expansion of the white middle class meant they could create new forms of de facto segregation to replace the old, unwieldy de jure ones: moving to wealthy suburbs, sending their children to private schools, joining private clubs, entering white-collar industries—all the while professing an allegiance to a color-blind society that just happened not to have any black people in it. It also goes without saying that the white South's acceptance of the letter of the Civil Rights Act did not mean the majority embraced its spirit. Russell's fear that the act would lead to a tsunami of interracial marriages notwithstanding, many Southern whites found it possible, even morally comfortable, to pay lip service to blacks' political equality while rejecting the idea that they could ever be social equals.

Still, Title II of the Civil Rights Act stands as a landmark: not only because it took down Jim Crow, but because it left the high-water mark of the New Deal tide of federal power. On December 14, 1964, the Supreme Court ruled unanimously against the Heart of Atlanta motel, which had argued that Congress had gone beyond the limits of the Commerce Clause in crafting Title II. In retrospect, the Heart of Atlanta was a poor candidate to test the law, since it was a 216-room motel located near an interstate, along which it frequently advertised, and some 75 percent of its guests were from out of state—if ever there was a public accommodation involved in interstate commerce, this was it. But the nature of this particular establishment proved less important to the court than the reality of modern travel. As Justice Hugo Black noted in his concurrence, the fact that many of the nation's 20 million blacks could and often did travel across state lines meant that very few businesses were not at least potentially involved in interstate commerce. "Certainly it would seriously discourage such travel by them if, as evidence before the Congress indicated has been true in the past, they should in the future continue to be unable to find a decent place along their way in which to lodge or eat," Black wrote. By that standard, the court actually went further than Congress did, to find that the federal government had the power to regulate practically any commercial activity at all, or even any activity that intersected with commercial operations.[28]

Titles II and III—the bans on discrimination in public accommodations and publicly owned facilities—were only the most immediately visible parts of the bill. Other titles were more or less effective. Title I, for example, which banned the unequal application of voter qualification tests, came with a very weak enforcement mechanism and provided no help for blacks who were intimidated or unfairly rejected by local registrars. On July 3, a group of blacks tried to register to vote in Jackson but were denied. It was only with the Voting Rights Act of 1965 that the federal government gained real powers to stamp out voting discrimination.[29]

The ongoing struggles of African Americans to access the ballot box was not lost on Johnson. He now fully embraced the need for action on moral grounds—and political grounds as well. In the late 1950s, earlier than almost everyone else, Johnson had seen that the white South, the traditional base for the Democratic Party, would soon enough shift to the Republicans, and that his party needed a new base to keep up. Having already spent decades tilting, outside the South at least, toward black voters, he knew that an act to protect and extend their franchise would lock them in as solid Democratic supporters for generations.

At the signing ceremony on July 2, Johnson was already planning to tackle voting. He took Katzenbach aside and said, "What are we going to do next year in civil rights?"[30]

Katzenbach glared back. "Jesus Christ, Mr. President, we just spent two years on this bill and practically nothing else happened," he said.

"Let's get a bill," Johnson said. "Let's get a voting rights bill."

Another plank, Title IV, required schools to develop desegregation plans and gave them assistance to do so. It also empowered the attorney general to sue if they did not. Title IV was broadly effective, creating, at least temporarily, a biracial educational system in the South. But more important to school desegregation was Title VI, ostensibly not a schools provision at all. It did, however, ban federal funds from going to segregated state and local programs, including schools—a provision that gained enormous weight with the Primary and Secondary Education Act of 1965, which opened the taps for federal largesse to flow to the nation's school districts. With billions of dollars as a tempting carrot, many Southern school districts fell over themselves to desegregate.

Aside from Title II, the most important part of the bill was Title VII, banning employment discrimination. And yet at the time, many observers wrote it off as fatally weakened by compromise. Richard Berg, who worked for the Equal Employment Opportunity Commission for the first few months of its existence, wrote: "Title VII was the principal victim of the legislative compromises necessary to achieve passage of the entire bill." Michael I. Sovern, a law professor at Columbia (and later its president), called it a "poor, enfeebled thing." Without a commission empowered to sue on behalf of plaintiffs, they said, the law had little in it to compel compliance. "Impotence will frequently be met with intransigence," Sovern wrote.[31]

It did not help that President Johnson dragged his feet on naming the EEOC staff and members, or that its budget was so thin that at times it had to beg other agencies to lend staff and support. When it opened its doors in July 1965, it was inundated with cases, part of a strategy by the NAACP Legal Defense Fund to highlight the commission's inadequacy. Eventually, so many cases had been on hold for so long that courts decided it was acceptable to ignore the sixty-day statute of limitations for complainants waiting for a review. And the early members of the commission looked askance at the addition of sex discrimination to the title, on the premise that it had been an ill-considered legislative accident.[32]

Over time, though, the EEOC, and Title VII enforcement generally, began to gain strength. Like the unexpected impact on school desegregation from Title VI, the provision within Title VII to cover plaintiffs' legal costs proved serendipitous: it fueled the emergence of an enormous civil rights bar, with thousands of lawyers specializing in workplace discrimination suits. According to Sean Farhang, a professor of public policy at the University of California, Berkeley, workplace discrimination suits today constitute about 18 percent of all litigation in federal courts, second only to petitions by prisoners requesting to be set free. Moreover, through the 1960s and 1970s, Congress and the courts regularly expanded and deepened Title VII's reach; in 1971 the Supreme Court decided, in *Griggs v. Duke Power*, that under the Civil Rights Act, employers could not use tests or other tools that disparately affected a minority group—in effect going against the bill's own authors, who insisted, after the Motorola case, that Title VII clearly allowed such tests. It was no longer necessary to prove that an employer had actively, purposely discriminated; it was enough to prove that minorities were adversely affected by company decisions, regardless of intention. And, in 1972, the EEOC won the power to sue, a power that had been stripped from it in the Senate negotiations with Dirksen.[33]

It is beyond the scope of this book to examine the entire post-enactment history of the Civil Rights Act. But one thing can be said with certainty: the act revolutionized American society by placing the federal government undeniably and forcefully on the side of African Americans. Though blacks had long benefited from federal policies, they had also been explicitly excluded from many of the New Deal public welfare programs, and they had sought in vain federal intervention against gross civil rights violations in the South. Congress had refused to pass legislation to enforce the 1954 *Brown* decision, and both the 1957 and 1960 civil rights acts were relatively toothless; it did not take a cynic to conclude that Congress had passed the acts more to win over black voters in the next election than out of any conviction on behalf of black America. No one could lay that charge against the 1964 act or the people who made it possible. Thanks to them, the relationship between blacks and the federal government—and between both of them and white America— changed forever.

ON THE COPY of the signing speech that Johnson gave to Humphrey, the president had inscribed, "Without whom it couldn't have happened." On an identical copy that he gave to Dirksen, he wrote simply, "Thanks."[34]

The president could afford to be personally magnanimous to those who labored so hard to pass the bill, because he knew a truism about American political memory: no matter how many people worked to get a bill through Congress, it was the man in the Oval Office who would get the credit. And, almost immediately, accolades for the president's performance began pouring in. In a July 5 news analysis, the *New York Times* credited Johnson as "the man who pushed [the bill] through Congress." In its endorsement of Johnson for president that October, the *Baltimore Afro-American* likewise praised Johnson for breaking the filibuster.[35]

However, this was not an opinion shared by insiders, even those with an interest in promoting the achievements of the president. Without denying that the president played an important symbolic role, they cast doubt on the notion that he was the hard-driving general behind the bill. "I don't recall that he had to get deeply involved as this played out," said Larry O'Brien. Humphrey agreed: "We did not bother the president very much. We did give him regular reports on the progress of civil rights over at the Tuesday morning breakfasts. But the president was not put on the spot. He was not enlisted in the battle particularly. I understand he did contact some of the senators, but not at our insistence."[36]

The press reported much the same during the filibuster. "As majority leader, the president was all muscle and scant conversation. In the present impasse, the criticism is freely heard that the reverse is true," wrote the columnist Doris Fleeson in the *Washington Star*. "Reporters covering the civil rights story in detail agree that they have seen no traces of the old brooding and impatient Johnson presence that they learned to know so well during the Eisenhower years."[37]

Meanwhile, those on the Senate side bristled at the suggestion that Johnson had played a central role in passing the bill. "Aside from reinforcing his support for the House bill and pushing Mansfield and Humphrey to get tough with the Southern Democrats, President Johnson did not become deeply involved in the detailed planning and negotiations," wrote John Stewart. Frank Valeo was even sharper, saying that Johnson's vaunted legislative skills were of little advantage when it came to passing the bill: "He never understood how it would be possible to do it by cloture. He'd already been away from the Senate for a period of time, and things change, attitudes change so fast. Unless you're there all the time, listening to what's going on and picking up reactions to the news everyday, you very quickly lose touch with the changing trends."[38]

And while Valeo had every interest in promoting the role of his boss, Mike Mansfield, his account accords with what people were saying at the time about the president's involvement—even what Johnson himself was saying. Johnson had tried to force Mansfield to pursue a more aggressive filibuster strategy; when the majority leader refused, Johnson took a backseat, either because he realized his influence was limited or because he thought Mansfield's plan was a time bomb and he did not want to be too close to the pyrotechnics when it exploded. "Whatever Dirksen and the attorney general agree on," he said in April, "I am for." In other words, Johnson positioned himself so that he could plausibly claim the bill as his own should it pass, but just as plausibly distance himself should it fail.[39]

Nevertheless, over the decades, Johnson's role in the bill's passage has grown to mythic proportions. Recent accounts have him lobbying senators, handing out orders, and drawing the grand strategies that would carry the bill to his desk. The equal and in some cases even more vital roles played by Dirksen, Humphrey, McCulloch, Katzenbach, and the Kennedys, among many others, have been diminished or forgotten, while the important but hardly singular role played by the president has ballooned to the point where "Civil Rights Act" is more often than not preceded by the possessive "Johnson's."

But as the record shows, while Johnson did play an important role—most notably getting Harry Byrd to release the tax cut bill so that it could clear the Senate before the filibuster—he was just one of a cast of dozens. (Even his maneuverings with Byrd were of only hypothetical importance; the tax cut bill presented no procedural obstacle to the civil rights bill, only a political one, and no one can be sure what would have happened had the filibuster begun with the tax cut bill on hold). Meanwhile, Johnson's personal lobbying efforts were few, and—like his efforts to win over Robert Byrd—as often as not failures. The only instance in which his efforts made a clear difference was in getting Carl Hayden to agree to withhold his vote against cloture—a helpful, but hardly decisive, achievement. And finally, Johnson's strategic advice, though it makes for colorful anecdotes, was neither original nor particularly well heeded. By the time he told Humphrey to "spend time with Dirksen!" in February 1964, the Senate leadership had already spent six months devising a plan for winning over the minority leader. And Mansfield simply ignored the president's insistence that he "get out the cots" and force a round-the-clock filibuster.

None of this is to suggest that Johnson did not play a central role in the bill's success. His decision to put the full weight of the presidency behind the bill from virtually the moment he took office was courageous; though he saw political gain to be had from aligning himself and his party with the civil rights movement, he also understood the risks involved. What made the difference was his fundamental belief in the moral rightness of the bill, and his urgency to see that rightness turned into action immediately. Had Johnson wavered—had he even once suggested, in a press conference or interview, that Congress should cut bait and negotiate—he would have done immense harm to the legislation.

But it is important to remember that while Johnson played a central role, he did not play *the* central role. Humphrey, Dirksen, McCulloch, and Katzenbach—not to mention Rauh, Mitchell, and King—were arguably much more important. At the same time, we must remember that there was no single central character, no prime mover, but rather dozens of contributors. And while this lesson is particularly true for the Civil Rights Act, it is also true for the history of American lawmaking in general. One reason Johnson's role in the bill became shorthand for the success of the bill itself is precisely that: when we talk about important actions by the federal government through history, we tend to let the presidents' names become proxies for the dizzying complexity of a law's actual history. Thus we remember it was Lincoln who freed the slaves, even though dozens of congressmen wrote and supported the laws that pushed him to sign the Emancipation Proclamation. We remember the New Deal as Franklin Roosevelt's doing, as if he wrote and negotiated and revised every change in each law himself, rather than recognizing the critical work done by his staff and allies in Congress, let alone the social movements outside of the government that made them possible.

Nowhere is this disjunction more true than with regard to the Civil Rights Act, and yet there are few pieces of legislation that we more closely associate with a single executive figure. Johnson was pushed by the civil rights movement and its congressional allies as much as or more than he pushed them. And he came into the story in the middle. The Civil Rights Act was not his bill by any stretch. But the reason to recognize that fact is not in order to dismiss Johnson, who does deserve a large amount of credit. Rather, it is to come to a better understanding of how legislation works, and in doing so to grasp more firmly the course of American political history.

On the evening of July 2, after Johnson had signed the bill, Bill Moyers found his boss in a state of "melancholy." According to Moyers, Johnson then uttered what has become the single most famous line associated with the Civil Rights Act: "We just delivered the South to the Republican Party for a long time to come." The line has come to symbolize Johnson's political savvy, his recognition of the high political price the Democrats would pay for the bill, and his foresight into the future of the American South.[40]

Moyers's anecdote gets to a fundamental truth about all landmark legislation: the larger and more pathbreaking it is, the higher its opportunity costs. There can be little doubt that the Civil Rights Act helped cleave the South from the Democratic Party. But this was a process that was already well under way and would have continued with or without the bill. The Northern Democrats did not suddenly "get" civil rights religion in 1963, nor did the South wake up to the realization that its beloved Democratic Party was moving away from it on July 2, 1964. At the presidential level, the South had been voting Republican since Eisenhower won four states of the former Confederacy in 1952. By 1964, John Tower had been in his Texas senator's office for two years; Republicans had run competitive, if losing, congressional and state-level races in several Deep South states; and Strom Thurmond was on the verge of bolting the party after serving as a "Democrat in Name Only" for several years. And the white South was, despite its occasional populism, always Republican in spirit, if not allegiance: with just a few cities speckled across a rural, religion-soaked population, it better resembled the Republican heartland of small Midwestern towns than it did the industrialized urbanism that had long dominated the Democratic Party. Moreover, the South was always more wary of activist government than the modern Democratic agenda could safely allow—and not just because of race, though certainly that was a key driver of its suspicions. As Robert Penn Warren wrote in 1955, "I remember another lawyer, hired by another group: 'Hell, all Southerners are Republicans at heart, conservative, and just don't know they're Republican.'" The Civil Rights Act, to the extent that it made a difference in the Southern realignment, simply added fuel to a fire that had been burning for decades.[41]

But there is another, more significant cost paid by the authors of the Civil Rights Act that needs examining. For a variety of reasons, they repeatedly considered and rejected the possibility of including substantial measures to combat economic inequality as well as discrimination. Some felt it was too much to ask for in any single piece of legislation; and, besides, the pressing issue of the moment (to them) was Jim Crow, not the largely Northern ghetto. In the end they argued, unconvincingly, that Title VII's ban on employment discrimination would eventually provide sufficient opportunity for blacks to climb out of poverty. But it is one very good thing to remove a man's shackles; it is another very pernicious thing to insist that, having done so, he should be able to compete with men who have spent their entire lives in freedom. The Civil Rights Act would not erase the legacies of a century of enforced black poverty on its own. In his book *A Thousand Days*, a memoir-cum-history of the Kennedy administration, Arthur M. Schlesinger Jr. wrote, "To the Negroes of the North the rights it offered were those they nominally possessed already. And to the heart of the now boiling Northern unrest—to the frustrations in the black ghettos of the cities—it offered nothing." The very notion of civil rights legislation, as it had come to be understood in Washington, "had little to say to the unemployed, undereducated, untrained Negroes wandering aimlessly down the gray streets of Harlem or Watts, to boys and girls in their teens abandoned by their fathers and adrift in a desolation of mistrust and corruption, to the hoods and junkies and winos and derelicts."[42]

Neither Kennedy nor Johnson was blind to this fact—nor were many members of Congress, nor were their administrations. As Secretary of Labor Willard Wirtz said in a speech in Chicago on the same day Johnson signed the act, "The plain fact is that freedom and groceries are both important, and neither is enough without the other." Kennedy had already been planning a major push against poverty for his second term, and Johnson picked up that flag and kept marching. In a May 1964 commencement speech at the University of Michigan, Johnson outlined his plan for a "great society" initiative that "demands an end to poverty and racial injustice, to which we are totally committed in our time" through federal programs to improve education, urban areas, rural communities, and job opportunities. A year later, at Howard University, he said, "It is not enough just to open the gates of opportunity. All our citizens must have the ability to walk through those gates. This is the next and the more profound stage of the battle for civil rights. We seek not just freedom but opportunity. We seek not just legal equity but human ability, not just equality as a right and a theory but equality as a fact and equality as a result."[43]

These two speeches announced and outlined the Great Society, and in particular the War on Poverty. And yet those grand initiatives, though they achieved much, were nowhere near large enough to approach, let alone resolve, the problem of black economic inequality. With fewer and fewer jobs available in the inner cities, with crime rates rising and the quality of schools plummeting, the administration's efforts amounted to little more than pilot programs, single sorties when a full-on assault was required.

In the end, the Civil Rights Act was aimed explicitly and exclusively at the South, largely because its supporters believed that was the only way to win over enough votes from non-Southern skeptics. And they may have been right. But what they did not consider was the amount of political capital they would have to spend to get any bill through Congress, and what the opportunity cost of spending that capital on a region-specific, rights-focused piece of legislation would be. Nor did they sufficiently appreciate the struggles facing blacks outside the South, either because of direct, explicit discrimination or the lingering effects of slavery and racism. In a tragic counterpoint to the triumph of July 2, two weeks later, Harlem and parts of Brooklyn erupted in three days of rioting. The violence was touched off by the police shooting of an unarmed black teenager, but it also gave vent to black anger over unemployment, police brutality, school and housing discrimination, and poor city services in minority neighborhoods. Similar rioting broke out in South Central Los Angeles the next year, Cleveland the year after, Newark and Detroit in 1967, and in more than a hundred cities, including Washington,

Baltimore, and Chicago, after the April 4, 1968, assassination of Martin Luther King Jr. Each riot had its unique flashpoint, but each followed a similar pattern of looting and destruction that spoke to the depths of black frustration with ghetto life. There is no saying whether an even larger Civil Rights Act, with provisions to address issues such as housing discrimination and the job market, could have prevented the violence. The point is that their occurrence underlined the failure of Congress, at the critical moment, even to try.

The simple fact is that in the early to mid-1960s, the federal government faced a unique moment—what the political scientists Robert Weisbrot and G. Calvin McKenzie call the "liberal hour"—when it was able to greatly expand its powers and purview over the nation's political, economic, and social life. The moment was fleeting and would not return for a long time. The decisions made regarding which laws to push for, which programs to create, are difficult to question—given the urgency of the racial situation in mid-1963, Title II was rightly the most important thing on the federal agenda. And yet the decision to pursue purely legal change, and to leave economic relationships alone, says much about the intellectual and moral limitations of midcentury liberalism. For too many legislators, it really was enough to simply remove the chains from the black man's hands.

And yet such criticisms—which are really just observations about the tragic logic of American politics—cannot diminish the historic achievement of the Civil Rights Act. It did not put an end to American racism, nor did it eliminate the unique challenges of African American life. But it did much to alleviate both, and it reoriented the country—both the government and the people— onto a path toward true racial equality. That point may never be reached, but thanks to the Civil Rights Act, the country has moved very far along. For all the bill's lost opportunities and negotiated shortcomings, the Civil Rights Act of 1964 remains the single most important piece of legislation passed in twentieth-century America.

ACKNOWLEDGMENTS

No one can write a book of serious historical research without the help of countless archivists and librarians. The people at the Library of Congress, the National Archives, the Kennedy Library and Museum, the Lyndon B. Johnson Library and Museum, the Presbyterian Historical Society, the Center for Jewish History, the University of California, Berkeley, the University of Georgia, the Ohio State University, Wayne State University, the University of Montana, and the University of Buffalo deserve my deepest gratitude. I am especially indebted to Allen Fisher and his colleagues at the Johnson Library. Rodolfo Villarreal-Ríos at the University of Montana and Lindsey Patterson at the Ohio State University provided critical research assistance into the papers of Mike Mansfield and William McCulloch, respectively.

I also thank all the people who lent their time to speak with me about their experiences working on the bill, including Birch Bayh, Al Bronstein, John Doar, David Filvaroff, Nicholas Katzenbach, Robert Kimball, Roger Mudd, Jack Rosenthal, Lee White, and Ben Zelenko.

Adam Goodheart, the C. V. Starr Center for the Study of the American Experience, and Washington College were kind enough to give me a Frederick Douglass Fellowship in the spring of 2013, which supported me during the outset of my writing. Jeff Shesol and David Greenberg read parts or drafts of the book and provided me with invaluable feedback; for that I am very thankful.

My agent, Heather Schroder, gave me the initial impetus to pursue a book about the 1964 Civil Rights Act, and she later helped me shape my proposal and find it a home. Fortunately, that home was with Peter Ginna and the people at Bloomsbury Press, who helped turn my awkward manuscript into what I hope is a compelling narrative.

I would be remiss if I did not thank all of my coworkers at the *New York Times* op-ed department, who provided me with encouragement and inspiration.

Finally, to my family—Talia, Elliot, Joanna, Mom, Dad, Michael, and the rest: thanks for being there, and for putting up with me for all these years, and not just the ones when I was writing this book.

BIBLIOGRAPHY

AUTHOR INTERVIEWS

Birch Bayh, Al Bronstein, John Doar, David Filvaroff, Jack Greenberg, Nicholas Katzenbach, Robert Kimball, Roger Mudd, Jack Rosenthal, Michael I. Sovern, Lee White, Ben Zelenko.

ARCHIVES

Center for Jewish History, New York, N.Y.
  American Jewish Congress Papers
Dirksen Congressional Center, Pekin, Ill.
  Everett M. Dirksen Papers
Lyndon B. Johnson Library and Museum, Austin, Tex.
  Administrative History Files
  Horace Busby Office Files
  Legislation Background Files
  Mike Manatos Office Files
  Bill Moyers Office Files
  Lawrence O'Brien Office Files
  George Reedy Office Files
  Presidential Statements
  Reports on Enrolled Legislation
  Reports on Pending Legislation
  Vice Presidential Office Files
  Lee White Office Files
  White House Central Files
  Henry Hall Wilson Office Files
John F. Kennedy Presidential Library and Museum, Boston, Mass.
  Robert F. Kennedy Papers
  Burke Marshall Office Files
  Victor Navasky Papers
  Presidential Office Files
  Arthur M. Schlesinger Jr. Papers
  Theodore Sorensen Office Files
  Lee White Office Files

Library of Congress, Washington, D.C.
  Emanuel Celler Papers
  Leadership Conference on Civil Rights Papers
  NAACP Papers
  Joseph L. Rauh Jr. Papers
Mississippi Department of Archives and History Online Collection
  Mississippi State Sovereignty Commission Papers
National Archives
  House Judiciary Committee Papers
Ohio Congressional Archives, Ohio State University, Columbus, Ohio
  William M. McCulloch Papers
Presbyterian Historical Society, Philadelphia, Penn.
  National Council of Churches Archives
  United Presbyterian Church Archives
The University of Buffalo Library—Special Collections, Buffalo, N.Y.
  David B. Filvaroff and Raymond E. Wolfinger Civil Rights Act Papers
The University of California, Berkeley, Special Collections, Berkeley, Calif.
  Harry Kingman Papers
  Thomas H. Kuchel Papers
The University of Montana Archives and Special Collections, Missoula, Mont.
  Mike Mansfield Papers
Wayne State University Archives, Detroit, Mich.
  United Auto Workers Community Action Program Files
  United Auto Workers Special Projects Department Files
  Walter P. Reuther Papers

Books and Dissertations

Bass, Jack, and Walter De Vries. *The Transformation of Southern Politics: Social Change and Political Consequence Since 1945*. New York: Basic Books, 1976.

Berman, Daniel M. *A Bill Becomes a Law: The Civil Rights Act of 1960*. New York: MacMillan, 1962.

Berman, William C. *The Politics of Civil Rights in the Truman Administration*. Columbus: Ohio State University Press, 1970.

Bernstein, Irving. *Promises Kept: John F. Kennedy's New Frontier*. New York: Oxford University Press, 1991.

Bernstein, Shana. *Bridges of Reform: Interracial Civil Rights Activism in Twentieth-Century Los Angeles*. New York: Oxford University Press, 2011.

Boyle, Kevin. *The U.A.W. and the Heyday of American Liberalism, 1945–1968*. Ithaca: Cornell University Press, 1998.

Bradlee, Benjamin C., and John F Kennedy. *Conversations with Kennedy*. New York: W. W. Norton, 1984.

Branch, Taylor. *Parting the Waters: America in the King Years, 1954–63*. New York: Simon and Schuster, 1988.

———. *Pillar of Fire: America in the King Years, 1963–65*. New York: Simon and Schuster, 1998.

Bryant, Nick. *The Bystander: John F. Kennedy and the Struggle for Black Equality*. New York: Basic Books, 2006.

Caro, Robert A. *The Years of Lyndon Johnson: Master of the Senate.* New York: Alfred A. Knopf, 2002.

———. *The Years of Lyndon Johnson: The Passage of Power.* New York: Alfred A. Knopf, 2012.

Carter, Dan T. *The Politics of Rage: George Wallace, the Origins of the New Conservatism, and the Transformation of American Politics.* Baton Rouge: Louisiana State University Press, 1995.

Chen, Anthony S. *The Fifth Freedom: Jobs, Politics, and Civil Rights in the United States, 1941–1972.* Princeton: Princeton University Press, 2009.

Coser, Lewis A. *Men of Ideas: A Sociologist's View.* First Free Press Paperbacks ed. New York: Free Press, 1997.

Countryman, Matthew. *Up South: Civil Rights and Black Power in Philadelphia.* Philadelphia: University of Pennsylvania Press, 2006.

Crespino, Joseph. *In Search of Another Country: Mississippi and the Conservative Counterrevolution.* Princeton: Princeton University Press, 2007.

———. *Strom Thurmond's America.* New York: Hill and Wang, 2012.

Dallek, Robert. *Flawed Giant: Lyndon Johnson and His Times.* New York: Oxford University Press, 1999.

Dichter, Mark S., David A. Cathcart, and Barbara Lindemann. *Employment Discrimination Law.* Foreword by Norbert A. Schlei. Washington D.C.: American Bar Association, Section of Labor and Employment Law, Bureau of National Affairs, 1987.

Dierenfield, Bruce J. *Keeper of the Rules: Congressman Howard W. Smith of Virginia.* Charlottesville: University Press of Virginia, 1987.

Douglas, Paul H. *In the Fullness of Time: The Memoirs of Paul H. Douglas.* New York: Harcourt Brace Jovanovich, 1972.

Eagles, Charles W. *The Price of Defiance: James Meredith and the Integration of Ole Miss.* Chapel Hill: University of North Carolina Press, 2009.

Ervin, Sam J. *Preserving the Constitution: The Autobiography of Senator Sam J. Ervin, Jr.* Charlottesville, Va.: Michie Co., 1984.

Finch, L. Boyd. *Legacies of Camelot: Stewart and Lee Udall, American Culture, and the Arts.* Norman: University of Oklahoma Press, 2008.

Findlay, James F. *Church People in the Struggle: The National Council of Churches and the Black Freedom Movement, 1950–70.* New York: Oxford University Press, 1993.

Finley, Keith M. *Delaying the Dream: Southern Senators and the Fight Against Civil Rights, 1938–1965.* Baton Rouge: Louisiana State University Press, 2010.

Fite, Gilbert C. *Richard B. Russell, Jr., Senator from Georgia.* Chapel Hill: University of North Carolina Press, 2002.

Freedman, Eric, and Edward Hoffman. *John F. Kennedy, in His Own Words.* New York: Kensington, 2005.

Garrow, David J. *Bearing the Cross: Martin Luther King, Jr., and the Southern Christian Leadership Conference.* New York: Perennial Classics, 2004.

Gillon, Steven M. *Politics and Vision: The A.D.A. and American Liberalism, 1947–1985.* New York: Oxford University Press, 1987.

Goldsmith, John A. *Colleagues: Richard B. Russell and His Apprentice, Lyndon B. Johnson.* Washington, D.C.: Seven Locks Press, 1993.

Goodwin, Doris Kearns. *Lyndon Johnson and the American Dream.* New York: Harper and Row, 1976.

Graham, Hugh Davis *The Civil Rights Era: Origins and Development of National Policy*. New York: Oxford University Press, 1990.

──. *Civil Rights and the Presidency: Race and Gender in American Politics, 1960–1972*. Abridged edition. New York: Oxford University Press, 1992.

Grofman, Bernard. *Legacies of the 1964 Civil Rights Act*. Charlottesville: University Press of Virginia, 2000.

Guthman, Edwin O. *We Band of Brothers*. New York: Harper and Row, 1971.

Guthman, Edwin O and Jeffrey Shulman. *Robert Kennedy: In His Own Words*. New York: Bantam Books, 1988.

Hulsey, Byron C. *Everett Dirksen and His Presidents*. Lawrence: University Press of Kansas, 2000.

Humphrey, Hubert H *The Education of a Public Man: My Life and Politics*. Garden City, N.Y.: Doubleday, 1976.

──. "Memorandum on Senate Consideration of the Civil Rights Act of 1964." In *The Civil Rights Act of 1964: The Passage of the Law That Ended Racial Segregation*. Albany: State University of New York Press, 1997.

Hustwit, William P. *James J. Kilpatrick: Salesman for Segregation*. Chapel Hill: University of North Carolina Press, 2013.

Johnson, Lyndon B. *The Vantage Point: Perspectives on the Presidency, 1963–1969*. New York: Holt, Rinehart and Winston, 1971.

Jones, William P. *The March on Washington: Jobs, Freedom, and the Forgotten History of Civil Rights*. New York: W. W. Norton, 2013.

Kabaservice, Geoffrey M. *Rule and Ruin: The Downfall of Moderation and the Destruction of the Republican Party, from Eisenhower to the Tea Party*. New York: Oxford University Press, 2012.

Kane, Peter E. "The Senate Debate on the 1964 Civil Rights Act." Unpublished dissertation. Purdue University, 1967.

Karabell, Zachary, and Jonathan Karabell. *Kennedy, Johnson, and the Quest for Justice: The Civil Rights Tapes*. New York: W. W. Norton, 2003.

Katzenbach, Nicholas deB. *Some of It Was Fun: Working with RFK and LBJ*. New York: W. W. Norton, 2008.

Kennedy, John F., Caroline Kennedy, and Robert F. Kennedy. *Profiles in Courage*. New York: Perennial/HarperCollins, 2006.

Kotz, Nick. *Judgment Days: Lyndon Baines Johnson, Martin Luther King Jr., and the Laws That Changed America*. New York: Houghton Mifflin, 2005.

Lichtenstein, Nelson. *Walter Reuther: The Most Dangerous Man in Detroit*. Urbana: University of Illinois Press, 1997.

Loevy, Robert D. *To End All Segregation: The Politics of the Passage of the Civil Rights Act of 1964*. Lanham, Md.: University Press of America, 1990.

──. *The Civil Rights Act of 1964: The Passage of the Law That Ended Racial Segregation*. Albany: State University of New York Press, 1997.

Mackenzie, G. Calvin, and Robert Weisbrot. *The Liberal Hour: Washington and the Politics of Change in the 1960s*. New York: Penguin, 2008.

MacLean, Nancy. *Freedom Is Not Enough: The Opening of the American Workplace*. Cambridge, Mass.: Harvard University Press, 2006.

Mann, Robert. *The Walls of Jericho: Lyndon Johnson, Hubert Humphrey, Richard Russell, and the Struggle for Civil Rights*. New York: Harcourt Brace, 1996.

Martin, John Frederick. *Civil Rights and the Crisis of Liberalism: The Democratic Party, 1945–1976.* Boulder, Colo.: Westview Press, 1979.

May, Gary. *Bending Toward Justice: The Voting Rights Act and the Transformation of American Democracy.* New York: Basic Books, 2013.

McWhorter, Diane. *Carry Me Home: Birmingham, Alabama, the Climactic Battle of the Civil Rights Revolution.* New York: Simon and Schuster, 2002.

Moreno, Paul D. *From Direct Action to Affirmative Action: Fair Employment Law and Policy in America, 1933–1972.* Baton Rouge: Louisiana State University Press, 1999.

Mudd, Roger. *The Place to Be: Washington, CBS, and the Glory Days of Television News.* New York: PublicAffairs, 2008.

Navasky, Victor S. *Kennedy Justice.* New York: Atheneum, 1971.

Nichols, David A. *A Matter of Justice: Eisenhower and the Beginning of the Civil Rights Revolution.* New York: Simon and Schuster Paperbacks, 2008.

O'Brien, Lawrence F. *No Final Victories: A Life in Politics—from John F. Kennedy to Watergate.* New York: Ballantine, 1975.

Perlstein, Rick. *Before the Storm: Barry Goldwater and the Unmaking of the American Consensus.* New York: Hill and Wang, 2001.

Poinsett, Alex. *Walking with Presidents: Louis Martin and the Rise of Black Political Power.* Lanham, Md.: Rowman & Littlefield, 1997.

Purnell, Brian. *Fighting Jim Crow in the County of Kings: The Congress of Racial Equality in Brooklyn.* Lexington: University Press of Kentucky, 2013.

The Presidential Recordings: Lyndon B. Johnson: The Kennedy Assassination and the Transfer of Power, November 1963–January 1964. 3 vols. New York: W. W. Norton, 2005.

The Presidential Recordings: Lyndon B. Johnson: Toward the Great Society, February 1, 1964–May 31, 1964. 3 vols. New York: W. W. Norton, 2007.

Rauh, Joseph L., Jr. "The Role of the Leadership Conference on Civil Rights in the Civil Rights Struggle of 1963–1964." In *The Civil Rights Act of 1964: The Passage of the Law That Ended Racial Segregation.* Albany: State University of New York Press, 1997.

Reed, Merl Elwyn. *Seedtime for the Modern Civil Rights Movement: The President's Committee on Fair Employment Practice, 1941–1946.* Baton Rouge: Louisiana State University Press, 1991.

Reedy, George E. *Lyndon B. Johnson: A Memoir.* New York: Andrews and McMeel, 1982.

Reeves, Richard. *President Kennedy: Profile of Power.* New York: Simon and Schuster, 1994.

Rosenberg, Jonathan and Zachary Karabell. *Kennedy, Johnson, and the Quest for Justice: The Civil Rights Tapes.* New York: W. W. Norton, 2003.

Russo, Gus. *The Outfit: The Role of Chicago's Underworld in the Shaping of Modern America.* New York: Bloomsbury, 2003.

Scheele, Henry Z. *Charlie Halleck: A Political Biography.* Hicksville, N.Y.: Exposition Press, 1966.

Schlesinger, Arthur M., Jr. *A Thousand Days: John F. Kennedy in the White House.* Boston: Houghton Mifflin, 1965.

———. *Robert Kennedy and His Times.* Boston: Houghton Mifflin, 1978.

———. *Journals, 1952–2000.* New York: Penguin, 2007.

Shesol, Jeff. *Mutual Contempt: Lyndon Johnson, Robert Kennedy, and the Feud That Defined a Decade.* New York: W. W. Norton, 1997.

Small, William. *To Kill a Messenger: Television News and the Real World.* New York: Hastings House, 1970.

Sokol, Jason. *There Goes My Everything: White Southerners in the Age of Civil Rights, 1945–1975*. New York: Vintage Books, 2007.

Sovern, Michael I. *Legal Restraints on Racial Discrimination*. New York: Twentieth Century Fund, 1966.

Stern, Mark. *Calculating Visions: Kennedy, Johnson, and Civil Rights*. New Brunswick, N.J.: Rutgers University Press, 1992.

Stewart, John G. "Independence and Control: The Challenge of Senatorial Party Leadership." Unpublished dissertation. University of Chicago, 1968.

———. "The Civil Rights Act of 1964: Strategy." In *The Civil Rights Act of 1964: The Passage of the Law That Ended Racial Segregation*. Albany: State University of New York Press, 1997.

———. "The Civil Rights Act of 1964: Tactics I." In *The Civil Rights Act of 1964: The Passage of the Law That Ended Racial Segregation*. Albany: State University of New York Press, 1997.

———. "The Civil Rights Act of 1964: Tactics II." In *The Civil Rights Act of 1964: The Passage of the Law That Ended Racial Segregation*. Albany: State University of New York Press, 1997.

———. "The Senate and Civil Rights." In *The Civil Rights Act of 1964: The Passage of the Law That Ended Racial Segregation*. Albany: State University of New York Press, 1997.

———. "Thoughts on the Civil Rights Bill." In *The Civil Rights Act of 1964: The Passage of the Law That Ended Racial Segregation*. Albany: State University of New York Press, 1997.

Sugrue, Thomas J. *Sweet Land of Liberty: The Forgotten Struggle for Civil Rights in the North*. New York: Random House, 2008.

Sullivan, Patricia. *Days of Hope: Race and Democracy in the New Deal Era*. Chapel Hill: University of North Carolina Press, 1996.

———. *Lift Every Voice: The NAACP and the Making of the Civil Rights Movement*. New York: New Press, 2010.

Thomas, Evan. *Robert Kennedy: His Life*. New York: Simon and Schuster, 2000.

Thompson, Kenneth W. *The Kennedy Presidency: 17 Intimate Perspectives of John F. Kennedy*. Lanham, Md.: University Press of America, 1985.

Thurber, Timothy N. *The Politics of Equality: Hubert H. Humphrey and the African American Freedom Struggle*. New York: Columbia University Press, 1999.

Valeo, Francis R. *Mike Mansfield, Majority Leader: A Different Kind of Senate, 1961–1976*. Armonk, N.Y.: M. E. Sharpe, 1999.

Warren, Robert Penn. *Segregation: The Inner Conflict in the South*. Athens: University of Georgia Press, 1994.

Watson, Denton L. *Lion in the Lobby: Clarence Mitchell, Jr.'s Struggle for the Passage of Civil Rights Laws*. Lanham, Md.: University Press of America, 2002.

Webb, Clive. *Fight Against Fear: Southern Jews and Black Civil Rights*. Athens: University of Georgia Press, 2003.

Whalen, Charles, and Barbara Whalen. *The Longest Debate: A Legislative History of the 1964 Civil Rights Act*. Cabin John, Md.: Seven Locks Press, 1985.

White, Theodore H. *The Making of the President 1964*. New York: HarperCollins, 2010.

White, William S. *The Professional: Lyndon B. Johnson*. New York: Houghton Mifflin, 1964.

Wilkins, Roy, and Tom Mathews. *Standing Fast: The Autobiography of Roy Wilkins*. New York: Da Capo Press, 1994.

Woods, Randall Bennett. *Fulbright: A Biography*. Cambridge, U.K., and New York: Cambridge University Press, 2006.

Wright, Gavin. *Sharing the Prize: The Economics of the Civil Rights Revolution in the American South*. Cambridge, Mass.: Belknap Press of Harvard University Press, 2013.

JOURNAL ARTICLES

Berg, Richard K. "Equal Employment Opportunity Under the Civil Rights Act of 1964." *Brooklyn Law Review* 31 (1964): 62–97.

———. "Title VII: A Three-Years' View." *Notre Dame Law Review* 44 (1969): 311–43.

Bird, Robert C. "More Than a Congressional Joke: A Fresh Look at the Legislative History of Sex Discrimination of the 1964 Civil Rights Act." *William and Mary Journal of Women and the Law* 3 (1997): 137–61.

Birnbaum, Owen. "Equal Employment Opportunity and Executive Order 10925." *Kansas Law Review* 11, no. 1 (October 1962): 17–30.

Denning, Brannon P. "Book Review: 'Civil Rights and Public Accommodations: The Heart of Atlanta Motel and McClung Cases'." *Law Library Journal* 94 (Winter 2002): 141–60.

Farhang, Sean. "The Political Development of Job Discrimination Litigation, 1963–1976." JSP/ Center for the Study of Law and Society Faculty Working Papers, 2008. http://escholar-ship.org/uc/item/3pk6v8sk.

Fleming, Harold C. "The Federal Executive and Civil Rights: 1961–1965." *Daedalus* 94, no. 4 (October 1, 1965): 921–48.

Freeman, Jo. "How 'Sex' Got into Title VII: Persistent Opportunism as a Maker of Public Policy." *Law and Inequality: A Journal of Theory and Practice* 9, no. 2 (March 1991): 163–84.

Goluboff, Risa Lauren. "The Lost Promise of Civil Rights." *Virginia Law Review* 93 (June 4, 2007): 85–103.

Laville, Helen. "'Women of Conscience' or 'Women of Conviction'? The National Women's Committee on Civil Rights." *Journal of American Studies* 43, no. 2 (2009): 277–95.

Lytle, Clifford M. "The History of the Civil Rights Bill of 1964." *The Journal of Negro History* 51, no. 4 (October 1966): 275–96.

Osterman, Rachel. "Origins of a Myth: Why Courts, Scholars, and the Public Think Title VII's Ban on Sex Discrimination Was an Accident." *Yale Journal of Law and Feminism* 20, no. 2 (2009): 409–40.

Pittman, R. Carter. "Equality Versus Liberty: The Eternal Conflict." *American Bar Association Journal* 46 (August 1960): 873–80.

Stevens, Arthur G., Jr., Arthur H. Miller, and Thomas E. Mann. "Mobilization of Liberal Strength in the House, 1955–1970: The Democratic Study Group." *American Political Science Review* 68, no. 2 (June 1974): 667–81.

Thompson, Llewellyn E. II. "The Civil Rights Act of 1964: Present at Its Birth." *University of San Francisco Law Review* 29 (Spring 1995): 681–84.

GOVERNMENT DOCUMENTS

U.S. Congress. House of Representatives. Committee on the Judiciary, Subcommittee No. 5. HR 405, 2999, 4031, and Similar Bills to Prohibit Discrimination in Employment in Certain Cases Because of Race, Religion, Color, National Origin, Ancestry, or Age. 88th Congress, 1st Session, 1963.

U.S. Congress. House of Representatives. Committee on the Judiciary, Subcommittee No. 5. Miscellaneous Proposals Regarding the Civil Rights of Persons Within the Jurisdiction of the United States. 88th Congress, 1st Session, 1963.

U.S. Congress. House of Representatives. Committee on the Judiciary. HR 7152, as Amended by Subcommittee No. 5. 88th Congress, 1st Session, 1963.

U.S. Congress. House of Representatives. Committee on Rules. HR 7152, Part 1 of 2. 88th Congress, 2nd Session, 1964.

U.S. Congress. House of Representatives. Committee on Rules. HR 7152, Part 2 of 2. 88th Congress, 2nd Session, 1964.

U.S. Congress. Senate. Committee on Labor and Public Welfare, Subcommittee on Employment and Manpower. S.773, S.1210, S.1211, and S.1937, Bills Relating to Equal Employment Opportunity. 88th Congress, 1st Session, 1963.

NOTES

Introduction

1 *Lawrence Journal World*, July 3, 1964, 2.

2 *Reporter*, August 13, 1964, 44; *Time*, July 17, 1964, 39.

3 "Compliance with Title II: A Summary of Field Reports from Southern States," box 27, Burke Marshall Papers, John F. Kennedy Library.

4 Fite, *Richard B. Russell*, 415.

5 Martin Luther King Jr., "Hammer of Civil Rights," *Nation*, March 9, 1964, http://www .thenation.com/article/157742/hammer-civil-rights#axzz2fqfOSRLD, accessed September 24, 2013.

Chapter 1: Bad Beginnings to a Big Year

1 *Christian Science Monitor*, February 14, 1963, 6; *Cleveland Call and Post*, February 23, 1963, 1c; *New Journal and Guide*, February 16, 1963, B1.

2 *New Journal and Guide*, ibid.

3 *New Journal and Guide*, February 16, 1963, B1; *Jet*, February 28, 1963, 12–13.

4 *Atlanta Daily World*, February 21, 1963, 2; *Jet*, ibid, 10.

5 *Washington Post*, February 28, 1988, B10; *Chicago Defender*, January 5, 1964, 4.

6 Martin Luther King Jr., "A Bold Guide for a New South," *Nation*, March 6, 1963, http:// www.thenation.com/article/157763/archive-bold-design-new-south#axzz2fqfOSRLD, accessed September 24, 2013.

7 *New York Amsterdam News*, May 19, 1962, 1; Branch, *Parting the Waters*, 686. To be fair, the president did issue an executive proclamation on December 17, 1962, to mark the centennial of Lincoln's famous document. It noted that "Negro citizens are still being denied rights guaranteed by the Constitution" and proclaimed "that the Emancipation Proclamation expresses our Nation's policy, founded on justice and morality, and that it is therefore fitting and proper to commemorate the centennial of the historic Emancipation Proclamation throughout the year 1963." Proclamation 3511, Code of Federal Regulations of the United States.

8 Poinsett, *Walking with Presidents*, 110; Reeves, *President Kennedy*, 464.

9 *Jet*, March 7, 1963, 12.

10 Ibid.

11 Berman, *Politics of Civil Rights*, 62; http://www.trumanlibrary.org/civilrights/srights1

.htm, accessed April 20, 2013; http://www.presidency.ucsb.edu/ws/?pid=78208, accessed April 20, 2013.

12 Graham, *Civil Rights Era*, 19; *Atlanta Daily World*, April 4, 1950, 1.

13 *Atlanta Daily World*, January 8, 1952, 1.

14 Gillon, *Politics and Vision*, 83.

15 Ibid., 84 and 101.

16 Interview with Frank Valeo by Donald Ritchie, September 18, 1985. Oral History Project, Senate Historical Office.

17 Graham, *Civil Rights and the Presidency*, 79.

18 Caro, *Lyndon Johnson: Master*, 914–15.

19 *New York Times*, July 3, 1957, 10.

20 Statement by Senator Paul H. Douglas Prior to Vote on Final Passage of Civil Rights Bill, August 7, 1957, box 26, Joseph L. Rauh Jr. Papers, Library of Congress; transcript, Joseph Rauh Jr. oral history interview, August 8, 1969, by Paige Mulhollan, Lyndon B. Johnson Library.

21 *New York Times*, January 6, 1957, E6; Caro, *Lyndon Johnson: Master*, 993.

22 *New Journal and Guide*, December 27, 1958; *Chicago Daily Defender*, January 15, 1959, 25.

23 *Washington Post*, April 24, 1960, 73.

24 *New York Times*, April 9, 1960, 1.

25 Notes on the 1963 Civil Rights Commission Report by Raymond Wolfinger, n.d., box 23, David B. Filvaroff and Raymond E. Wolfinger Civil Rights Acts Papers, University Archives, State University of New York at Buffalo; *Washington Post*, September 7, 1959, A12.

26 Green Book, box 466, Emanuel Celler Papers, Library of Congress; House Rules Committee Hearing on HR 7152, part 1 of 2, January 14, 1964, 89.

27 *Chicago Defender*, August 16, 1958, 9.

28 Cited by Rep. William T. Cahill, Hearings Before Subcommittee No. 5 of the House Judiciary Committee, May 8, 1963, 942.

29 Sugrue, *Sweet Land*, 163–69; *New York Times*, October 23, 1963, 1.

30 Sovern, *Legal Restraints*, 4–5; cited in Hearings Before the Subcommittee on Employment and Manpower of the Committee on Labor and Public Welfare, July 24, 25, 26, 29, 31 and August 2 and 20, 1963, 333–38.

31 Wilkins and Mathews, *Standing Fast*, 285.

32 *Baltimore Afro-American*, April 4, 1959, 3.

33 Branch, *Pillar of Fire*, 32.

34 *Los Angeles Times*, September 23, 1963, 1.

35 *Cleveland Call and Post*, September 16, 1961, 2C.

36 Wilkins and Mathews, *Standing Fast*, 285.

37 *Los Angeles Times*, July 16, 1960, 3.

38 *New York Times*, July 16, 1960, 1.

39 http://www.presidency.ucsb.edu/ws/?pid=29602, accessed April 23, 2013.

40 October 7, 1960 Debate Transcript, the Commission on Presidential Debates, http://www.debates.org/index.php?page=october-7-1960-debate-transcript, accessed September 24, 2013; Freedman and Hoffman, *John F. Kennedy*, 87.

41 Wilkins and Mathews, *Standing Fast*, 227; Statement by Senator Joseph S. Clark and Representative Emanuel Celler Concerning the Democratic Party Civil Rights Legislation in 1961, September 16, 1960, box 462, Emanuel Celler Papers, Library of Congress.

42 Wilkins and Mathews, *Standing Fast*, 279.

43 Reeves, *President Kennedy*, 63; Joseph L. Rauh Jr. oral history interview by Charles T. Morrissey, December 23, 1965, John F. Kennedy Archives.

44 Interview with Harris Wofford, by Raymond Wolfinger, November 16, 1966, box 22, David B. Filvaroff and Raymond E. Wolfinger Civil Rights Acts Papers, University Archives, State University of New York at Buffalo; interview with Lee White, by Milton Gwirtzman, May 26 and 28, 1964, John F. Kennedy Library.

45 *New York Times*, February 4, 1963, 1.

46 Kane, "Senate Debate," 40.

47 Caro, *Lyndon Johnson: Master*, 857.

48 *New York Times*, January 16, 1963, 1; *New York Times*, February 4, 1963; Caro, ibid.

49 *Washington Post*, February 8, 1963, A13.

50 Joseph L. Rauh to Francis Biddle, February 11, 1963, box 43, Papers of Joseph L. Rauh Jr., Library of Congress.

51 Guthman and Shulman, *Robert Kennedy*, 67.

52 Thurber, *Politics of Equality*, 66; Mann, *Walls of Jericho*, 98–99.

53 Mann, *Walls of Jericho*, 92; Humphrey, *Education*, 268.

54 Schlesinger, *Thousand Days*, 931; Guthman and Shulman, *Robert Kennedy*, 149, interview with Anthony Lewis.

55 Stern, *Calculating Visions*, 70.

56 Kennedy, Kennedy, and Kennedy, *Profiles*, 119.

57 Memo from Lee White to Ted Sorensen, November 13, 1961, box 30, Ted Sorensen Papers, John F. Kennedy Library.

58 Bryant, *The Bystander*, 298–302; *Pittsburgh Post-Gazette*, May 15, 1962, 2.

59 Guthman and Shulman, *Robert Kennedy*, 149, interview with Anthony Lewis.

60 Burke Marshall, interview with Anthony Lewis, June 20, 1964, John F. Kennedy Library; Burke Marshall, interview with Anthony Lewis, June 13, 1964, John F. Kennedy Library.

61 *Chicago Tribune*, February 1, 1961, 1.

62 Eleanor Clift, "Inside Kennedy's Inauguration, 50 Years On," *Daily Beast*, January 20, 2011.

63 Thompson, *Kennedy Presidency*, 89; Roy Wilkins Oral History Interview, by Berl I. Bernard, August 13, 1964, John F. Kennedy Library.

64 Ralph Dungan to John F. Kennedy, March 3, 1963, box 97, series 8, Presidential Office Files, John F. Kennedy Library.

65 Report of the Attorney General to the President on the Department of Justice Activities in the Field of Civil Rights, December 29, 1961, box 96, series 8, Presidential Office Files, Lyndon B. Johnson Library, http://www.eeoc.gov/eeoc/history/35th/thelaw/eo-10925.html, accessed April 27, 2013.

66 Birnbaum, 1962, 19.

67 Shesol, *Mutual Contempt*, 83.

68 Memo from Nicholas Katzenbach to Lee White, October 20, 1961, box 30, Theodore Sorensen Papers, John F. Kennedy Library.

69 Schlesinger, *Thousand Days*, 939.

70 *Chicago Tribune*, July 13, 1951, 1.

71 Interview with Lee White, by Milton Gwirtzman, May 26 and 28, 1964, John F. Kennedy Library.

72 *Wall Street Journal*, November 21, 1962, 18.

73 *New York Times*, June 30, 2003, A1.

74 Schlesinger, *Robert Kennedy*, 237.

75 *New York Herald Tribune*, February 18, 1961, 8; Stern, *Calculating Visions*, 50–51; *Afro-American*, September 16, 1961, 6.

76 *Chicago Defender*, December 30, 1961, 1; Navasky, *Kennedy Justice*, 25.

77 Bryant, *The Bystander*, 315; Navasky, *Kennedy Justice*, 205.

78 Burke Marshall to Clarence Mitchell, January 25, 1962, box 48, Records of the U.S. House of Representatives, 88th Congress, Committee on the Judiciary, National Archives and Records Administration; address by Assistant Attorney General Burke Marshall before the 53rd Annual Convention of the NAACP, Atlanta, Ga., July 2, 1962, box 10, Victor Navasky Papers, John F. Kennedy Library.

79 President's News Conference, August 1, 1962. http://www.presidency.ucsb.edu/ws/index.php?pid=8799&st=&st1, accessed May 2, 2013.

80 Bryant, *The Bystander*, 323.

81 Eagles, *Price of Defiance*, 340–70.

82 Ibid.

83 Ibid.

84 Schlesinger, *Thousand Days*, 944; Schlesinger, *Robert Kennedy*, 298.

85 Memo from Burke Marshall to Nicholas Katzenbach, October 30, 1962, box 8, David B. Filvaroff and Raymond E. Wolfinger Civil Rights Act Papers, University of Buffalo Library.

86 Interview, Fred Sontag, with Raymond Wolfinger, August 30, 1965, David B. Filvaroff and Raymond E. Wolfinger Civil Rights Act Papers, University of Buffalo Library; Robert Kimball, interview with the author, September 4, 2013.

87 Mann, *Walls of Jericho*, 341.

88 Letter from Joseph Clark, Paul Douglas, Hubert Humphrey, and Harrison Williams to John F. Kennedy, January 8, 1963, box 15, David B. Filvaroff and Raymond E. Wolfinger Civil Rights Act Papers, University of Buffalo Library; memo from Louis Martin to Ted Sorensen, January 30, 1963, box 30, Theodore Sorensen Office Files, John F. Kennedy Library.

89 Lee White interview with Milton Gwirtzman, May 26 and 28, 1964, John F. Kennedy Library; *Jet*, January 17, 1963, 6.

90 "A Report on the Progress in the Field of Civil Rights by Attorney General Robert F. Kennedy to the President," January 24, 1963, box 22, Lee White Office Files, John F. Kennedy Library.

91 http://www.presidency.ucsb.edu/ws/?pid=9138, accessed May 1, 2013.

92 http://www.presidency.ucsb.edu/ws/?pid=9581, accessed May 1, 2013.

93 Wilkins and Mathews, *Standing Fast*, 287; *Los Angeles Times*, March 9, 1963, 3; Schlesinger, *Robert Kennedy*, 327.

94 Mann, *Walls of Jericho*, 342; Americans for Democratic Action Newsletter, April 8, 1963, box 17, David B. Filvaroff and Raymond E. Wolfinger Civil Rights Act Papers, University of Buffalo Library.

95 Mann, *Walls of Jericho*, 343; Schlesinger, *Robert Kennedy*, 328.

96 Joseph L. Rauh Jr. interview, Charles T. Morrissey, December 23, 1965, John F. Kennedy Library.

97 Martin Luther King Jr., "Fumbling on the New Frontier," *Nation*, March 3, 1962, 191.

CHAPTER 2: "A NATIONAL MOVEMENT TO ENFORCE NATIONAL LAWS"

1 Branch, *Parting the Waters*, 756–57.

2 Ibid.

3 McWhorter, *Carry Me Home*, 22.

4 Garrow, *Bearing the Cross*, 263.

5 McWhorter, *Carry Me Home*, 316.

6 *New York Times*, March 29, 1963, 1.

7 Robert F. Kennedy Press Conference, April 2, 1963, box 8, Burke Marshall Papers, John F. Kennedy Library; Presidential News Conference, April 3, 1963. http://www.jfklibrary.org/ Research/Research-Aids/Ready-Reference/Press-Conferences/News-Conference-53.aspx, accessed May 4, 2013.

8 Branch, *Parting the Waters*, 708 and 711.

9 *New York Times*, April 13, 1963, 1; McWhorter, *Carry Me Home*, 348.

10 "Annual Message to the Congress on the State of the Union," January 14, 1963, http:// www.presidency.ucsb.edu/ws/?pid=9138#ixzz2fxWRSPj4, accessed September 25, 2013; *New York Times*, April 17, 1963, 1; *Chicago Tribune*, April 18, 1963, D3; "Letter to the Chairman in Response to a Report on Mississippi by the Civil Rights Commission," April 19, 1963, http:// www.presidency.ucsb.edu/ws/?pid=9155, accessed August 8, 2013.

11 *Chicago Tribune*, April 25, 1963, 1; President's News Conference, April 24, 1963, http:// www.presidency.ucsb.edu/ws/index.php?pid=9165, accessed May 10, 2013.

12 Memo from Burke Marshall to Robert F. Kennedy, April 23, 1963, box 8, Burke Marshall Papers, John F. Kennedy Library; *Time*, April 19, 1963, 30–31.

13 *New York Times*, May 4, 1963, 8; *New York Times*, May 7, 1963, 5.

14 *New York Times*, May 8, 1963, 29.

15 Branch, *Parting the Waters*, 772, 780.

16 *New York Times*, May 9, 1963, 14; *New York Times*, May 7, 1963, 32; *New York Times*, May 15, 1963, 26; *Washington Post*, May 30, 1963, A7; Perlstein, *Before the Storm*, 207 and 213.

17 Tape 85, Americans for Democratic Action, May 4, 1963, John F. Kennedy Library, http://www.jfklibrary.org/Asset-Viewer/Archives/JFKPOF-MTG-085-002.aspx, accessed May 6, 2013; Schlesinger, *Thousand Days*, 959; Schlesinger, *Journals*, 189.

18 Schlesinger, *Journals*, 191; *Washington Post*, May 28, 1963, A19.

19 *New York Times*, May 8, 1963, 1; *Los Angeles Times*, May 10, 1963, 14.

20 President's News Conference, May 8, 1963, http://www.jfklibrary.org/Research/Research-Aids/Ready-Reference/Press-Conferences/News-Conference-55.aspx, accessed May 5, 2013.

21 *Los Angeles Times*, May 12, G1.

22 Tape 86, May 12, 1963, John F. Kennedy Library, http://www.jfklibrary.org/Asset-Viewer/Archives/JFKPOF-MTG-086-002.aspx, accessed May 6, 2013.

23 Ibid.

24 Branch, *Parting the Waters*, 796–800; "Radio and Television Remarks Following Renewal of Racial Strife in Birmingham," May 12, 1963, http://www.presidency.ucsb.edu/ws/ index.php?pid=9206&st=&st1, accessed May 5, 2013.

25 Burke Marshall interview with Anthony Lewis, June 20, 1964, John F. Kennedy Library.

26 Lee White to Lawrence O'Brien, April 17, 1963, box 21, Lee White Office Files, John F. Kennedy Library; Bryant, *The Bystander*, 401.

27 McWhorter, *Carry Me Home*, 447.

28 Norbert Schlei interview with Raymond Wolfinger, August 27, 1965, box 22, David B. Filvaroff and Raymond E. Wolfinger Civil Rights Act Papers, University of Buffalo Library.

29 *New York Times*, May 19, 1963, 1; *Washington Post*, May 24, 1963, A6.

30 "Legislative Possibilities," May 20, 1963, box 30, Theodore Sorensen Office Files, John F. Kennedy Library; Tape 88, Civil Rights Legislation, May 20, 1963, http://www.jfklibrary.org/Asset-Viewer/Archives/JFKPOF-MTG-088-004.aspx, accessed September 25, 2013.

31 Grofman, *Legacies*, 13–14; Dichter, Cathcart, and Lindemann, *Employment Discrimination Law*, ix–xi.

32 "Legislative Possibilities," May 20, 1963, box 30, Theodore Sorensen Office Files, John F. Kennedy Library; tape 88, Civil Rights Legislation, May 20, 1963, http://www.jfklibrary.org/Asset-Viewer/Archives/JFKPOF-MTG-088-004.aspx, accessed September 25, 2013.

33 Tape 88, ibid.

34 Ibid.

35 Ibid.

36 Kenneth O'Donnell interview, Raymond Wolfinger, April 11, 1967, box 22, David B. Filvaroff and Raymond E. Wolfinger Civil Rights Act Papers, University of Buffalo Library.

37 Ibid.

38 Baltimore *Sun*, May 22, 1963, 1; President's Press Conference, May 22, 1963, http://www.presidency.ucsb.edu/ws/index.php?pid=9233, accessed May 10, 2013.

39 Burke Marshall interview, Raymond Filvaroff, April 7 and 8, 1967, box 22, David B. Filvaroff and Raymond E. Wolfinger Civil Rights Act Papers, University of Buffalo Library; Schlesinger, *Thousand Days*, 960.

40 Marshall interview.

41 Schlesinger, *Robert Kennedy*, 345.

42 Ibid., 331.

43 Ibid., 333.

44 Guthman, *Band of Brothers*, 220.

45 Schlesinger, *Robert Kennedy*, 332.

46 Schlesinger, *Thousand Days*, 963.

47 Harry Belafonte interview with Vicki Daitch, May 20, 2005, John F. Kennedy Library; Guthman, *Band of Brothers*, 221.

48 Transcript, President's Committee on Equal Employment Opportunity, May 29, 1963, box 11, Civil Rights, Vice Presidential Office Files, Lyndon B. Johnson Library.

49 Schlesinger, *Robert Kennedy*, 349.

50 Interview with George Reedy, Michael L. Gillette, October 27, 1982, Lyndon B. Johnson Library.

51 Remarks of Vice President Lyndon B. Johnson, Memorial Day, Gettysburg, Pennsylvania, May 30, 1963, Lyndon B. Johnson Library, http://www.lbjlib.utexas.edu/johnson/archives.hom/speeches.hom/630530.asp, accessed May 6, 2013.

52 Ibid.

53 Dichter et al., *Employment Discrimination Law*, viii; Norbert Schlei interview with John Stewart, February 20–21, 1968, John F. Kennedy Library.

54 Dichter et al., *Employment Discrimination Law*, xi.

55 Agenda for civil rights meeting, June 1, 1963, box 30, Theodore Sorensen Office Files, John F. Kennedy Library.

56 White House Meeting, June 1, 1963, Tape 90, John F. Kennedy Library, http://www.jfklibrary.org/Asset-Viewer/Archives/JFKPOF-MTG-090-003.aspx, accessed May 7, 2013.

57 Thompson, *Kennedy Presidency*, 92–93; Louis Martin interview, Ronald J. Grele, March 14, 1966, John F. Kennedy Library.

58 Ibid.

59 Caro, *Lyndon Johnson: Passage*, 258.

60 Transcript of phone call between Lyndon B. Johnson and Theodore Sorensen, June 3, 1963, Lyndon B. Johnson Library.

61 Memo for the Attorney General: Comments of the Vice President on the Civil Rights Legislation Proposals, box 1, General Papers, Robert F. Kennedy Papers, John F. Kennedy Library; Norbert Schlei interview with John Stewart, February 20–21, 1968, John F. Kennedy Library.

62 Memo from John F. Kennedy to Willard Wirtz and Anthony Celebrezze, June 4, 1963, box 30, Theodore Sorensen Papers, John F. Kennedy Library.

63 Thompson, *Kennedy Presidency*, 94.

64 United States Decennial Census, U.S. Census Bureau, http://www.census.gov/prod/www/decennial.html, accessed September 25, 2013; *New York Times*, June 1, 1963, 6.

65 Branch, *Parting the Waters*, 814.

66 *Time*, June 7, 1963, 17; *Chicago Daily Defender*, May 29, 1963, 1; *New York Times*, May 29, 1963, 1; Branch, ibid.

67 *Time*, ibid.; *Time*, June 21, 1963, 17.

68 Branch, *Parting the Waters*, 816–17.

69 *New York Times*, May 30, 1963, 32; *Cleveland Call and Post*, June 8, 1963, 1c; memo from Robert F. Kennedy to District Attorneys, May 27, 1963, box 31, Burke Marshall Papers, John F. Kennedy Library.

70 Morris Abram interview, Michael Gillette, March 20, 1984, John F. Kennedy Library.

71 "Record of Presidential Meetings with Leadership Groups," n.d., box 23, Lee White Papers, John F. Kennedy Library.

72 Findlay, *Church People*, 148.

73 Civil Rights Statement, July 1963. Civil Rights 1963–1964, Everett M. Dirksen Papers, Dirksen Congressional Center.

74 Kane, "Senate Debate," 46.

75 *Wall Street Journal*, June 3, 1963, 1; *Today*, June 9, 1963, transcript, box 11, Victor Navasky Papers, John F. Kennedy Library.

76 Baltimore *Sun*, June 1, 1963, 1.

77 Carter, *Politics of Rage*, 110, 112; Bryant, *The Bystander*, 417.

78 Katzenbach, *Some of It*, 110–18.

79 President's News Conference, May 8, 1963, http://www.presidency.ucsb.edu/ws/index.php?pid=9192, accessed May 9, 2013; Drew, Robert "Crisis: Behind a Presidential Commitment." Directed by Charles Drew. Sharon, Conn. Drew Associates, 1963.

80 "Crisis," ibid.

81 Katzenbach, *Some of It*, 113.

82 Ibid., 114–18.

83 "Crisis: Behind a Presidential Commitment."

84 Katzenbach, *Some of It*, 113–15; *Time*, June 21, 1963, 17–18; Thomas, *Robert Kennedy*, 248.

85 Branch, *Parting the Waters*, 822.

86 Burke Marshall interview with Anthony Lewis, June 20, 1964, John F. Kennedy Library.

87 Burke Marshall interview with Anthony Lewis, June 13, 1964, John F. Kennedy Library; Guthman and Shulman, *Robert Kennedy*, 176.

88 Address on Civil Rights, June 11, 1963, http://millercenter.org/president/speeches/detail/3375, accessed May 10, 2013.

89 Telegram from Martin Luther King Jr. to John F. Kennedy, June 10, 1963, John F. Kennedy

Library, http://www.jfklibrary.org/Asset-Viewer/fXbXxZHwaUmJqbxW_5IrQg.aspx, accessed September 25, 2013; Bryant, *The Bystander*, 424.

90 Mann, *Walls of Jericho*, 366; Crespino, *Thurmond's America*, 138–39.

91 Bryant, *The Bystander*, 425.

92 Bryant, *The Bystander*, 424; *Time*, June 21, 1963, 18.

93 *Los Angeles Times*, February 6, 1994, 1; *Boston Globe*, December 23, 1990, 71.

94 Schlesinger, *Robert Kennedy*, 339. Schlesinger added in a footnote: "Alas, he had been taught thus by the Harvard history department."

CHAPTER 3: AN IDEA BECOMES A BILL

1 Memorandum from Bobby G. Baker to Senator Mansfield, June 12, 1963, box 9, David B. Filvaroff and Raymond E. Wolfinger Civil Rights Act Papers, University of Buffalo Library.

2 "Questions of Tactics," Theodore Sorensen, June 14, 1963, box 53, series 4, Presidential Office Files, John F. Kennedy Library.

3 Memo by Senator Mansfield on Conference with Senator Dirksen, June 13, 1963, box 53, series 4, Presidential Office Files, John F. Kennedy Library; memo from Mike Mansfield to John F. Kennedy, June 18, 1963, box 30, Theodore Sorensen Office Files, John F. Kennedy Library.

4 Memo from Lee White to John F. Kennedy, June 13, 1963, box 22, Lee White Office Files, John F. Kennedy Library; Meeting of the President with Religious Leaders, June 17, 1963, box 97, series 8, Presidential Office Files, John F. Kennedy Library.

5 Supplemental Message on Civil Rights, June 19, 1963, box 97, series 8, Presidential Office Files, John F. Kennedy Library.

6 James O'Hara interview, Raymond Wolfinger, September 23, 1965, box 22, David B. Filvaroff and Raymond E. Wolfinger Civil Rights Act Papers, University of Buffalo Library.

7 Ibid.

8 Nicholas Katzenbach interview with Anthony Lewis, November 29, 1964, John F. Kennedy Library.

9 Memo from G. Mennen Williams to Theodore Sorensen, June 15, 1963, box 30, Theodore Sorensen Papers, John F. Kennedy Library.

10 Remarks Upon Signing the Juvenile Delinquency and Youth Offenses Control Act, September 22, 1961, http://www.presidency.ucsb.edu/ws/?pid=8347#axzz2g3PKPI9b, accessed September 26, 2013; Thomas, *Robert Kennedy*, 305.

11 Memo from Lawrence J. O'Brien and Theodore C. Sorensen to John F. Kennedy, June 18, 1963, box 53, series 4, Presidential Office Files, John F. Kennedy Library; *Atlanta Daily World*, June 19, 1963, 1.

12 Memo from Chuck Daly to Larry O'Brien, June 14, 1963, box 30, Theodore Sorensen Office Files, John F. Kennedy Library.

13 Katzenbach, *Some of It*, 123.

14 *Atlanta Daily World*, June 13, 1963, 8; *Chicago Daily Defender*, June 13, 1963, 6; *Chicago Tribune*, June 13, 1963, S8; *Christian Science Monitor*, June 13, 1963, 1; *Los Angeles Times*, June 13, 1963, 1.

15 *New York Times*, June 15, 1963, 1.

16 Ibid.

17 *Atlanta Daily World*, June 14, 1963, 1; transcript of telephone call from Thelton Henderson, June 13, 1963, box 31, Burke Marshall Papers, John F. Kennedy Library.

18 *Atlanta Daily World,* June 13, 1963, 1; *Chicago Tribune,* June 16, 1963, 1; Bryant, *The Bystander,* 426.

19 Bryant, *The Bystander,* 425–26.

20 Sol Lindenbaum interview with Raymond Wolfinger, September 15, 1965, box 22, David B. Filvaroff and Raymond E. Wolfinger Civil Rights Act Papers, University of Buffalo Library; *Wall Street Journal,* June 20, 1963, 12.

21 Rauh Jr., "Role of the Leadership," 53; *New York Times,* June 24, 1963, 20; *Meet the Press,* August 25, 1963, transcript, http://archives.nbclearn.com/portal/site/k-12/flatview?cuecard=4570, accessed May 14, 2013.

22 Crespino, *In Search,* 92; *New York Times,* June 20, 1963, 18; *Washington Post,* June 25, 1963, A1; *New York Times,* June 25, 1963, 1; *Congressional Quarterly Weekly Report,* June 21, 1963, 997.

23 *New York Times,* June 20, 1963, 32.

24 *Atlanta Daily World,* June 20, 1963, 8.

25 *Indianapolis Recorder,* June 20, 1963, 1; *Baltimore Sun,* June 20, 1963, 1.

26 *New York Times,* June 20, 1963, 1; *Chicago Tribune,* June 20, 1963, 1.

27 Branch, *Parting the Waters,* 837–38.

28 Ibid., 839.

29 Ibid., 839–40; Schlesinger, *Thousand Days,* 968–71; Schlesinger, *Journals,* 196–98.

30 Joseph Rauh interview with Charles T. Morrissey, December 23, 1965, John F. Kennedy Library; *Los Angeles Times,* June 23, 1963, E1.

31 *New York Times,* June 23, 1963, 1.

32 Wilkins and Mathews, *Standing Fast,* 291–92.

33 Whalen and Whalen, *Longest Debate,* 29; Ben Zelenko, interview with author, April 20, 2012; *Washington Post,* June 2, 1972, B15.

34 Zelenko interview.

35 Ibid.

36 www.williammcculloch.org, accessed September 5, 2013.

37 William McCulloch, interview with Raymond Wolfinger, September 19, 1965, box 22, David B. Filvaroff and Raymond E. Wolfinger Civil Rights Act Papers, University of Buffalo Library.

38 *Cleveland Call and Post,* July 13, 1957, 2D.

39 Whalen and Whalen, *Longest Debate,* 10; *Cleveland Call and Post,* July 13, 1957, 2D.

40 *Washington Post,* February 5, 1960, A2.

41 *New York Times,* March 16, 1962, 19.

42 William M. McCulloch interview with Raymond Wolfinger, September 15, 1965, box 22, David B. Filvaroff and Raymond E. Wolfinger Civil Rights Act Papers, University of Buffalo Library.

43 Miscellaneous Proposals Regarding the Civil Rights of Persons Within the Jurisdiction of the United States, vol. 2 of 3, Subcommittee No. 5 of the Committee on the Judiciary, 907–10.

44 *New York Times,* June 27, 1963, 1; *Chicago Tribune,* June 27, 1963, 1; Whalen and Whalen, *Longest Debate,* 3–6.

45 Miscellaneous Proposals, 1378.

46 Miscellaneous Proposals, 1374 and 1376; *New York Times,* June 27, 1963, 1.

47 Miscellaneous Proposals, 1383.

48 Ibid., 1400.

49 Ibid., 1413–15.

50 Ibid.

51 Robert Kimball, interview with the author, September 4, 2013; Nicholas deB. Katzenbach interview with Raymond Wolfinger, September 18, 1965, box 22, David B. Filvaroff and Raymond E. Wolfinger Civil Rights Act Papers, University of Buffalo Library.

52 Miscellaneous Proposals, 1422; *New York Times*, June 19, 1963, 1.

53 Miscellaneous Proposals, 1372–1422.

54 *New York Times*, June 27, 1963, 1; Baltimore *Sun*, June 27, 1963, 1; *Los Angeles Times*, June 30, 1963, K4.

55 Memo from Nicholas Katzenbach to Robert Kennedy, June 29, 1963, box 11, General Correspondence, Robert F. Kennedy Papers, John F. Kennedy Library.

56 Whalen and Whalen, *Longest Debate*, 10–12.

57 Leadership Breakfast Statement on Civil Rights, July 9, 1963, box 53, series 4, Presidential Office Files, John F. Kennedy Library.

58 Jones, *March on Washington*, 173.

59 Arnold Aronson interview, August 13, 1965, box 22, David B. Filvaroff and Raymond E. Wolfinger Civil Rights Act Papers, University of Buffalo Library.

60 http://www.civilrights.org/about/video/lccr_history_text.html, accessed September 25, 2013.

61 Aronson interview.

62 *Crisis*, June–July 1964, 360.

63 Louis Martin interview with Ronald J. Grele, March 14, 1966, John F. Kennedy Library.

64 Findlay, *Church People*, 20.

65 Findlay, *Church People*, 22; "Will D. Campbell 1952 B.D.," Yale Divinity School Web site, http://divinity.yale.edu/will-d-campbell-1952-bd, accessed May 18, 2013.

66 *Disciples World Magazine*, October 2004, http://www.disciplesworldmagazine.com/node/7143, accessed May 19, 2013.

67 Findlay, *Church People*, 29–30.

68 General Board Discussion of the Report of the President's Temporary Committee of Six on Race, June 7, 1963, box 48, record group 6, National Council of Churches Archives, Presbyterian Historical Society; Findlay, ibid.

69 Memo from Jon Regier to Robert Spike, July 14, 1963, box 48, record group 6, National Council of Churches Archives, Presbyterian Historical Society.

70 Summary of Meeting at the University Club, New York City, with Representatives of the Justice Department and Religious Organizations, July 9, 1963, box 48, record group 6, National Council of Churches Archives, Presbyterian Historical Society.

71 Memo from Nicholas Katzenbach to Robert Kennedy, June 29, 1963, box 9, David B. Filvaroff and Raymond E. Wolfinger Civil Rights Act Papers, University of Buffalo Library.

72 Findlay, *Church People*, 53–54; S.773, S.1210, S.1211, and S.1937, Bills Relating to Equal Employment Opportunity, Subcommittee on Employment and Manpower of the Committee on Labor and Public Welfare.

73 *Time*, October 31, 1969, 77; Crespino, *In Search*, 93; White, *Making*, 191.

74 "Rough Memo Concerning Preparation for Work of the Committee to Defeat the Civil Rights Act of 1963," box 17, David B. Filvaroff and Raymond E. Wolfinger Civil Rights Act Papers, University of Buffalo Library.

75 John Synon interview with Raymond Wolfinger, September 7, 1965, box 22, David B. Filvaroff and Raymond E. Wolfinger Civil Rights Act Papers, University of Buffalo Library.

76 *Wall Street Journal*, June 11, 1999, A1; Crespino, *Thurmond's America*, 170–71; Crespino, *In Search*, 96–99; Hustwit, *James J. Kilpatrick*, 129–30.

77 Whalen and Whalen, *Longest Debate*, 23.

78 Baltimore *Sun*, June 30, 1963, 3.

79 Memo from Robert G. Baker to Senator Mansfield, June 27, 1963, box 10, David B. Filvaroff and Raymond E. Wolfinger Civil Rights Act Papers, University of Buffalo Library.

80 *Chicago Defender*, June 22, 1963, 1; *Los Angeles Times*, May 19, 1963, M2.

81 *Chicago Tribune*, July 3, 1963, 4; Crespino, *Thurmond's America*, 192.

82 *Chicago Tribune*, July 11, 1963, 15.

83 *New York Times*, July 16, 1963, 16; Crespino, *Thurmond's America*, 139; Carter, *Politics of Rage*, 160.

84 Loevy, *To End All Segregation*, 40.

85 Schlesinger, *Robert Kennedy*, 381; *Chicago Tribune*, July 21, 1963, 9; Loevy, *To End All Segregation*, 40.

86 Navasky, *Kennedy Justice*, 227; John Douglas interview with Raymond Wolfinger, April 5, 1963, box 22, David B. Filvaroff and Raymond E. Wolfinger Civil Rights Act Papers, University of Buffalo Library.

87 Garrow, *Bearing the Cross*, 278.

88 *Washington Post*, June 25, 1963, A14; *New York Times*, August 21, 1963, 24; memo from Joe Dolan to Robert F. Kennedy, July 17, 1963, box 13, David B. Filvaroff and Raymond E. Wolfinger Civil Rights Act Papers, University of Buffalo Library.

89 *Washington Post*, June 25, 1963, A14; memo from Joe Dolan to Robert Kennedy, July 17, 1963, box 13, David B. Filvaroff and Raymond E. Wolfinger Civil Rights Act Papers, University of Buffalo Library; Jones, *March on Washington,* 181.

90 *Congressional Quarterly Weekly Report*, August 30, 1963, 1495; Mudd, *Place to Be*, 116; *Washington Post*, August 29, 1963, A1.

91 Jones, *March on Washington*, 183; Mudd, *Place to Be*, 116–17; *New York Times*, August 29, 1963, 1.

92 Jones, *March on Washington*, 194–200.

93 http://www.archives.gov/press/exhibits/dream-speech.pdf, accessed September 25, 2013.

94 Jones, *March on Washington*, 203.

95 Branch, *Parting the Waters*, 883–86; Jones, *March on Washington*, 203–4; Garrow, *Bearing the Cross*, 285.

96 Branch, Jones, and Garrow, ibid.

97 *Washington Post*, August 29, 1963, A1; Katzenbach, *Some of It*, 126.

98 Memo No. 5, August 30, 1963, box 37, part 1, Leadership Conference on Civil Rights Papers, Library of Congress.

99 Report of the Executive Director to the Committee on Religion and Race of the National Council of Churches, July 26, 1963, box 11, record group 6, National Council of Churches Archives, Presbyterian Historical Society; interview with James Hamilton, September 21, 1964, by Raymond Wolfinger, box 22, David B. Filvaroff and Raymond E. Wolfinger Civil Rights Act Papers, University of Buffalo Library; memo to file, August 9, 1963, box 367, Walter P. Reuther Papers, Wayne State University Library.

100 "Labor Views on Administration Civil Rights Program," June 7, 1963, box 9, David B. Filvaroff and Raymond E. Wolfinger Civil Rights Act Papers, University of Buffalo Library.

101 Andrew Biemiller interview with Gerald Stern, May 24, 1979, John F. Kennedy Library.

102 Memo from Nicholas Katzenbach to Robert Kennedy, August 19, 1963, box 8, David B. Filvaroff and Raymond E. Wolfinger Civil Rights Act Papers, University of Buffalo Library.

103 Memo from William Geoghegan to Nicholas Katzenbach, August 6, 1963, box 10, David B. Filvaroff and Raymond E. Wolfinger Civil Rights Act Papers, University of Buffalo Library Archives; Schlesinger, *Thousand Days*, 967–68.

104 Garrow, *Bearing the Cross*, 279.

105 Miscellaneous Proposals Regarding the Civil Rights of Persons Within the Jurisdiction of the United States, vol. 2 of 4, Subcommittee No. 5 of the Committee on the Judiciary, 2128; Ben Zelenko, interview with the author, April 20, 2013; minutes of the Leadership Conference Meeting, July 31, 1963, box 34, part 1, Leadership Conference on Civil Rights Papers, Library of Congress.

106 Memo of the White House Meeting, July 29, 1963, box 8, David B. Filvaroff and Raymond E. Wolfinger Civil Rights Act Papers, University of Buffalo Library.

107 Loevy, *To End All Segregation*, 57; Memorandum on Civil Rights Bill, August 30, 1963, box 1, part 1, Leadership Conference on Civil Rights Records, Library of Congress.

108 Minutes, Subcommittee No. 5, Committee on the Judiciary, August 14, 1963, box 402, Records of the U.S. House of Representatives, 88th Congress, Committee on the Judiciary, National Archives.

109 Tape from David Filvaroff to Raymond Wolfinger, n.d., box 22, David B. Filvaroff and Raymond E. Wolfinger Civil Rights Act Papers, University of Buffalo Library.

110 George Meader interview with Raymond Wolfinger, September 21, 1965, box 22, David B. Filvaroff and Raymond E. Wolfinger Civil Rights Act Papers, University of Buffalo Library.

111 Minutes, Subcommittee No. 5, Committee on the Judiciary, passim, box 402, Records of the U.S. House of Representatives, 88th Congress, Committee on the Judiciary, National Archives.

112 William McCulloch interviews with Raymond Wolfinger, September 15, 19, 23, and 24, 1965, box 22, David B. Filvaroff and Raymond E. Wolfinger Civil Rights Act Papers, University of Buffalo Library.

113 Ibid.

114 *Chicago Tribune*, September 5, 1963, 1; *New York Times*, September 10, 1963, 1; *New York Times*, September 11, 1963, 1.

115 Statement by the President on the Sunday Bombing in Birmingham, September 16, 1963, http://www.presidency.ucsb.edu/ws/?pid=9410, accessed May 22, 2013.

116 Statement by Roy Wilkins, September 18, 1963, box 119, part IX, NAACP Papers, Library of Congress; memorandum from Robert Spike, September 18, 1963, box 48, record group 6, National Council of Churches Archives, Presbyterian Historical Society; Memo No. 7, Leadership Conference on Civil Rights, September 20, 1963, box 37, part 1, Leadership Conference on Civil Rights Papers, Library of Congress.

117 Whalen and Whalen, *Longest Debate*, 34–35; Meader interview.

118 *Wall Street Journal*, September 26, 1963, 6; Whalen and Whalen, *Longest Debate*, 35.

119 Minutes, Subcommittee No. 5, Committee on the Judiciary, September 24, 1963, box 402, Records of the U.S. House of Representatives, 88th Congress, Committee on the Judiciary, National Archives; Robert Kimball, interview with the author, September 4, 2013.

120 *New York Times*, October 3, 1963, 194; *Washington Post*, October 1, 1963, A2.

121 Bryant, *The Bystander*, 448; *Christian Science Monitor*, October 6, 1963, 68.

122 Katzenbach, *Some of It*, 124.

CHAPTER 4: THE OCTOBER CRISIS

1 Memo from Nicholas Katzenbach to Robert Kennedy, October 1, 1963, box 13, David B. Filvaroff and Raymond E. Wolfinger Civil Rights Act Papers, University of Buffalo Library.

2 Guthman and Shulman, *Robert Kennedy*, 217–18.

3 Ibid.

4 Ibid.

5 Memo from Nicholas Katzenbach to Robert Kennedy, October 1, 1963, box 13, David B. Filvaroff and Raymond E. Wolfinger Civil Rights Act Papers, University of Buffalo Library; Grofman, *Legacies*, 18.

6 Grofman, ibid.

7 Nicholas Katzenbach interview with Raymond Wolfinger, September 25, 1965, box 22, David B. Filvaroff and Raymond E. Wolfinger Civil Rights Act Papers, University of Buffalo Library.

8 Nicholas Katzenbach interview with Anthony Lewis, November 29, 1964, John F. Kennedy Library.

9 ADA Legislative Newsletter, October 11, 1963, box 18, David B. Filvaroff and Raymond E. Wolfinger Civil Rights Act Papers, University of Buffalo Library; letter from Clarence Mitchell to Charles M. Mathias Jr., October 8, 1963, box 231, NAACP Papers, Library of Congress; *Chicago Tribune*, October 24, 1963, 3.

10 Rosenberg and Karabell, *Kennedy, Johnson, and the Quest for Justice*, 176; Guthman and Shulman, *Robert Kennedy*, 209.

11 O'Brien, *No Final Victories*, 130.

12 Rosenberg and Karabell, *Kennedy, Johnson, and the Quest for Justice*, 178.

13 Ibid., 181.

14 Andrew Biemiller interview with Sheldon Stern, May 24, 1979, John F. Kennedy Library; D. B. Hardeman interview with Raymond Wolfinger, September 13, 1965, box 22, David B. Filvaroff and Raymond E. Wolfinger Civil Rights Act Papers, University of Buffalo Library; Garrison Nelson, "Unraveling the Reinvention of Speaker John W. McCormack," *New England Journal of Public Policy* XV (Fall/Winter 1999/2000), 7–34.

15 John W. McCormack interview with Raymond Wolfinger, April 4, 1967, box 22, David B. Filvaroff and Raymond E. Wolfinger Civil Rights Act Papers, University of Buffalo Library.

16 John McCormack, ibid.; Katzenbach, *Some of It*, 126.

17 HR 7152, as amended by Subcommittee No. 5, Committee on the Judiciary, House of Representatives, October 15–16, 1963, 2653–86.

18 Statement by Attorney General Robert F. Kennedy on HR 7152 before the House Judiciary Committee, October 15, 1963, box 97, series 8, Presidential Office Files, John F. Kennedy Library.

19 Press Conference of Attorney General Robert F. Kennedy, October 15, 1963, box 30, Theodore Sorensen Papers, John F. Kennedy Library.

20 HR 7152, 3697.

21 Ibid., 2762.

22 *Chicago Daily Defender*, October 16, 1963, 3; *Los Angeles Sentinel*, October 17, 1963,

A11; Loevy, *To End All Segregation*, 62; press release, October 21, 1963, box 170, American Jewish Congress Papers, American Jewish Congress Archives.

23 *Chicago Tribune*, October 16, 1963, 14; *New York Times*, October 16, 1963, 1.

24 *New York Times*, ibid.; *New York Times*, October 17, 1963, 1.

25 Nicholas Katzenbach interview with Anthony Lewis, November 29, 1964, Oral History Collection, John F. Kennedy Library.

26 Guthman and Shulman, *Robert Kennedy*, 217; Katzenbach interview with Lewis.

27 *New York Times*, October 18, 1963, 1.

28 Russo, *The Outfit*, 23; *Time*, November 1, 1963, 23–24.

29 *Time*, ibid.

30 *Harvard Crimson*, October 22, 1963, http://www.thecrimson.com/article/1963/10/22/lobbyists-press-for-civil-rights-bill/, accessed May 28, 1963.

31 Bess Dick interview with Raymond Wolfinger, September 23, 1966, box 22, David B. Filvaroff and Raymond E. Wolfinger Civil Rights Act Papers, University of Buffalo Library.

32 Ibid.

33 Minutes of Meeting No. 23, House Judiciary Committee, October 22, 1963, box 465, Emanuel Celler Papers, Library of Congress.

34 Nicholas Katzenbach interview with Anthony Lewis, November 29, 1964, Oral History Collection, John F. Kennedy Library.

35 William McCulloch interview with Raymond Wolfinger, September 23, 1965, box 22, David B. Filvaroff and Raymond E. Wolfinger Civil Rights Act Papers, University of Buffalo Library.

36 Katzenbach, *Some of It*, 127.

37 McCulloch interview.

38 Rosenberg and Karabell, *Kennedy, Johnson, and the Quest for Justice*, 199.

39 Norbert Schlei interview with Raymond Wolfinger, September 2, 1965, box 22, David B. Filvaroff and Raymond E. Wolfinger Civil Rights Act Papers, University of Buffalo Library.

40 Rosenberg and Karabell, *Kennedy, Johnson, and the Quest for Justice*, 190; Scheele, *Charlie Halleck*, 217–18.

41 Whalen and Whalen, *Longest Debate*, 52.

42 Bradlee and Kennedy, *Conversations*, 218.

43 Press Conference, October 24, 1963. Civil Rights 1963–1964, Everett M. Dirksen Papers, Dirksen Congressional Center.

44 Whalen and Whalen, *Longest Debate*, 53.

45 Don Edwards interview with Raymond Wolfinger, September 23, 1964, box 22, David B. Filvaroff and Raymond E. Wolfinger Civil Rights Act Papers, University of Buffalo: Whalen and Whalen, *Longest Debate*, 53.

46 Whalen and Whalen, *Longest Debate*, 52–53.

47 O'Brien, *No Final Victories*, 148.

48 Robert Kimball, interview with the author, September 4, 2013.

49 Ibid.

50 Letter from Arnold Aronson and James Hamilton, October 7, 1963, box 1, part 1, Leadership Conference on Civil Rights Records, Library of Congress.

51 Nicholas Katzenbach interview with Raymond Wolfinger, September 25, 1965, box 22, David B. Filvaroff and Raymond E. Wolfinger Civil Rights Act Papers, University of Buffalo Library.

52 Kimball interview.

53 William Copenhaver interview with Raymond Wolfinger, August 23, 1964, box 22, David B. Filvaroff and Raymond E. Wolfinger Civil Rights Act Papers, University of Buffalo Library; William Edwards interview with Raymond Wolfinger, September 23, 1964, box 22, David B. Filvaroff and Raymond E. Wolfinger Civil Rights Act Papers, University of Buffalo Library.

54 James Byrnes interview with Raymond Wolfinger, September 13, 1965, box 22, David B. Filvaroff and Raymond E. Wolfinger Civil Rights Act Papers, University of Buffalo Library.

55 Time line by Raymond Wolfinger, n.d., box 23, David B. Filvaroff and Raymond E. Wolfinger Civil Rights Act Papers, University of Buffalo Library.

56 Robert Kastenmeier interview with Raymond Wolfinger, September 23, 1964, box 22, David B. Filvaroff and Raymond E. Wolfinger Civil Rights Act Papers, University of Buffalo Library.

57 Whalen and Whalen, *Longest Debate*, 63.

58 Katzenbach, *Some of It*, 128.

59 Ibid.

60 Ibid.; memo from Nicholas Katzenbach to Emanuel Celler, October 28, 1963, box 13, David B. Filvaroff and Raymond E. Wolfinger Civil Rights Act Papers, University of Buffalo Library.

61 Ben Zelenko, interview with the author, April 4, 2013.

62 Katzenbach, *Some of It*, 128; Zelenko interview.

63 *New York Times*, October 30, 1963, 1; *Washington Post*, October 31, 1963, F2; statement, October 29, 1963, box 1, part 1, Leadership Conference on Civil Rights Papers, Library of Congress.

64 *New York Times*, October 31, 1963, 1.

65 Dictabelt 28.a3, October 29, 1963, Presidential Recordings, John F. Kennedy Library.

66 Clarence Brown interview with Raymond Wolfinger, September 24, 1964, box 22, David B. Filvaroff and Raymond E. Wolfinger Civil Rights Act Papers, University of Buffalo Library; Albert Quie interview with Raymond Wolfinger, August 27, 1964, box 22, David B. Filvaroff and Raymond E. Wolfinger Civil Rights Act Papers, University of Buffalo Library; *New Journal and Guide*, October 31, 1963, 8.

67 Sol Mosher interview with Raymond Wolfinger, September 9, 1965, box 22, David B. Filvaroff and Raymond E. Wolfinger Civil Rights Act Papers, University of Buffalo Library; Robert Ellsworth interview with Raymond Wolfinger, September 2, 1965, box 22, David B. Filvaroff and Raymond E. Wolfinger Civil Rights Act Papers, University of Buffalo Library.

68 Report on the Civil Rights Act of 1963, November 20, 1963, box 462, Emanuel Celler Papers, Library of Congress.

69 Leadership Conference on Civil Rights Newsletter, vol. 1, no. 6, box 1, part 1, Leadership Conference on Civil Rights Papers, Library of Congress.

70 Statement by Senator Dirksen, Joint Senate-House Republican Leadership, November 21, 1963. Civil Rights 1963–1964, Everett M. Dirksen Papers, Dirksen Congressional Center.

CHAPTER 5: "LET US CONTINUE"

1 Mann, *Walls of Jericho*, 381; *Presidential Recordings: Lyndon B. Johnson: The Kennedy Assassination and the Transfer of Power, November 1963–January 1964*, 2005a, 129.

2 Mann, *Walls of Jericho*, 160.

3 Goldsmith, *Richard B. Russell*, 103.

4 *Presidential Recordings: Lyndon B. Johnson: The Kennedy Assassination and the Transfer of Power, November 1963–January 1964*, 2005a, 120, 138, and 161–62.

5 Humphrey, *Education*, 265.

6 Ibid.

7 George Reedy interview with Michael L. Gillette, October 27, 1982, Lyndon B. Johnson Library.

8 *New York Times*, November 28, 1963, 20.

9 Address Before a Joint Session of Congress, November 27, 1963, *Public Papers of the Presidents of the United States: Lyndon B. Johnson, 1963–64*, vol. 1, entry 11, 8–10; Schlesinger, *Journals*, 210.

10 Caro, *Lyndon Johnson: Passage*, 432.

11 President's Thanksgiving Day Address to the Nation, November 28, 1963. http://www.presidency.ucsb.edu/ws/?pid=25999, accessed June 4, 2013.

12 *New York Times*, November 28, 1963, 1; letter from Arnold Aronson to Lyndon Johnson, November 27, 1963, box 67, LE HU 2, White House Central Files, Lyndon B. Johnson Library; Mann, *Walls of Jericho*, 384.

13 Joseph Rauh interview with Paige Mulhollan, August 8, 1969, Lyndon B. Johnson Library.

14 *Washington Post*, July 5, 1964, E7; Rauh interview.

15 Rauh interview; *Presidential Recordings: Lyndon B. Johnson: The Kennedy Assassination and the Transfer of Power, November 1963–January 1964*, 2005a, 386.

16 Loevy, *To End All Segregation*, 98–99.

17 Memo No. 18, December 1963, box 37, part 1, Leadership Conference on Civil Rights Papers, Library of Congress; *Congressional Quarterly Weekly Report*, December 6, 1963, 2129; "Deschler's Precedents," vol. 5, 3207–15, http://www.gpo.gov/fdsys/pkg/GPO-HPREC-DESCHLERS-V5/html/GPO-HPREC-DESCHLERS-V5-1-2.htm, accessed September 29, 2013.

18 Larry O'Brien interview with Michael Gillette, December 5, 1985, Lyndon B. Johnson Library; *Congressional Quarterly Weekly Report*, December 6, 1963, 2118.

19 *Presidential Recordings: Lyndon B. Johnson: The Kennedy Assassination and the Transfer of Power, November 1963–January 1964*, 2005a, 263, 300–301.

20 Ibid.

21 *Presidential Recordings: Lyndon B. Johnson: The Kennedy Assassination and the Transfer of Power, November 1963–January 1964*, 2005b, 151; Scheele, *Charlie Halleck*, 231.

22 Whalen and Whalen, *Longest Debate*, 79; Larry O'Brien interview with Michael Gillette, December 5, 1985, Lyndon B. Johnson Library.

23 *Presidential Recordings: Lyndon B. Johnson: The Kennedy Assassination and the Transfer of Power, November 1963–January 1964*, 2005a, 143–44 and 278–81.

24 Memo from Roy Wilkins to all NAACP branches, November 20, 1963, box 25, NAACP Papers, Library of Congress; Leadership Conference on Civil Rights Newsletter, December 16, 1963, box 37, part 1, Leadership Conference on Civil Rights Papers, Library of Congress.

25 Shesol, *Mutual Contempt*, 161; Schlesinger, *Robert Kennedy*, 673–74.

26 Caro, *Lyndon Johnson: Passage*, 489–91.

27 Ibid.

28 *National Review*, September 24, 1963, 231–36.

29 Letter from John Satterfield to William Loeb, December 3, 1963, box 17, David B. Filvaroff and Raymond E. Wolfinger Civil Rights Act Papers, University of Buffalo Library.

30 *New York Times*, December 12, 1963, 40.

31 *Congressional Quarterly Weekly Report*, December 13, 1963, 2150; Loevy, *To End All Segregation*, 94; *New York Times*, December 12, 1963, 40.

32 Kabaservice, *Rule and Ruin*, 103.

33 Caro, *Lyndon Johnson: Passage*, 496; Whalen and Whalen, *Longest Debate*, 86.

34 Loevy, *To End All Segregation*, 94–95.

35 Findlay, *Church People*, 51–52.

36 James Hamilton interview with Raymond Wolfinger, September 21, 1964, box 22, David B. Filvaroff and Raymond E. Wolfinger Civil Rights Act Papers, University of Buffalo Library; Findlay, *Church People*, 54; Kotz, *Judgment Days*, 144.

37 Findlay, *Church People*, 53.

38 *New York Times*, January 12, 1964, E3; Memo Number 20, January 13, 1964, box 2, part 1, Leadership Conference on Civil Rights Records, Library of Congress.

39 Baltimore *Sun*, December 6, 1963, 1.

40 Leadership Conference on Civil Rights Memo No. 19, December 23, 1963, box 37, part 1, Leadership Conference on Civil Rights Papers, Library of Congress; Whalen and Whalen, *Longest Debate*, 91.

41 *New York Times*, January 10, 1964, 1; *New York Times Magazine*, January 12, 1964, SM13.

42 Annual Message to the Congress on the State of the Union, January 8, 1964, http://www.presidency.ucsb.edu/ws/index.php?pid=26787, accessed June 10, 2013.

43 Mackenzie and Weisbrot, *Liberal Hour*, 56.

44 Hearing on HR 7152, Rules Committee, House of Representatives, January 9–29, 1964, 1.

45 Whalen and Whalen, *Longest Debate*, 92.

46 Hearing on HR 7152, 90.

47 Ibid., 99.

48 Ibid., 125.

49 Ibid., 211.

50 Ibid., 257; Loevy, *Civil Rights Act*, 64.

51 Hearing on HR 7152, 418, 465, and 521.

52 Caro, *Lyndon Johnson: Passage*, 475–554.

53 Garrow, *Bearing the Cross*, 310; *Presidential Recordings: Lyndon B. Johnson: The Kennedy Assassination and the Transfer of Power, November 1963–January 1964*, 2005a, 618; *Chicago Tribune*, January 19, 1964, 7; *Los Angeles Times*, January 19, 1964, D15.

54 Loevy, *Civil Rights Act*, 62.

55 *Los Angeles Times*, January 21, 1964, 4; Caro, *Lyndon Johnson: Passage*, 559.

56 *Washington Post*, January 22, 1964, A2; *New York Times*, January 22, 1964, 19.

57 *Los Angeles Times*, January 26, 1964, K4; *New York Times*, January 26, 1964, E4.

58 *Chicago Tribune*, January 24, 1964, 8; *New York Times*, January 24, 1964, 1.

59 *Congressional Record*, 88th Congress, 2nd Session, 1964, 110, pt. 2:1511–52.

60 Ibid.

61 Memo from William Foley to Emanuel Celler, January 28, 1963, box 465, Emanuel Celler Papers, Library of Congress; Katzenbach, *Some of It*, 138.

62 Katzenbach, *Some of It*, 137; interview with David Filvaroff by the author, November 17, 2012.

63 Filvaroff interview.

64 Notes from the DSG Files, by Raymond Wolfinger, box 23, David B. Filvaroff and

Raymond E. Wolfinger Civil Rights Act Papers, University of Buffalo Library; Katzenbach, *Some of It*, 138.

65 Watson, *Lion in the Lobby*, 20; *Congressional Quarterly Weekly Report*, February 21, 1964, 365.

66 Guide to Meetings with Senators and Congressmen, Religion Action Center, Union of American Hebrew Congregations, January 31, 1964, box 2, part 1, Leadership Conference on Civil Rights Records, Library of Congress.

67 Memorandum, February 11, 1964, box 37, part 1, Leadership Conference on Civil Rights Papers, Library of Congress.

68 *Congressional Quarterly Weekly Report*, February 7, 1964, 250; *New Republic*, February 29, 1964, 17.

69 Baltimore *Sun*, February 4, 1; Baltimore *Sun*, February 5, 1964, 1; *Presidential Recordings: Lyndon B. Johnson: Toward the Great Society, February 1, 1964–May 31, 1964*, 2007, 206–7.

70 Ben Zelenko, interview with the author, April 4, 2013.

71 *Congressional Quarterly Weekly Report*, February 14, 1963, 293.

72 Ibid.

73 *Meet the Press*, January 26, 1964, transcript in box 15, David B. Filvaroff and Raymond E. Wolfinger Civil Rights Act Papers, University of Buffalo Library.

74 *Congressional Quarterly Weekly Report*, February 14, 1964, 293; for the number of women in Congress, see http://www.senate.gov/CRSReports/crs-publish.cfm?pid='0E%2C* PLS%3D%22%40%20%20%0A; Dierenfield, *Keeper of the Rules*, 195.

75 *Time*, February 21, 1964. 24; Dierenfield, *Keeper of the Rules*, 194–96.

76 Chronology, by Raymond Wolfinger, n.d., box 23, David B. Filvaroff and Raymond E. Wolfinger Civil Rights Act Papers, University of Buffalo Library.

77 Dierenfield, *Keeper of the Rules*, 196.

78 *New York Times*, February 11, 1964, 1.

79 Joe Rauh interview, with Paige Mulhollan, August 8, 1969, Lyndon B. Johnson Library.

80 *Congressional Record*, 88th Congress, 2nd Session, 1964, 110, pt. 2:2803–4.

81 Findlay, *Church People*, 54.

82 *Congressional Record*, February 10, 1964, 2804–5.

83 *Time*, February 14, 1964, 26.

84 Katzenbach, *Some of It*, 137.

85 *Presidential Recordings: Lyndon B. Johnson: The Kennedy Assassination and the Transfer of Power, November 1963–January 1964*, 2005a, 190; Shesol, *Mutual Contempt*, 162.

CHAPTER 6: A BATTLE IS LOST

1 Frank Valeo interview, Donald Ritchie, September 18, 1985, Senate Oral History Project, United States Senate Historical Office.

2 *Palm Beach Post*, June 10, 1957, 10A.

3 "The Charge Up Capitol Hill: North and South Prospects for November," *Advance*, March 1962, 29–30; Crespino, *Thurmond's America*, 133.

4 Memo from Lee White to Larry O'Brien, October 30, 1963, box 21, Lee White Office Files, John F. Kennedy Library.

5 Meg Greenfield, "The Man Who Leads the Southern Senators," *Reporter*, May 21, 1964, 17.

6 *Newsweek*, August 19, 1963, 20–24.

7 Fite, *Richard B. Russell*, 407; George Reedy interview with Joe B. Frantz, February 14, 1972, Lyndon B. Johnson Library.

8 Richard B. Russell to constituent, December 9, 1963, box 15, section C.I, Richard B. Russell Papers, University of Georgia Library.

9 *Congressional Quarterly Weekly Report*, March 13, 1964, 491.

10 Grofman, *Legacies*, 15.

11 *Time*, March 20, 1964, 28; Valeo, *Mike Mansfield*, 19–21.

12 Valeo, *Mike Mansfield*, 35; Whalen and Whalen, *Longest Debate*, 128; Frank Valeo interview with Donald Ritchie, September 18, 1985, U.S. Senate Historical Office Oral History Project.

13 *New York Times*, October 6, 2001, A1.

14 Valeo, *Mike Mansfield*, 59.

15 Kotz, *Judgment Days*, 120.

16 Mike Mansfield Speech on Civil Rights, June 18, 1963, box 109, series 9, Mike Mansfield Papers, University of Montana Library.

17 Memo from Kenneth Teasdale to Mike Mansfield and Frank Valeo, August 15, 1963, box 32, series 18, Mike Mansfield Papers, University of Montana Library; memo from Kenneth Teasdale to Mike Mansfield, October 30, 1963, box 32, series 18, Mike Mansfield Papers, University of Montana Library.

18 Text and audio versions of the speech are available at the Minnesota Historical Society, http://www.mnhs.org/library/tips/history_topics/42humphreyspeech/transcript.htm, accessed September 30, 2013.

19 *Presidential Recordings: Lyndon B. Johnson: Toward the Great Society, February 1, 1964– May 31, 1964*, 2007a, 452–54. *Congressional Record*, 88th Congress, 2nd Session, 1964, 110, pt. 3:2882–86.

20 *Congressional Record*, ibid.

21 Ibid.

22 James Hamilton interview with Raymond Wolfinger, September 21, 1964, box 22, David B. Filvaroff and Raymond E. Wolfinger Civil Rights Act Papers, University of Buffalo Library.

23 *Presidential Recordings: Lyndon B. Johnson: Toward the Great Society, February 1, 1964– May 31, 1964*, 2007a, 477–78.

24 Notes on meeting with Senator Russell, February 19, 1964, box 28, series 22, Mike Mansfield Papers, University of Montana Library.

25 Meeting on Civil Rights—two memos, February 19, 1963, box 99, series 22, Mike Mansfield Papers, University of Montana Library; Conclusions of Cloture Study, February 20, 1964, box 14, David B. Filvaroff and Raymond E. Wolfinger Civil Rights Act Papers, University of Buffalo Library.

26 Letter from Everett Dirksen to Hubert Humphrey, February 3, 1964. Civil Rights 1963– 1964, Everett M. Dirksen Papers, Dirksen Congressional Center.

27 Hubert Humphrey interview with Michael Gillette, June 21, 1977, Lyndon B. Johnson Library.

28 Two Letters from Everett Dirksen to Louella Dirksen, both dated July 31, 1924, Civil Rights 1924–1954, Everett M. Dirksen Papers, Dirksen Congressional Center.

29 For various bill texts, see the folders "Civil Rights 1924–1954" and "Civil Rights 1955– 1959," Everett M. Dirksen Papers, Dirksen Congressional Center.

30 Chronology by Raymond Wolfinger, n.d., box 23, David B. Filvaroff and Raymond E. Wolfinger Civil Rights Act Papers, University of Buffalo Library.

31 *Chicago Tribune*, various articles from February 20 to February 29, 1963.

32 Report on the Coordinating Committee for Fundamental American Freedoms, March 1964, box 110, part 1, Leadership Conference on Civil Rights Records, Library of Congress; file memo, May 6, 1964, box 6, series 10, Richard B. Russell Papers, University of Georgia Library.

33 See various constituent letters in box 109, series 9, Mike Mansfield Papers, University of Montana Library; Patricia Connell interview with Raymond Wolfinger, August 28, 1965, box 22, David B. Filvaroff and Raymond E. Wolfinger Civil Rights Act Papers, University of Buffalo Library.

34 *Congressional Record*, 88th Congress, 2nd Session, 1964, 110, pt. 3:3689–720.

35 *Washington Post*, April 26, 1964, M2; *Washington Post*, January 17, 1964, A15.

36 *Congressional Quarterly Weekly Report*, February 28, 1964, 385; February 28, 1964, Stephen Horn periodic log maintained during the discussions concerning the passage of the Civil Rights Act of 1964.

37 Humphrey, *Education*, 247.

38 Minutes of Meeting with Katzenbach, et al., February 28, box 28, series 22, Mike Mansfield Papers, University of Montana Library.

39 *New York Times*, November 24, 1994, D18.

40 Minutes of civil rights meeting, 4:00 p.m., February 28, 1964, box 10, David B. Filvaroff and Raymond E. Wolfinger Civil Rights Act Papers, University of Buffalo Library.

41 Ibid.

42 February 28, 1964, Stephen Horn periodic log maintained during the discussions concerning the passage of the Civil Rights Act of 1964; minutes of civil rights meeting, February 28, 1964, box 10, David B. Filvaroff and Raymond E. Wolfinger Civil Rights Act Papers, University of Buffalo Library.

43 Ibid.

44 Remarks at Miami Beach at a Democratic Party Dinner, February 27, 1964, http://www.presidency.ucsb.edu/ws/index.php?pid=26086&st=&st1, accessed June 21, 2013; President's News Conference, February 29, 1964, http://www.presidency.ucsb.edu/ws/index.php?pid=26090&st=&st1, accessed June 21, 2013; *Presidential Recordings: Lyndon B. Johnson: Toward the Great Society, February 1, 1964–May 31, 1964*, 2007a, 468–70; Remarks to Members of the Southern Baptist Christian Leadership Seminar, March 25, 1964, http://www.presidency.ucsb.edu/ws/?pid=26130#ixzz2gQlXP3Is, accessed September 30, 2013.

45 *Congressional Quarterly Weekly Report*, March 13, 1964, 491.

46 President's News Conference, March 7, 1964, http://www.presidency.ucsb.edu/ws/index.php?pid=26101&st=&st1, accessed June 22, 2013.

47 *Presidential Recordings: Lyndon B. Johnson: Toward the Great Society, February 1, 1964–May 31, 1964*, 2007b, 941–46.

48 *Los Angeles Times*, March 8, 1964, G13.

49 March 7, 1964, Stephen Horn periodic log maintained during the discussions concerning the passage of the Civil Rights Act of 1964.

50 *Congressional Record*, 88th Congress, 2nd Session, 1964, 110, pt. 4:4741–68.

51 Ibid.

52 Ibid., 4640 and 6207. This analysis of the phony filibuster debate borrows from points made in Kane, "Senate Debate."

53 Ibid., 6225.

54 *New Republic*, August 31, 1963, 20; *Chicago Tribune*, March 1, 1964, 1.

55 *Congressional Record*, 88th Congress, 2nd Session, 1964, 110, pt. 4:5340.

56 Ibid., 4828.

57 Ibid., 4590.

58 Ibid., 4598–99.

59 Loevy, *To End All Segregation*, 180.

60 The agenda for Democratic Floor Leader Conference, March 12, 1964, box 10, David B. Filvaroff and Raymond E. Wolfinger Civil Rights Act Papers, University of Buffalo Library; March 18, 1964, Stephen Horn periodic log maintained during the discussions concerning the passage of the Civil Rights Act of 1964.

61 *Washington Post*, March 27, 1964, A1; March 24, 1964, Stephen Horn periodic log maintained during the discussions concerning the passage of the Civil Rights Act of 1964.

62 *Los Angeles Times*, March 29, 1964, N4.

63 *Congressional Record*, 88th Congress, 2nd Session, 6455.

CHAPTER 7: THE SOUTH TAKES ITS STAND

1 Mudd, *Place to Be*, 141.

2 Small, *To Kill a Messenger*, 257; Mudd, *Place to Be*, 143; Roger Mudd interview with the author, April 22, 2012.

3 Memo from Hubert Humphrey to John Stewart, March 30, 1964, box 15, David B. Filvaroff and Raymond E. Wolfinger Civil Rights Act Papers, University of Buffalo Library.

4 Clarence Mitchell interview with Thomas Baker, April 30, 1969, Lyndon B. Johnson Library; Whalen and Whalen, *Longest Debate*, 141.

5 Mudd, *Place to Be*, 144; Caro, *Lyndon Johnson: Passage*, 567; *Los Angeles Times*, March 29, 1964, 1.

6 *New York Times*, March 31, 1964, 1.

7 *New York Times*, ibid.; Mudd, *Place to Be*, 144.

8 Manger memo, box 22, Burke Marshall Papers, John F. Kennedy Library; Julius Manger Jr. obituary by John Manger, http://www.cowpensvets.org/manger.html, accessed August 25, 2013.

9 Larry O'Brien to Robert Kennedy, August 26, 1963, box 30, Burke Marshall Papers, John F. Kennedy Library; memos from Harold C. Fleming to ad hoc committee members, March 26 and April 7, 1964, box 27, Burke Marshall Papers, John F. Kennedy Library; Report of the Executive Director to the Committee on Race and Reconciliation of the National Council of Churches, July 26, 1963, box 6, RG 11, National Council of Churches Papers, Presbyterian Historical Society.

10 Letter from Luther Holcomb to Hobart Taylor June 9, 1964, box 8, Burke Marshall Papers, John F. Kennedy Library.

11 Leadership Conference on Civil Rights Memo Number 32, April 6, 1964, box 2, part 1, Leadership Conference on Civil Rights, Library of Congress; notes from May 11, 1964, by Raymond Wolfinger, box 23, David B. Filvaroff and Raymond E. Wolfinger Civil Rights Act Papers, University of Buffalo Library.

12 Memo from Violet Gunther to all participants in the LCCR, March 13, 1964, box 119, part IX, NAACP Papers, Library of Congress.

13 *Washington Post*, April 1, 1964, A2; *Atlanta Daily World*, October 27, 1963, 13; *Chicago Daily Defender*, May 28, 1964, 5.

14 Caro, *Lyndon Johnson: Passage*, 565.

15 Kotz, *Judgment Days*, 132; Findlay, *Church People*, 132; Mann, *Walls of Jericho*, 413.

16 Dan O'Brien interview with Raymond Wolfinger, September 21, 1965, box 22, David B. Filvaroff and Raymond E. Wolfinger Civil Rights Act Papers, University of Buffalo Library; letter from Ernest Reuter, February 28, 1964, box 232, part IX, NAACP Papers, Library of Congress.

17 Mudd, *Place to Be*, 144; *New York Times*, April 1, 1964, 1.

18 Frank Valeo to Mike Mansfield, April 9, 1964, box 99, series 22, Mike Mansfield Papers, University of Montana Library.

19 *New York Times*, April 4, 1964; Bipartisan Civil Rights Newsletter, April 3, 1964, box 32, series 18, Mike Mansfield Papers, University of Montana Library.

20 Whalen and Whalen, *Longest Debate*, 157–58; Thurber, *Politics of Equality*, 136; Statement by Senator Mansfield, April 7, box 28, series 22, Mike Mansfield Papers, University of Montana Library; notes by Raymond Wolfinger, April 9, 1964, box 23, David B. Filvaroff and Raymond E. Wolfinger Civil Rights Act Papers, University of Buffalo Library.

21 April 7, 1969, Stephen Horn periodic log maintained during the discussions concerning the passage of the Civil Rights Act of 1964.

22 Carter, *Politics of Rage*, 208.

23 Ibid., 211; *National Review*, April 16, 1964, 348.

24 *Time*, April 17, 1964, 42.

25 Hulsey, *Everett Dirksen*, 34; Whalen and Whalen, *Longest Debate*, 152 and 154.

26 Katzenbach, *Some of It*, 129.

27 Dichter, Cathcart, and Lindemann, *Employment Discrimination Law*, 10; Dirksen press conference, February 20, 1964, Civil Rights 1963–1964 file, Everett M. Dirksen Papers, Dirksen Congressional Center.

28 *Reporter*, January 27, 1964, 26–29; Clyde Flynn interview with Raymond Wolfinger, November 16, 1966, box 22, David B. Filvaroff and Raymond E. Wolfinger Civil Rights Act Papers, University of Buffalo Library.

29 Hulsey, *Everett Dirksen*, 188.

30 The Civil Rights Bill: Some Observations by Senator Everett McKinley Dirksen, March 26, 1964, Civil Rights 1963–1964, Everett M. Dirksen Papers, Dirksen Congressional Center.

31 Notes by Raymond Wolfinger, April 9, 1964, box 23, David B. Filvaroff and Raymond E. Wolfinger Civil Rights Act Papers, University of Buffalo Library.

32 *Chicago Tribune*, April 7, 1964, 2.

33 *Los Angeles Times*, April 10, 1964, 3.

34 Horn log, Thursday, 10:30 A.M., April 9.

35 *Congressional Record*, 88th Congress, 2nd Session, 1964, 110, pt. 6:7375–80.

36 *Los Angeles Times*, April 14, 1964, 2.

37 Loevy, *To End All Segregation*, 194; Finch, *Legacies*, 78.

38 Senate Letter No. 5, April 10, 1964, box 231, part IX, NAACP Papers, Library of Congress.

39 Horn log, April 13.

40 Ibid., April 16.

41 Loevy, *Civil Rights Act*, 232.

42 *Los Angeles Times*, April 11, 1964, A2; Horn log, April 16; *Washington Post*, April 11, 1964, A2.

43 Horn log, April 13.

44 *Los Angeles Times*, April 12, 1964, 1.

45 *Presidential Recordings: Lyndon B. Johnson: Toward the Great Society, February 1, 1964–May 31, 1964,* 2007a, phone call with Robert Byrd, April 10, 1964, 956–61.

46 Horn log, March 9; memo from Harry Kingman to Chancellor Dean E. McHenry, University of California, Santa Cruz, April 13, 1964, box 2, part 1, Leadership Conference on Civil Rights Records, Library of Congress.

47 *New Yorker,* May 13, 1964, 33–34.

48 The *San Francisco Sunday Chronicle,* February 5, 1961, page 6; Letter to Chancellor Dean E. McHenry from Harry and Ruth Kingman, April 13, 1964, box 2, part 1, Leadership Conference on Civil Rights, the Library of Congress.

49 *New York Times,* April 16, 1964, 1.

50 Purnell, *Fighting Jim Crow,* 355.

51 For history on the World's Fair, see http://www.nywf64.com/index.html, accessed June 29, 2013.

52 Purnell, *Fighting Jim Crow,* 362–63.

53 White, *Making,* 196; Purnell, *Fighting Jim Crow,* 370; *Chicago Defender,* April 22, 1964, 1; *New York Times,* April 16, 1964, 1.

54 Joint statement by Senators Humphrey and Kuchel, April 15, 1964, box 463, Thomas Kuchel Papers, University of California Library.

55 White, *Making,* 198.

56 *New York Times,* April 23, 1964, 1; President's News Conference, April 23, 1964, http://www.presidency.ucsb.edu/ws/?pid=26182#axzz2gQlWDCI7, accessed on October 1, 2013.

57 *Washington Post,* April 21, 1964, A1.

58 For the extended initial debate over the Talmadge amendment, see *Congressional Record,* April 21, 1964, 8613–66.

59 Ibid.

60 Whalen and Whalen, *Longest Debate,* 167–68; Horn log, April 22; thoughts on the Civil Rights Bill dictated Wednesday, April 21, 1964, by Raymond Wolfinger, box 23, David B. Filvaroff and Raymond E. Wolfinger Civil Rights Act Papers, University of Buffalo Library.

61 Ibid.; *Presidential Recordings: Lyndon B. Johnson: Toward the Great Society, February 1, 1964–May 31, 1964,* 2007b, 174–75.

62 Baltimore *Sun,* April 25, 1964, 1; chronology, box 23, David B. Filvaroff and Raymond E. Wolfinger Civil Rights Act Papers, University of Buffalo Library.

63 Stewart, "Strategy," 109.

64 Program, National Interreligious Convocation on Civil Rights, April 28, 1964, box 48, record group 6, National Council of Churches Papers, Presbyterian Historical Society; Julian Smith, "The Challenge to Religion," box 48, record group 6, National Council of Churches Papers, Presbyterian Historical Society.

65 Eugene Carson Blake, "Human Dignity—Have We Not All One Father?" box 48, record group 6, National Council of Churches Papers, Presbyterian Historical Society.

66 Civil Rights Timeline, http://www.congresslink.org/civilrights/1964.htm, Dirksen Congressional Center, accessed October 1, 2013; Whalen and Whalen, *Longest Debate,* 171.

67 *Chicago Tribune,* April 29, 1964, B8; *Presidential Recordings: Lyndon B. Johnson: Toward the Great Society, February 1, 1964–May 31, 1964,* 2007b, 325–26.

68 *New York Times,* April 29, 1964, 1; Mann, *Walls of Jericho,* 231.

69 Mann, ibid.

70 *New Republic,* May 2, 1964, 9–11.

71 Horn log, May 5, 1965.

72 Loevy, *Civil Rights Act*, 110–11, 120.

73 Valeo, *Mike Mansfield*, 123–24; Katzenbach, *Some of It*, 141.

74 Loevy, *Civil Rights Act*, 110; notes from April 30 9:30 meeting, box 23, David B. Filvaroff and Raymond E. Wolfinger Civil Rights Act Papers, University of Buffalo Library.

75 Press release, May 6, 1964, box 578, Walter P. Reuther Papers, Wayne State University Archives; *Presidential Recordings: Lyndon B. Johnson: Toward the Great Society, February 1, 1964–May 31, 1964*, 2007b, 419; *Baltimore Afro-American*, May 16, 1964, 13.

76 Michael Rogin, "Politics, Emotion, and the Wallace Vote," *British Journal of Sociology*, vol. 20, no. 1, March 1969, 27–49; *Nation*, May 4, 1964, 451.

77 Kotz, *Judgment Days*, 145; memo from Stewart L. Udall to the president, May 7, 1964, box 1, Legislative Background, Lyndon B. Johnson Library; memo from Mike Manatos to Larry O'Brien, May 11, 1964, box 6, Manatos Office Files, Lyndon B. Johnson Library.

78 *Wall Street Journal*, May 7, 1964, 2.

79 "Notes on the Civil Rights Bill Dictated May 6, 1964" and "May 6 9:30 Meeting," both by Raymond Wolfinger, box 23, David B. Filvaroff and Raymond E. Wolfinger Civil Rights Act Papers, University of Buffalo Library.

80 Notes for May 11, 1964, by Raymond Wolfinger, box 23, David B. Filvaroff and Raymond E. Wolfinger Civil Rights Act Papers, University of Buffalo Library.

81 Notes for May 11, 1964, by Raymond Wolfinger, box 23, David B. Filvaroff and Raymond E. Wolfinger Civil Rights Act Papers, University of Buffalo Library; Horn log, May 7, 10:45.

82 Charles Ferris interview with Raymond Wolfinger, September 24, 1965, box 22, David B. Filvaroff and Raymond E. Wolfinger Civil Rights Act Papers, University of Buffalo Library.

83 *Presidential Recordings: Lyndon B. Johnson: Toward the Great Society, February 1, 1964–May 31, 1964*, 2007b, 594–95; *Time*, May 22, 1964, 23.

84 "Notes on the Civil Rights Bill," May 13, 1964, by Raymond Wolfinger, box 15, David B. Filvaroff and Raymond E. Wolfinger Civil Rights Act Papers, University of Buffalo Library.

85 Ibid.; *New York Times*, May 14, 1964, A1.

86 *New York Times*, May 14, 1964, 1.

87 "Notes on the Civil Rights Bill," May 13, 1964, by Raymond Wolfinger, box 15, David B. Filvaroff and Raymond E. Wolfinger Civil Rights Act Papers, University of Buffalo Library.

88 "Notes on the Civil Rights Bill," May 19, 1964, by Raymond Wolfinger, box 15, David B. Filvaroff and Raymond E. Wolfinger Civil Rights Act Papers, University of Buffalo Library; minutes of the Senate Democratic Conference, May 19, 1964, U.S. Senate Historical Office; *New York Times*, May 19, 1964, 1.

89 Minutes of the Senate Republican Conference, May 19, 1964, U.S. Senate Historical Office; *New York Times*, May 19, 1964, 1.

90 *New York Times*, ibid.

91 Chen, *Fifth Freedom*, 185–86; Herbert Liebenson interview with Raymond Wolfinger, July 29, 1965, box 22, David B. Filvaroff and Raymond E. Wolfinger Civil Rights Act Papers, University of Buffalo Library.

92 Moreno, *From Direct Action*, 154.

93 Letter from Walter Carey, May 12, 1964, box 17, David B. Filvaroff and Raymond E. Wolfinger Civil Rights Act Papers, University of Buffalo Library; Chen, *Fifth Freedom*, 185–86.

94 Graham, *Civil Rights and the Presidency*, 78; Whalen and Whalen, *Longest Debate*, 186; May 21, 1964, 11:30 A.M. presession meeting notes by Raymond Wolfinger, box 23, David B. Filvaroff and Raymond E. Wolfinger Civil Rights Act Papers, University of Buffalo Library.

95 *Los Angeles Times*, May 20, 1964, A5; *New York Times*, May 20, 1964, 1.

96 *Washington Post*, May 21, 1964, A8; Loevy, *Civil Rights Act*, 285; *New York Times*, May 25, 1964, 1; Wilkins and Mathews, *Standing Fast*, 301.

97 "Ray's Running Journal," May 25, 1964, box 23, David B. Filvaroff and Raymond E. Wolfinger Civil Rights Act Papers, University of Buffalo Library.

98 Baltimore *Sun*, May 27, 1964, 1; *Congressional Record*, 88th Congress, 2nd Session, 1964, 110, pt. 9:11917–43.

99 Baltimore *Sun*, ibid.

100 *Washington Post*, May 28, 1964, 1.

101 *Atlanta Daily World*, June 3, 1964, 1.

102 "Notes on June 2," by Raymond Wolfinger, box 23, David B. Filvaroff and Raymond E. Wolfinger Civil Rights Act Papers, University of Buffalo Library.

103 *New York Times*, June 6, 1964, 1.

104 *Chicago Tribune*, June 6, 1964, 3.

CHAPTER 8: BREAKING THE FILIBUSTER

1 *Washington Post*, June 7, 1964, 1; Humphrey, "Memorandum," 91.

2 *Washington Post*, ibid.

3 Ibid.

4 *Washington Post*, June 8, 1964, 1.

5 *Atlanta Daily World*, June 10, 1964, 1; notes from June 9, 1964, by John Stewart, box 23, David B. Filvaroff and Raymond E. Wolfinger Civil Rights Act Papers, University of Buffalo Library.

6 "Final Dictated Thoughts on the Civil Rights Debate," by Raymond Wolfinger. June 11, 1964, box 15, David B. Filvaroff and Raymond E. Wolfinger Civil Rights Act Papers, University of Buffalo Library.

7 *Chicago Tribune*, June 11, 1964, 1; *Congressional Record*, 88th Congress, 2nd Session, 1964, 110, pt. 10:13125–219; "Memorandum Dictated Shortly After Cloture," by Hubert Humphrey, n.d., box 15, David B. Filvaroff and Raymond E. Wolfinger Civil Rights Act Papers, University of Buffalo Library.

8 Loevy, *To End All Segregation*, 278; Baltimore *Sun*, June 11, 1964, 1.

9 http://www.senate.gov/artandhistory/history/minute/Key_Pittman_Barely_Elected.htm, accessed July 11, 2013; Jack Biedler interview with Raymond Wolfinger, n.d., box 22, David B. Filvaroff and Raymond E. Wolfinger Civil Rights Act Papers, University of Buffalo Library.

10 Thurber, *Politics of Equality*, 144; Humphrey, "Memorandum," 91.

11 Woods, *Fulbright*, 330–31.

12 *Washington Post*, June 11, 1964, B5; *Chicago Tribune*, June 11, 1964, 1.

13 Baltimore *Sun*, June 11, 1964, 1; *Congressional Record*, 88th Congress, 2nd Session, 1964, 110, pt. 10:12855–68.

14 Ibid.

15 "Civil Rights Speech," June 10, 1964, Civil Rights 1963–1965, Everett M. Dirksen Papers, Dirksen Congressional Center; *New York Times*, June 11, 1964, A1.

16 *Congressional Record*, 88th Congress, 2nd Session, 1964, 110, 87, 10:12853–64.

17 Ibid.

18 Mudd, *Place to Be*, 155.

19 Baltimore *Sun*, June 11, 1964, 1.

20 Thompson II, "The Civil Rights Act of 1964," 681–91.

21 John J. Synon interview with Raymond Wolfinger, September 7, 1965, box 22, David B. Filvaroff and Raymond E. Wolfinger Civil Rights Act Papers, University of Buffalo Library.

22 Thurber, *Politics of Equality*, 144.

23 Kotz, *Judgment Days*, 151.

24 Larry O'Brien interview with Michael Gillette, February 12, 1986, Lyndon B. Johnson Library.

25 Bipartisan Civil Rights Newsletter, June 11, 1964, box 32, series 18, Mike Mansfield Papers, University of Montana Library.

26 *Congressional Record*, 88th Congress, 2nd Session, 1964, 110, pt. 10:13330–419.

27 Stewart, "Strategy," 130–31.

28 Humphrey, *Education*, 284.

29 Stewart, "Tactics I," 130.

30 "Final Dictated Thoughts," by Raymond Wolfinger, box 15, David B. Filvaroff and Raymond E. Wolfinger Civil Rights Act Papers, University of Buffalo Library; Stewart, "Tactics I," 131.

31 Stewart, "Tactics I," 131.

32 "June 16, 1964, "by Raymond Wolfinger, box 23, David B. Filvaroff and Raymond E. Wolfinger Civil Rights Act Papers, University of Buffalo Library; *Congressional Quarterly Weekly Report*, June 19, 1964, 1205.

33 *Chicago Tribune*, June 14, 1964, 26; Baltimore *Sun*, June 14, 1964, 1.

34 "Final Dictated Thoughts," by Raymond Wolfinger, box 15, David B. Filvaroff and Raymond E. Wolfinger Civil Rights Act Papers, University of Buffalo Library.

35 *Chicago Tribune*, June 17, 1964, 7.

36 *New York Times*, June 16, 1964, 18.

37 Notes from June 16, 1964, by John Stewart, box 15, David B. Filvaroff and Raymond E. Wolfinger Civil Rights Act Papers, University of Buffalo Library.

38 Ibid.

39 "Final Dictated Thoughts," by Raymond Wolfinger, box 15, David B. Filvaroff and Raymond E. Wolfinger Civil Rights Act Papers, University of Buffalo Library.

40 Ibid.

41 Ibid.; *New York Times*, June 17, 1964, 1.

42 Whalen and Whalen, *Longest Debate*, 210.

43 *Congressional Record*, 88th Congress, 2nd Session, 1964, 110, pt. 11:14240; *Atlanta Daily World*, June 16, 1964, 1; *Chicago Tribune*, June 18, 1964, 4.

44 Thurber, *Politics of Equality*, 145.

45 For the entire proceedings of June 18, see *Congressional Record*, 88th Congress, 2nd Session, 1964, 110, pt. 11:14275–336.

46 *New York Times*, June 19, 1964, 18.

47 *Time*, June 26, 1964, 20; *Chicago Tribune*, June 19, 11.

48 Ibid.; *Washington Post*, June 28, 1964, E7; *Newsweek*, June 29, 1964, 17.

49 *Los Angeles Times*, June 19, 1964, 10.

50 *Washington Post*, June 20, 1964, 1.

51 For the entire proceedings of that historic day, see *Congressional Record*, 88th Congress, 2nd Session, 1964, 110, pt. 11:14432–511.

52 Stewart, "Independence and Control," 181; Thurber, *Politics of Equality*, 181. Late that evening, the Senate's celebratory mood was derailed when news arrived that two of its

members—Edward Kennedy and Birch Bayh of Indiana—had been in a plane crash in Massachusetts. Though the pilot and one of Kennedy's aides died, Bayh and his wife survived relatively unhurt, while Kennedy was seriously injured but managed to recover quickly.

53 *Chicago Tribune*, June 23, 1964, 6; Baltimore *Sun*, June 23, 1964, 8.

54 Baltimore *Sun*, June 8, 1964, 8; *New York Times*, June 23, 1964, 14; memo from Bill Moyers to Lyndon Johnson, June 29, 1964, box 112, Statements, Lyndon B. Johnson Library.

55 *New York Times*, July 1, 1964, 1; *Wall Street Journal*, July 1, 1964, 3.

56 *Wall Street Journal*, July 1, 1964, 3.

57 *New York Times*, July 3, 1964, 9.

CHAPTER 9: A BILL BECOMES A LAW

1 *Chicago Tribune*, July 3, 1964, 1.

2 See various drafts and memos in box 125, Bill Moyers Office Files, Lyndon B. Johnson Library.

3 *Chicago Tribune*, July 3, 1964, 1; Dierenfield, *Keeper of the Rules*, 198.

4 Memo No. 44, from Leadership Conference on Civil Rights, July 6, 1964, box 37, part 1, Leadership Conference on Civil Rights Papers, Library of Congress; *Congressional Record*, 88th Congress, 2nd Session, 1964, 110, pt. 12:15869–97; *Washington Post*, July 3, 1964, A1; *Los Angeles Times*, July 3, 1964, 1.

5 *Los Angeles Times*, July 3, 1964, 1.

6 *New York Times*, July 3, 1964, 1.

7 "Civil Rights: President Signs Historic Bill," Universal newsreel, July 2, 1964, http://www.youtube.com/watch?v=ZaRUca7FyAc, accessed July 16, 2013; *Los Angeles Times*, July 3, 1964, 3.

8 "Radio and Television Remarks Upon Signing the Civil Rights Bill," July 2, 1964, http://www.presidency.ucsb.edu/ws/index.php?pid=26361, accessed July 16, 2013.

9 Shesol, *Mutual Contempt*, 165.

10 *New York Times*, July 3, 1964, 1; memo to the files by Lee White, July 4, 1963, box 2, Ex Gen HU 2, White House Central Files, Lyndon B. Johnson Library.

11 Stewart, "Independence," ii and 289.

12 Webb, *Fight Against Fear*, 109–11; *Reporter*, August 13, 1964, 44.

13 *Reporter*, ibid.

14 *Time*, July 10, 1964, 27; *Time*, July 17, 1964, 39.

15 *New York Times*, July 7, 1964, 20; *New York Times*, July 7, 1964, 1; *New York Times*, July 10, 1964, 10; *Washington Post*, July 4, 1964, 1; *Washington Post*, July 5, 1964, 1.

16 *Los Angeles Times*, July 5, 1964, D1.

17 *Tuscaloosa News*, May 1, 2011, http://www.tuscaloosanews.com/article/20110501/news/110439984, accessed July 19, 2013; "Compliance with Title II: A Summary of Field Reports from Southern States," box 27, Burke Marshall Papers, John F. Kennedy Library.

18 "Compliance with Title II."

19 *Congressional Quarterly Weekly Report*, July 10, 1964, 1454.

20 Ibid.; *Reporter*, August 13, 1964, 44; press release from Bill Fulbright, July 8, 1964, box 110, part 1, Leadership Conference on Civil Rights Records, Library of Congress; text of radio address recorded by Senator Allen J. Ellender, July 4, 1964, box 110, part 1, Leadership Conference on Civil Rights Records, Library of Congress.

21 *New York Times*, July 3, 1964, 9.

22 *New York Times*, June 24, 1964, 23; *New York Times*, July 4, 1964, 1.

23 *Wall Street Journal*, May 13, 1963, 1.

24 "Compliance with Title II"; *New York Times*, July 4, 1964, 1.

25 "Compliance with Title II"; *Washington Post*, July 30, 1964, A5.

26 *Christian Science Monitor*, February 8, 1964, 4; *Christian Science Monitor*, April 30, 1964, 11.

27 For an excellent review of the white South's experience during the civil rights movement, see Sokol, *There Goes My Everything*.

28 *Heart of Atlanta Motel, Inc. v. United States*, 379 U.S. 241, 1964, Supreme Court of the United States, http://www.law.cornell.edu/supct/html/historics/USSC_CR_0379_0241_ZS.html, accessed July 19, 2013.

29 *New York Times*, July 4, 1964, 1.

30 Stern, *Calculating Visions*, 184.

31 Sovern, *Legal Restraints*, 205 and 80. Years later, Sovern admitted, in an interview with the author, that he had been too hasty in his criticism of Title VII, and that he later developed a much more positive view of it. See also Berg, "Equal Employment Opportunity," 311–43.

32 Berg, ibid.; interview with Jack Greenberg by the author, November 28, 2012; Osterman, "Origins of a Myth."

33 Farhang, "Political Development," 1.

34 *Los Angeles Times*, July 3, 1964, 3.

35 *New York Times*, July 5, 1964, 1; *Baltimore Afro-American*, October 24, 1964, 1.

36 Larry O'Brien interview with Michael L. Gillette, February 12, 1986, Lyndon B. Johnson Library; "Memorandum Dictated Shortly After Cloture," n.d., Hubert Humphrey, box 15, David B. Filvaroff and Raymond E. Wolfinger Civil Rights Act Papers, University of Buffalo Library.

37 *Washington Star*, April 22, 1964. See article in box 65, LE HU 2, White House Central Files, Lyndon B. Johnson Library.

38 Frank Valeo interview with Donald A. Ritchie, September 18, 1985, Oral History Project, U.S. Senate Historical Office.

39 Stewart, *Civil Rights Act*, 197; Schlesinger, *Robert Kennedy*, 674.

40 Bill Moyers, "Second Thoughts: Reflections on the Great Society," *New Perspectives Quarterly*, vol. 4, no. 1, 1987, http://www.digitalnpq.org/archive/1987_winter/second.html, accessed July 17, 2013.

41 Warren, *Segregation*, 23.

42 Schlesinger, *Thousand Days*, 974–75.

43 Speech by Secretary Wirtz before the National Conference on Negro Policy in Chicago, July 2, 1964, box 465, Thomas Kuchel Papers, University of California, Berkeley; remarks at the University of Michigan, May 22, 1964, http://www.lbjlib.utexas.edu/johnson/archives.hom/speeches.hom/640522.asp, accessed July 19, 2013; commencement address at Howard University, June 4, 1965, http://www.lbjlib.utexas.edu/johnson/archives.hom/speeches.hom/650604.asp, accessed July 19, 2013.

INDEX

A NOTE ON THE AUTHOR

CLAY RISEN IS A STAFF editor for the *New York Times* op-ed section. Previously he served as an editor at the *New Republic* and as the managing editor of the noted quarterly *Democracy: A Journal of Ideas*. His journalism has also appeared in a wide variety of publications, including the *Atlantic*, *Smithsonian*, and the *Washington Post*. His first book, *A Nation on Fire: America in the Wake of the King Assassination*, published in 2009, received much critical acclaim; he is also the author of *American Whiskey, Bourbon and Rye: A Guide to the Nation's Favorite Spirit* and a coeditor of *The New York Times: Disunion: Modern Historians Revisit and Reconsider the Civil War from Lincoln's Election to the Emancipation Proclamation*. He lives in New York.